Alexander Sperber:
Collected Essays on Biblical Hebrew Grammar, 1935 - 1948

Volume One of Three

edited by
Eric Chevlen

Borromean Books
Youngstown, OH

Cover images: Leningrad Codex, 1008 CE. The story of the
Tower of Babel.

ISBN 978-0-9830559-3-8

Library of Congress Control Number: 2018950680

Library of Congress subject headings:
    Hebrew language--Grammar, Historical.
    Bible. Old Testament. Greek. Septuagint.
    Masorah.
    Hebrew language--Phonology.
    Bible. Pentateuch. Aramaic. Onkelos.
    Sperber, A. (Alexander), 1897-

Table of Contents

Volume One

Volume Two

Volume Three

My fascination with the scholarship of Alexander Sperber started with a dot. Actually, it started with a dot that wasn't there.

By way of introduction:

The Hebrew language, as it appears in a Torah scroll or in Israeli newspapers and books, is written without vowels. The structure of the language is such that the meaning of a word is usually easily understood without explicit vowel markings. However, some texts, for example prayer books and printed editions of the Hebrew Bible, explicitly mark the vowels to prevent any misunderstanding. One of the diacritical marks which are printed along with vowels is a tiny dot which appears within some consonants. That dot is called a dagesh, and it can serve a number of syntactic and phonemic functions. For example, when a substantive (noun or gerund) is preceded by the affixed definite article ה, the consonant after the ה almost always is marked with a dagesh. For reasons which do not bear elaboration here, that's just the rule.

I was standing in synagogue, minding my own spiritual business, when I noticed that a dagesh was missing from one of the words in the prayer I was reciting. The word והמרחם means "and the compassionate one." It should have a dagesh in the מ. It didn't. That bothered me. I noticed that the same paragraph had another word in which a dagesh should appear in the מ, and indeed there it was: המסורים ("the ones which are committed") sported a proper dagesh in its מ. Why the inconsistency, I wondered?

As I continued to read the prayer book, I found other examples of grammatical solecisms that I had never noticed before. Eventually, these grammatical conundra began to accumulate to the point of distracting me from my prayers.

To understand what was going on, I turned to *A Historical Grammar of Biblical Hebrew—A Presentation of Problems with Suggestions to Their Solution* (1966) by Alexander Sperber. I soon realized that the problem of grammatical anomalies was far more convoluted than I had realized.

For example, another function of the dagesh is to change the sound of some consonants. A ב without a dagesh is pronounced like a V, but the same letter with a dagesh is pronounced like a B. There are rules—or so I had learned—governing when certain consonants should be marked with this phonemic dagesh. But Sperber cites hundreds of examples which violate that rule. For example, in Genesis 36:22 we find וַיִּהְיוּ בְנֵי with no dagesh in the ב. But in the same chapter, verse 11, the same words appear with a dagesh in the ב : וַיִּהְיוּ בְּנֵי. Similarly, in 2 Samuel 13:5, we find תָּבֹא נָא תָמָר, but in the next verse a dagesh appears in Tamar's name: תָּבוֹא-נָא תָּמָר. (Why a makkeph [hyphen] appears in the second cited verse but not the first is another puzzling irregularity.)

Oh, but wait, there's more!

Sperber points out hundreds of other grammatical "errors" in our received text. While a few might be blamed on scribal or printing errors, the huge number of them, and their irregular distribution through the texts, militate against such an interpretation. Sperber points to sentences in which the subject and predicate do not agree in number. One example is Genesis 13:7, in which the Masoretic text reads והכנעני והפרזי אז ישב בארץ. Another example is in Genesis 10:25: ולעבר ילד שני בנים. Curiously, the Samaritan Pentateuch shows both of those verbs in the plural, in agreement with their subjects.

Other problems which Sperber highlights are widespread inconsistencies in use of some consonants to represent vowel sounds. (The technical name for this is *matres lectionis*.) Nagging questions about pronunciation and vocalization (vowel placement) of Hebrew words do not escape Sperber's assessment. Here, he relies on early Greek translations and transliterations of the (then extant) Hebrew text. Since Greek has the letters sigma, tau, and theta, the translator's choice of which consonant to use in translating personal names, such as Ruth, can give us an idea as to how the letter ת was pronounced at that time.

One of the strongest points of Sperber's book is his criticism of modern efforts to edit our received text so as to correct "obvious" grammatical errors. He points out that the only way we can have a theory of Biblical Hebrew grammar—this does not necessarily apply to post-biblical Hebrew grammar—is to base it on the primary text itself. Once we use the "data" in the Hebrew Bible to create a theory of its grammar, we cannot go back to change the data upon which that theory is based. Sperber concludes that the Masoretes, working in the 6th to 10th centuries to create an authentic and accurate vocalized text, were in fact basing their working on two vorlages (and perhaps redactions of them), representing a dialectical difference in the Hebrew spoken in the kingdom of Judah vs the kingdom of Israel.

The elephant-in-the-room in Biblical Hebrew grammar is the waw-consecutive (also called vav-consecutive). Attaching the conjunction waw (which usually translates "and") to the beginning of a verb is, in the standard paradigm criticized by Sperber, understood to change the aspect or tense of the verb. Thus, while שמר means "he watched," ושמר means "and he will watch." Similarly, ישמר means "he will watch," but וישמר means "and he watched." As far as I know, this bizarre linguistic phenomenon does not occur in any other Semitic language. Sperber's iconoclastic conclusion is that the waw-consecutive is a vestige of the two dialects underlying our received text, and is not necessarily an indicator of a tense switch.

Sperber concludes the book by answering the implicit question "Who cares?" Perhaps not the only reason, but the major reason why we should care about the grammatical analysis is that the grammar is the key to understanding the meaning of the text. Sperber shows that his critical grammatical analysis can, in many passages, actually change the exegesis of the text. Many people care about that very much.

2

After I completed reading Sperber's magnum opus, I remained unsettled. Yes, by then I understood some of the historical forces which had led to the grammatical irregularities, and I had learned a fair bit about the history and ongoing challenges of Masoretic studies. But I was still hoping that there might be a guide to biblical Hebrew grammar which would explain when and why I should expect to find grammatical forms which defied the standard grammar textbooks I had studied over the years. What I wanted, of course, was a paradox: regular rules to describe irregularities.

In his 1966 book, Sperber had recommended the inquisitive reader to read his 1959 text, *A Grammar of Masoretic Hebrew, a General Introduction to the Pre Masoretic Bible.* In that book, I quickly learned that Sperber saw his mission not merely as a builder of grammar, but as a destroyer and re-builder. In his introduction to the book he wrote, "This is a grammar for grammarians: for Hebrew scholars who are well-read in the Bible, sensitive to the problems which it presents to the philologian, and who do not find the current grammars appealing to their philological taste: neither in the way they pose the problems, nor in the solutions which they offer...And my aim is to present a new kind of grammar...The constructive work, which is presented here, is not built in the void; it is built upon the ruins of prevailing theories, which I have reduced to shambles in my previous publications."

In the 1959 book, Sperber intends to establish three points which he feels are foundational for a proper understanding of pre-Masoretic Hebrew:

1. In the Hebrew Bible we possess only a part of the original lexicon of Hebrew. Consequently, no work on any branch of Biblical philology may claim to be an exhaustive presentation of the problems in the respective field. Thus, many words, occurring but rarely in the text, may appear to be inflected forms of infinitive verbs, but are in reality inflected forms derived from different roots altogether.

2. Similarly, the pronunciation of Biblical Hebrew words cannot be reconstructed from only the Masoretic vocalizations, but must also take into account vocalizations found in pre-Masoretic transliterations in Greek and Latin, and on findings from the Dead Sea Scrolls.

3. The Hebrew Bible reflects two dialects of Hebrew as spoken in Biblical days: Judaean and Israelitish, respectively.

The evidence which Sperber offers to support these claims is formidable. He does not discuss Origen's Hexapla as much in this book as he does in his much longer summarizing book of 1966. (The Hexapla is a critical edition of the Hebrew Bible in six versions, four of them translated into Greek, preserved only in fragments. It was an immense and complex word-for-word comparison of the original Hebrew Scriptures with the Greek Septuagint translation and with other Greek translations. It was compiled by the theologian and scholar Origen, sometime before the year 240 CE.) However, Sperber makes ample use of the newly discovered Dead Sea Scrolls in supporting his claims about the Hebrew in use around the time of the destruction of the Second Temple and earlier.

What had led Sperber to conclusions so iconoclastic that Waltke and O'Connor would later describe him as "an erratic but diligent scholar"?[1] In his introduction to *A Historical Grammar of Biblical Hebrew*, Sperber himself describes his intellectual journey: "In September 1934 I joined the Faculty of the Jewish Theological Seminary of America, and thus the treasures of its famous Library became easily accessible to me. This resulted in an almost complete re-orientation in my Biblical studies. For up till then, while in Bonn, my research was based upon the well-known printed Bibles, which were in general use at that time...and which claimed to be faithful reproductions of Jacob ben Chayim's First Masoretic Bible...

But upon coming to America, I could fill the shelves of my study...with all the genuine, old Bible editions, both Hebrew and polyglot...The first result was utter confusion on my part! I saw the cherished rules of Hebrew grammar crumble, one after the other, since the actual facts as exhibited in these Bibles did not uphold them. I then tried to concentrate on the re-examination of specific, individual problems according to the new findings, and to present the outcome of such studies in separate monographs, whenever I felt that the material which I had assembled, allowed for the formulation of definite conclusion..."

H.L. Ginsberg's biographical sketch of Sperber's career (see page 6) tells us about Sperber the scholar, but gives little information about Sperber the man. In fact, the public record has little to say about that. However, just as Sperber was able to learn about the past from documents which had been unavailable in earlier years, so we too may now glean some information from archives which were unavailable when Ginsberg wrote his sketch.

We learn from his Social Security application that Sperber's parents were named Israel Sperber and Leah R. Kramer. The passenger list from the S.S. Kosciussko tells us that Sperber first set foot in American on August 29, 1934. He had come from British Mandate Palestine via the Polish port Gadyna. He cited as his closest relative his brother-in-law (sister's husband), Colcher Meer, who lived in Tel Aviv. Sperber arrived with $100 in his pocket, but knew that his destination was the Jewish Theological Seminary (JTS) at Broadway and 122nd Street, New York.

Less than two months after his arrival (October 11, 1934), Sperber declared his intention to become a United States citizen in the Southern District Court of New York. He then lived at 3080 Broadway, which was not coincidentally, the address of the JTS. At that time he described himself as being 5 feet 7 inches tall, and weighing 171 pounds. He said that he had a dark complexion, brown hair, and brown eyes. (See photo from his declaration of intent document on the opposite page.)

His petition for citizenship was dated February 19, 1940, and was witnessed by Joseph B. Abrahams, the secretary of the JTS, and Michael Higger, a rabbi at the same institution.

---

1. Bruce K. Waltke and M. O'Connor, *An Introduction to Biblical Hebrew Syntax*, Eisenbrauns, Winona Lake, Indiana, 1990, p. 462.

Sperber continued to live at the JTS until at least 1947. However, by 1953 the New York phone directory listed him as living at 608 West 139th Street. He was still living there in 1960.

There is no evidence in any of the documents I could find in American archives that Sperber ever married. He was unmarried on his arrival to America at age 37, and was still unmarried at the time of the 1940 census, when he was 43 years old. Perhaps he would have been a difficult man to live with. His writings reveal a scholar who was polite to others in his field who disagreed with his theories, but steadfast in his certainty that his work had left theirs largely unsupported.

The essays collected in this volume are the above-mentioned separate monographs which Sperber published from 1935 to 1948. It is ironic that this span of academic creativity begins around the time that the malign forces of European antisemitism were gathering to extirpate Jews from the face of the earth, and concludes around the time that the Jewish people re-established a state in its historic homeland. As these events were unfolding, Sperber was exploring the origins, as represented in its philology, of the foundational text which had defined that nation for millennia.

Although they are fascinating and persuasive, these essays are certainly not ones which I recommend for the casual reader. In fact, there are times when I wonder whom Sperber had in mind as his audience. He frequently quotes whole paragraphs (of prior scholars) in German or Latin, and doesn't bother to translate those passages. Early Greek translations are often cited (in Greek, of course) at length. No doubt Sperber simply expected his readers to be as adept in these scholarly languages as he was. He was writing for a readership of scholars of Semitic languages, not for curious dilettantes, such as the editor of this collection of essays. That nonetheless these essays can so demand our attention and respect, and perhaps even our reluctant acquiescence, is a testimony to the power of Sperber's scholarship and analysis.

—Eric Chevlen

Dr Alexander Sperber

5

Proceedings of the American Academy for Jewish
Research, Vol. 38/39 (1970-1971), pp. xxi-xxiii
ALEXANDER SPERBER
(September 15, 1897–July 15, 1970)

Alexander Sperber was born in what is now the city of Chernovtsy
in the Ukrainian Soviet Socialist Republic. At the time of his
birth, however, it was Austrian (Czernowitz), and in between
(1919–40) it was Rumanian (Cernăuti). As a child, he was taught
to write German in Hebrew characters, expressing the *umlauts*
precisely by means of diacritical modifications. He received a
Gymnasium education in Vienna. In Vienna, too, he pursued higher
learning from 1916 to 1918 at the University and at the Jewish
Theological Seminary; this was continued from 1919 to 1922 at
the University and at the Rabbinical Seminary in Berlin. After
earning the degree of Ph.D. at the University of Bonn in 1924,
he was appointed Resident Fellow of the Berlin Academy for
Jewish Research; and in 1928 he became, in addition, *Privatdozent*
at the University of Bonn. Both these positions came to an end
in 1933, the year that National Socialism triumphed in Germany.
Meanwhile, from 1925 to 1928 he resided in England for the
purpose of copying manuscripts at English libraries. Until his
departure from Germany in 1933, he contributed variants from
the Targums to the third edition of *Biblia Hebraica*; and since the
fascicles containing Genesis, Exodus, Leviticus, Isaiah, Jeremiah,
Ezekiel, Psalms and Job-Proverbs were published in the years
1929–32, the variants from the Targums included in the critical
apparatuses to those parts of BHK–3ff. (or BHKK [= Biblia-
Hebraica ed. Kittel-Kahle], as Sperber usually designates it) were
obviously contributed by him. Another publication of his pre-
Hitler years is his *Septuagintaprobleme*, 1929. The English of the
second half of his life bore the imprint of his *Neuhochdeutsch* past.

In the academic session 1933–34, Sperber was a Fellow at the
Hebrew University of Jerusalem. From Palestine his career took
him to the United States. From 1934 to 1938 he was both Visiting
Professor at the Jewish Theological Seminary in New York and
Visiting Lecturer at The Dropsie College of Hebrew and Cognate
Learning in Philadelphia; and he remained on a permanent basis

with the former, at which he was appointed Lecturer in Bible Versions in 1938, Reader in Bible Versions in 1941, and Research Fellow in 1948. The latter status he retained to the end, but from 1965 on his home was in Tel Gannim, a suburb of Ramat Gan, Israel.

Sperber's publications fall into two main divisions: 1. the editing of Targums and 2. textual and linguistic studies in biblical philology.

His enduring importance is due to the first division, the basic work on which seems to have been completed by the end of his European phase. It bears the name of *The Bible in Aramaic, based on old manuscripts and printed texts*. Vol. I, titled *The Pentateuch according to Targum Onkelos*, came out in the year 1959 (Brill, Leiden); Vol. II, *The Former Prophets according to Targum Jonathan*, likewise in 1959; Vol. III, *The Latter Prophets according to Targum Jonathan*, in 1962; and Part A (comprising Chronicles and the Five Megilloth) of Vol. IV, *The Hagiographa — Transition from Translation to Midrash*, in 1968. The rest of the Hagiographa (presumably Psalms, Job, and Proverbs, since Targums may well be wanting, to [the Hebrew parts of] Daniel and Ezra–Nehemiah) are promised for Part B. Though one may have some reservations about the editing of the — in any case, late — Targums in IV A (there are no apparatuses, though obvious errors in the Five Megilloth could have been corrected by means of variants from the editions of Jacob b. Hayyim-Lagarde, Qâfih ["Kapah" — the Canticles, Ruth, and Ecclesiastes Targums in his Hamesh Megillot] and R. H. Melamed [Canticles]), Vols. I–III bid fair to become classics, thanks to their excellent texts with supralinear vocalization and their double — in the case of the Prophets, triple — apparatuses.

To the second division of Sperber's publications belong the items mentioned at the end of the first paragraph of this article, sundry papers in MGWJ, HUCA, JBL, PAAJR, etc., and the following major items: 1. *The Pre-Masoretic Bible* (I. The Codex Reuchlinianus, II. The Parma Pentateuch, III. The Parma Bible [photographic reproductions]), Copenhagen 1956–59, of which a fourth volume, The London Bible, is planned; 2. *A Grammar of Masoretic Hebrew*, Copenhagen 1959, 209 pp., 4to, of which the first three chapters were also published, in an earlier form, as Introduction to Vol. I of *The Pre-Masoretic Bible*; 3. *A Historical Grammar of Biblical Hebrew*, A Presentation of Problems with Suggestions to Their Solution, Leiden 1966, XIII + 705 pp. 4to. In all of this area, his conclusions are controversial. But firstly, the material itself — not only the photographed medieval manuscripts of the Bible, but all citations of forms wherever the source is given, in particular the "Hebrew Dictionary" on pp. 124–170 of *A Historical Grammar* — is valuable. Secondly, even scholars who are not convinced by the author's inferences from his data often find his argumentation of heuristic value. And thirdly, nothing could be more characteristic of the man than his choice of a motto for the Introduction to Volume I of *The Pre-Masoretic Bible* and for its expansion and outgrowth, *A Grammar of Masoretic Hebrew*. The motto, he tells us, is a quotation from "Gotthold Ephraim Lessing in his 'Duplik gegen Goeze'; with a slight stylistic change." An attempt by the undersigned to render it in English follows:

"If God, holding enclosed in his right hand all truth and in his left only the unrelaxing urge for truth though coupled with the warning that it entailed the risk of repeatedly erring, were to command me, 'Choose!' — I should in all humility grasp his left hand and say, 'Father, give this; pure truth is after all for You alone.'"

H. L. Ginsberg

Journal of Biblical Literature, Vol. 54, No. 2 (Jun., 1935), pp. 73-92

THE PROBLEMS OF THE SEPTUAGINT RECENSIONS

ALEXANDER SPERBER

JEWISH THEOLOGICAL SEMINARY

A LL the research work that has been done in the field of the Septuagint in the last fifty years is based upon the fundamental investigations which Paul de Lagarde has made, and upon the results he has arrived at. But to Lagarde the study of the Septuagint in itself and the explanation of its various readings was not the last aim. He considered it only as a help for the better understanding of the Hebrew Bible. Therefore the Hebrew text was the starting point for his research work in the field of the Septuagint; and consequently he applied his theory concerning the development of the Hebrew *textus receptus* even to the history of the Septuagint. As to this *textus receptus*, an examination of the numerous *variae lectiones* noted down in Kennicott's *Vetus Testamentum Hebraicum cum variis lectionibus* (Oxonii 1776/80) as the result of a collation of hundreds of Mss. of the Hebrew Bible proved to him that they are of rather little importance for textual criticism. In most cases they only refer to the spelling of a given Hebrew word, whether *plene* or *defectiv*, whether to add or to omit a *waw copulativum*, and similar details. But there is practically not a single *varia lectio* to give a changed meaning to the whole connection of the Biblical sentence. This negative result of the value of the *variae lectiones* for the early history of the Hebrew text led him, then, to the conclusion that in reality they did not represent different textual forms, but were only mistakes of the many scribes in the different centuries, and that all the Mss. of the Hebrew Bible go back to only one Original which had served as prototype to

10

all later copies. This Hebrew prototype of all Hebrew Bible Mss. in existence he called the Archetype of the Bible.

According to this uniformity that has to be presupposed for the Hebrew Bible, Lagarde assumed that even the Septuagint was originally known in a single form. This was the Greek rendering of the Hebrew Archetype, and he called it the Original Septuagint (*Urseptuaginta*). But a statement, which St. Jerome made in his *praefatio* to Chronicles, and which Lagarde was the first to come across, seemed to be in contradiction to the afore-mentioned theory. This statement reads as follows: "Nunc vero, cum pro varietate regionum diversa ferantur exemplaria . . . Alexandria et Aegyptus in Septuaginta suis Hesychium laudat auctorem; Constantinopolis usque Antiochiam Luciani martyris exemplaria probat. Mediae inter has provinciae Palaestinos codices legunt, quos ab Origene elaboratos Eusebius et Pamphilus vulgaverunt; totusque orbis hac inter se trifaria varietate compugnat." But according to Lagarde's explanation there is really no contradiction between his theory and St. Jerome's statement. For he interpreted St. Jerome's words to mean that Origen, Lucian, and Hesychius were not the authors of respective new translations of the Bible into Greek; they only transformed the one existing Greek translation, namely the Septuagint, by all kinds of additions and omissions, as well as other changes of language and style. Thus the formerly uniform text of the Original Septuagint was subdivided into three different forms, which he called recensions. Hence the final aim of all Septuagint study ought to be to restore that text of the Original Septuagint in its utmost purity, so as to enable us to draw conclusions as to its Hebrew prototype, i. e. the Archetype.

Consequently Lagarde demanded, that all Septuagint Mss. should be classified and thus distributed to the respective recension according to St. Jerome's statement. The next step to be taken should be to publish editions of parts of the Greek Bible according to one of those recensions, and not to base the editions upon a more or less limited number of Mss. belonging to different groups, as editors used to do. To set an example, Lagarde himself published an edition of the Pentateuch according to Lucian (*Librorum Veteris Testamenti Canonicorum pars prior Graece*,

Goettingae 1883). Thus the way would be paved for the final task, the edition of the Septuagint itself. Now, since the large number of existing Septuagint Mss. would be classified and with the three recensions of the Septuagint being restored, the editor of the Septuagint would not have to deal any longer with a mass of single Mss. for preparing his text, but only with the three recensions. Having before him the Greek Bible in the three forms of Origen, Lucian, and Hesychius respectively, the editor of the Septuagint should be aware of the fact that wherever all three of them agree in their readings they have preserved the Original Septuagint, and this means that in these points the final aim of the Septuagint study would be reached.

This theory of Lagarde has been adopted as the fundamental basis for all further research in the field by his disciple Alfred Rahlfs, who succeeded him in Göttingen; the publications of the *Göttinger Septuaginta-Unternehmen* are the results of those investigations. But these publications prove that in practice it is impossible to work on the principles laid down by Lagarde. Rahlfs himself admits this failure in plain words in the introduction to his edition of the book of Genesis (*Septuaginta Societatis Scientiarum Gottingensis* auctoritate edidit A. Rahlfs, I. Genesis, Stuttgart 1928). He says that if we intend to get along in our Septuagint studies we must not consider ourselves bound to any theory. This statement of Rahlfs refers only to the impossibility of putting into practice Lagarde's theoretical demands; but this does not affect in his eyes the correctness of those demands from a strictly theoretical point of view. Although he admits that he is unable to reconcile theory and practice, the theory still seems to him to be true.

In a paper entitled "Problems of an Edition of the Septuagint," which will appear in the Jubilee Volume on the occasion of Professor Kahle's sixtieth birthday, I have tried to prove by theoretical reasoning, that in the present state of Septuagint research it is futile to think of restoring even the three recensions referred to by St. Jerome. Until now a certain Septuagint Ms. was assigned to one out of the three recensions according to the agreement of its readings with the Bible quotations of a certain Church Father. If, for instance, a Church Father, who lived in Syria, quoted in his works a biblical passage in the same form as we find it in a certain Ms., this fact would lead to the conclusion that the Ms. in question belongs to Lucian's recension. But I should think that for such a far-reaching conclusion it ought to be proved also that the same biblical passage occurs in the writings of an Egyptian Church Father in a different form; for only then could we assume with certainty that this verse was known in these two provinces in two various forms. But even in this case we should have only one instance by which we could attribute a certain passage to one recension or to the other. And still we would have no criteria in general to enable us to assign Septuagint Mss., containing the whole Bible or parts of it, in their entirety. As long as the contrary is not proved to be true, we must assume that the authors of the recensions did not confine themselves to changing the Greek wording of single verses and passages, which they happened to come across merely by accident. On the contrary they must surely have gone through at least one entire biblical book, transforming its readings according to their respective principles. These principles no doubt must have been the same for all biblical books. Now if, for instance, we knew Lucian's recension of Genesis in all its details, we would be in a position to draw final conclusions as to what should be understood under the name of the Lucianic character of a book; so that if we happen to see a Septuagint Ms. containing say the Psalms, we ought to be able to decide whether this Ms. in question is Lucianic or not. This is the only way of thinking Lagarde's theory to a logical end.

We must be aware of the fact that we are lacking all preliminary requirements for such a classification of the Mss., since we know too little about the true character of the recensions. It may suffice to point out that we still do not know whether Lucian and Hesychius based their works upon the text as prepared by Origen or upon the pre-Origenic text. That is, whether Origen remained as an independent recension, or whether his work has disappeared and its influence is to be recognized only in the two later recensions; so that instead of looking out for three recensions we would have to establish only two independent recensions. This argument serves the purpose, to prove purely theoretically that at present we can not even think of applying Lagarde's principles, and that consequently Rahlfs and his entire staff of collaborators would do better to refrain from any attempt at editing Septuagint texts in the footsteps of Lagarde.

I would like to go now one step further and to ask whether Lagarde's presuppositions which led him to formulate his theories are still valid now, after a lapse of fifty years. In this period between Lagarde's days and now even Biblical studies have made remarkable progress, so that it may be that the very starting point of Lagarde has now to be considered as antiquated. In such a case the conclusions he arrived at would have to be discarded.

Lagarde assumes that originally the Septuagint was known in only one form, thus being the only translation of the Bible in Greek. It was not until a comparatively late date that this uniform text underwent changes which resulted in the establishing of three different recensions. Against this supposition I have proved in a paper entitled "The New Testament and the Septuagint"(published in the Hebrew Quarterly תרביץ, Jerusalem, Vol. VI, 1934, pp. 1–29) that at as early a time as the New Testament period, the Greek Bible must have been known and published in several translations. To this end I had collected all Old Testament quotations in the New Testament and compared them with the corresponding readings of Codex B of the Septuagint; I then eliminated those quotations which I found in literal agreement with Codex B and brought the others, which differed from the renderings of Codex B, in a certain order, methodically classifying them according to the points in which they differ. The result of this investigation is that the differences in the vocabulary and style prove that in the days of the New Testament the Septuagint was far from being the only Greek Bible translation. Of course one could reason now with the same arguments which Lagarde used in his days for proving the existence of a Hebrew Archetype. In most cases which I dealt with in my paper, the differences of vocabulary or style leave the meaning of the context untouched. But we must realize that it is a wrong procedure to take the Hebrew Bible, to compare it with the two ways of translating the same passage as preserved in the Septuagint and in the New Testament quotations and to find out that after all there can be no reason for rejecting either of those translations, since both of them are quite good in their methods of translating the Hebrew text. Let us bear in mind that the Greek Bible translation was meant for the masses of the population who had no longer enough knowledge of the Hebrew language to understand the Bible in the original. To them the Greek was therefore not a mere translation but an original, just as the average English speaking reader of the Bible would not refer to King James' Version as to only a translation, but as to an original. From this point of view it makes a lot of difference, whether you use ἐρεύγομαι instead of φθέγγομαι, or διασκορπίζομαι instead of ἐκσπάω (cf. my paper in the תרביץ, pp. 9 sq). This is not merely replacing one word by another synonymon; it results in a different verse altogether, and those who knew the Bible according to the Septuagint would hardly have recognized a quotation from their Holy Scriptures in this changed form. So we are led to the conclusion, that already in the New Testament Period the Septuagint could not have been the Greek Bible Version κατ' ἐξοχήν.

For a later period there is no reason whatsoever to assume the existence of such a unique form of a Greek Bible translation as Lagarde's theory of an Original Septuagint presupposes. To prove this, I should now like to come back to the statement of St. Jerome, and I find it rather strange that Lagarde could interpret the passage that speaks of Origen, Lucian, and Hesychius as being the authors of three different texts, to mean that their texts were merely recensions of only one original text. To disprove this interpretation of Lagarde, I shall deal here in detail with the meaning of St. Jerome's expression of the *trifaria varietas.*

The importance of the Bible quotations in the writings of the Church Fathers for the establishing of the text of the Septuagint or, to use the phrase of Lagarde, for the characterization of the recensions, has been admitted long ago. But in practice we meet with the great difficulty that in very many cases those Bible quotations have not come down to us in exactly the same form as the Church Father may originally have quoted them. The scribes of the Middle Ages who copied those Mss. were mostly monks with a very sound knowledge of the Bible; and when in the course of their copying such a Ms. they came across a quotation which differed from the wording of the Septuagint, they looked upon such a *varia lectio* as upon a simple mistake that had to be corrected. Therefore, whenever we find a Church Father quoting the Bible in full agreement with the Septuagint, this does not prove original uniformity. Consequently those various readings which escaped the attention of the scribes and remained unwittingly unchanged, are very valuable to us.

The various books of the Old Testament have often been commentated upon by the Greek Church Fathers. It was of course the Greek translation that served as the basis for their commentaries, and not the Hebrew text. Considering now St. Jerome's statement that the Greek Bible was spread in his days in different forms in each of the three provinces, we shall assume that a Father who lived somewhere in Asia Minor used the text of Lucian as a basis for his commentary, while his colleague who lived in Egypt will most likely have based his explanations upon the text of Hesychius. Comparing now the two texts underlying such commentaries, the resulting differences would show us the genuine variants of the renderings of Lucian and Hesychius. This of course is only true on the supposition that such commentaries did not undergo corrections by later scribes. Indeed, this is the fact in most cases. But fortunately at least one biblical book remained uncensored in this sense; and this book is sufficient for the sake of this investigation.

The Minor Prophets have been commented upon by Cyril of Alexandria (i. e. an Egyptian) and by Theodoret of Kyros (i. e. of Asia Minor). In their commentaries they first quote the verse (naturally in Greek) and then comment upon it. Thus in Cyril's work the entire book of the Minor Prophets has been preserved in Hesychius' text, while about one-third of it has come down to us according to Lucian's Bible in Theodoret's commentary. I collated both texts very closely and here I cite the differences in their readings, systematically arranged, so as

16

to enable us to draw conclusions with regard to the characteristics of the texts of Lucian and Hesychius. I start with noting those variants that originate in misunderstanding of the Hebrew text, either with regard to consonants or vowels, thus giving rise to translations that have no sense at all in the context. Such misconceptions are the best linguistic proof that the texts, which served the basis for Cyril and Theodoret, go back each to an independent translation. The Hebrew text that has to be presupposed as the prototype of those two translations is practically identical, the differences between the Hebrew Original of Cyril and that of Theodoret being of very minor significance. Since Cyril represents the text of Hesychius and Theodoret that of Lucian, the conclusions we arrived at have to be applied to them. Accordingly we shall henceforth no longer speak of the recensions of Lucian and Hesychius but of the translations, thus indicating that the texts in question do not represent two recensions of one single Greek text (a meaning connected with the word recension), but two entirely different texts.

Now it may be of interest to find out whether it is possible at all to assign Codex B, the oldest Septuagint Ms. available, to one of the newly established translations of Lucian and of Hesychius. I, therefore, noted the readings of this Codex at all passages which I quoted in this paper, from paragraph I till paragraph XI; the result is that in most instances the Ms. agrees with the readings of Cyril, but there is still a considerable number of instances left, where it is found to be in accordance with Theodoret. In other words: Codex B to the Minor Prophets follows to a very large extent the translation of Hesychius, but indicates also a remarkable Lucianic influence. This may serve as evidence that at least at the time when this Ms. was written, the two translations were already used promiscuously, the scribes being no longer aware of the fact that they were confusing readings originating in two different translations.

We have now three texts before us (Cyril, Theodoret and Codex B), representing at least two translations. I say "at least two translations," because the problem as to whether Codex B is the representative of a further independent translation can not be solved on the basis of the material collected here, but only upon a very close investigation of all the Minor Prophets according to Codex B as compared with Cyril and, as far as possible, with Theodoret. And just as I could prove in a general way that Codex B has readings originating in either of the two translations, it may, theoretically speaking, be possible to prove also that neither of the Church Fathers forming the basis of this investigation represent their translation in its original purity. Up to a certain degree the correctness of this supposition may be proved by referring to paragraph IV, where Theodorets renderings can not be explained otherwise than as a result of putting together two different translations. In this connection it may be worth while to point to the passage Zech. 13 7 which shows that Theodorets rendering is already a further development of the reading of Codex B. The mere fact that Theodoret has doublets in five places is a proof that his text, being originally the text of Lucian, has undergone a revision according to the text of Hesychius. Some more mistakes in Theodoret I showed in paragraph V; and it is noteworthy that Theodoret and Codex B have three of these misspellings (Hos. 7 4, 9 10; Amos 6 3) in common. Incidentally this is a further proof that Codex B was influenced by Lucian. Mistakes of this kind occur also in many other places in Codex B; for instance:

Amos 1 11: רַחֲמָיו: Cyril: μήτραν (derived from רָחָם); Codex B: μητέρα.

Jonah 2 5: הֵיכָל: Cyril: ναόν; Codex B: λαόν.

Mic. 4 14: שֵׁפֶט: Cyril: φυλάς (=שֵׁבֶט; cf. 7 14); Codex B: πύλας.

"   5 1: מִמְּךָ: Cyril: ἐκ σοῦ; Codex B: ἐξ οὗ.

Hab. 1 13: לֹא תוּכַל: Cyril: οὐ δυνήσῃ Codex B: ὀδύνης.

Zech. 14 6: יְקָרוֹת: Cyril: ψύχος; Codex B: ψυχή.

Apparently Codex B represents here corruptions of Cyril. But since we are missing Theodoret's equivalents to these words, the problem can not be solved as to whether Codex B really followed Hesychius, or that there was no difference here in the renderings of Lucian and Hesychius, so that even Lucian's text may be assumed as the prototype of Codex B.

Referring to Zech. 13 7 I showed that although Theodoret has to be considered as representing on the whole the text of

Lucian, he does not preserve it in its absolute purity. The same is true of Cyril as a representative of Hesychius; cf. Mic. 7 14: בְּשִׁבְטֶךָ, which is rendered in Cyril's commentary by: ῥάβδῳ φυλήν; this is a combination of two translations; one of them, ῥάβδῳ;, is to be found in Codex B; the origin of the second translation I could not yet trace. This fact in itself proves that the original text of Hesychius has already undergone changes in Cyril; and perhaps these changes were influenced by the text of Lucian, for I suppose that originally Lucian had here φυλήν and Hesychius ῥάβδῳ, and Cyril combined both readings.

Now I bring a classified list of the differences between the translations of the two Church Fathers, whose commentaries are the basis for this investigation:

I. The Hebrew word is incorrectly spelled:

Hos. 8 1: אל חכך: Cyril: εἰς κόλπον αὐτῶν (B)=אֶל חֵקָם; Theodoret: ἐπὶ φάρυγγι αὐτῶν=אֶל חַכָּם.

Nah. 3 3: לגויה: Cyril: τοῖς σώμασιν; Theodoret: τοῖς ἔθνεσιν (B) =לַגּוֹיִם.

Obad. 1 16: ולעו: Cyril: καταβήσονται (B)=וְעָלוּ; Theodoret: καταπίονται.

Hab. 3 12: תצעד: Cyril: ὀλιγώσεις (B) =תְּצָעֵר; Theodoret: συμπατήσεις.

Zech. 12 10: דקרו: Cyril: κατωρχήσαντο (B)=רָקָדוּ; Theodoret: ἐξεκέντησαν.

II. The Hebrew word is incorrectly vocalized:

Hos. 13 3: מֵאָרֻבָּה: Cyril: ἐκ καπνοδόχης; Theodoret: ἀπὸ ἀκρίδων=מֵאַרְבֶּה (B: ἀπὸ δακρύων!).

Amos 1 15: מַלְכָּם: Cyril: οἱ βασιλεῖς αὐτῶν (B); Theodoret: Μελχομ=מִלְכֹּם.

Amos 6 2: כַּלְנֶה: Cyril: πάντες (B)=כֻּלָּנָה; Theodoret: εἰς Χαλανην.

19

Zeph. 1 5: בְּמַלְכָּם: Cyril: τοῦ βασιλέως αὐτῶν (B);; Theodoret: Μελχωμ = בְּמַלְכָּם.

Zech. 9 1: מְנֻחָתוֹ: Cyril: ἀνάπαυσις; Theodoret: θυσία (B) = מְנֻחָתוֹ.

III. Translation—Transliteration:

Hos. 4 15: אָוֶן: Cyril: τῆς ἀδικίας; Theodoret: Ὤν (B).

Amos 6 2: רַבָּה: Cyril: Ῥαββα (B); Theodoret: τὴν μεγάλην.

IV. Doublets in Theodoret:

Nah. 1 14: כִּי קַלּוֹת: Cyril: ὅτι ταχεῖς (B); Theodoret: ὅτι ἠτιμώθης ὅτι ταχεῖς.

Zech. 6 7; ויבקשו Cyril: καὶ ἔβλεπον (cf. B); Theodoret: καὶ ἐξήτουν και ἐπέβλεπον.

Zech. 7 3: הַנָּזֵר: Cyril: τὸ ἁγίασμα (B) = הַנָּזֵר; Theodoret: τὸ ἁγίασμα ἢ νηστεύω = הַנָּזֵר + הַנָּזֵר.

Zech. 13 7: הצערים: Cyril: ποιμένας = הָרֹעִים; Codex B: μικρούς = הַצְּעִירִים; Theodoret: μικροὺς ποιμένας.

Zech. 14 4: וימה: Cyril: θάλασσαν (B); Theodoret: δύσιν θάλασσαν

V. Greek Corruptions in Theodoret:

Hos. 2 1: אשר יאמר: Cyril: οὗ ἐρρέθη (B); Theodoret: ᾧ ἐρρέθη.

" 4 19: אותה: Cyril: σὺ εἶ (B); Theodoret: συριεῖ.

" 7 4: בצק: Cyril: σταιτός; Theodoret: στέατος (B).

" 9 10: כבכורה: Cyril: ὡς σῦκον; Theodoret: ὡς σκοπόν (B).

Amos 6 3: המנדים: Cyril: εὐχόμενοι; Theodoret: ἐρχόμενοι (B).

Nah. 2 9: כברכת מים: Cyril: ὡς κολυμβήθρα ὕδατος (B); Theodoret: ὡς ὕδατα κολυμβήθρας

Zech. 4 10: קטנות: Cyril: μικράς (B); Theodoret: μακράς.

Zech. 7 3: האבכה: Cyril: εἰ εἰσελήλυθεν (B); Theodoret: εἰ εἰσῆλθεν

VI. Differences in the Exegesis of the same Hebrew word:

אבן: Zech. 5 8: Cyril: λίθος (B); Theodoret: τάλαντον.

בטן: Hab. 3 16: Cyril: καρδία; Theodoret: κοιλία (B).

ברדים: Zech. 6 6: Cyril: ποικίλος (B); Theodoret: πυρρός.

זנח: Hos. 8 5: Cyril: ἀποτρέπω (B); Theodoret: ἀπορρίπτω.

טרף: Hos. 6 1: Cyril: ἁρπάζω (B); Theodoret: παίζω.

מבט: Zech. 9 5: Cyril: ἐλπίς; Theodoret: παράπτωμα (B).

נוס: Amos 2 16: Cyril: διώκω (B); Theodoret: φεύγω.

הסג: Mic. 6 14: Cyril: καταλαμβάνω; Theodoret: ἐκνεύω (B).

סוף: Amos 3 15: Cyril: προστίθεμαι (B); Theodoret: ἀφανίζομαι.

עם: Mic. 6 8: Cyril: μετά (B); Theodoret: ὀπίσω.

פעל: Hos. 7 1: Cyril: ἐργάζομαι (B); Theodoret: ἀγαπάω.

צבאות: Zech. 1 3: Cyril: παντοκράτωρ (B); Theodoret: τῶν δυναμέων.

קדש: Mic. 3 5: Cyril: ἐγείρω (B); Theodoret: ἁγιάζω.

קרחה: Mic. 1 16: Cyril: χηρεία (B); Theodoret: ξύρησις

הַרְאָה: Mic. 7 15: Cyril: ὁράω (B); Theodoret: δείκνυμι.

הַרְאָה: Zech. 9 14: Cyril: εἰμί (B); Theodoret: ὁράομαι.

הרבה: Hos. 8 14: Cyril: ποιέω; Theodoret: πληθύνω (B).

הרחב: Amos 1 13: Cyril: ἐμπλατύνω (B); Theodoret: ἐμπληθύνω.

רפא: Hos. 5 13: Cyril: ἰάομαι (B); Theodoret: ῥύομαι.

שוב: Jonah 3 9: Cyril: μετανοέω (B); Theodoret: ἐπιστρέφω
Zech. 4 1: Cyril: ἐπιστρέφω (B); Theodoret: προσέρχομαι.

השב: Zech. 13 7: Cyril: ἐπάγω (B); Theodoret: ἐπιστρέφω.

שדד: Hos. 10 14: Cyril: οἴχομαι (B); Theodoret: φανίζομαι.

שחת: Hos. 13 9: Cyril: διασπορά; Theodoret: διαφθορά (B).

שמד: Amos 2 9: Cyril: ξηραίνω; Theodoret: ἐξαίρω (B).

Without a Hebrew equivalent:

Hos. 14 8: Cyril: μεθύσκω (B); Theodoret: στηρίζω.
Mic. 7 12: Cyril: ὁμαλισμός (B); Theodoret: συγκλεισμός·

VII. Greek Synonyma:

און: Hos. 12 9: Cyril: ἀναψυχή (B); Theodoret: ἀνάπαυσις.

כאשר: Zech. 14 5: Cyril: καθώς (B); Theodoret: ὃν τρόπον.

Mic. 7 20: Cyril: καθότι (B); Theodoret: καθάπερ.

היה: Amos 7 3: Cyril: εἶναι (B); Theodoret: γίνεσθαι.

חלק: Mic. 2 4: Cyril: διαμετρέω (cf. B); Theodoret: διαμερίζω.

חמדה: Zech. 7 14: Cyril: ἐκλεκτός (B); Theodoret: ἐπιθυμητός.

חמס: Mic. 6 12: Cyril: ἀσεβεία (B); Theodoret: ἀδικία.

חנית: Mic. 4 3: Cyril: ζιβύνη; Theodoret: δόρυ (B).

חרב: Mic. 4 3 (bis); Nah. 2 14: Cyril: ῥομφαία (B); Theodoret: μάχαιρα.

חרד: Hos. 11 11: Cyril: ἐκπέτομαι (B); Theodoret: ἥκω.

יצא: Joel 4 18: Cyril: ἐξέρχομαι (B); Theodoret: πορεύομαι.

: Jonah 4 5: Cyril: ἐξέρχομαι (B); Theodoret: καταλείπω.

הכחד: Zech. 11 16: Cyril: ἐκλιμπάνω (B); Theodoret: ἐκλείπω.

כסה: Mic. 7 10: Cyril: περιβάλλω (B); Theodoret: καλύπτω.

הכרת: Mic. 5 11: Cyril: ἐξαίρω; Theodoret: ἐξολοθρεύω (B).

מגפה: Zech. 14 18: Cyril: πτῶσις (B); Theodoret: πληγή.

מגרים: Mic. 1 4: Cyril: φερόμενον (B); Theodoret: καταγόμενον.

מות: Amos 7 11: Cyril: τελευτάω (B); Theodoret: πίπτω.

נאם: Zech. 2 9: Cyril: φημί; Theodoret: λέγω (B).

הביט: Zech. 12 10: Cyril: ἐπιβλέπω (B); Theodoret: ὁράω.

הטיף: Mic. 2 6: Cyril: κλαίω (B); Theodoret: δακρύω.

הכה: Amos 3 15: Cyril: συγχέω (B); Theodoret: συντρίβω.

נמס: Nah. 2 11: Cyril: θραυσμός (B); Theodoret: θόρυβος.

נקה: Joel 4 21: Cyril: ἐκδικέω; Theodoret: ἐκζητέω (B).

עוד: Joel 2 27: Cyril: ἕτερος; Theodoret: ἔτι (B).

עון: Hos. 7 1: Cyril: κακία; Theodoret: ἀδικία (B).

: Mic. 7 18: Cyril: ἀνομία (B); Theodoret: ἀδικία.

: Mic. 7 19: Cyril: ἀδικία (B); Theodoret: ἁμαρτία.

לפני: Hos. 6 2: Cyril: ἐνώπιον (B); Theodoret: ἐναντίον.

פשע: Mic. 7 18: Cyril: ἀδικία; Theodoret: ἀσεβεία (B).

קצר: Hos. 10 12: Cyril: τρυγάω (B); Theodoret: θερίζω.

רוח: Zech. 6 8: Cyril: θυμός (B); Theodoret: πνεῦμα.

רצץ: Hos. 5 11: Cyril: καταπατέω; Theodoret: καταδυνα-
στεύω (B).

רשע: Mic. 6 11: Cyril: ἄνομος (B); Theodoret: ἄδικος.

שכן: Zech. 8 3: Cyril: κατασκηνόω (B); Theodoret: κατοικέω.

שסה: Hos. 13 15: Cyril: καταξηραίνω (B); Theodoret: ἐρημόω.

שפלים: Mal. 2 9: Cyril: παρειμένοι; Theodoret: ἀπερριμένοι (B).
Hos. 13 4: Cyril: κτίζω (B); Theodoret: πλάσσω.

VIII. Various declensions of the same root:

Amos 6 10: Cyril: ἡ οἰκία; Theodoret: ὁ οἶκος (B).
Hos. 7 2: Cyril: ἡ κακία (B); Theodoret: τὸ κακόν.
Mic. 1 7: Cyril: πορνεία (B); Theodoret: πόρνη.
Hos. 14 7: Cyril: ὄσφρανσις; Theodoret: ὀσφρανσία (B).
Hos. 2 21; 6 6; Zech. 7 9: Cyril: τὸ ἔλεος (B); Theodoret: τὸ ἔλεον.
Mic. 6 8; 7 20: Cyril: τὸ ἔλεος; Theodoret: τὸ ἔλεον (B).
Nah. 3 17: Cyril: ὁ πάγος; Theodoret: τὸ πάγος (B).
Hos. 7 4: Cyril: κατάκαυμα (B); Theodoret: κατάκαυσις.

IX. Differences in dialect:

Mal. 3 15: Cyril: ἄνομον (B); Theodoret: ἀνόμημα.
Hos. 13 8: Cyril: ἄρκτος; Theodoret: ἄρκος(B).
Zeph. 2 11: Cyril: ἐπιφανής εἰμι; Theodoret: ἐπιφαίνομαι.
Mic. 7 15: Cyril: θαυμαστά (B); Theodoret: θαυμάσια.
Zech. 5 7.8: Cyril: μόλιβος (B); Theodoret: μόλιβδος.
Zeph. 3 12; Zech. 9 9: Cyril: πραύς (B); Theodoret: πρᾶος.
Hos. 6 8: Cyril: ταράσσω (B); Theodoret: ταράττω.
Hos. 9 11: Cyril: τόκος (B); Theodoret: τοκετός.
Amos 4 13: Cyril: ὕψη (B); Theodoret: ὑψηλά.
Zech. 9 12: Cyril: παροικεσία (B); Theodoret: παροικία.
Zech. 10 1: Cyril: χειμερινός (B); Theodoret: χειμέριος.
Mal. 3 14: Cyril: πλέον (B); Theodoret: πλεῖον.

X. Nouns and Compounds:

Hos. 4 6: Cyril: γνῶσις (B); Theodoret: ἐπίγνωσις.
Hag. 1 6: Cyril: δεσμός (B); Theodoret: ἀπόδεσμος.
Mic. 2 13: Cyril: κοπή; Theodoret: διακοπή (B).
Nah. 2 11: Cyril: ἐκβρασμός (cf. B); Theodoret: βρασμός.
Amos 9 6: Cyril: ἀνάβασις (B); Theodoret: ἐπίβασις.
Mic. 5 7: Cyril: ὑπόλειμμα (B); Theodoret: κατάλειμμα.
Amos 9 11: Cyril: κατεσκαμμένα (B); Theodoret: ἀνεσκαμμένα.

XI. Verbs and Compounds:

a.) Cyril: Verb—Theodoret: Compound:

Joel 1 12; Zech. 9 5: Cyril: αἰσχύνω (B); Theodoret: καταισχύνω.

Nah. 3 17; Mal. 2 4: Cyril: γιγνώσκω; Theodoret: ἐπιγιγώσκω (B: Nah. = Cy; Mal. = Theo).

Hab. 1 6: Cyril: ἐγείρω; Theodoret: ἐξεγείρω (B).

Hos. 13 8: Cyril: ἐσθίω; Theodoret: κατεσθίω (B).

Hos. 13 11: Cyril: ἔχω (B); Theodoret: ἀνέχω.

Hos. 10 12: Cyril: ζητέω; Theodoret: ἐκζητέω (B).

Zech. 11 7: Cyril: καλέω (B); Theodoret: ἐπικαλέω.

Amos 2 7: Cyril: πατέω (B);Theodoret: καταπατέω.

Mic. 5 6: Cyril: πίπτω (B); Theodoret: ἐπιπίπτω.

Hab. 2 16: Cyril: σαλεύω (B); Theodoret: διασαλεύω.

Mal. 2 3: Cyril: σκορπίζω (B); Theodoret: διασκορπίζω.

Hos. 8 7: Cyril: σπείρω (B); Theodoret: συσπείρω.

Mal. 3 3: Cyril: χέω (B); Cyril: Theodoret: ἐκχέω.

b.) Cyril: Compound—Theodoret: Verb:

Hos. 7 2: Cyril: συνᾴδω (B); Theodoret: ᾄδω.

Zech. 6 15: Cyril: εἰσακούω (B); Theodoret: ἀκούω.

Mic. 2 2: Cyril: διαρπάζω (B); Theodoret: ἀρπάζω.

Hag. 1 9: Cyril: ἐπιβλέπω (B); Theodoret: βλέπω.

Zech. 6 8: Cyril: ἀναβοάω (B); Theodoret: βοάω.

Hos. 14 10; Zech.2 15; 6 15: Cyril: ἐπιγιγνώσκω; Theodoret: γιγνώσκω (B. Hos. 14 10, Zech. 2 15 = Cy; Zech. 6 15 = Th).

Nah. 3 19; Zech. 12 9: Cyril: ἐπέρχομαι; Theodoret: ἔρχομαι (B: Nah. = Cy; Zech. = Theod.).

Amos 7 2: Cyril: κατεσθίω (B); Theodoret: ἐσθίω.

Hos. 3 5; 7 10: Cyril: ἐκζητέω; Theodoret: ζητέω (B: 3 5: ἐπιζητέω; 7 10 = Cy).

Hos. 12 4: Cyril: ἐνισχύω (B); Theodoret: ἰσχύω.

Hab. 2 14: Cyril: κατακαλύπτω (B); Theodoret: καλύπτω.

Zech. 10 12: Cyril: κατακαυχάομαι (B); Theodoret: καυχάομαι.

Zeph. 3 1: Cyril: ἀπολυτρόω (B); Theodoret: λυτρόω.

Mal. 2 14: Cyril: διαμαρτύρομαι (B); Theodoret: μαρτύρομαι.

Hos. 2 1: Cyril: ἐκμετρέω (B); Theodoret: μετρέω.

Hab. 2 14: Cyril: ἐμπίμπλημι (B); Theodoret: πίμπλημι.

Hos. 1 2: Cyril: ἐκπορνεύω (B); Theodoret: πορνεύω.
Zech. 14 12: Cyril: ἐκρέω; Theodoret: ῥέω (B).
Zech. 2 4; 11 16: Cyril: διασκορπίζω; Theodoret: σκορπίζω (B: 2 4
  = Cy; 11 16 = Theod.).
Hag. 1 10: Cyril: ὑποστέλλομαι (B); Theodoret: στέλλομαι.
Hos. 12 2: Cyril: διατίθεμαι (B); Theodoret: τίθεμαι.
Hos. 7 16: Cyril: ἐντείνω (B); Theodoret: τείνω.
Hos. 10 14: Cyril: περιτειχίζω (B); Theodoret: τειχίζω.
Obad. 12: Cyril: ἐπιχαίρω (B); Theodoret: χαίρω.

c.) Different Compounds:

Hab. 2 5: Cyril: εἰσδέχομαι (B); Theodoret: προσδέχομαι.
Hab. 3 12: Cyril: κατάσσω (B); Theodoret: πατάσσω.
Zeph. 2 15: Cyril: διαπορεύω (B); Theodoret: παραπορεύω.
Zeph. 3 14: Cyril: κατατέρπω (B); Theodoret: εὐτέρπω.
Hos. 2 9: Cyril: ὑποστρέφω; Theodoret: ἐπιστρέφω (B).
Zech. 10 11: Cyril: ἀφαιρέω (B); Theodoret: καθαιρέω.
Nah. 1 8; Zech. 9 13: Cyril: ἐπεγείρω; Theodoret: ἐξεγείρω
  (B: Nah. = Cy; Zech. = Th.).
Jonah 4 5: Cyril: ἀφοράω (B); Theodoret: ἐφοράω.
Amos 6 10: Cyril: ὑπολείπω (B); Theodoret: ἀπολείπω.
Hos. 7 16: Cyril: ἀποστρέφω (B); Theodoret: ἐπιστρέφω.

d.) Compound and Decompound:

Hos. 4 14: Cyril: συναναφύρω; Theodoret: συμφύρω (B).
Mic. 6 12: Cyril: κατοικέω (B); Theodoret: ἐνκατοικέω.
Zech. 6 15: Cyril: ἀποστέλλω (B); Theodoret: ἐξαποστέλλω.
Amos 1 4: Cyril: ἐξαποστέλλω (B); Theodoret: ἀποστέλλω.

XII. The Use of the Particles:

1.) Cyril: οὕτως—Theodoret: οὕτω: Amos 4 12 (bis); 5 14; Nah.
    1 12; Zech. 7 13.
   Cyril: οὕτω—Theodoret: οὕτως: Joel 2 4; Mic. 3 4.
2.) Cyril: διότι—Theodoret: ὅτι: Hos. 4 4, 14 10; Joel 4 12;
    Obad. 18; Zeph. 2 9; Zech. 2 13.17; 6 15; 9 1.2; Zech.
    10 2.5; 11 11; 13 5; Mal. 3 19.
   Cyril: ὅτι—Theodoret: διότι: Hos. 2 2; Jonah 1 14.
   Cyril: διότι—Theodoret: διό: Hab. 1 6.

3.) Cyril: διότι—Theodoret: γάρ: Hos. 8 13; Amos 3 7; Mic. 1 3; 4 4.

    Cyril: ὅτι—Theodoret: γάρ: Zech. 9 17.

4.) Cyril: (ὅς)ἄν—Theodoret: (ὅς)ἐάν: Mic. 6 14; Hag. 2 14; Zech. 14 16.

    Cyril: ἐάν—Theodoret: ἄν: Amos 3 7; Zech. 14 19.

5.) Cyril: ἐπί—Theodoret: ἐν: Hos. 10 10; Joel 1 17; Amos 6 6; 9 15; Mic. 3 4; 7 7; Zeph. 3 17; Zech. 12 2.

    Cyril: ἐν—Theodoret: ἐπί: Hag. 1 14; Zech. 6 8.

6.) Cyril: εἰς—Theodoret: ἐν: Amos 7 8; Mic. 6 14; Zeph. 3 8.

7.) Cyril: ἐκ—Theodoret: ἀπό: Hos. 2 4; 13 14; Jonah 3 9; Mic. 3 6; 7 13.

    Cyril: ἀπό—Theodoret: ἐκ: Amos 9 15; Zech. 9 5.

8.) Cyril: ἐπί—Theodoret: εἰς: Hos. 3 1; Zech. 10 3.

    Cyril: εἰς—Theodoret: ἐπί: Hab. 1 9.

9.) Cyril: πρός—Theodoret: εἰς: Jonah 2 8; Zech. 11 10.

10.) Cyril: οὐ μή—Theodoret: οὐ: Hab. 2 3; Zeph. 3 13; Zech. 11 16.

    Cyril: οὐ μή—Theodoret: μή: Zeph. 1 12; Mal. 2 16.

    Cyril: οὐ—Theodoret: οὐ μή: Amos 7 3; 9 8; Hab. 1 2 (bis).

11.) Cyril: ὡσεί—Theodoret: ὡς: Hos. 7 11; Zech. 12 10.

12.) Cyril: ὥσπερ—Theodoret: ὡς: Hos. 13 3; Mal. 3 3.

13.) Cyril: καθώς—Theodoret: κατά: Mic. 7 14; Mal. 3 4 (bis).

14.) Cyril: ὡς—Theodoret: εἰς: Hos. 7 16; Mic. 1 6 (bis); 3 12.

    Cyril: εἰς—Theodoret: ὡς: Mic. 2 11.

XIII. Addition of Particles:

1.) Theodoret adds γάρ: Hos. 3 1; 4 12.18; 5 10; 6 3; 7 7; 9 11; 13 13.15; Joel 1 8; Obad. 1 5; Jonah 1 12.14; 2 1; Mic. 7 10,17; Nah. 2 10,14 Hab. 1 11; 3 16; Hag. 1 9; Zech. 8 16,17.

2.) Theodoret adds δέ: Hos. 9 10; Amos 5 2; Hab. 3 7; Zech. 9 2; 14 9.

    Cyril adds δέ: Zeph. 3 5.

3.) Cyril adds δή: Joel 1 2; Amos 4 5; Hag. 1 1,5.

4.) Theodoret adds ἐπειδή: Hos. 4 6.

5.) Theodoret adds νῦν δέ: Hos. 6 3.

6.) Theodoret adds τοίνυν: Joel 1 14; Amos 3 1.
7.) Theodoret adds οὖν: Amos 5 14.
8.) Cyril adds οὕτως: Hos. 4 16.
9.) Theodoret adds ὡς: Joel 1 6; Nah. 3 12; Zech. 9 13.

XIV. Syntactic Differences:

1.) Cyril: καὶ (εἶπεν etc.)—Theodoret: (εἶπεν etc.) γάρ:
   Hos. 1 4; 2 1,9,16; 3 5; 10 14; Joel 2 3; Amos 2 11; 8 2;
   9 4; Jonah 3 4,10; 4 8; Mic. 7 14; Nah. 2 6; Zeph. 1 13;
   Zech. 4 7; 8 16; 12 10.
2.) Cyril: καὶ (εἶπεν etc.)—Theodoret: (εἶπεν etc.) δέ: Hos. 13 7;
   Joel 4 19; Obad. 19.
   Cyril: (εἶπεν etc.) δέ—Theodoret: καὶ (εἶπεν etc.): Hos. 7 13;
   8 13; Amos 7 11; Obad. 13.

XV. Cases following Verbs:

ἀκούω: Cyril: c. gen.—Theodoret: c. acc.: Mic. 6 1.
   Cyril: c. acc.—Theodoret: c. gen.: Zech. 7 12.
ἀκούομαι: Cyril: c. acc.—Theodoret: c. dat.: Hos. 2 24.
μιμνήσκομαι: Cyril: c. acc.—Theodoret: c. gen.: Hos. 2 19; 7 2; 8 13.

XVI. Cases following ἐπί:

Cyril: c. dat.—Theodoret: c. acc.: Hos. 8 5; Zech. 14 18.
Cyril: c. acc.—Theodoret: c. dat.: Zech. 12 10.
Cyril: c. acc.—Theodoret: c. gen.: Jonah 1 12; Mic. 3 5; Zech. 14 12.

XVII. Differences in Spelling:

Hos. 1 4: Cyril: 'Ιεσραελ; Theodoret: 'Ιεζραελ.
Hos. 2 18: Cyril: Βααλειμ; Theodoret: Βααλιμ.
Mic. 1 10: Cyril: 'Ενακειμ; Theodoret: 'Ενακιμ.
Hos. 10 11: Cyril: νῖκος; Theodoret: νεῖκος.
Amos 1 4: Cyril: θεμέλια; Theodoret: θεμέλεια.
Hos. 11 8: Cyril: Σεβοειμ; Theodoret: Σεβωιμ.
Hos. 1 7: Cyril: οὔτε; Theodoret: οὐδέ.

Hos. 3 5: Cyril: Δαυειδ; Theodoret: Δαβιδ.
Hos. 6 9: Cyril: Σικιμα; Theodoret: Σικημα.
Amos 6 2: Cyril: Αἱμαθ; Theodoret: Ἐμαθ.
Amos 6 14: Cyril: Αἱμαθ; Theodoret: Ἡμαθ.
Zech. 9 1: Cyril: Ἐδραχ; Theodoret: Ἀδραχ.
Zech. 7 2: Cyril: Βαιθηλ; Theodoret: Βεθηλ.

XVIII. Corruptions of Proper Names:

Hos. 1 4: Cyril: Ἰουδα; Theodoret: Ἰηου (MT).
Hos. 5 13; 10 6: Cyril: Ἰαρειμ; Theodoret: Ἰαρειβ (MT).
Hos. 6 8: Cyril: Γαλααδ (MT); Theodoret: Γαλγαλα.
Hos. 10 14: Cyril: Ἱεροβααλ; Theodoret: Ἀρβεηλ (MT).
Amos 3 13: Cyril: Ἰακωβ (MT); Theodoret: Ἰσραηλ.
Mic. 1 11: Cyril: Σεννααρ; Theodoret: Αἰναν (MT: צַאֲנָן).
Mic. 1 15: Cyril: Ἰσραηλ; (MT); Theodoret: Σιων.
Zeph. 1 1: Cyril: Ἀμως; Theodoret: Ἀμων (MT).
Zech. 14 5: Cyril: Ἀσαηλ; Theodoret: Ἰασσα MT: אָצַל).
Zech. 14 10: Cyril: Γαβελ; Theodoret: Γαβαα (MT).

XIX. Differences resulting from Hebrew variae lectiones:

Hos. 1 4: אֵלָיו > Theodoret:
Hos. 2 9: תִמְצָא: Cyril: εὕρη αὐτούς = תִּמְצָאֵם.
Hos. 2 10: וְכָסֶף: Theodoret: ἀργύριον καὶ χρυσίον = כֶּסֶף וְזָהָב.
Hos. 2 20: וְהִשְׁכַּבְתִּים: Cyril: καὶ κατοικιῶ σε = וְהִשְׁכַּבְתִּיךְ.
Hos. 2 25: אֱלֹהָי: Cyril: κύριος ὁ θεὸς μου = יהוה אלהי.
Hos. 7 2: לִלְבָבָם: Theodoret: ἐν ταῖς καρδίαις αὐτῶν = בִּלְבָבָם.
Hos. 7 7: וְאָכְלוּ: Theodoret: πῦρ γὰρ κατέφαγεν = אֵשׁ אָכְלָה.
Hos. 8 12: נֶחְשָׁבוּ: Cyril: ἐλογίσθησαν αὐτῷ = נֶחְשְׁבוּ־לוֹ.
Hos. 9 1: מֵעַל אֱלֹהֶיךָ: Theodoret: ἀπὸ κυρίου θεοῦ σου = מעל יהוה אלהיך.
Hos. 9 13: וְאֶפְרַיִם לְהוֹצִיא: Theodoret: καὶ ἐξήγαγεν = וְהוֹצִיא.
Hos. 10 10: וְאָסְרָם: Theodoret adds: κατὰ τὴν ἐπιθυμίαν μου = + בְּאַוָּתִי.
Hos. 10 12: וְעֵת: Theodoret: ὡς ἔτι καιρός = וְעֹד עֵת.

28

Hos. 10 15: נִדְמָה: Theodoret: ὡς ὄρθρος ἀπερρίφη = כַּשַׁחַר נִדְמָה.

Hos. 12 14: מִמִּצְרָיִם: Theodoret: ἐκ γῆς Αἰγύπτου = מֵאֶרֶץ‖מִצְרָיִם.

Joel 1 14: אֱלֹהֵיכֶם: Cyril: θεοῦ ἡμῶν = אֱלֹהֵינוּ.

Joel 2 8: יִבְצָעוּ: Theodoret: συντελεσθῶσιν = יְבָצֵעוּ.

Amos 4 3: יהוה: Cyril: κύριος ὁ θεός = יְהוָה אֱלֹהִים.

Amos 5 22: אֶרְצֶה: Cyril: προσδέξομαι αὐτά = אֶרְצֵם.

Mic. 4 6: בַּיּוֹם הַהוּא: Theodoret: ἐν ταῖς ἡμέραις καὶ ἐν τῷ καιρῷ
ἐκείνῳ = בַּיָּמִים הָהֵם וּבָעֵת הַהִיא.

Hab. 2 14: הָאָרֶץ: Cyril: σύμπασα γῆ = כָּל־הָאָרֶץ.

Zech. 9 15: יַיִן: Theodoret: ὕδωρ = מָיִם.

Zech. 13 6: יָדֶיךָ: Theodoret: ὤμων σου = שְׁכְמֶיךָ.

Zech. 13 8: בְּכָל־הָאָרֶץ > Cyril.

Zech. 14 5: וְנַסְתֶּם 2° > Cyril.

Proceedings of the American Academy for Jewish Research,
Vol. 6 (1934 - 1935), pp. 309-351

THE TARGUM ONKELOS

in its Relation to the
Masoretic Hebrew text

ALEXANDER SPERBER

The various Aramaic Versions of the Hebrew Bible as a means of help for the better understanding of the Masoretic Hebrew Text began to interest me, when I was still in my undergraduate years. I just happened to be reading the book of Jeremiah, when the passage in the chapter 11 verse 14 startled me. ואתה אל תתפלל בעד העם הזה ואל תשא בעדם רנה ותפלה כי אינני שמע בעת קראם אלי: "Pray not thou for this people, neither lift up cry nor prayer for them; for I will not hear (them) in the time that they cry unto me." For the first half of the verse the prophet is referred to as he, who does the praying (note the second person in ואתה תשא . . .), while the suffix of the third person in קראם in the second half of the verse implies, that Israel is praying to the Lord. This difficulty becomes even more obvious, when we consider the following verse 15: מה לידידי בביתי עשותה המזמתה: "What hath My beloved to do in My house, (seeing) she hath wrought lewdness." Far from repenting her ways "she," i. e. Israel, continues to sin; and it is only "My beloved," i, e. the prophet, who comes "in My house," surely to "cry unto Me."

The key to the solution of this difficulty is to be found in chapter 7 verse 16: ואתה אל תתפלל בעד העם הזה ואל תשא בעדם רנה ותפלה ואל תפגע בי כי אינני שמע אתך: "Pray not thou for this people, neither lift up cry nor prayer for them, neither make intercession to Me, for I will not hear thee." Both verses, 7.16 and 11.14, are nearly identical, except for the last words; instead of בעת קראם אלי in 11.14, which does not fit in the context, as we have seen, 7.16 reads אתך. It is the prophet, according to this reading, who prays to God for his people, and whose prayer the Lord would not accept, because of Israel's sins.

Looking up the ancient versions I found the Septuagint
offering no help: ὅτι οὐκ εἰσακούσομαι ἐν τῷ καιρῷ ἐν ᾧ
ἐπικαλοῦνταί με is an exact translation of the Masoretic
Text to 11.14; and as for 7.16, the Septuagint has there only:
ὅτι οὐκ εἰσακούσομαι, and this means, that the Greek equivalent for the Hebrew word אתך is missing in the Septuagint,
unfortunately; for it is this word in 7.16, which corresponds to
קראך אלי in 11.14. After this failure of the Septuagint I was
gladly surprised to find the Aramaic Targum most helpful:
ארי לא רעוא קדמי בעידן דאת מצלי עליהון; in other words; the Targum
read: בעת קָרְאָךְ אֵלַי in 11.14.

Since I did not find in the modern commentaries any hint to
this textual difficulty or any reference to the Targum as evidence
of the aforementioned *varia lectio*, I surmised that the importance
of the Targum for the exegesis of the Bible might not be fully
realized by the biblical commentators. I, therefore, decided to
make a thorough investigation of all the Aramaic Bible Versions
as to their relation to the Masoretic Hebrew Text. The results
of these studies were gradually embodied in the *apparatus criticus*
of the new (third) edition of R. Kittel's *Biblia Hebraica*, while
I served there as assistant editor for the Ancient Versions; cf.
Kittel's Preface to *Isaia*, the first book to be published in the
third edition, and P. Kahle in his *Masoreten des Westens*, II,
Stuttgart 1930, page 11*, note 1.

As a basic Aramaic text for this comparison with the Masoretic
Hebrew Text I had to use Lagarde's print of the codex Reuchlinianus (*Prophetae Chaldaice*, 1872); as for the Pentateuch, I
had to refer to Berliner's reprint of the Sabbioneta text of the
Targum Onkelos (*Targum Onkelos*, 1884). Both publications
are merely reprints of only one textual form and are not in the
least entitled to be considered critical editions of the respective
Targumim. I fully realized this disadvantage, which made
the value of my study rather questionable from a purely scientific
point of view. I was, therefore, glad, when after my graduation
at Bonn University, the Berlin *Academy for Jewish Research*
invited me to prepare a critical edition of the Aramaic Targumim for publication under its auspices. At this occasion
I wish to extend my sincerest thanks to the Ex-Trustees and

Directors of that learned body, which ceased to exist as a result of the political changes in Germany; and especially to Professor Julius·Guttmann, who is now at the Hebrew University in Jerusalem—for their generous help and assistance during a period of nearly ten years. Owing to the great interest, which Professor Guttmann took in my work, I was able to spend two years and a half in England, and one summer in Italy, to work on the Targum manuscripts of the various libraries of these countries. As a result of these years of research, I prepared critical editions of the Targum Onkelos to the Pentateuch and of the Targum Jonathan to the former prophets, based upon all available manuscripts and old printed editions.

When in the year 1931 the economic situation in Germany became very serious, it was obvious that it would be impossible for the Jewish Academy to cover the printing expenses of these Targum editions— although the *Notgemeinschaft Deutscher Wissenschaft*, a federal government institution for the advancement of pure research, agreed to subsidize the print with a considerable contribution. Then the well known publisher, Kohlhammer in Stuttgart, after having consulted Professors Kahle (Bonn) as a Semitic Philologist, Alt (Leipzig) as an Old Testament authority and G. Kittel (Tübingen) as a New Testament and Rabbinic scholar, declared himself ready to bring the editions out at his own expenses. The recent development of the political situation in Germany cast all these plans into the discard.

Since it does not seem very likely that these editions will appear in the near future, I should like to submit here to the scholarly world at least one chapter of the introduction to the Targum Onkelos, which is in the course of preparation, to indicate the nature of the contribution of my edition towards the advancement of biblical scholarship. For this purpose I selected the chapter dealing with the *variae lectiones* of the Targum Onkelos as compared with the Masoretic Text. A comparison of the collection presented here with the material which I offered in Kittel's *Biblia Hebraica* will prove, to what degree my edition reveals progress in this field. It may be of interest to note, that out of the 650 various readings contained in this paper, only about 270 are derived from the Ms. y, which serves as the basic text for my edition, whilst some 380 variants go back to the other texts as used in the *apparatus criticus*. This fact shows the importance of the critical apparatus not only for the solution of the problem in question, but also for all other problems connected with the text of Targum Onkelos, which underwent many changes in the course of the centuries. On this point see my paper "Peschitta und Onkelos" in the forthcoming *Jewish Studies in Memory of George A. Kohut*.

The variant readings which I derived from the manuscripts and printed editions of Targum Onkelos I compared with all the Non-Masoretic Bible Texts as indicated in the second part of my Table of Sigla. It is noteworthy that evidence for a very large proportion of these variants is found in these texts. This proves that Bible Mss. with such Non-Masoretic readings actually existed in the early centuries of the common era.

Similarly, even the other *variae lectiones* which are not found in the Non-Masoretic Bible texts, are well founded, since they are based on well established philological principles. The fact that they are not recorded in the Non-Masoretic Bible texts does not diminish their importance. For even these Non-Masoretic Bible texts are not preserved in their original form; they themselves underwent a series of changes to the effect of harmonizing them more and more with the more authoritative Masoretic Text. This statement can be applied not only to the Hebrew manuscripts collated by Kennicott and de Rossi, but to the Septuagint as well. And even the Hebrew Pentateuch of the Samaritans now offers sometimes a text, which differs from the original reading. This becomes evident, when we compare some of the readings of these texts with quotations found in St. Jerome's writings.

I should like to demonstrate the correctness of this assertion by referring to a statement made by Jerome in his *Quaestiones Hebraicae in libro Geneseos* (editio Lagarde, Leipzig 1868). To Gen. 5.25–27 Jerome remarks: *"Et uixit Mathusalam annis CLXVII et genuit Lamech. et uixit Mathusala, postquam genuit Lamech, annos DCCCII et genuit filios et filias. et fuerunt omnes dies Mathusalae, quos uixit, anni DCCCCLXVIIII et mortuus est.* famosa quaestio et disputatione omnium ecclesiarum uentilata quod iuxta diligentem subputationem XIIII annos post diluuium Mathusala uixisse referatur. etenim cum esset Mathusala annorum CLXVII, genuit Lamech. rursum Lamech, cum esset annorum CLXXXVIII, genuit Noe. et fiunt usque ad diem natiuitatis Noe anni uitae Mathusalae CCCLV. sexcentesimo autem anno uitae Noe diluuium factum est. ac per hoc habita subputatione per partes DCCCCLV anno Mathusalae diluuium fuisse conuincitur. cum autem supra DCCCCLXVIIII annis uixisse sit dictus, nulli dubium est XIIII eum annos uixisse post diluuium. et quo modo uerum est quod octo tantum animae in arca saluae factae sunt? restat ergo ut quomodo in plerisque, ita et in hoc sit error in numero. siquidem et in hebraeis et Samaritanorum libris ita scriptum repperi *et uixit Mathusala CLXXXVII annis et genuit Lamech. et uixit Mathusala, postquam genuit Lamech. DCCLXXXII annos, et genuit filios et filias. et fuerunt omnes dies Mathusalae anni DCCCCLXVIIII et mortuus est. et uixit Lamech CLXXXII annos et genuit Noe.* a die ergo natiuitatis Mathusalae usque ad diem natiuitatis Noe sunt anni CCCLXIX: his adde DC annos Noe, quia in sexcentesimo uitae eius anno diluuium factum est: atque ita fit, ut DCCCCLXIX anno uitae suae Mathusala mortuus sit, eo anno quo coepit esse diluuium."

In short: according to Jerome, the Septuagint records that Methuselah was 167 years old, when he begat Lamech, and that he lived afterwards 802 years, so that all his days were 969 years. Now Lamech was 188 years of age, when he begat Noah. Methuselah, therefore, was 355 years old, when Noah was born. When Noah was 600 years old, the flood came. How old was then Methuselah? 355+600=955 years. But since Methuselah lived 969 years, it would mean, that he survived the flood for 14 years, in contradiction to the biblical narrative, which does not include him amongst the persons saved in Noah's ark. The solution of this problem Jerome finds in the data given in the Hebrew and in the Samaritan Bible. Both texts are referred to as stating that Methuselah was 187 years old when he begat Lamech, while Lamech was 182 years of age when he begat

Noah. Methuselah, therefore, was 369 years old at Noah's birth. Adding to it 600 years—for Noah was 600 years old when the flood came—we find, that the flood began, when Methuselah was 969 years of age; this means, that Methuselah died, when the flood came.

Let us now test Jerome's assertions: The Septuagint reads: Verse 25: καὶ ἔζησεν Μαθουσαλα ἑκατὸν καὶ ὀγδοήκοντα ἑπτὰ ἔτη, καὶ ἐγέννησεν τὸν Λαμεχ. Methuselah lived 187 years, and he begat Lamech. This reading agrees exactly with the Masoretic Hebrew text in the most essential point, which gave rise to Jerome's question. The original reading of the Septuagint, as presupposed by Jerome, is still to be found in a quotation of a Church Father in Field's *Origenis Hexaplorum quae supersunt* (Oxford 1875) and in some Septuagint Mss. of the cursive type, as quoted in the Cambridge edition of the Septuagint. This is a further instance for the importance of this group of Septuagint Mss.; cf. my *Septuagintaprobleme* (Stuttgart 1929, page 56). As to the Samaritan Pentateuch, it offers in verse 25 and verse 28, where the ages of Methuselah and Lamech are recorded at the time of birth of Lamech and Noah respectively, readings which have nothing in common with the entire numerical system of the Masoretic Hebrew text.

We have seen, that in the passage in question Jerome had in the Septuagint and in the Samaritan Pentateuch readings before him, which differ materially from those readings, which we find there now. It is only logical to assume, that just as these particular verses have undergone such important changes in these Non-Masoretic Bible texts, in the same way many other passages may have shared this fate, although that for the time being we are lacking evidence from old sources such as Jerome to prove it. The agreement in the reading of a certain biblical passage between the Masoretic Text and any of the Non-Masoretic texts is, therefore, no proof whatsoever, that this passage always read in this way. On the contrary, it may very often be assumed, that this agreement is only the result of the harmonizing efforts of later scribes.

TABLE OF SIGLA

1) Targum Mss. and early printed editions:

a	Ms. No. 282 in the possession of Mr. D. S. Sassoon, London
b	The First Biblia Rabbinica, ed. Bomberg, Venice 1517
c	Ms. Or. 9400 in the British Museum
d	Ms. Solger No. 2 in the Stadtbibliothek of Nuremberg, Germany
g	The Second Biblia Rabbinica, ed. Bomberg, Venice 1524/25
h	Biblia Hebraica, shelf-mark I 1363, University Library, Freiburg i/Br., Germany
i	Mss. Or. 2228, 2229 and 2230 in the British Museum (one Ms. in three volumes)
j	Ms. Or. 1467 in the British Museum
k	Biblia Hebraica, Lisbon 1491
l	Biblia Hebraica, Ixar 1490
n	Biblia Sacra Complutensia, 1517
s	Biblia Hebraica, Sabbioneta 1557
v	Ms. Socin No. 84, library of the Deutsche Morgenländische Gesellschaft, Halle, Saale, Germany
y	Ms. Or. 2363 in the British Museum
T	Agreement of the readings of all texts with Tiberian punctuation (a b c d g h k l n s)
Y	Agreement of the readings of all texts with supralinear punctuation (j i v, as against y)
Trg	The basic Targum text of my edition
a	behind a Ms. indicates: prima manus
b	behind a Ms. indicates: secunda manus
1	behind a Ms. indicates: marginal note

36

2) Masoretic and Non-Masoretic Bible texts:

MT   The Masoretic Hebrew Text, according to Kittel's
          Biblia Hebraica, 1905

Ms. K   Variants of MT, according to Kennicott's *Vetus
          Testamentum Hebraicum cum variis lectionibus*,
          2 vols. Oxford 1776–80.

Ms. R   Variants of MT, according to de Rossi's *Variae
          lectiones Veteris Testamenti*, 4 vols. Parma
          1784–88.

S   The Samaritan Hebrew Pentateuch, according to
          von Gall: *Der Hebräische Pentateuch der Sam-
          aritaner*. Giessen 1914–18.

LXX   The Septuagint, according to Brooke—Mc Lean:
          The Old Testament in Greek. Vol. I, Cambridge
          1906–1911

S (Ms.) or LXX (Ms.) refers to the critical apparatus of these
          editions

P   Peshitta, according to *Pentateuchus Syriace* post
          Samuelem Lee . . . edidit G. E. Barnes, London
          1914.

Genesis

I

11: לְמִינוֹ / לְמִינֵהוּ=לְזנוהי :k l n; cf. Lev 11.15, 22; Dt 14.14.

12: לְמִינֵהוּ 1° / לזניה=לְמִינוֹ :h.

21: למיניהם / לזנוהי :1=לְמִינֵהוּ.

26: כדמותנו / בדמותנא :h=בִּדְמוּתֵנוּ; 6 Mss R.

30: רומש / דרחיש :Trg=הָרוֹמֵשׂ; S, P.

31: הששי / שתיתי :Trg=שִׁשִּׁי; 1 Ms K, LXX, P.

II

6: מן / על :Trg=עֵל.

7 ויהי האדם / והות באדם :Trg=וַתְּהִי בָאָדָם.

11.13: הסבב / מקיף :Trg=סֹבֵב.

11: החוילה / חוילה :Trg=חֲוִילָה; S.

14: ההלך / מהליך :Trg=הַהֹלֵךְ.

15: לעבדה ולשמרה / למפלח ולמנטר :k=לעבדה ולשמרה; cf.
Theodoret: ἐργάζεσθαι καὶ φυλάσσειν.

17: תמות / תמותון :h=תָּמוּתוּן; LXX.

23: מאיש / מבעלה :Trg=מֵאִישָׁה; S, LXX.

לקחה / נסיבא :Trg=לֻקֳחָה; P; difference in the vocalization, cf. 7.20, 9.16, 21.2, 34.31, Ex 5.23, 10.21, 23.7,
35.22, Lev 8.31, 9.4, Num 8.12, 18.11, 19, Dt 32.10.

III

7: עלה / טרפי :Trg=עֲלֵי; 13 Mss K, 5 Mss R, S, LXX.

16: אל האשה / ולאיתתא :1=וְאֶל הָאִשָּׁה; 4 Mss K, 2 Mss R,
S, LXX, P.

24: וישכן / ואשרייה :Trg=וישכן אתו; LXX; the missing object
is added; cf. Ex 2.3.

IV

1: את 3° / Trg: מֵאֵת=מן קדם; LXX; cf. Dt 28.12.

6: ולמה / 1 n: וְלָמָה זֶה=ולמא דנן; cf. 27.46.

7: from ואליך תשוקתו until the end of the verse > Trg.

22: לטש / Trg: הוּא הָיָה אָבִי=הוא הוה רבהון; cf. v. 21.

25: ותקרא / h 1: וַתִּקְרָא=וקרא; 1 Ms K, S; cf. 19.37, 38; 30.18, 21, 24; 38.3.

 כי 1° / Trg: כִּי אָמְרָה=ארי אמרת; LXX.

V

1: אדם 2° / 1: אֶת הָאָדָם=ית אדם; nota accusativi added, cf. 9.11, 21.10, 24.46, 34.27, 38.30, 39.6, 9, Ex 1.18, 2.9, 16, 4.21, 7.19, 8.16, Lev 4.28, 18.29, 19.27, Num 13.25, 18.28, 23.7, Dt 5.26, 11.14, 22.4.

3: כצלמו / 1: בְּצַלְמוֹ=בצלמיה; 17 Mss K, 25 Mss R.

23: ויהי / Trg: וַיִּהְיוּ=והוו; 20 Mss K, 1 Ms R, S, LXX, P.

31: ויהי / Trg: וַיִּהְיוּ=והוו; 11 Mss K, 4 Mss R, S, LXX, P.

VI

3: ידון / Trg: יָדוּר=יתקיים ?; cf. LXX: καταμείνῃ; P: תעמר.

7: עד 1° / 1: וְעַד=ועד; 9 Mss K, P.

 עד 2° / Trg: וְעַד=ועד; 3 Mss K, LXX, P.

 ועד / k: עַד=עד; 1 Ms K, 2 Mss R, S, LXX.

VII

2: ומן / 1: מִן=מן.

9.15: אל / Trg: אֶת=עם; P.

20: ויכסו / n: וַיְכַסּוּ=וחפו; LXX; cf. 2.23.

21: ובחיה / n: בְּחַיָּה=בחיתא.

23: עד 1° / d: וְעַד=ועד; 5 Mss K, P.

 עד 2° / c: וְעַד=ועד; 1 Ms K, LXX, P.

VIII

19: כל 2° / n: וכל=וְכָל; 5 Mss K, 1 Ms R, S, LXX, P.

כל 3° / h l: וכל=וְכָל; 11 Mss K, 3 Mss R, P.

20: במזבח / Trg: על מדבחא=עַל הַמִּזְבֵּחַ; LXX, P.

21: ולא / Trg: לא=לָא; 4 Mss K.

IX

2: בכל / l: ובכל=וּבְכָל; 1 Ms K, 1 Ms R, S, LXX, P.

9: ואני / h: אנא=אֲנִי; LXX, P.

10: בבהמה / i c h k l: ובבעירא=וּבַבְּהֵמָה; 24 Mss K, 14 Mss R, S, LXX, P.

11: הארץ / d: ית ארעא=אֶת הָאָרֶץ; cf. 5.1.

16: לזכר / Trg: לדוכרן=לְזֵכָר; P; cf. S: לאזכרה; cf. 2.23.

18: וחם 1° / k: חם=חָם; 1 Ms K, S.

19: נפצה כל / Trg: אתבדרו בכל=נָפְצוּ בְכָל; LXX, P.

X

1: חם / c h k n: וחם=וְחָם; 20 Mss K, 31 Mss R, P.

8: גבר / b d g k l: גיבר תקיף=גִּבֹּר צַיִד; cf. v. 9.

19: ואדמה / k: אדמה=אַדְמָה; 18 Mss K, 12 Mss R, LXX.

20: בגויהם / k: לעממיהון=לְגוֹיֵהֶם; 2 Mss R, S; cf. v. 31.

25: ילד / Trg: אתילידו=יֻלְּדוּ; S, LXX, P; cf. 35.26, 41.50, 46.27.

31: לגויהם / g k: בעממיהון=בְּגוֹיֵהֶם; 7 Mss K, S, LXX, P; cf. v. 20.

32: הגוים / k: נגות עממיא=אִיֵּי הַגּוֹיִם; S, LXX; cf. v. 5.

XII

6: אלון / Trg: מישרי=אֵלוֹנֵי; cf. 18.1.

12: אשתו / h: איתתי=אִשְׁתִּי.

13: נא / לִי = עֲלַי :l.

19: למה / d: וְלָמָה = ולמה ; S, P.

XIII

3: הֹיֶה / Trg: נָטָה = דפרסיה.

XIV

4: ושלש / l n: וּבְשָׁלֹשׁ = ובתלת ; S, LXX, P.

6: בהררם / Trg: בָּהָרֲרִי = דבטוריא ; i b g: דבטורא = בָּהָר.

7: הוּא / Trg: עַד = עד.

12: רכשו / Trg: כָּל רְכֻשׁוֹ = כל קנייניה.

24: בלעדי Trg > ; LXX, P.

XV.

6: צדקה / Trg: לִצְדָקָה = לזכו ; LXX, P.

8: אירשנו / l: יִירָשֶׁנוּ = יירתינה ; S.

9: ואיל / h: אַיִל = דכרין.

10: איש בתרו / Trg: הַבְּתָרִים אִישׁ = פלגיא פלג.

14: יעבדו / Trg: יַעֲבֹדוּם = דיפלחון בהון ; cf. 1 Ms K: יעבודון.

17: אשר עבר / Trg: אֲשֶׁר = עדא ; אשר Trg > ; 1 Ms K ; cf. Ex 39.1, Num 31.12.

18: מנהר / Trg: מִנַּחַל = מנחלא / ; עד / b d g: וְעַד = ועד ; 1 Ms K, P.

21: ואת יַת / 1° את = יָת ; l.

XVI.

6: הטוב / b d g l n: כַּטּוֹב = כדתקין ; 1 Ms K, 1 Ms R, LXX.

12: ועל / b c l: עַל = על ; 20 Mss K.

XVII.

5: אב / Trg: לְאָב = לאב ; cf. v. 4.

6: ומלכים / c: מְלָכִים = מלכין ; cf. v. 16.

41

12: מֵאֵת בֶּן=מן בר / 1: מן בר=מכל בן; 1 Ms K.

16: וּבְרַכְתִּיךָ=ואברכינך / Trg: וברכתיה; 1 Ms K.

וּמְלָכִי=ומלכין / h k l s: מלכי; 9 Mss K, 7 Mss R, S, LXX, P.

17: אִם=אם / h: ואם; P.

19: וּלְזַרְעוֹ=ולבנוהי / k l n: לזרעו; 57 Mss K, 18 Mss R, S, LXX, P.

XVIII.

13: הַאַף הָאֻמְנָם=הבקושטא / Trg: הַאֻמְנָם=הָאֻמְנָם; cf. S(Mss): האף האמנם.

19: הֵבִיא=דאייתי / n: הבִיא; mistake, cf. 19.15 and 23.9.

XIX.

3: אֵפֹה לָהֶם=אפא להון / Trg: אפה; LXX, P; the object is added; cf. 22.2, Ex 18.16, 21.13, 23.1, Num 15.34, 19.22, 23.7, Dt 17.16.

4: מִקָצֵהוּ=מסופיה / Trg: מקצה; P.

8: יָדְעָן=ידעונין / Trg: ידעו?; P.

10: וְהַדֶלֶת-=ודשא / 1: ואת הדלת; nota accusativi omitted, cf. 33.5, Num 7.11, 9.15, 14.36, 18.28, 30.15, 33.52, Dt 20.19, 31.28, 29.

12: חֲתָנֶיךָ=חתנך / h n: חתן; P.

15: הַנִמְצָאֹת=דאשתכחת / 1: הנמצאת; mistake, cf. 18.19.

17: כְּהוֹצִיאוֹ=כד אפיק / Trg: כהוציאם.

20: שָׁם 1°=תמן / b d l: שמה; cf. 23.13, 24.6, 8, 29.3, 42.2, Ex 10.26, 26.33, Lev 18.3, 20.22, Num 15.18, 35.6, 11, 15, Dt 1.38, 4.14, 26, 42, 6.1, 11.8, 11, 29, 19.3, 23.21, 28.37, 30.1, 3, 16, 18, 31.13, 32.47, 52, 34.4.

21: הָפֹךְ=למיהפך / T: הפכי; LXX.

33: הוא / 1: ההוא=הַהוּא; 4 Mss K, S, LXX, P.

ותבא / i: וקמת=וַתָּקָם cf. v. 35.

37.38: ותקרא / 1: וקרא=וַיִּקְרָא; cf. 4.25.

XX.

2: אל / Trg: על=עַל; LXX, P.

3: על / Trg: על עיסק=על אודת=עַל אֹדֹת; S, P; cf. v. 11 and 18.

13: אל כל / 1: בכל=בְּכָל; 1 Ms K, P.

XXI.

2: אתו / 1: עימיה=אִתּוֹ; cf. 2.23.

10: גרש / g n: תריך ית=גרש אֶת; 12 Mss K, S; cf. 5.1.

17: אל קול / k: ית קליה=אֶת קוֹל; 8 Mss K, 16 Mss R, S; cf. the beginning of the verse.

XXII.

2: והעלהו / Trg: ואסיקהי קדמי=והעלהו לי; cf. 19.3.

8: לו >Trg.

13: אחר >Trg; 1 Ms K; g l: חדא=אָחָד; 32 Mss K, 13 Mss R, S, LXX, P.

XXIII.

9: ויתן / 1: ויהב=וַיִּתָּן; mistake; cf. 18.19.

13: שמה / Trg: תמן=שָׁם; S, P; cf. 19.20.

18: בכל / d l: לכל=לְכָל; 11 Mss K, 12 Mss R, S.

XXIV.

6: שמה / 1: תמן=שָׁם; cf. 19.20.

8: ואם / h: אם=אִם.

שמה / b l: תמן=שָׁם; cf. 19.20.

10: אל עיר / h: קרתא=עִיר.

43

27: אחי / Trg: אחוהי=אָחִי; LXX.

40: אלי >Trg.

46: גמליך / b d g: לגמלך=לְגַמְלִיךְ 2 Mss K, P; cf. v. 14, 19, 44.
הגמלים / n: ית גמליא=אֶת הַגְמַלִים; cf. 5.1.

55: אחר / d: ובתר=וְאַחַר; 8 Mss K, 7 Mss R, S, LXX, P.

XXV.

8: ושבע / v l n: וסבע יומין=וּשְׁבַע יָמִים; 3 Mss K, 1 Ms R,
S, LXX, P; cf. 35.29.

26: ויקרא / l n: וקרו=וַיִּקְרְאוּ; 1 Ms R, S; cf. v. 25.

XXVI.

21: ויחפרו / l: וחפר=וַיַּחְפֹּר; LXX; cf. v. 18, 22.

22: ופרינו / Trg: ויפשיננא=וְיַּפְרֵנוּ; cf. LXX.

XXVII.

1: אליו 2°>Trg; 1 Ms K, P.

12: והבאתי / l: ותהי מייתי=וְהֵבֵאת (!); S, P.

46: למה / l: למא דנן=לְמָה זֶה; cf. 4.6.

XXIX.

3: שמה / Trg: תמן=שָׁם; S; cf. 19.20.

24: שפחה / Trg: לאמהו=לְשִׁפְחָה; 2 Mss K, 3 Mss R, S; cf. v. 29.

XXX.

11: בגד / Trg: אתא גד=בָּא נָד; 8 Mss K, P.

13: באשרי / Trg: תושבחתא הות לי=בָּא אָשְׁרִי?

15: ולקחת / c h k l n s: וְלָקַחְתְּ=ותיסבין; S (וְלָקַחְתִּי), P.

18.21. 24: ותקרא / l: וקרא=וַיִּקְרָא; cf. 4.25.

40: אֶל פְּנֵי . . . כָּל=בריש . . . כל / Trg: פני (הצאן) אל.

41: יחם / Trg: עידן דמיתיחמן=עֵת יַחֵם; 1 Ms K, P; cf. 31.10.

XXXI.

13: אשר (נדרת) / Trg: וְאַשר=ודקיימתא; 1 Ms K, 4 Mss R, S, LXX, P.

18: מקנה קנינו / Trg: מִקְנֵהוּ וְקִנְיָנוֹ=גיתוהי וקניניה; cf. 1 Ms K: וקנינו.

39: אנכי אחטנה Trg<.

XXXII.

19: והנה גם / Trg: וְגַם=ואף; cf. 42.28.

XXXIII.

3: עד 2° / Trg: אֶל=לות; P.

4: ויבכו / Trg: וַיֵּבְךְּ=ובכא; 1 Ms K.

5: את 1°<Trg; 3 Mss K, S; cf. 19.10.

XXXIV.

27: העיר / 1: אֶת הָעִיר=ית קרתא; 5 Mss K; cf. 5.1.

31: יעשה / Trg: יֵעָשֶׂה=יתעביד; P; cf. 2.23.

XXXV.

26: ילד / Trg: יֻלְּדוּ=דאתילידו; 3 Mss K, 3 Mss R, S, LXX, P; cf. 10.25.

XXXVII.

27: וישמעו / Trg: וְישמעו אֵלָיו=וקבילו מניה; P; cf. Num 27.20.

36: והמדנים / Trg: וְהַמְּדָנִים ומדינאי; S, LXX, P; cf. v. 27.

XXXVIII.

1: עד / Trg: אֶל=לות; P; cf. LXX: ἕως πρός, uniting both readings.

3: ויקרא / h: וַתִּקְרָא=וקרת; 10 Ms K, 5 Mss R, S; cf. 4.25.

12: על / c h n s: אֶל=לות; S, P.

14: ותכס / Trg: וַתִּתְכָּס=ואתכסיאת; 1 Mss K, S, LXX, P.

30: שמו / 1: אֶת שמו=ית שמיה; 2 Mss K; cf. 5.1.

XXXIX.

4: יש / Trg: דאית=אֲשֶׁר יש; 2 Mss K, 1 Ms R, S, LXX, P; cf. v. 5 and 8; cf. 50.13, Ex 13.20, 18.20.

6: ויעזב / Trg: ושבק ית=וַיַעֲזֹב אֶת; 1 Ms K; cf. 5.1.

9: אעשה / 1: אעביד ית=אֶעֱשֶׂה אֶת; cf. 5.1.

XLI

5: בריאות / 1: מליאן=מְלֵאוֹת; 2 Mss K, LXX, P; cf. v. 7.

45: על / h: על כל=עַל כָּל; 1 Mss R, P; cf. בכל 2 Mss K, 3 Mss R; cf. v. 41.

50: ילד / Trg: אתילידו=יֻלַּד; S, LXX, P; cf. 10.25.

XLII

2: שמה / 1: תמן=שם; S; cf. 19.20.

21: צרת / Trg: בעקת=בְּצָרַת; 1 Ms R, S, P.

28: וגם הנה / Trg: והא=וְהִנֵּה; 1 Ms K; cf. 32.19.

33: רעבון / Trg: עיבורא דחסיר=שֶׁבֶר רַעֲבוֹן; LXX, P; cf. v. 19.

34: את 2° / d: וית=וְאֶת; 1 Ms K, 3 Mss R, LXX, P.

XLIV.

8: כסף / Trg: כספא=הַכֶּסֶף; S, LXX, P.

XLV.

1: אל אחיו / 1: ית אחוהי=אֶת אֶחָיו; 10 Mss K.

3: אתו / Trg: יתיה פתגם=אֹתוֹ דָבָר; P.

8: אָב . . . וְאָדוֹן=אב . . . ורבון / לאב . . . ולאדון; P; cf. ומשל.

XLVI.

27: ילד / Trg: דאיתילידו=יֻלַּד 4 Mss K, 2 Mss R, S, LXX, P; cf. 10.25.

34: ועד / b d g: עד=עַד; LXX.

XLVII.

3: רעה / רְעִי=רען :Trg; 34 Mss K, 12 Mss R, S, LXX, P.

15: ולמה / 1: למה=למה; 12 Mss K.

15.16: כסף / הַכְּסַף=כספא :Trg; S, LXX, P.

18: לא 2° / 1: וְלֹא=ולא; 1 Ms K, LXX, P.

XLVIII.

21: הנה אנכי / 1: הנה=אנא; >1: 1 Ms K; cf. Ex 4.14.

22: ואני / i: וַאֲנִי הֲנָא=ואנא הא; 2 Mss K, 2 Mss R, P.

XLIX.

4: עלה / עָלִיתָ=סליקתא :Trg; LXX, P.

13: על / עַד=עד :Trg; 7 Mss K, 12 Mss R, LXX, P.

L.

11: אָבֵל / אָבֵל=אֹבֵל :Trg.

13: על / אֲשֶׁר עַל=דעל :Trg; 2 Mss K, P; cf. 39.4.

18: לפניו / a: קדמוהי על אפיהון=עַל פְּנֵיהֶם=--; לפניו על פניו cf. in S.

Exodus.

I.

18: עשיתן / b d: עשיתן אֶת=עבדתין ית; 7 Mss K, S, cf. Gn 5.1.

22: הילוד / דיתיליד ליהודאי=הילוד לָעְבְרִים :Trg; S, LXX.

II.

3: ותשם 2° / ושויתה=ותשם אֹתָה :Trg; LXX, P; cf. Gn 3.24.

4: לו / k: בֹו=ביה?

6: ותראהו / וחזת=וַתֵּרָא :Trg; S, LXX; or=וַתִּרְאֶה, 1 Ms K.

47

9: הילד 2° / a b l n: אֶת הילד=ית רביא; 17 Ms K, S; cf. Gn 5.1.

16: להשקות Trg: לאשקאה ית=אֶת להשקות; 3 Mss K, S; cf. Gn 5.1.

22: אמר>Trg.

24: את 4° / k: וְאֶת=ודעם; 2 Mss K, 3 Mss R, S, LXX, P.

III.

10: ממצרים / Trg: מארעא דמצרים=מֵאֶרֶץ מצרים; 3 Mss K, 2 Mss R, LXX.

15: לדר / Trg: לכל דר=לְכָל דר.

IV.

 6: נא>Trg; 1 Ms K, LXX, P.

14: הנה>Trg; cf. Gn 48.21.

21: ראה / b g h l s: חזי ית=ראה אֶת; 1 Ms K, S; cf. Gn 5.1.

V.

17: נזבחה /c: ונדבח=וְנִזְבְּחָה; 4 Mss K, 2 Mss R, S, LXX (Mss).

22: למה 2° / a b d g l: ולמה=וְלָמָה; 25 Mss K, 32 Mss R, S, LXX, P.

23 הרע / Trg: אתבאש=הֲרַע; P; cf. Gn 2.23.

VI.

3: נודעתי / Trg: הודעית=הוֹדַעְתִּי; LXX, P.

13: ואל . . . על / l: ועל . . . על 2° / אל . . . וְעַל=עַל.

VII.

15: הנה / c: והא=וְהִנֵּה; 4 Mss K.

19: קח / a l: סב ית=קח אֶת; 6 Mss K, S; cf. Gn 5.1.

על 3° / Trg: ועל=וְעַל; 12 Mss K, 12 Mss R, S, LXX, P.

VIII.

3: את> d; 2 Mss K, S.

5: ולעבדיך / לעבדיך = עַל עַבְדֶּךָ :d; 1 Ms K.

16: שלח / שְׁלַח אֶת = שלח יַת :h l s; 9 Mss K, S; cf. Gn 5.1.

24: העתירו / a b d g h k n: הַעְתִּירוּ גַם = צַלוּ אַף; LXX, P.

X.

12: הארץ / l: הַשָּׂדֶה = דחקלא; 1 Ms K.

21: וימש / Trg: וַיָּמֶשׁ = בתר דייעידי; cf. Gn 2.23.

26: שמה / b: תמן = שָׁם = שם; S (Mss); cf. Gn 19.20

XI.

1: כשלחו / Trg: בְּשַׁלְּחוֹ = בשלחותיה; 1 Ms K.

XII.

16: וביום 1° / Trg: בַּיּוֹם = ביומא = ביום; 5 Mss K, 9 Mss R, S, P.

46: תוציא / Trg: תוֹצִיאוּ = תפקון; S, LXX, P.

XIII.

20: בקצה / Trg: אֲשֶׁר בקצה = דבסטר; S, P; cf. Gn 39.4.

XIV.

20: את / Trg: כָּל = כל; P.

XV.

1: אשירה / Trg: נָשִׁירָה = נשבח; LXX, P.

2: וזמרת / Trg: וְזִמְרָתִי = ותושבחתי; 3 Mss K, S.

22: וילכו / Trg: וַיֵּלְכוּ דָרֶךְ = ואזלו מהלך; 1 Ms K, P.

XVI.

3: הזה 1° > Trg.

23: שבתון שבת / Trg: שַׁבַּת שַׁבָּתוֹן = שבא שבתא; 1 Ms K.

31: בית / a: בְּנֵי = בני; 5 Mss K, 7 Mss R, LXX, P; cf. Lev 17.3, 22.18.

XVIII.

16: וְהוֹדַעְתִּי / Trg: וּמְהוֹדַעְנָא לְהוֹן=וְהוֹדַעְתִּי לָהֶם; LXX, P; cf.
S (וְהוֹדַעְתִּיו); cf. v. 20; cf. Gn 19.3.

20: יֵלְכוּ / Trg: דִיהְכוּן=אֲשֶׁר יֵלְכוּ; 11 Mss K, 10 Mss R, S, P;
cf. Gn 39.4.

21: שָׂרַי 2° / b d b g h: וְרַבְנִי=וְשָׂרַי; 12 Mss K, 23 Mss R, S,
LXX, P.

25: שָׂרַי 2° / Trg. וְרַבְנִי=וְשָׂרַי; 5 Mss K, S, LXX, P.

XIX.

12: עָלוֹת / Trg: מְלַמֵּיסַק=מַעֲלוֹת.

XX.

10: עַבְדְּךָ / Trg: וְעַבְדָּךְ=וְעַבְדְּךָ; 36 Mss K, 39 Mss R, P.

21: אֶת צֹאנְךָ וְאֶת בְּקָרְךָ / Trg: מִן עָנָךְ וּמִן תּוֹרָךְ=מִצֹּאנְךָ;
וּמִבְּקָרֶךָ S.

הַמָּקוֹם / Trg: אֲתַר=מָקוֹם; 1 Ms K, LXX, P.

שָׁמִי / Trg adds: לְתַמָּן=שָׁמָּה; S, LXX, P; 1 adds: תַּמָּן=שָׁם;
1 Ms K, S (Ms).

XXI.

13: צֵדָה / Trg: כְּמָן לֵיהּ=צֵדָה לוֹ; P; cf. Gn 19.3.

XXII.

8: עַל 5° / l: וְעַל=וְעַל; 13 Mss K, 8 Mss R, LXX, P.
עַל 6° / a: וְעַל=וְעַל; 14 Mss K, 11 Mss R, LXX, P.

16: אִם / l: וְאִם=וְאִם; 6 Mss K, 5 Mss R, S, LXX, P.

20: תּוֹנֶה / Trg: תּוֹנוּן=תּוֹנוּ; S, LXX, P.
תִּלְחָצֶנּוּ Trg: תְּעִיקוּן=תִּלְחָצוּ; S, LXX, P.

24: לֹא 2° / a: וְלֹא=וְלֹא; 8 Mss K, P.

29: בַּיּוֹם / i a c h n: וּבְיוֹמָא=וּבַיּוֹם; 29 Mss K, 28 Mss R, S,
LXX, P.

XXIII.

1: להיות / Trg: למהוי ליה= להיות לו; P; cf. Gn 19.3.

8: פקחים / Trg: עיני חכימין=עֵינֵי פקחים; 5 Mss K, 4 Mss R, S, LXX, P; cf. 2 Mss K: עיני חכמים.

10: ושש / l: שית=שש; 3 Mss K, LXX, P.

13: לא 2° / a c l: ולא=וְלֹא; 20 Mss K, 44 Mss R, S, LXX, P.

17: אל פני / Trg: קדם= אֶת פני; 11 Mss K, S.

21: אל / Trg: ולא=וְאֶל; 1 Ms K, LXX.

27: והמתי / l: ואקטול=וְהֵמַתִּי; cf. Gn 2.23.

28: את 3° / a l: וית=וְאֶת; 31 Mss K, 32 Mss R, S, LXX, P.

31: ועד / a c n s: עד=עַד; 7 Mss K, LXX.

עד / Trg: ועד=וְעַד; 3 Mss K, S, P.

את 2° / l: ית כל=אֶת כל; 7 Mss K, 10 Mss R.

XXIV.

5: שלמים >Trg; 2 Mss K.

XXV.

22: אל / l: על=עַל; P.

37: והעלה / Trg: ותדליק=וְהַעֲלִיתָ; S, LXX.

והאיר / Trg: ויהון מנהרין=וְהָאִירוּ; S, LXX, P.

XXVI.

31: יעשה / l: תעביד=תַעֲשֶׂה; 5 Mss K, 2 Mss R, LXX.

33: שמה / b h l: תמן=שָם; S; cf. Gn 19.20.

XXVII.

5: עד / Trg: על=עַל.

7: והובא / Trg: ותעיל=וְהַבֵאתָ; S, LXX, P.

XXVIII.

‏3: מלאתיו / Trg: מלאתים=דאשלימית עמהון‎; LXX, P.

‏6: תולעת / Trg: ותולעת=וצבע‎; 18 Mss K, 16 Mss R, S, P; cf. v. 8.

‏17: טור / Trg: טור ראשׁון=סדרא קדמאה‎; P; cf. 39.10.

‏43: והיו / Trg: וְהָיָה=ויהי‎.

XXIX.

‏43: ונקדש / Trg: ונקדשׁתי=ואתקדש‎; LXX, P.

XXX.

‏4: והיה / i: וְהָיוּ=ויהון‎; 2 Mss K, 4 Mss R, S, LXX, P.

‏לבתים / 1: בתים=אתרא‎; LXX, P; cf. 37.27, 38.5.

‏8: לפני יהוה‎ >Trg.

XXXI.

‏2: ראה / h: רְאוּ=חזו‎; cf. Dt 1.8, 11.26.

‏3: ובתבונה / 1: בתבונה=בסוכלתנו‎; 13 Mss K, 7 Mss R.

‏ובדעת / h: בדעת=במדע‎.

‏4: ובכסף / Trg: בכסף=בכספא‎; 2 Mss K.

‏8: ואת 1° / Trg: את=ית‎; 2 Mss K, 4 Mss R, S.

‏ואת 2° / 1: ואת כל=וית כל‎; 81 Mss K, 27 Mss R, S, LXX, P.

‏כל‎ >1; 1 Ms K, 3 Mss R.

XXXII.

‏7: רד / 1: רד מִזֶּה=חות מיכה‎; LXX, P; cf. Dt 9.12.

‏12: לעמך / Trg: אֲשֶׁר דִּבַּרְתָ לַעֲשׂוֹת=דמלילתא למעבד לעמך‎; לעמך‎; cf. v. 14.

‏20: דק / 1: דק לְעָפָר=דקיק לעפרא‎; 2 Mss K, P; cf. Dt 9.21.

‏26: המחנה / 1: הָאֹהֶל=משכנא‎; P.

XXXIII.

2: החוי / Trg: וחיואי = וְהַחִוִּי; 14 Mss K, 23 Mss R, S, LXX, P.

3: בקרבך / Trg: מבינך = מִקִּרְבְּךָ.

15: הלכים / Trg: מהלכא בינא = הלכים בְּקִרְבֶּנוּ; P.

XXXIV.

3: גם / d l: ואף = וְגַם; 6 Mss K, 2 Mss R, S, LXX.

18: אשר צויתך / d g l n: כמא דפקידתך = כַּאֲשֶׁר צִוִּיתִךָ; 11 Mss K, 19 Mss R, S, LXX, P; cf. 39.32.

19: לי / Trg: דילי הוא = לִי הוּא; 1 Ms K.

XXXV.

5: יביאה / Trg: ייתי = יָבִיא; S, P.

11: את 3°–5°, ואת 2° and 3° > Trg.

את 2° / c d l: וית = וְאֶת; 7 Mss K, 15 Mss R, S, LXX, P.

12: את 2° / a c l n: וית = וְאֶת; 31 Mss K, 40 Mss R, S, LXX, P.

19: את 1° / l: וית = וְאֶת; 7 Mss K, 8 Mss R, LXX, P.

22: ויבאו / Trg: ומיתן = וַיָּבִאוּ; S, LXX, P; cf. Num 31.12, 54; cf. Gn 2.23.

25: ואת 1° / b g: ית = אֶת.

את 2° / Trg: וית = וְאֶת; 33 Mss K, 49 Mss R, S, LXX.

31: בתבונה / Trg: ובסוכלתנו = וּבִתְבוּנָה; 5 Mss K, 5 Mss R, S, LXX, P.

32: ולחשב / l: לאלפא = לַחְשֹׁב; LXX, P.

35: כל 1° / l: בכל = הְרָל; 26 Mss K, 39 Mss R.

XXXVII.

27: לבתים / h: אתרא = בתים; P; cf. 30.4.

XXXVIII.

3: אֵת: 3° / b c d g h k l n s: וית = וְאֵת; 28 Mss K, 58 Mss R, S, P.

5: בתים / 1: לאתרא = לְבתים; cf. 30.4.

24: בכל / 1: לכל = לְכל.

ויהי / 1: והוה כל = וְיהי כָל; 1 Ms K.

XXXIX.

1: אשר (לאהרן) > Trg; P; cf. Gn 15.17.

3: וקצץ / Trg: וקציצו = וְקִצְצוּ; S, P.

10: טור / Trg: סדרא קדמאה = טוּר רָאשׁוֹן; P; cf. 28.17.

15: ויעשו / 1: ועבד = וַיַּעַשׂ.

22: ויעש / Trg: ועבדו = וַיַּעֲשׂוּ; 1 Ms K, S, P.

24: משזר / 1: ובוץ שזיר = וְשֵׁשׁ מָשְׁזָר; 3 Mss K, 1 Ms R, S, P.

32: ככל אשר (צוה) / 1: כמא = כַּאֲשֶׁר; 1 Ms R, S; cf. 34.18, 40.16,
   Num 2.34, 4.49, 8.20.

34: פרכת / 1: כפורתא = כַּפֹּרֶת.

35–41: את and ואת differ very often in Trg.

40: את 3° / Trg: וית = וְאֵת; 12 Mss K, 17 Mss R, S, P.

41: ואת / Trg: ית = אֵת; 3 Mss K, P.

XL.

16: ככל אשר (צוה) / 1: כמא = כַּאֲשֶׁר; 1 Ms R; cf. 39.32.

Leviticus.

I.

7: הכהן / c: כהניא = הַכֹּהֲנִים; 2 Mss K, 3 Mss R, S, LXX, P.

8: את 2° / b d: וית = וְאֵת; 4 Mss K, 3 Mss R, S, LXX, P.

12: ואת 1° / c k l n: ית = אֵת; 15 Mss K.

17: לא / a: ולא = וְלֹא; 8 Mss K, 7 Mss R, S, LXX, P.

54

III.

9: ואת 1° / Trg: את=ית; 19 Mss K, 23 Mss R, S.

IV.

21: את 1° / Trg: את כָּל=ית כל; 1 Ms K; cf. v. 12.

27: ממצות / l: מכל פיקודיא=מִכָּל מִצְוֹת; 3 Mss K, 1 Ms R, S, LXX.

28: והביא / c$_b$ k l: והביא אֶת=וייתי ית; 16 Mss K, S, cf. Gn 5.1.

31: חלב / Trg: חלב הַכָּשָׂב=תרב אימר; 1 Ms K; cf. v. 35; cf. 1 Ms K: חלב הכבש.

35: על חטאתו / a b g: מָחטאתו=מחובתיה; 2 Mss K; cf. v. 26.

V.

2: טמא / k: יָדַע=ידע; 3 Mss K.

3: ידע / i: טָמֵא=מסאב; 1 Ms K.

24: וחמשתיו / i g h k l n s: וַחֲמִישָׁתוֹ=וחמשיה; 29 Mss K, 23 Mss R, S, LXX, P.

VI.

3: מדו / Trg: מַדָּי=לבושין; S, LXX, P.

VII.

21: שקץ / a b g h l: שָׁרֶץ=רחיש; 5 Mss K, 2 Mss R, S, LXX, P.

25: יקריב / Trg: יַקְרִיבוּ=דיקרבון; 6 Mss K, 14 Mss R, S.

34: שלמיהם / h: שלמיכָם=קודשיכון; 4 Mss K, LXX.

37: למנחה / a k n=וְלַמִנחה; 7 Mss K, 15 Mss R, S, LXX, P.

38: במדבר / l: בְּהַר=בטורא; 1 Ms K.

VIII.

30: על 3° / h k n: וְעַל=וְעַל; 38 Mss K, 38 Mss R, S, LXX, P.
וְעַל 1° / h: עַל=עַל.
אֵת 2° / b d h k l: וְיַת=וְאֵת; 19 Mss K, 34 Mss R, S, LXX, P.

31: צויתי / Trg: דְאִתְפַּקֵדִית=צַוֵּיתִי; LXX, P; cf. v. 35; cf. Gn 2.23.

IX.

4: נראה / Trg: מִתְגְלֵי=נִרְאָה; cf. Gn 2.23.
10: ואת 2° / Trg: מִן=מִן.

XI.

2: לאמר / Trg: לְמֵימַר לְהוֹן=לֵאמֹר אֲלֵהֶם?; P.
13: שקץ / l: אֲרֵי שִׁקְצָא=כִּי שֶׁקֶץ; P.
15: למינו / a l: לִזְנוֹהִי=לְמִינֵהוּ; cf. Gn 1.11.
22: את 1° / s: וְיַת=וְאֵת; LXX.
למינו / l: לִזְנוֹהִי=לְמִינֵהוּ; 2 Mss K, S, cf. Gn 1.11.
ואת 2° / c: יַת=אֵת.
26: בהם / k n: בְּנִבְלָתְהוֹן=בְּנִבְלָתָם; 3 Mss K, 3 Mss R, LXX; cf. v. 24, 27./
38: על / l: עַל כָּל=עַל כָּל; 1 Ms K, 1 Ms R, LXX.
42: כל 1° / Trg: וְכֹל=וְכֹל; 6 Mss K, 2 Mss R, LXX, P.

XIII.

16: ובא / i l: וְיתִיתִי=וְהוּבָא; P; cf. v. 9.
54: והסגירו / Trg: וְיַסְגְרִינֵיה כַּהֲנָא=וְהִסְגִּירוֹ הַכֹּהֵן; 3 Mss K, 3 Mss R, LXX, P; cf. v. 5, 21, 26.

XIV.

41: יקצע / Trg: יִקְלְפוּן=יַקְצִעוּ; 1 Ms K, S, LXX, P.

XV.

19: וכל / c d: כֹל=כָּל; 31 Mss K, 33 Mss R, S, LXX.

XVI.

1: בְּהַקְרִיבָם אֵשׁ = בקריביהון אישתא נוכריתא / Trg: בקרבתם
זָרָה; LXX, P; cf. 10.1.

XVII.

3: מִבְּנֵי = מבני / l: מבית; 1 Ms R, LXX, P; cf. Ex 16.31.

8: בְּתוֹכְכֶם = ביניכון / g h k: בתוכם; 1 Ms K, 1 Ms R, LXX, P.

10: בְּתוֹכְכֶם = ביניכון / b g h: בתוכם; 1 Ms K, 1 Ms R, LXX, P.

13: בְּתוֹכְכֶם = ביניכון / a b c g h l: בתוכם; 1 Ms K, LXX, P.

14: אֲכָלוֹ = דייכליניה / Trg: אכליו; S, LXX, P; cf. 19.8.

XVIII.

3: שָׁם = תמן / l: שמה; cf. Gn 19.20.

28: הַגּוֹיִם = עממיא / Trg: הגוי; LXX.

29: כִּי אֶת = ארי ית / l: כי; 8 Mss K; cf. Gn 5.1.

XIX.

8: וְאֲכָלוֹ = ודייכליניה / Trg: ואכליו; S, LXX, P; cf. 17.14.

13: וְלֹא = ולא / c: לא 2°; 17 Mss K, 24 Mss R, S, LXX.

16: וְלֹא = ולא / c d l: לא 2°; 20 Mss K, 23 Mss R, S, P.

20: תִּהְיֶה בָהּ = תהי בה / Trg: תהיה; cf. S (לֹן), LXX (αὐτοῖς),
P (עליהון).

21: אַיִל לְאָשָׁם = דכרא לאשמא / Trg: איל אשם.

27: וְלֹא = ולא / Trg: לא; 1 Ms K, 1 Ms R, S, LXX, P.
תקפו אֶת = תקפון ית / j: תקפו; S; cf. Gn 5.1.

31: וְאֶל = ולא / b d: אֶל 2°; 4 Mss K, 4 Mss R, LXX, P.

33: אֶתְכֶם = עימכון / Trg: אתך; 1 Ms K, 2 Mss R, S, LXX, P.

XX.

8: אֱלֹהֵיכֶם = אלהכון / h: מקדשכם; cf. v. 7.

22: שָׁם = תמן / b d g h l s: שמה; S (Ms); cf. Gn 19.20.

XXI.

20: בְּעֵינָיו=בעינוהי :Trg / בעינו ;S, LXX, P.

XXII.

18: מְבְּנֵי=מבני :b d g l / מבית ;LXX; cf. Ex 16.31.

29: תִזְבָחֵהוּ=תכסוניה :h / 2° תזבחו ;4 Mss K, 1 Ms R, S, LXX, P.

XXIII.

2: מְקְרָא=מערע :Trg / מקראי ;cf. v. 4, 37.

4: מְקְרָא=מערע :j c k n / מקראי ;1 Ms K.

5: עֶשֶׂר יוֹם=עסרא יומא :h / עשר ;3 Mss K, 12 Mss R, S, LXX.

17: שְׁתַּיִם חַלּוֹת=תרתין גריצן :Trg / שתים ;S, LXX, P.

37: מְקְרָא=מערע :Trg / מקראי ;S (Ms); cf. v. 2.

43: אֶתְכֶם=יתכון :l / אותם.

XXIV.

22: כי >l.

23: וַיּוֹצֵא=ואפיק :h / ויוציאו.

XXV.

14: תִמְכֹּר=תזבין :Trg / תמכרו ;S, LXX, P.

XXVI.

20: את >l; 6 Mss K.

39: אֹיְבֵיהֶם=דסנאיהון :Trg / איביכם ;23 Mss K, 48 Mss R, S, LXX, P.

XXVII.

9: יַקְרִיב=די יקרב :a / יקריבו ;9 Mss K, 6 Mss R, S.

Numeri.

II.

1: ואל אהרן 1<; 8 Mss K.

34: (צוה) כאשר ככל אשר / i: כמא=כַּאֲשֶׁר; 4 Mss K, S (Ms); cf. Ex 39.32.

III.

13: עד / j c: וְעַד=ועד; 17 Mss K, P.

36: ובריחיו / k n: עברוהי=בריחיו.

ועמדיו / k n: עמודוהי=עמדיו.

IV.

3: בא / Trg: דאתי=הַבָּא; 9 Mss K, S, LXX, P.

14: את 3° / Trg: וית=וְאֶת; 35 Mss K, 48 Mss R, LXX, P.

15: אלה / Trg: דין=זֶה; cf. the sing. in v. 28 and 33.

26: ועל המזבח h<; LXX.

28: משפחת 1<; 2 Mss K, 1 Ms R, LXX.

42: לבית / 1: ולבית=וּלְבֵית; 10 Mss K.

49: (צוה) אשר / i a: כמא=כַּאֲשֶׁר; 2 Mss K, S, LXX, P; cf. Ex 39.32.

V.

10: איש / k: וגבר=וְאִישׁ; 13 Mss K, 2 Mss R, S, LXX, P.

16: אתה / h: יתה לות=אַתָּה אֶל; S (Ms).

VII.

11: את h<; cf. Gn 19.10.

VIII.

12: ועשה / b d g: ויעביד=וְעָשָׂה; LXX; cf. Gn 2.23.

19: נתנים / h: מסירין יהיבין=נתנים נתנים; LXX.

20: (צוה) ככל אשר / a: כמא=כַּאֲשֶׁר; LXX, P; cf. Ex 39.32.

25: ולא / 1: לא=לֹא; 7 Mss K.

IX.

3: בחדש / j b d: לְחֹדֶשׁ=לירחא; 7 Mss K, 18 Mss R; cf. 10.11;
לַחֹדֶשׁ הָרִאשׁוֹן=לירחא קדמאה :1; LXX.

תעשו 1° / b d: יַעֲשׂוּ=יעבדון; 2 Mss K, 3 Mss R, S, LXX
(Mss), P.

15: הקים / Trg: הוּקַם=דאיתקם; S, LXX.
את 1°>Trg; cf. Gn 19.10.

21: עד / b g: וְעַד=ועד; 19 Mss K, P.

X.

9: מלחמה / Trg: לְמִלְחָמָה=לאגחא קרבא; 1 Ms K, LXX.
11: בחדש 2° / i b d g: לַחֹדֶשׁ=לירחא; LXX; cf. 9.3.

XI.

31: פני / c d h s: פְּנֵי כָל=אפי כל; 10 Mss K, 23 Mss R.

XIII.

22: ויבא / Trg: וַיָּבֹאוּ=ואתו; 2 Mss K, S, LXX, P.
25: מתור / a g k l n s: מְתוֹר אֶת=מלאללא ית; S; cf. Gn 5.1.

XIV.

6: את >Trg.
14: נראה אתה / Trg: רָאוּ אֹתְךָ=חזו שכינת יקרך.
15: הגוים / h: כָּל הַגּוֹיִם=כל עממיא; 1 Ms K, 1 Ms R.
18: חסד / b d_b: חֶסֶד וֶאֱמֶת=טבון וקשוט; 3 Mss K, 2 Mss R,
S, LXX; cf. Ex 34.6.
ופשע / .a_1 b c d_b g n: וּפֶשַׁע וְחַטָּאָה=ולמרוד ולחובין; 1 Ms
K, 1 Ms R, S, LXX; cf. Ex 34.7.
24: יורשנה / Trg: יִירָשֶׁנָּה=יירתונה; S, LXX, P; cf. 32.39, Dt
2.21.
34: תנואתי / Trg: תְּלוּנֹתֵיכֶם עָלָי=דאתרעמיתון עלי; P.
36: את 2°>l; 3 Mss K; cf. Gn 19.10.

XV.

18: שמה / 1: תמן=שם; cf. Gn 19.20.

29: בתוכם / i b 1: בְּיֵנִיכוֹן=בְּתוֹכְכָם; LXX (Mss), P.

34: פרש / Trg: אתפריש להון=פָּרַשׂ לָהֶם; cf. Gn 19.3.

39: והיה / a b d g: ויהון=וְהָיוּ; S, P.

אתו / i a: יתהון=אֹתָם; 1 Ms K, S, LXX, P.

XVI.

1: ויקח / Trg: ואתפליג=וַיֵּחָלֵק; P.

32: ואת 2° / 1: ית=את.

XVII.

2: השרפה / Trg: יקידיא=הַשְּׂרֵפִים; LXX, P; cf. v. 4.

5: וכעדתו / b d h 1: וכנישתיה=וַעֲדָתוֹ; LXX.

24: ויראו / Trg: ואשתמודעו=וַיַּכִּירוּ.

28: הקרב הקרב / Trg: דקריב מקרב=הקרב קָרַב.

XVIII.

5: ושמרתם / b d: ויטרון=וְשָׁמְרוּ; LXX (Mss), P; cf. v. 4.

9: כל / Trg: לכל=לְכָל; 8 Mss K, 3 Mss R, P; cf. LXX (ἀπὸ πάντων).

11: תנופת / Trg: ארמות=תְּנוּפַת; cf. Gn 2.23.

19: תרומת / Trg: אפרשות=תְּרוּמַת; 1 Ms R, LXX; cf. Gn 2.23.

23: לדרתיכם / Trg: לדריהון=לְדֹרֹתָם; S (Mss), LXX, P.

28: אתם / b d: אתון ית=אתם אָת; 4 Mss K, S; cf. Gn 5.1.

את>a b d h s; 7 Mss K; cf. Gn 19.10.

XIX.

17: ונתן / 1: ויתנון=וְנָתְנוּ; S, LXX, P.

18: הנפשות / s: כל נפשתא=כָּל הַנְפָשׁוֹת; 4 Mss K, 3 Mss R, P.

22: הנגעת / Trg: דיקרב ביה=הנגעת בּוֹ=דנקרוב; 1 Ms K; cf. P (לה); cf. Gn 19.3.

XX.

10: ויאמר / ‏a d:‏ וַיֹּאמְרוּ=ואמרו‏; 1 Ms R.

XXI.

1: האתרים / Trg: מאלליא=הַתָרִים‏; P.

18: במחקק / Trg: ספריא=מְחֹקֵק‏ or מְחֹקְקִים.

22: לא 2° / Trg: וְלֹא=ולא‏; 5 Mss K, P.

XXII.

11: העם היצא / Trg: עמא נפק=עַם יָצָא‏; S, LXX, P; cf. v. 5;
   cf. 1 Ms K (עם) and 1 Ms K (יצא).

28: מה / Trg: מא דא=מַה זֹּאת‏; cf. Gn 42.28.

33: אולי / Trg: אילו פון לא=לוּלֵי‏; LXX, P.

39: ויבאו / Trg: ואעליה=וַיְבִאֵהוּ‏; S, P.

XXIII.

6: והנה / ‏k n:‏ והא הוא=וְהִנּוֹ‏; cf. v. 17.

7: זעמה Trg: תריך לי=זעמה לִי‏; LXX, P; on account of the
   parallelism; and cf. Gn 19.3.

   ישראל / ‏k n:‏ ‏ית ישראל=אֶת ישראל‏; cf. Gn 5.1.

17: והנו / Trg: והוא=וְהֹוּא‏; LXX, P.

XXV.

17: והכיתם / Trg: ותקטיל=וְהִכִּיתָה‏; P.

XXVI.

3: וידבר / ‏a:‏ ומנא=וַיִּפְקֹד.

   הכהן / Trg. adds: אמרו לממני=add. לִפְקֹד.

60: את 2° / 1: וְאָת=וית‏; 19 Mss K, 12 Mss R, LXX, P.

XXVII.

1: נעה / Trg: ונעה=וְנֹעָה‏; 2 Mss K, 1 Ms R, S, LXX, P.

   וחגלה / ‏i a c a:‏ חגלה=חָגְלָה‏; 9 Mss K, 5 Mss R, S.

   ומלכה / ‏i:‏ מלכה=מִלְכָּה‏ 3 Mss K, 4 Mss R, S.

2: וכל / h s: וקדם=וְלִפְנֵי; cf. 1 Ms K (ולפני כל), LXX (καὶ ἔναντι πάσης), P (וקדם כלה).

20: ישמעו / Y b c d g h k l n s: דיקבלון מניה=יִשְׁמְעוּ אֵלָיו; LXX, P; cf. Gn 37.27.

XXVIII.

5: למנחה / Trg: מנחתה=מנחה; 1 Ms K, P.

10: בשבתו / Trg: בשבא=בְּשַׁבַּת; S, LXX, P.

27: איל / b d g k n: ודכר=וָאִיל; 39 Mss K, 30 Mss R, S, P.

31: התמיד / a: צפרא=הַבֹּקֶר; cf. 29.38.

XXIX.

3: לאיל / h: לדכרא חד=לָאַיִל הָאֶחָד; 1 Ms R, LXX, P; cf. 1 Ms K (לאיל האחד תעשו); cf. v. 9, 14.

4: ועשרון / k: ועשרונא עשרונא=וְעִשָּׂרוֹן עִשָּׂרוֹן; S, LXX; cf. v. 15.

5: חטאת / b: לחטאתא=לְחַטָּאת; 10 Mss K, 4 Mss R, S, LXX, P; cf. v. 11, 25.

8: איל / a: ודכר=וְאַיִל; 3 Mss K, 3 Mss R, S (Mss), P.

9: לפר / k: לתורא חד=לְפַר הָאֶחָד; LXX; cf. v. 14.

11: חטאת 1° / k l n: לחטאתא=לְחַטָּאת; 6 Mss K, 6 Mss R, S, LXX; cf. v. 5.

ומנחתה / h: מנחתה=מנחתה.

16: מנחתה / i: ומנחתה=וּמִנְחָה; 10 Mss K, 11 Mss R, S, P.

19: ומנחתה / h: מנחתה=מנחתה; 1 Ms K, LXX.

25: חטאת / l: לחטתא=לְחַטָּאת; 3 Mss K, 4 Mss R, S, LXX, P; cf. v. 5.

מנחתה / s: ומנחתה=וּמִנְחָתָהּ; 10 Mss K, 14 Mss R, S, P.

34: ונסכה / b g: ונסכהא=וּנְסָכֶיהָ; 1 Ms K, S, LXX, P; cf. v. 31.

38: התמיד / a: צפרא=הַבֹּקֶר; cf. 28.31.

XXX.

3: ככל / כל=כָּל :s; LXX, P.

6: אתה (bis) / אָתָם=יתהון :Trg; P.

9: אתה / אָתָם=יתהון :Trg; P.

נדרה / נְדָרֶיהָ=נידרהא :a b g h; S, LXX, P.

12: אתה / אָתָם=יתהון :Trg; P.

יקום / יָקוּמוּ=יקומון :Trg; S, LXX, P.

13: ולאסר / לֶאְסֹר=לאיסר :h.

15: את 1°>l; 1 Ms K; cf. Gn 19.10.

XXXI.

6: לצבא 1°>l.

12: אשר על / אשר>Trg; עַל :Trg; 1 Ms K; cf. Gn 15.17.

16: למסר מעל / לְמָעַל מעל=לשקרא שקר :Trg; 1 Ms K.

22: ואת 1° / יָת=אֵת :c.

את 2° / וְאֵת=וית :i; 16 Mss K, 17 Mss R, LXX, P.

את 3° / וְאֵת=וית :b d; 32 Mss K, 26 Mss R, S, LXX, P.

28: ומן 1° / מִן=מן :h; 8 Mss K.

29: ונתתה / וּנְתַתָּם=ותתנון :i v; P.

30: מן 4° / וּמִן=ומן :c; 3 Mss K, 5 Mss R, S, LXX, P

XXXII.

8: אבתיכם / אֲבֹתֵיהֶם=אבההתון :h.

15: להניחו / לְהָנִיחֲכָם=לאחרותכון :h; P.

25: ויאמר / וַיֹּאמְרוּ=ואמרו :h k l n s; 7 Mss K, 11 Mss R, S, LXX, P.

39: ויורש / וַיְיָרָשׁ=וארִיתו :s; 11 Mss K; cf. 14.24.

XXXIII.

52: את 1°>k n; cf. Gn 19.10.

XXXIV.

24: ולמטה / Trg: למטה=לשבטא; 1 Ms K, S, LXX, P.

XXXV.

5: להם / j c h k n: לְכֶם=לכון; 22 Mss K 32 Mss R, S, LXX, P.

6: שמה / b d g k n: שָׁם=תמן; S (Mss); cf. Gn 19.20.

11: שמה / b d g: שָׁם=תמן; S (Mss); cf. Gn 19.20.

12: מגאל / Trg: מגאל הדם=מגאיל דמא; 1 Ms K, LXX, P; cf. v. 19, 21, 24, 25, 27.

15: בתוכם / b d g: בְּתוֹכְכֶם=ביניכון; 1 Ms K, LXX, P.
שמה / b d: שָׁם=תמן; cf. Gn 19.20.

33: אשר אתם / k: אֲשֶׁר אַתֶּם יֹשְׁבִים=דאתון יתבין; 1 Ms K, 3 Mss R, S, LXX, P.

34: תטמא / Trg: תְטַמְּאוּ=תסאבון; 2 Mss K, 2 Mss R, S, LXX, P.

Deuteronomium.

I.

1: ישראל / Trg: בְּנֵי יִשְׂרָאֵל=בני ישראל.

7: ובשפלה / k n: בַּשְּׁפֵלָה=בשפלתא; 10 Mss K.

8: ראה / Trg: רְאוּ=חזו; 1 Ms K, S, LXX, P; cf. Ex 31.2.

28: ענקים / Trg: עֲנָק=גיברא; 1 Ms K: cf. Num 13.33.

35: לאבתיכם / Trg: לַאֲבֹתֵיהֶם=לאבהתהון; 1 Ms K, 1 Ms R, LXX, P.

37: שם / Trg: שָׁמָּה=לתמן; 9 Mss K, 13 Mss R, S, P.

38: שמה / d: שָׁם=תמן; cf. Gn 19.20.

II.

13: עתה / וְעַתָּה=וכען :d; 4 Mss K, 2 Mss R, S, LXX.

19: בם / בם מִלְחָמָה=למעבד עמהון קרב :Trg; cf. v. 9 and 29.

21: ויירשם / וַיוֹרָשֵׁם=ותריכונון :Trg; P; cf. Num 14.24.

36: ועד / עד=עד :c; 12 Mss K.

III.

6: הנשים / וְהנשים=ונשיא :Trg; 8 Mss K, LXX, P; cf. 2.34.

12: נחל / שְׂפַת נחל=כיף נחלא :b d; 7 Mss K, 5 Mss R, S, LXX, P.

17: הערבה / הערבה וּגְבֻל=דמישרא ותחומא :1.

IV.

14: שמה / שם=תמן :v b d g l; S (Mss); cf. Gn 19.20.

26: שמה / שם=תמן :d g l; S (Mss); cf. Gn 19.20.

29: ובקשתם / וּבְקַשְׁתָּ=ותתבע :Trg; S.

32: ולמקצה / מקצה=למסיפי :c; 5 Mss K, P.

ועד / עד=עד :c; 1 Ms K, LXX.

34: לעיניך / לְעֵינֵיכֶם=לעיניכון :Trg; 1 Ms K, S, P.

37: ותחת / תחת=חלף :h; LXX.

39: יהוה / יהוה אֱלֹהֶיךָ=יוי אלהך :1; LXX; cf. 16.2, 18.12.

42: שמה / שם=תמן :c; S (Mss); cf. Gn 19.20.

V.

5: דבר / דְּבָרַי=פתגמיא :Trg; 1 Ms K, S, LXX, P.

8: כל / וְכל=וכל :d h; 23 Mss K, 38 Mss R, S, LXX, P.

18: ולא / לא=לא :c; 5 Mss K, 6 Mss R, S, LXX, P.

21: שורו / וְשׁורו=ותוריה :j k n; 16 Mss K, 18 Mss R, LXX, P.

26: שמע / שמע אֶת=דשמע ית :k n; cf. Gn 5.1.

28: כל >1; 11 Mss K.

VI.

1: החקים / k n: וקימיא=וְהַחֻקִּים: 7 Mss K, LXX, P.

לעשות / c: למעבד יתכון = לַעֲשׂוֹתְכֶם; 1 Ms K, P.

שמה / b d g: תמן=שם; S (Mss); cf. Gn 19.20.

19: יהוה> b g.

VII.

1: והגרגשי / s: גרגישאי=הגרגשי; 3 Mss K.

4: בנך / Trg: בנך=בָּנֶיךָ; P.

10: לא / k l n: ולא=וְלֹא; 20 Mss K, 20 Mss R, LXX.

12: לך >Trg; 3 Mss K.

נשבע / Trg: דקיים יוי=נשבע יהוה.

13: ותירשך / l: חמרך=תירשך; 6 Mss K, 7 Mss R, S; cf. 11.14, 12.17.

19: והאתת / d a h s: אתיא=הָאֹתֹת; 8 Mss K, 2 Mss R, S, LXX, P.

VIII.

2: לנסתך / i: ובדיל לנסיותך=וּלְמַעַן נַסֹּתְךָ; cf. v. 16.

9: כל >k n.

17: את / l: ית כל=אֶת כָּל; 2 Mss K.

IX.

27: ואל רשעו / b c d g: לחוביהון=אֶל רשעו; 13 Mss K.

X.

10: ההוא / k n: הדא=הַזֹּאת.

15: בכם >Trg; 1 Ms K, P.

21: אתו / Trg: וקדמוהי=וְאֹתוֹ; 20 Mss K, 34 Mss R, S, LXX, P.

XI.

2: את 4° / Trg: וית=וְאֶת; 26 Mss K, 46 Mss R, S, LXX, P.

6: כל 2° / Trg: בני=בְּנֵי.

8: שמה / b d g n: תמן=שם; 1 Ms K; cf. Gn 19.20.

11: שמה / c d g: תמן=שם; S (Ms); cf. Gn 19.20.

13: מצותי / 1: הַמִּצְוֹת=לפיקודיא; LXX, P.

14: ונתתי / h: וְנָתַתִּי אֶת=ואיתין ית; cf. Gn 5.1.

ותירשך / 1: תִּירשֶׁךָ=חמרך; 1 Ms K, S; cf. 7.13.

22: ללכת / k n: וְלָלֶכֶת=ולמהך; S (Mss), LXX, P; cf. 30.16.

בכל דרכיו / k n: בִּדְרָכָיו=בארחן; 1 Ms K.

24: ועד / 1: עַד=עד; 5 Mss K, 5 Mss R.

26: ראה / Trg: רְאוּ=חזו; P; cf. Ex 31.2.

29: שמה / g: תמן=שם; cf. Gn 19.20.

XII.

2: את 2° / b c d: וְאֵת=וית; 4 Mss K, P.

5: ובאת / Trg: וּבָאתָם=ותיתון; S, LXX, P.

17: ותירשך / Trg: תִּירשֶׁךָ=חמרך; 9 Mss K, 5 Mss R, S; cf. 7.13.

XIII.

1: תסף / Trg: תֹסִיפוּ=תוספון; 1 Ms K, S.

תגרע / Trg: תִגְרְעוּ=תמנעון; 1 Ms K, S.

XIV.

7: ואת 1° / c 1: אֵת=ית.

מעלה / Trg: מַעֲלֵי=מסקי; 5 Mss K, S, LXX.

14: למינו / 1: לְמִינֵהוּ=לזנוהי; cf. Gn 1.11.

16: את הכוס / Y b: וְאֵת הכוס=וקדיא; 27 Mss K, 33 Mss R, S, LXX, P.

20: כל / c: וְכֹל=וכל; 1 Ms K, P.

21: תאכלו / b n: תֹאכַל=תיכול; 1 Ms K.

XV.

2: לא / c s: וְלֹא=ולא; 6 Mss K, LXX.

11: לעניך / c: וְלַעֲנִיֶּךָ=ולעניך; 4 Mss K.

14: ומגרנך / j b c d 1: מִגָּרְנְךָ=מאידרך; 13 Mss K.

XVI.

2: יהוה / יהוה אֱלֹהֶיךָ=יוי אלהך :j l / ‏;יהוה אֱלֹהֶיךָ=יוי אלהך 2 Mss R, S, LXX, P; cf. 4.39.

16: יראה 1° / Trg: יֵרָאוּ=יתחזון‏; P.

יראה 2° / Trg: יֵרָאוּ=יתחזון‏; 1 Ms K, S; cf. Ex 23.15, 34.20.

19: לא 2° / l: וְלֹא=ולא‏; 14 Mss K, 18 Mss R, S, P.

XVII.

2: את > Trg; 4 Mss K.

3: ולשמש / b d: לשמש=לשמשא‏; 5 Mss K, LXX.

או לירח / k n: וְלַיָּרֵחַ=ולסיהרא‏; 1 Ms R.

8: ובין / Trg: בֵּין=בין‏; 17 Mss K.

9: הלוים / k: וְאֶל הַלְוִיִּם=ולות ליואי‏; P; cf. 2 Mss K (והלוים).

16: הרבות / Trg: הַרְבֹּת לוֹ=לאסגאה ליה‏; LXX, P; cf. Gn 19.3.

19: בו / Trg: בָּהּ=בה‏; S, P.

XVIII.

3: מאת 2° / h: וּמֵאֵת=ומן‏; 3 Mss K.

אם 2° / c: וְאִם=ואם.

4: תירשך / h: וְתִירֹשְׁךָ=וחמרך‏; 10 Mss K, LXX, P.

12: יהוה 1° / c: יהוה אֱלֹהֶיךָ=יוי אלהך‏; 3 Mss K, 7 Mss R, S, LXX, P; cf. 4.39.

15: מאחיך / c: וּמֵאַחֶיךָ=ומאחך.

XIX.

3: שמה / b d g l: שָׁם=תמן‏; S (Ms); cf. Gn 19.20.

כל > k.

9: וללכת / h: לָלֶכֶת=למהך‏; 9 Mss K, 6 Mss R, S, LXX.

17: לפני 2° / k n: וְלִפְנֵי=וקדם‏; 6 Mss K, 4 Mss R, S (Mss), LXX, P.

הכהנים / l: הַכֹּהֲנִים וְהַלְוִיִּם=כהניא וליואי.

69

XX.

14: כל / c: וכל=וְכָל; 20 Mss K, 12 Mss R, LXX, P.

19: את>b d; 2 Mss K; cf. Gn 19.10.

XXI.

14: לא 3° / c: ולא=וְלָא; 3 Mss K, P.

18: כי / c: וארי=וְכִי; 1 Ms K, LXX, P.

19: ואל שער / c: לתרע=אל שער; 1 Ms K, 3 Mss R, S.

XXII.

4: או / b d: או ית=אוֹ אָת; 3 Mss K, S; cf. Gn 5.1.

12: תכסה / Trg: דתתכסי=חֲכָסָה; LXX, P.

21: וסקלוה / j 1: וירגמונה כל=וסקלוה כָל; 12 Mss K, 11 Mss R.

29: תחת אשר ענה>1; 2 Mss K.

XXIII.

8: לא 2° / 1: ולא=וְלָא; 10 Mss K, 14 Mss R, S, P.

21: שמה / n: תמן=שם; cf. Gn 19.20.

22: אלהיך 1°>1; 1 Ms K.

XXIV.

5: לכל / b d: כל=כָל; 3 Mss K, LXX.

8: ולעשות / h: למעבד=לעשות; 2 Mss K, S, LXX.

17: יתום / b c d ƀ 1: ויתם=וְיתוֹם; 2 Mss K, LXX, P.

XXVI.

5: עצום / b g: ותקיף=וְעָצום; 4 Mss K.

13: ולגר / k l n: לגיורא=לגר; 23 Mss K, 48 Mss R, S.

16: היום הזה / j: ארי=כִּי.

XXVIII.

12: את 2° / l: מֵאֵת=מן; cf. Gn 4.1.

20: את 2° / Trg: וְאָת=וית; 40 Mss K, 49 Mss R, S, LXX.

29: אַך >h; P.

37: שמה / l: שם=תמן; cf. Gn 19.20.

57: בשעריך / c: בְּכָל שְׁעָרֶיךָ=בכל קירוך; 4 Mss K, P.

63: יהוה 2°>h.

68: לאיביך / Trg: לְאֹיְבֶיכָם=לבעלי דבביכון; S, LXX, P.

XXIX.

1: אל כל / l: אֶל כָּל בָּנֵי=לכל בני; LXX; c: לכל זקני (!)(=לכל); זְקֵנָי.

באר ץ מצרים >l.

9: שבטיכם / c: וְשִׁבְטֵיכֶם=ושבטיכון; 1 Ms K, LXX.

13: ולא / s: לֹא=לא; P.

17: ללכת >Trg.

XXX.

1: שמה / l: שם=תמן; 1 Ms K; cf. Gn 19.20.

3: שמה / l: שם=תמן; S (Mss); cf. Gn 19.20.

16: ללכת / k n: וְלָלֶכֶת=וללכת ולמהך; 3 Mss K, 3 Mss R, S (Ms), P; cf. 11.22.

16.18: שמה / l: שם=תמן; S (Ms); cf. Gn 19.20.

XXXI.

12: והנשים / d: הנשים=נשיא.

13: שמה / b d g k n: שם=תמן; cf. Gn 19.20.

28: את 1°>l; cf. Gn 19.10.

את 2° / j: אֵת כָּל=ית כל; 6 Mss K, 6 Mss R, LXX.

בם / Trg: בְּכָם=בכון; P.

29: את >k; 3 Mss K; cf. Gn 19.10.

XXXII.

10: ימצאהו / Trg: סופיק צורכיהון =יַמְצְאֵהוּ; cf. S (Ms: ימיצהו);
cf. Gn 2.23.

13: ויאכל / Trg: ואוכילינון =יַאֲכִילָהוּ; S, LXX, P.

35: ושלם / Trg: ואנא אשלים =וַאֲנִי אֲשַׁלֵם; cf. N T (Heb 10.30
and Rom 12.19): ἐγὼ ἀνταποδώσω; cf. LXX, P.

38: יהי / Trg: יהון =יְהָיוּ; S, LXX, P.

47: שמה / b d g l: תמן =שָׁם; cf. Gn 19.20.

52: ושמה / l: ותמן =וְשָׁם; S (Ms); cf. Gn 19.20.

XXXIV.

4: ושמה / k: ותמן =וְשָׁם; S (Mss); cf. Gn 19.20.

Hebrew Union College Annual, Vol. 12/13 (1937-1938),
pp. 103-274

HEBREW BASED UPON GREEK AND LATIN
TRANSLITERATIONS

ALEXANDER SPERBER

Jewish Theological Seminary, New York and Dropsie College, Philadelphia

INTRODUCTION

I. The Methodical Approach

THE present study is an endeavor to give, as fully as the
sources permit, an outline of a Hebrew Grammar and
Dictionary based upon the Greek and Latin transliterations of
Hebrew words and their respective derivatives. The sources of
these transliterations date from the third century B.C.E. to the
beginning of the fifth century C.E. Thus the end of this period
antedates by several centuries the beginnings of the activities
of the Masoretic school of Tiberias. Because of this, while arranging the transliterations, I did not consider the vocalization which
the Masorites of Tiberias gave to the Hebrew words in question.
For the better understanding of the transliteration I had put
in juxtaposition merely the Hebrew consonants of the word to
which the transliteration referred, without originally vocalizing
these consonants, since the transliteration was meant to indicate
how these consonants should be vocalized and read; for instance:
מבלעדי μεββελαδη would mean that the word has to be read as
מִבְּלְעֲדִי, and not מִבַּלְעֲדִי as the Masorites vocalized it; יחבל ιεβαλ
would be = יֶחְבָּל, as against יַחְבָּל of the Masorites. But for
reasons of practical utility, in the course of my work, I aband-
oned this method of leaving the Hebrew equivalents of the
transliterations unvocalized, and I vocalized them with the
Tiberian vowel signs. Although these vowel signs, which I added
to the Hebrew consonants, are Tiberian, I did not always follow
the Tiberian rules in applying them. Sometimes I used the Tiberian system to indicate the vowels which are presupposed by the
transliterated text; for instance: חֻפְצִי, דְּלַף instead of the Tiberian

way of vocalizing these forms as יַדְלֹף, חַפַּצ׳. This method I followed in the relatively numerous cases, where the transliteration presupposes a word, different from that found in the Masoretic text; for instance: צָפוּן, רָשָׁע as compared with their corresponding Masoretic forms רָשָׁע, צָפוּן. Of course this method could not be followed throughout, since I could not vocalize a word like חֲלוֹם to read חֵלֶם, thus following the transliteration *helem*, although this form has its parallel in the Aramaic חילמא, since such a procedure would definitely diminish the intelligibility and practical utility of this study.

The necessity for vocalizing the Hebrew consonants first arose while dealing with those words, in which the transliteration yielded forms differing not only in pronunciation from the Masoretic reading, but actually changing the meaning of the Hebrew word as intended by the Masorites; for instance: מַשְׁכִּים instead of מְשַׁכִּים, or שְׁעָרִים instead of שָׂעָרִים. In order to bring into sharp relief the distinction between the Masoretic and the transliterated word, it was necessary to vocalize the Masoretic word too. The Tiberian system was used for this purpose, since this system covers—unlike the Babylonian or Palestinian system—the entire biblical Hebrew vocabulary. The Tiberian vocalization, therefore, serves only a practical end and is irrelevant for an appreciation of the problems dealt with in this study. Cf. also paragraphs XXV and XXVIII.

II. The Sources

The material upon which this investigation is based, is to be found in three sources: 1) the transliterations of proper names in the *Septuagint*; 2) the material preserved from the *Second Column of Origen's Hexapla*; and 3) the transliterations of *St. Jerome*.

III. Previous Attempts

Each of these sources has already been dealt with in special monographs; so for instance the Septuagint by Cl. Könnecke in his paper *Die Behandlung der hebräischen Namen in der Septua-*

ginta, Stargard 1885; the Hexaplaric material most recently by O. Pretzl in *Biblische Zeitschrift* 1932, pp. 4–32; and Jerome by C. Siegfried in *ZAW*, IV, 1884, pp. 34–83. But all of them missed the point; for they considered the Masoretic textus receptus with its Tiberian vocalization as the Hebrew text which served as the basis for the Septuagint, St. Origen and St. Jerome respectively for their transliterations. In the early days of Könnecke and Siegfried one could hardly expect a more critical standpoint as regards the Masoretic text; and when we find that for instance Siegfried went sometimes even so far as to "correct", according to the Masoretic text, Jerome's spelling of a Hebrew word in his transliteration without noting down, that his citation is based upon such a "correction"—e. g. דעה deah instead of dea; רוח ruah instead of rua; מלככם malchechem instead of melchechem—we may excuse it out of this consideration. But even Pretzl, who criticizes Max L. Margolis' approach to the problem (in the latters paper "The pronunciation of שוא according to new Hexaplaric material," *AJSL*, XXVI, p. 62 sq.), shows just the same misconception; cf. f. i. p. 8 in his paper, §I 3β where he advances a theory that the Greek ε was pronounced like "a" since it is used to indicate a pataḥ, as f. i. in δερχω for דרכו, δερχι for דרכי, ρεγλαι for רגלי. I am rather doubtful as to whether such a procedure is methodically justifiable. For I think that Pretzl would first have to prove from purely Greek sources that ε could have had the phonetic value of an *a*. But even then, a mere comparison of the words in question with their equivalent forms in the Babylonian vocalization would have taught him that according to this system דרך and רגל belong to the qitl-class, cf. דֹרכֹם. Prov. 1.31; דֹרכֹי ib. 3.17; דֹרכֹו ib. 11.5 (in Ms. Ec 1); further רֹגלֹי Ps. 40.3 (in Ms. Ec 1) and רֹגלֹי Ex. 25.26 (in Ms. Ea 5). In these cases the Greek transliteration and the Babylonian vocalization of Hebrew are in full agreement between themselves and both presuppose a pronunciation of Hebrew, different from what the Tiberian Masorites offer us. This most essential point Pretzl failed to see. I deal with these details at length so as to show that all the research that has been done in this field until now could not spare me the trouble of starting my own investigation from the very beginning, i. e. to go through the sources indicated above for collecting my material. And may I be permitted here to say that it was not an easy task at all to find the proper method for arranging and classifying the large amount of material, which first seemed to contradict itself in nearly every detail. I did my best to present the results of long years of continuous study in such a form, as may interest the serious minded student of Hebrew Grammar, without making him aware of the uncountable difficulties which I had to overcome before I found my way out of this labyrinth.

IV. HEBREW PROPER NAMES IN THE SEPTUAGINT

In the first chapter of my *Septuagintaprobleme* (Kohlhammer, Stuttgart 1929) I dealt only with such forms of transliterated proper names as indicated an accumulating corruption in the Greek spelling in the various Mss. The thesis was there advanced that the growing inaccuracies in such spellings were proofs of the later date of the more corrupt Ms. At the present time however we are concerned only with those transliterations which accurately reproduce the Hebrew consonants. This consideration applies only to the consonants, since the vocalization of the Tiberian Grammarians is irrelevant to a study of the systems of vocalization used by the transliterators. Thus, to give an instance, if the Masoretic text reads צְלָפְחָד and the Septuagint renders it $\Sigma a\lambda\pi aa\delta$, then the only possible conclusion is that in the time of the Septuagint the name was still pronounced צְלָפְחָד, which corresponds to צְלָפְחָד in the Tiberian system (cf. *B.-L.* §14z and g'), or even צְלָפְחָד, cf. the form בְּצַלְאֵל. Thus the name צלפחד proves to be a theophorous name-form, meaning "the shadow of פַּחַד"; cf. Gen. 31.53, where פחד is referred to as the god of Isaac.

Hebrew proper names are for the most part either nominative or verbal forms; sometimes a combination of both; cf. f. i. אבימלך, ראובן, פדהאל; יורח, יבחר; אבשלום. The study of the transliterations, may therefore, indicate how any given noun or verb was pronounced in that particular period.

Of Septuagint Mss. I have selected for this study the codices B and A (according to Henry B. Swete: *The Old Testament in*

Greek, 3 vols., Cambridge 1901 sq.), since they contain the most characteristic grammatical tendencies. In codex B there are preserved the oldest transliterated forms known to us, whereas in codex A we have the transition to the period of the Second Column (see paragraph V). It is well to note the frequent rendering of ח by χ (cf. חבר χαβερ in B and αβερ in A, חפה χοφφα in B and οφφα in A), of ז by σ (cf. אחז αχας in B and αχαζ in A, יורע ισρα in B and ιζρα in A), of long י‧ by ει (cf. אבי αβει in B and αβι in A, אחי αχει in B and αχι in A) in codex B; cf. also paragraph XXVId on the Article. This estimate of the comparative age of the basic texts of these two codices is valid only if they are considered in their totality, but is no indication of the age of any particular transliteration. There are any number of forms in codex B which are late (cf. חפצי αψει and חריף αρειφ; זכרי ζεχρει and זמה ζεμμα; אהלי οολι), and correspondingly there are forms in codex A which are early (cf. חותם χωϑαμ and חלק χελεκ; יריב ιαρειβ and ישב ιασειβ) (cf. ¶ XXXII). I have arranged my material in such a way that this is obvious in any particular instance. We can, therefore, apply here the statement which is elaborated in my *Septuagintaprobleme* (p. 46) to the effect that the uniformity of a given Ms. indicates nothing as to the uniformity of the Ms. from which it is derived, nor is there any possibility of determining the age of the basic text by ascribing the Ms. to any particular period.

V. Origen's Hexapla

For the Second Column of the Hexapla I used the citations in Fridericus Field: *Origenis Hexaplorum quae supersunt* (2 vols., Oxford 1875) and the fragments discovered by *Mercati* (cf. Alfred Rahlfs: *Verzeichuis der griechischen Handschriften des Alten Testaments*, Berlin 1914, p. 130 sq., under the symbol O. 39 sup.). These fragments have been printed by Franz X. Wutz in his commentary *Die Psalmen* (Munich 1925), but without any comment on them or even the slightest attempt to compare them with the corresponding text in Hebrew characters for the sake of mere textual criticism; cf. the final remarks in paragraph XXII. Fortunately I could verify his indications by reference to Hatch and Redpath: *A Concordance to the Septuagint* (Supplement, Oxford 1906, pp. 199–216). The understanding of these transliterations is made more difficult by the fact that very often words are rendered in forms that differ from those of the Masora; cf. Ps. 18.48: MT: וַיַּדְבֵּר Origen: ουιεδαββερ = וַיְדַבֵּר; ib. 46.6: MT: יַעְזְרֶהָ Origen: ουεζρα = וְעֶזְרָה. In regard to the method of rendering Hebrew words, the transliterations of the Second Column agree for the most part with the system of codex A of the Septuagint, but not infrequently they agree with codex B. This leads to the conclusion that the Second Column is very definitely not a uniform text. In this connection compare the subdivisions a and b of the respective paragraphs in the section dealing with the verb, f. i. §3a and b, §27a and b, §53a and b for the perfect; §7a and b, §10a and b, §31a and b for the imperfect; §15a and b for the participle; §78 and §79 for the waw as waw conjunctivum and waw consecutivum; cf. similarly the paragraphs headed "Nouns with varying vocalization" in the section dealing with the noun, f. i. §§83 and 88 for the formation of the noun; §§115 and 116 for the article and §117 sq. for the inseparable prepositions בכלם. I had, therefore, originally attempted to arrange the material from the Hexapla in such a way as to enable me to assign the various fragments which have been discovered by Mercati to different textual types; f. i. s. v. בקר as a qutl-form (to use the Tiberian terminology) בקר $\beta o\kappa\rho$ in Ps. 46.6 and as a qitl-form לבקר $\lambda\alpha\beta\epsilon\kappa\rho$ in Ps. 49.15; s. v. דרך as a qitl-form דרך $\delta\epsilon\rho\chi$ in Ps. 89.42 and as a qatl-form דרכם $\delta\alpha\rho\chi\alpha\mu$ in Ps. 49.14; s. v. קרב as a qutl-form בקרב $\beta\epsilon\kappa o\rho\beta$ in Ps. 36.2; as a qitl-form בקרבה $\beta\kappa\epsilon\rho\beta\alpha$ in Ps. 46.6 and as a qatl-form קרבם $\kappa\alpha\rho\beta\alpha\mu$ in Ps. 49.12. But as a result of this investigation I realized that any such attempt must finally prove to be a failure, since the fragments represent already a mixed type. Compare, f. i., s. v. חפץ: the participle forms החפץ $\alpha\alpha\varphi\eta s$ and חפצי $\omega\varphi\sigma\eta$, both occurring in the same verse (Ps. 35.27); s. v. מיד יד: $\mu\epsilon\iota\epsilon\delta$ and ידו $\iota\alpha\delta\omega$, both in the same chapter (Ps. 89); cf. further the paragraphs cited above which deal with the different ways of verbal formations, the examples for which are taken in large part from the very same biblical chapter.

VI. Jerome's Role

Numerically considered, the overwhelming majority of transliterated words is taken from St. Jerome. A glance at the arrangement of this study, in which instances are brought from Jerome for almost every subdivision of every paragraph, makes it evident that his transliterations must be based upon *Vorlagen* (originals) belonging to different periods. By merely external evidence, there are two main sources to which his references can be traced, namely the *Onomastica Sacra* which are merely a Latin transliteration of Greek texts, and his large Commentary to the various biblical books, where Jerome's own pronunciation of Hebrew or rather that of his Jewish teachers is given.

VII. The Onomastica Sacra Go Back to Greek *Vorlagen*

The Onomastica Sacra I have worked through in the edition of Lagarde (Goettingen 1887). When I had finished collecting my material from this source and sat down to classify it and to distribute the quotations to the various paragraphs where they belonged, I arrived at the conclusion that they are not genuine transliterations of Hebrew *Vorlagen*, but unquestionably go back to originals in Greek characters. How else could one account for the fact that he himself points out the divergencies between his transliteration and the corresponding Hebrew word? Cf. his remarks to עמרה, צער and חם in paragraph VIII. I discussed this problem with a scholarly friend and he raised objections against my conclusion. To meet his objections I once again took up the study of the Onomastica Sacra, and this time I found there a plain statement of Jerome to this effect, which must have escaped my attention on previous occasions. This statement reads as follows (editio Lagarde, p. 26): "Philo, uir disertissimus Iudaeorum, Origenis quoque testimonio conprobatur edidisse librum hebraicorum nominum eorumque etymologias iuxta ordinem litterarum e latere copulasse. qui cum uulgo habeatur a Graecis, et bibliothecas orbis impleuerit, studii mihi fuit in latinam eum linguam uertere." Cf. also the headline on p. 156 of *Philonis*

Iudaei Alexandrini omnes quae apud Graecos et Latinos extant libri (Basileae, per Henricum Petrum, 1538) reading: "Divi Hieronymi Presbyteri in librum Philonis Iudaei de nominibus Hebraicis praefatio." This work, thus ascribed to Philo, is only Pseudo-Philonic; cf. Leopold Cohn; *Einteilung und Chronologie der Schriften Philos*, VII. Supplementband des *Philologus* (Leipzig 1899, p. 426) and at full length Franz Wutz: *Onomastica Sacra*, I, Leipzig 1914, §2.

VIII. The Pronunciation of ח and ע Had Changed

The transliteration of the Greek *Vorlagen* of the Onomastica Sacra into Latin characters is the best indication of the exactness and punctiliousness of Jerome. In spite of the fact that the pronunciation of Hebrew had changed materially between the time of the writing of the Greek originals and the period of Jerome, and despite the fact that Jerome himself was fully aware of the incongruities between the transliteration and the contemporary pronunciation of Hebrew, he made no attempt to avoid these discrepancies by means of corrections, but rather reproduced his originals faithfully and limited himself to mere glosses. Thus he remarks while explaining the name עֲמֹרָה (ed. Lagarde, p. 33): "Gomorra populi timor (this would mean: עַם and מוֹרָא) siue seditio (probably: עַם and מוֹרָה, cf. Deut. 21.18: וּמוֹרֶה), sciendum quod ɢ litteram in hebraico non habet, sed scribitur per uocalem ע." Similarly he notes to צֹעַר (ib. in the Genesis list of names beginning with S): "Segor parua (cf. Gen. 19.20). ipsa est quae et supra Seor. sed sciendum quia ɢ. litteram in medio non habeat, scribaturque apud Hebraeos per uocalem ain." As regards this inconsistency in transliterating Hebrew words (Segor and Seor) cf. Jerome's preface (ed. Lagarde, p. 26). "uerum tam dissona inter se exemplaria repperi et sic confusum ordinem, ut tacere melius indicauerim quam reprehensione quid dignum scribere."

On the name חָם Jerome remarks (ib., p. 30): "Cham calidus. sed sciendum quod in hebraeo χ (this corresponds to "ch" in Jerome's transliteration; cf. paragraph X) litteram non habeat,

scribitur autem per ח, quae duplici adspiratione profertur."
He speaks at greater length concerning the question of transliterating the ח in his *Quaestiones hebraicae in libro Geneseos*
to Gen. 9.18: "frequenter LXX interpretes, non ualentes heth
literam quae duplicem aspirationem sonat, in graecum sermonem
uertere, chi graecam literam addiderunt, ut nos docerent in
istius modi uocabulis aspirare debere: unde et in praesenti loco
Cham transtulerunt, pro eo quod est Ham, a quo et Aegyptus
usque hodie Aegyptiorum lingua dicitur."

This manifests what Jerome understood by the duplex asp-
iratio: an H. His explanation of the fact that ח is transliterated
in the older texts by χ, is hardly correct. On the contrary, such
transliterations clearly indicate that ח had then the consonantal
value of χ. But when in the period of the ·Second Column ח
became merely a vowel, no change was made in the transliterations
tions of proper names which were utilized in the current texts.
That Jerome's explanation is not based upon any well founded
tradition, but rather upon his own fancy, is demonstrated by the
inconsistent manner in which he himself transliterates ח one
time with an h and another time simply as a vowel; cf. for
instance: חדלו hedalu, חדש hodes as compared with: חלד eled,
חנף oneph; even the same Hebrew word is transliterated in
different places in different ways, cf. חמר omer and homer, חרב
areb and hareb, חרוץ arus and harus. Moreover, even his transliteration of ח by h fails to satisfy completely his own demands
for a double aspirate, since h according to him is only a simple
aspirate; cf. Onomastica Sacra, p. 51: "H autem a plerisque
adspiratio putatur esse, non littera." Accordingly Jerome transliterates the ה—in so far as he deals with it not simply as a
vowel—equally by h; so for instance in his Quaestiones on
Gen. 14.5: "porro BAHEM, pro quo dixerunt (namely: the
Septuagint) $\mu\epsilon\tau$' $a\dot{v}\tauo\hat{i}s$ (hoc est cum eis) putauerunt scribi
per ה, ducti elementi similitudine, cum per heth scriptum sit.
BAHEM enim cum per tres literas scribitur, si mediam he habet,
interpretatur in eis, si autem heth (ut in praesenti) locum significat, id est Hom." As to the fact that Jerome read בחם here
instead of the Masoretic spelling בהם, cf. paragraph XVII.

IX. The *Vorlagen* Belong to Different Types

It is, therefore, explicable that Jerome sometimes renders the same Hebrew name forms, occurring in the various biblical books or even in the same book, differently; f. i. אחי achi and ahi, זבדי zabdi and zebdi, זמרי zamri and zemeri, מלכי melchi and malchi. It is obvious that his *Vorlagen* could not have been parts of a uniform tradition. This fact was naturally taken into consideration in the arrangement of the material utilized in this study; note for instance the order in which the transliterations are cited for אחז: $\alpha\chi\alpha\zeta$, achaz—$\alpha\alpha\zeta$, aaz; or for מעון: $\mu\alpha\omega\nu$, maon—$\mu\epsilon\omega\nu$, meon. Jerome himself definitely indicates these various possibilities of pronunciation (editio Vallarsi, vol. VI, p. 24C on Hos. 2.18): "בעלי. inter Beth et Lamed literas consonantes Ain uocalis litera ponitur, quae iuxta linguae illius proprietatem nunc BEEL, nunc BAAL legitur."

X. How to Reconstruct the Original Greek

One can reconstruct without any difficulty the Greek originals of Jerome's rendering of the Hebrew name lists in the Onomastica Sacra, when we keep in mind that the following are the Greek equivalents of his Latin characters: $a = \alpha$, $b = \beta$, $c = \kappa$, ch $= \chi$, $d = \delta$, $e = \epsilon$ or η, $f = \varphi$, $g = \gamma$, i and $j = \iota$, $l = \lambda$, $m = \mu$, $n = \nu$, $o = o$ or ω, $p = \pi$, ph $= \varphi$, $r = \rho$, $s = \sigma$, $t = \tau$, th $= \vartheta$, $u = ov$, $z = \zeta$. If our conjecture be correct, Jerome has permitted himself only one major deviation from the normal Greek spelling; that is between two vowels immediately following one another he inserts an h to indicate that they are to be pronounced separately; so for instance (in the name lists of the Genesis and of Exodus in the Onomastica Sacra): ישראל Israhel, בצלאל Beselehel, ימואל Iamuhel, מישאל Misahel, רעואל Raguhel, בעל פעור Behelfegor, בעל צפון Behelsefon, בעל מעון Bahalmeon. Compare also the passage in Quaestiones on Gen. 17.3, cited in paragraph XI, which states that by adding an a to the name Abram it became Abraham; the h inserted between the two a's does not count. Cases like אחר aher (cf. $\alpha\epsilon\rho$ B), נחלה nehela (cf. $\nu\epsilon\epsilon\lambda\alpha\vartheta\alpha\chi$ o), מרחם merehem (cf. $\mu\eta\rho\epsilon\mu$ o) have, therefore, to be treated similarly; an assumption that the h here corresponds to the Hebrew ח, would be unjustified.

XI. The Greco-Latin Alphabets Inadequate
for Transliteration

Jerome was quite aware of the incompatability of the Latin and Greek alphabets for rendering Hebrew sounds, insofar as the Greco-Latin alphabets have for one thing no exact equivalents for Semitic Gutturals or Sybillants. So he prefaces the list from Genesis with the following remark (p. 27): "Non statim, ubicumque ex A littera, quae apud Hebraeos dicitur aleph, ponuntur nomina, aestimandum est ipsam esse solam quae ponitur. nam interdum ex ain, saepe ex he, non numquam ex heth litteris, quae adspirationes suas uocesque commutant, habent exordium. sciendum igitur quod tam in Genesi quam ceteris in libris, ubi a uocali. littera nomen incipit, apud Hebraeos a diuersis (ut supra diximus) ·incohetur elementis, sed quia apud nos non est uocum tanta diuersitas, simplici sumus elatione contenti. unde accidit ut eadem uocabula, quae apud illos non similiter scripta sunt, nobis uideantur in interpretatione uariari." This general statement Jerome further elucidates in discussing the changes in the name forms of אברם—אברהם and שרה—שרי in Quaestiones on Gen. 17.3: "dicunt autem Hebraei quod ex nomine suo deus, quod apud illos tetragrammum est, he literam Abrahae et Sarae addiderit: dicebatur enim primum Abram, quod interpretatur pater excelsus (this means: composed of אָב and רָם) et postea uocatus est Abraham, quod transfertur pater multarum (i. e. אָב and הָמוֹן): nam quod sequitur, gentium, non habetur in nomine, sed subauditur. nec mirandum quare, cum apud Graecos et nos A litera uideatur addita, nos he literam hebraeam additam dixerimus: idioma enim linguae illius est, per E quidem scribere, sed per A legere: sicut e contrario A literam saepe per E pronuntiant." This conception is rounded out in his explanation to Gen. 17.15: "Sarai igitur primum uocata est per sin res ioth: sublata ergo ioth, id est I elemento, addita est he litera, quae per A legitur, et uocata est Saraa. causa autem ita nominis immutati haec est, quod antea dicebatur princeps mea, unius tantum modo domus mater familiae, postea uero dicitur absolute princeps, id est ἄρχουσα."

XII. GUTTURALS

Gutturals have, therefore, no independent consonantal value, but serve merely to carry the vowel sign. This yields a double conclusion: when two different Gutturals bear the same vowel signs we can have the result that two entirely distinct words may be pronounced identically and consequently be identical in transliteration. An example for such a case we find in Quaestiones to Gen. 30.13: "Aser ergo non diuitiae, sed beatus dicitur, dum taxat in praesenti loco. nam in aliis secundum ambiguitatem uerbi possunt et diuitiae sic uocari." The two Hebrew words Jerome refers to here, are: אָשֵׁר and עָשִׁיר. Similarly he explains in his Onomastica Sacra (p. 36) רעמה Gen. 10.7: "Rama tonans uel excelsa," i. e. רעמה (from רעם thunder) and ראמה (from רום; cf. Zech. 14.10: וראמה). But on the other hand, when the same Guttural appears in two etymologically different words with identical spelling, and the Guttural has different vowels, then the transliterations fail to indicate the identical consonantal spelling in the original Hebrew. So Jerome remarks in Quaestiones on Gen. 26.12: "licct enim eiusdem literis et aestimatio scribatur et hordeum, tamen aestimationes SAARIM leguntur, hordea uero SORIM," Jerome thinks here of שְׂעָרִים and שְׂעָרִים.

XIII. SYBILLANTS

Concerning the difficulty of rendering Hebrew Sybillants, Jerome discourses in his introduction to those explanations coming under the letter S (Onomastica, p. 36): "Quod in principio dixeramus in uocalibus litteris obseruandum eo, quod apud nos una sit interdum littera et apud Hebraeos uariis uocibus proferatur, hoc nunc quoque in s littera sciendum est. siquidem apud Hebraeos tres s sunt litterae: una, quae dicitur samech, et simpliciter legitur quasi per s nostram litteram describatur: alia sin, in qua stridor quidam non nostri sermonis interstrepit: tertia sade, quam aures nostrae penitus reformidant. sicubi ergo euenerit ut eadem nomina aliter atque aliter interpretentur, illud in causa est quod diuersis scripta sunt litteris." In another place (editio Vallarsi, vol. IV, p. 155E) Jerome nevertheless attempts to explain the pronunciation of the צ: "נצר. Sed sciendum quod hic NESER per SADE literam scribatur: cuius proprietatem et sonum inter z et s Latinus sermo non exprimit. Est enim stridulus et strictis dentibus vix linguae impressione profertur."

Due to the circumstance that in the Greek and Latin alphabets the three Hebrew letters ס, צ and שׂ can be rendered only by one character (σ, s), there results the situation in which two entirely different words are identical in transliteration. When the opportunity presents itself, Jerome himself indicates this; so for instance (Onomastica, p. 53): "Aser beatus, si per aleph et sin litteram scribitur; sin autem per heth et sade, atrium interpretatur." Jerome has in mind: אָשֵׁר and חָצֵר.

XIV. שׂ AND שׁ

From the passages of the Onomastica Sacra cited above and from all those other passages in which Jerome attempts to explain the pronunciation and transliteration of Semitic Sybillants (cf. especially Quaestiones on Gen. 26.12; 41.29), it is obvious that for him the שׂ had but one sound: sin. He is unfamiliar with the differentiation between שׂ and שׁ. In this connection cf. Jud. 12.6: in Ephraim (i. e. the klngdom of Israel) the שׁ had the same consonantal value as שׂ. Later on, maybe due to the inclusion of parts of Israel into the kingdom of Judah after the destruction of Samaria, (cf. Rudolf Kittel, *Geschichte des Volkes Israel*, 5. Auflage, Gotha 1922, p. 473 note 1 and p. 482 note 2, also the references cited there) we meet with this phenomenon even in Judah; cf., f.i., Jer. 23.38, 39: ואם מָשָׂא יהוה תאמרו....וְנָשִׁיתִי אתכם נָשֹׁא: a play on words: משא from the root נָשָׂא, with the verb נָשָׁה to forget, cf. Lam. 3.17 (tertiae ה and א are promiscuously used in that late period). Cf. also Talmud babli Šabbat 9a: הלא פרוש לרעב כתיב ב ש י ' ן (Isa. 58.7) לחמך as compared with the spelling of the Masoretic text: פָּרֹס, and with Rabbi Akiba Eger's remark (ib. 55b) on the passage: ובספרים שלנו כתיב ב ס י ן. Cf. also paragraph XXXIII 2. In the alphabetical arrangement of the word list beginning with שׁ I have therefore not considered the fact, whether according to the Tiberian grammatical system this sign is pronounced שׂ or שׁ, but have followed the conception of Jerome.

XV. Jerome's Commentaries Are Based upon the Hebrew Text

Jerome's Commentaries I have gone through in the edition of Vallarsi (Venice 1767 sq.); for the *Quaestiones hebraicae in libro Geneseos* I used also Lagarde's edition (Leipzig 1868). Whereas the Onomastica Sacra, considered as a unit, undoubtedly render Hebrew pronunciations as they were known before the time of Jerome, since they agree for the most part with codex A and frequently even with codex B, in the transliterations which appear in his commentaries we have a mixtum compositum, which includes, it is true, old material but at the same time a great deal that is purely contemporary; cf., f. i., ברורה barura (§19a) against דרושה drusa (§19c); בת bath and beth (§83); שרף saraph and seraph (§93); הרס ares and heres; (§96); עגור agor and agur (§109); הצדק asedec and השדמות asademoth (§115) against הגוי aggoi and המלך ammelech (§116); מבטן mebeten and מקדם mecedem (§121a) against מבית mebbeth and מכנף mecchenaph (§122); בסופה basupha and בקרב bacereb (§117a) against בגוים baggoim and בפוך baphphuch (§120). This results from the fact that Jerome in his commentaries has not limited himself to a mere explanation of the text offered by the Septuagint but has consulted the Hebrew text in every instance. This Hebrew text which he utilized must have consisted of unvocalized consonants (as was already pointed out by Wilhelm Nowack: *Die Bedeutung des Hieronymus für die alttestamentliche Textkritik*, Göttingen 1875, p. 55), since he frequently calls attention to the various possibilities for the pronunciation of the consonantal word; so for instance (editio Vallarsi, vol. IV, p. 856E): "רעים. Verbum enim REIM, quod quattuor literis scribitur RES, AIN, JOD, MEM, et amatores et pastores utrumque significat. Et si legamus REIM, amatores significat; si ROIM, pastores;" this means: רעים and רעים. He has also noticed that various Hebrew characters are sufficiently similar to be confused; note for instance his remark (ib., vol. VI, p. 818AB): "oculum eorum, quod Hebraice dicitur ENAM, et scribitur per AIN, JOD, NUN, MEM. Sive iniquitatem eorum; quae si per VAV literam scripta esset, recte legeretur ONAM, ut LXX putaverunt"; the two words referred to are: עֵינָם and עֹנָם.

In basing his work upon the original Hebrew text of the Bible, Jerome must have performed a task, which in his time was a mark of unusual scholarly achievement. Otherwise he would not have called special attention to this fact (ib., vol. V, p. 239): "Accedit ad hanc dictandi difficultatem, quod caligantibus oculis senectute et aliquid sustinentibus beati Isaac, ad nocturnum lumen nequaquam valeamus Hebraeorum volumina relegere, quae etiam ad solis dieique fulgorem literarum nobis parvitate caecantur." In instances, where Jerome felt doubtful as to his conception of the meaning of particular passages of the Bible, he followed the practice of turning to a Jew for advice and guidance; and in his explanations he calls attention to this procedure; so for instance (ib., vol. IV, p. 172A): "Hebraeus, quo ego praeceptore usus sum," or (ib., vol. VI, p. 288D; cf. also ib., pp. 383C, 550A, 570A, 637D): "Hebraeus autem, qui nos in Scripturis sanctis erudivit." In particularly difficult passages he was not satisfied with one such consultation, but would seek the advice of several Jews; note the plural for instance in the remark (ib., vol. VI, p. 808AB): "quid videatur Hebraeis, a quibus in veteri Testamento eruditi sumus."

XVI. Uncertainty of Etymology

These Jews who served as sources of information for Jerome and whom he so respectfully calls his teachers, must have been considered in their time authorities in matters of biblical exegesis; otherwise he would not have turned particularly to them for instruction. Consequently it is all the more interesting to read an answer like the following to one of his questions (ib., vol. VI, p. 934BC on Zech. 14.20 מְצִלּוֹת): "Verbum Hebraicum MESU-LOTH (this question implies that Jerome vocalized the word as מְצֻלּוֹת; cf. ib. 10.11), Aquila et Theodotio βυθόν interpretati sunt, id est profundum; Symmachus περίπατον σύσκιον, id est incessum umbrosum. Soli Septuaginta χάλινον, id est frenum, transtulerunt; quos et nos in hoc loco sequuti sumus, ne novum aliquid in quaestione vulgata videremus afferre. Quod quum ab

Hebraeo quaererem quid significaret, ait mihi, non debere nos
legere MESULOTH sed MESALOTH (i. e. מְצְהֲלוֹח; cf. Jer.8.16;
13.27. The word is, therefore, not a ἄπαξ λεγόμενον, as Jerome
says.), quod significat phaleras equorum et ornatum bellicum et
excepto hoc loco, in nullo penitus sanctarum Scripturarum
volumine hoc verbum reperiri."

Such suggestions indicate clearly that the Hebrew text of
the Bible itself, even in passages where Jerome's consonantal
text is identical with our *textus receptus*, could at that time be
read very differently from the vocalization to which we are
accustomed as a result of the activities of the Tiberian school
of grammarians. Both the pronunciation and the etymological
derivation of Hebrew words were at that time to a large extent
decidedly uncertain, as Jerome himself frequently remarks; for
instance in Quaestiones to Gen. 48.2: "ipsum uerbum METTA,
quod hic in lectulum transtulerunt, supra . . . uirgam potius
quam lectulum nominauerunt"; i. e. מִטָּה and מַטֶּה. Similarly to
Gen. 21.31: "septem enim dicuntur SABEE . . . et iuramentum
SABEE similiter appellatur," as compared with his assertion to
Gen. 41.29: "uerbum hebraicum SABEE . . . abundantiam siue
satietatem . . . interpretati sumus," i. e. שָׂבַע, שְׂבוּעָה and שֶׁבַע.
This explanation Jerome repeats in his commentary (editio
Vallarsi, vol. IV, pp. 64E and 945E): "licet iuxta Hebraei ser-
monis ambiguitatem, qui verbum SABA, nunc septem, nunc
plures, nunc iuramentum, interpretantur."

XVII. Variants against MT

But even in respect to the consonantal text the tradition was
fluctuating and uncertain, a fact which did not escape the attention of Jerome. Thus he remarks on Hab. 2.19 (ib., vol. VI,
p. 630BC): "וכל־דרוח. Unde et Aquila significantius vertit Hebraicum dicens: Et spiritus eius non est in visceribus sive in
medio eius. Propterea sciendum in quibusdam Hebraicis volu-
minibus non esse additum omnis, sed absolute spiritum legi";
these Mss. had, according to this statement, the reading: ורוח.
In this connection it is interesting to indicate the fact that in
the large collections of textual variations by Kennicott (*Vetus*

Testamentum cum variis lectionibus, 2 vols., Oxford 1776 and 1780), de Rossi (*Variae lectiones Veteris Testamenti*, 4 vols., Parma 1784–88), and Ginsburg (*The Old Testament . . . with the various readings from Mss.*, London 1926) there are still evidences for such non-Masoretic readings of Jerome:

Gen. 14.5: בְּהָם; Jerome: בְּחָם (cf. paragraph VIII); 7 Mss. de Rossi.

Isa. 29.4: כְּאוֹב; Jerome: כְּאב; 2 Mss. Kennicott.

Ezek. 29.10: מִגְדֹּל; Jerome: מִגְדָּל; 5 Mss. Ginsburg.

Ezek. 46.23: טִירוֹת; Jerome: טוּרוֹת; 1 Ms. Kennicott.

Micah 5.3: יָשֵׁבוּ; Jerome: יָשׁוּבוּ; 1 Ms. Kennicott, 2 Mss. de Rossi, 1 Ms. Ginsburg.

Zech. 12.5: אַמְצָה; Jerome: אָמְצָא; 2 Mss. de Rossi.

XVIII. Origen's Hebrew Text Differs from MT, too

A further indication of the importance of these collections of variants is the fact that they frequently substantiate the devia-tions from Masoretic readings which are already found in the Second Column of Origen's Hexapla:

Ps. 30.4: מִן שְׁאוֹל; Origen: מִשְּׁאוֹל; 4 Mss. Kennicott, 2 Mss. Ginsburg.

Ps. 31.25: חִזְקוּ; Origen: חָזַק; 1 Ms. Kennicott.

Ps. 31.25: הַמְיַחֲלִים; Origen: הַמְּיחלים; 2 Mss. Ginsburg.

Ps. 35.1: לְחֹם; Origen: לְחֹם; 1 Ms. Kennicott.

Ps. 35.25: בִּלַּעֲנוּהוּ; Origen: בִּלְבָבֵם; 4 Mss. Kennicott.

Ps. 36.2: לְבִּי; Origen: לְבוֹ; 2 Mss. Kennicott, 4 Mss. de Rossi, 1 Ms. Ginsburg.

Ps. 76.10: עֲנָוֵי; Origen: עֲנָיֵי; 1 Ms. Kennicott.

Ps. 89.36: בְּקָדְשִׁי; Origen: בְּקָדְשׁ; 1 Ms. Kennicott.

Ps. 89.47: תִּסָּתֵר; Origen: תִּסָּתִיר; 5 Mss. Kennicott.

The establishment of this fact is all the more important, since these collections are based on relatively late Hebrew Bible Mss. which otherwise follow almost entirely the Tiberian school. How numerous and wide-spread must have been such variae lectiones in the time of the transliterations, if in spite of the unifying activities of the Masorites of Tiberias, remnants of such readings could have been preserved in Mss. dating from a period possibly a thousand years later than that of the transliterations; see also my article "Targum Onkelos in its relation to the Hebrew Masoretic text," *Proceedings of the American Academy for Jewish Research*, vol. VI, 1934/5, p. 312 seq.

XIX. JEROME TRANSLATES WORDS, REGARDLESS OF THE CONTEXT

Attention has already been called to Jerome's commentary on Zech. 14.20 (paragraph XVI), where the explanation of the difficult word מצלות was referred to a Jew, who indicated the various possibilities of reading it. It is interesting that no attempt was made to explain this word so as to fit in its context. It was sufficient that the single word should be explained. This is not the only instance for such a procedure in Jerome. On the contrary, it is obvious from the manner both of the question and the answer that only single words and not the sense of the passages were the subjects of his inquiry. It made little difference at that time whether the words so explained fitted into the passages or not. We are thus in a position to understand how it could come about that sometimes the Septuagint offers translations of separate words based upon a vocalization of the Hebrew consonants, which in itself is quite possible, but which fails to make sense in the context. I have already brought instances of such renderings (see my articles "Das Alphabet der Septuaginta-Vorlage," *OLZ* 1929, p. 533 sq. and "The Problems of the Septuagint Recensions," *JBL* 1935, p. 82, paragraph II), and may I at this point add the following:

1 Sam. 11.5: הַבָּקָר; LXX: τὸ πρωί = הַבֹּקֶר.
Isa. 26.14: זֵכֶר; LXX: ἄρσεν = זָכָר.
Isa. 55.1: וְחָלָב; LXX: στέαρ = וְחֵלֶב.
Jer. 6.23: כְּאִישׁ; LXX: ὡς πῦρ = כָּאֵשׁ.
Jer. 6.23: וְאֵנֹשׁ; LXX: ἄνθρωπος = וְאֶנֹשׁ.
Jer. 18.14: שָׂדַי; LXX: μαστοί = שָׁדַי.

Ezek. 16.30: לִבָּתֵךְ: LXX: τὴν θυγατέρα σου = לְבִתֵּךְ.
Ezek. 24.17: דֹם; LXX: αἵματος = דָם.
Ezek. 26.10: מִבְקָעָה; LXX: ἐκ πεδίου = מִבִּקְעָה.
Ezek. 34.3: הַחָלָב; LXX: τὸ γάλα = הֶחָלָב.

Translations of this kind are generally referred to as obvious misconceptions; and there can hardly be any disagreement on this point. But it is a very important problem, whether they really originate in erroneous readings of the then undoubtedly unvocalized text. Going through the few instances which we have just listed, we note that in Isa. 55.1 the Septuagint misunderstood וְחָלָב as וְחֵלֶב, while in Ezek. 34.3 vice versa הַחֵלֶב was misconceived as הֶחָלָב These two facts combined advocate the assumption that in that early period חָלָב milk and חֵלֶב fat were similarly pronounced and could thus be confused with each other. The same may have been the case with וַכָּר and זָכָר (Isa. 26.14); cf., f. i., our remarks on רָשַׁע and רֶשַׁע in paragraph XXV; and in regard to שָׂדַי and שָׂדַי (Jer. 18.14), the explanation offered in paragraph XIV is of similar nature. These considerations lead us to the conclusion that mistranslations of this kind may largely be due not so much to a mistaken reading of the word in question as to a faulty etymology; cf. the similar case from b. Sanh. 5b, dealt with in paragraph XXXI. Bearing this in mind we may now try to solve some similar vexing problems: The word רְפָאִים is rendered by the Septuagint with γίγαντες; cf. Isa. 14.9; Job 26.5. However, in two passages, namely Isa. 26.14 and Ps. 88.11 they translate it: ἰατροί; this would correspond to a vocalization of the word as רֹפְאִים. Needless to emphasize that a meaning "healers" is quite out of place in these two verses. It is, therefore, all the more interesting to note that Jerome in the Deuteronomy Name List of his Onomastica Sacra (p. 51) remarks: "Raphaim medici uel gigantes." We have now to dispense with any attempt to explain the translation ἰατροί as based upon a mere mistake in the pronunciation, but have to admit that, speaking in the terms of the Tiberian Hebrew grammar, רְפָאִים shades and רֹפְאִים healers were similarly pronounced at least until Jerome's days. With the results of this study in mind we can easily account for it: 1) רפאים raphaim meaning: shades.

The Tiberian nominal plural form רְפָאִים presupposes a singular רְפָא, just as דְּבָרִים is the plural of דְּבָר. In paragraph XXVIa we will show that according to the system of the transliterations, the plur. masc. is formed by merely adding *im* to the noun without its undergoing any phonetic change as is the case in the Tiberian system. Thus, f. i., תמר ϑαμαρ is in the plural: thamarim; accordingly, to the sing. רְפָא rapha, shade, corresponds a plural רפאים raphaim. 2) רפאים raphaim meaning: healers. The Tiberian Hebrew grammar vocalizes רפא healer as a participle to רפא. But there is no reason why it should not be pronounced as a nominal form רְפָא like f. i. גֵּנָב (from גנב) or רָכָּב (from רכב). Now, in the Tiberian grammar, pataḥ is a short vowel and can not stand in an open syllable; the dagesh is therefore put in the immediately following consonant (נ and כ respectively) to close the preceding syllable with the pataḥ. But this rule does not hold true for the transliteration system; cf., f. i., in §80 the following plural forms without the gemination of the second radical, as required by the Tiberian grammar: s. v. גל: γαλειμ; s. v. ים: ιαμιμ; s. v. רב: ραβιμ; s. v. עם: αμιμ. We may thus assume a nominal singular form רפא rapha healer, to which the plural according to paragraph XXVIa would be: raphaim. On the Tiberian pluralis fractus רְפָאִים or דְּבָרִים see the discussion of שרפים at the end of paragraph XXVIa.

XX. Beginnings of Etymological Consideration

The variants on the Masoretic text as found in the transliterations belong to a certain extent to this category of words, being theoretically possible, but out of context in the particular passage. Such renderings are, therefore, impossible, not only because they fail to make sense in the context, which in those days was a matter of little importance as evidenced by the examples brought from the Septuagint, but also because they are etymologically unsound. However, an etymological sense was foreign to the contemporaries of Jerome; cf. his statement in Quaestiones on Gen. 17.16: "quidam pessime suspicantur ante eam lepram fuisse uocitatam et postea principem: cum lepra SARATH dicatur, quae in nostra quidem lingua uidetur aliquam habere similitudinem, in hebraeo autem penitus est diuersa. scribitur enim per SADE et AIN et RES et THAU: quod multum a superioribus tribus literis, id est SIN, RES et HE, quibus SARAA scribitur, discrepare manifestum est." If one could think of an etymological connection between צרעת and שרה, so that Jerome found it necessary to call attention to the different spelling of the two words in order to refute such an interpretation, it must be readily admitted that at that time etymological considerations played a very small role, indeed, in biblical exegesis.

XXI. Tracing Back of Jerome's Mistakes

The evidence for the various readings of the transliterations, which was brought from the Tiberian Bible Mss., indicates how long such variants were still current. On the other hand we can see from the agreement of the Septuagint with some of these variants that such texts are much older than the time when they were committed to writing by Origen and Jerome, since they served in part as *Vorlagen* for the Septuagint itself. For instance:

Gen. 26.12: שְׂעָרִים; Jerome: שְׂעָרִים; LXX: κριθήν.

Jer. 18.3: אֲבָנִים; Jerome: אֲבָנִים; LXX: τῶν λίθων.

Ezek. 23.23: פְּקוֹד; Jerome: פְּקוּד; LXX (3 Mss.): Φακουδ.

Ezek. 40.21: תָּאָו; Jerome: תָּא; LXX: ϑεέ.

Amos 5.26: סִכּוּת; Jerome: סָכּוֹת; LXX: τὴν σκηνήν.

Hag. 1.11: חֹרֶב; Jerome: חָרֶב; LXX: ῥομφαίαν.

Zech. 2.7: יָצָא; Jerome: יָצָא; LXX: ἱστήκει (tempus!).

Zech. 12.5: אַמְצָה; Jerome: אָמְצָא; LXX: εὑρήσομεν.

Mal. 2.13: מִיֶּדְכֶם; Origen: מִידֵיכֶם; LXX: ἐκ τῶν χειρῶν ὑμῶν.

Ps. 18.37: צַעֲדִי; Origen: צַעֲדִי; LXX: τὰ διαβήματά μου.

Ps. 36.2: לִבִּי; Origen: לִבּוֹ; LXX: ἐν ἑαυτῷ.

Ps. 46.3: אֶרֶץ; Origen: הָאָרֶץ; LXX: τὴν γῆν.

XXII. Variae Lectiones of Origen and Jerome

For the benefit of the biblical scholar who is interested in textual criticism, I consider it worth while to give here a full list of the variae lectiones of Origen and Jerome as compared with the Masoretic Hebrew text, based upon their transliterations of the

94

words in question. These transliterations are scattered all over the third part of this monograph, the Dictionary, and can be looked up there sub voce. Here I arrange them according to the order of the biblical books. Those variants, which have been dealt with in the preceding paragraphs, will be noted with a reference to the respective paragraph. The Variants from the Septuagint and the Onomastica Sacra referring to the pronunciation of Hebrew Proper Names, will easily be found with the help of the Alphabetical Index at the end of this monograph.

Gen. 14.5: בְּהֶם; cf. paragraph XVII.

Gen. 26.12: שְׂעָרִים; cf. paragraph XXI.

2 Ki. 23.7: הַקְּדֵשִׁים; Origen: הַ.קְּדֵשִׁים.

Isa. 7.14: קְרָאת; Jerome: קְרָאתִי.

Isa. 8.21: וּבֵאלֹהָיו; Origen: בֵּאלֹהָיו.

Isa. 24.16: זְמְרֹת; Jerome: זְמְרָת.

Isa. 26.3: יֵצֶר; Origen: יְצְרוֹ.

Isa. 26.10: רָשַׁע; Jerome: רָשַׁע; cf. paragraph XXV.

Isa. 29.4: כְּאוֹב; cf. paragraph XVII.

Isa. 38.10: דְּמִי; Jerome: דְּמִי.

Isa. 46.3: מִנִּי בֶטֶן; Jerome: מִבֶּטֶן.

Isa. 46.3: מִנִּי רָחַם; Jerome: מֵרָחַם.

Isa. 62.4: שְׁמָמָה; Jerome: שְׁמָמָה.

Jer. 4.19: הֹמָה; Jerome: הֹמָה.

Jer. 5.8: מַשְׁכִּים; Jerome: מַשְׁכִּים.

Jer. 5.26: יָשׁוּר; Jerome: יָשִׁיר.

Jer. 13.16: נָשַׁף; Jerome: נָשְׁפָּה.

Jer. 18.3: אֲבָנַיִם; cf. paragraph XXI.

Jer. 23.6: צִדְקֵנוּ; Jerome: צִדְקֵנוּ.

Ezek. 1.14: בָּזָק; Jerome: בָּזָק.

Ezek. 7.23: הָרַתּוּק; Jerome: הָרַתִּיק.

Ezek. 23.23: פְּקוֹד; cf. paragraph XXI.

Ezek. 29.10: מִגְדֹּל; cf. paragraph XVII.

Ezek. 30.17: אָוֶן; Jerome: אוֹן.

Ezek. 40.16: תִּמֹרִים; Jerome: תָּמָרִים.

Ezek. 40.16: אֲטֻמוֹת; Jerome: אַטֻמוֹת.

Ezek. 40.21: תָּאָו; cf. paragraph XXI.

Ezek. 40.24: אֵילָם; Jerome: אוּלָם.

Ezek. 46.23: טִירוֹת; cf. paragraph XVII.

Hos. 9.7: יָדְעוּ; Jerome: יָרְעוּ.

Hos. 11.1: וָאֹהֲבֵהוּ; Origen: וָאֹהֲבֵהוּ.

Hos. 12.5: וַיָּשַׁר; Jerome: יָשָׁר.

Amos 4.12: הִכּוֹן; Jerome: הַכִּין.

Amos 5.26: סִכּוּת; cf. paragraph XXI.

Amos 7.1: גִּי; Jerome: גּ.

Mic. 5.3: יְשׁוּבוּ; cf. paragraph XVII.

Hab. 1.5: רְאוּ; Jerome: רָאוּ.

Hab. 1.11: וְאָשֵׁם; Jerome: וְאָשֵׁם.

Hab. 3.13: לְיֵשַׁע; Jerome: לִישׁוּעָה.

Zeph. 1.5: מַלְכָּם; Jerome: מִלְכָּם.

Hag. 1.11: חֹרֶב; cf. paragraph XXI.

Zech. 2.7: וְיָצָא; cf. paragraph XXI.

Zech. 8.14: נִחָמְתִּי; Jerome: נִחָמְתִּי.

Zech. 12.5: אַמְצָה; cf. paragraph XVII and XXI.

Zech. 14.20: מְצִלּוֹת; Jerome: מְצוֹלוֹת and מְצָהֲלוֹת.

Mal. 2.13: פָּנוֹת; Origen: פָּנוֹת.

Mal. 2.13: מִיָּדְכֶם; cf. paragraph XXI.

Ps. 1.1: רְשָׁעִים; Origen: הָרְשָׁעִים.

Ps. 7.15: יְחַבֶּל; Origen: יַחְבְּל.

Ps. 9.1: לַבֵּן; Origen: בֵּן.

Ps. 9.1: עַל מוּת; Jerome: עֲלָמוֹת.

Ps. 9.7: חֳרָבוֹת; Origen: חָרְבוֹת.

Ps. 9.7: הֵמָּה; Origen: הֵם.

Ps. 12.9: כְּרֻם; Origen: כְּרָם.

Ps. 18.32: מִבַּלְעֲדֵי; Origen: מִבַּלְעֲדֵי.

Ps. 18.33: הַמְאַזְּרֵנִי; Origen: הַמְאַזְּרֵנִי.

Ps. 18.35: וְנִחֲתָה; Origen: וְנִחֲתָה.

Ps. 18.35: זְרוֹעֹתָי; Origen: זְרוֹעֹתָי.

Ps. 18.37: צַעֲדִי; cf. paragraph XXI.

Ps. 18.37: תַּחְתָּי; Origen: תַּחְתָּי.

Ps. 18.40: וַתְּאַזְּרֵנִי; Origen: וַתְּאַזְּרֵנִי.

Ps. 18.41: וּמְשַׂנְאַי; Origen: ומשנאי.

Ps. 18.48: וַיַּדְבֵּר; Origen: וַיַּדְבֵּר.

Ps. 28.6: שָׁמַע; Origen: שָׁמַע.

Ps. 28.9: וְרָעֵם ; Origen: וְהָרֵם.
Ps. 30.4: מִן שְׁאוֹל ; cf. paragraph XVIII.
Ps. 30.13: יִדֹּם ; Origen: יָדֹּם.
Ps. 30.13: אוֹדְךָ ; Origen: אוֹדְךָ.
Ps. 31.8: וְאֶשְׂמְחָה ; Origen: וְאֶשְׂמַח.
Ps. 31.21: מֵרִיב ; Origen: מְרִיבִי.
Ps. 31.24: וּמְשַׁלֵּם ; Origen: וְשָׁלֵם.
Ps. 31.25: חִזְקוּ ; cf. paragraph XVIII.
Ps. 31.25: הַמְיַחֲלִים ; cf. paragraph XVIII.
Ps. 35.1: לָחֶם ; cf. paragraph XVIII.
Ps. 35.2: וְקוּמָה ; Origen: וְקוּם.
Ps. 35.14: כְּאָבֵל ; Origen: כְּאָבֵל.
Ps. 35.19: שֹׂנְאַי ; Origen: שֹׂנְאַי.
Ps. 35.19: אֹיְבַי ; Origen: אֹיְבַי.
Ps. 35.22: תֶּחֱרַשׁ ; Origen: תֶּחֱרַשׁ.
Ps. 35.25: בִּלַּעֲנוּהוּ ; cf. paragraph XVIII.
Ps. 35.27: חֲפֵצֵי ; Origen: חֹפְצֵי.
Ps. 36.2: לָרָשָׁע ; Origen: לָרָשָׁע ; cf. paragraph XXV.
Ps. 36.2: לִבִּי ; cf. paragraph XVIII and XXI.
Ps. 46.1: עֲלָמוֹת ; Origen: עֲלָמוֹת.
Ps. 46.2: עֶזְרָה ; Origen: עֶזֶר.
Ps. 46.3: אֶרֶץ ; cf. paragraph XXI.
Ps. 46.5: יְשַׂמְּחוּ ; Origen: יְשַׂמְּחוּ.
Ps. 46.6: וְעֶזְרָהּ ; Origen: וְעֶזְרָהּ.
Ps. 46.9: שַׁמּוֹת ; Origen: שַׁמּוֹת.
Ps. 46.10: יְשַׁבֵּר ; Origen: יְשַׁבֵּר.
Ps. 48.3: צָפוֹן ; Origen: צָפוֹן.
Ps. 49.4: וְהָגוּת ; Origen: וְהָגִית.
Ps. 49.4: חָכְמוֹת ; Origen: חָכְמוֹת.
Ps. 49.6: יְסֻבֵּנִי ; Origen: יְסֻבֵּנִי.
Ps. 49.6: עֲקֵבַי ; Origen: עֲקֵבַי.
Ps. 49.9: וְחָדַל ; Origen: יֶחְדַּל.
Ps. 49.12: קָרְאוּ ; Origen: קָרְאוּ.
Ps. 49.12: בְּתֵימוֹ ; Origen: בְּתֵימוֹ.
Ps. 49.14: יִרְצוּ ; Origen: יִרְצוּ.
Ps. 49.15: וַיִּרְדּוּ ; Origen: וַיִּרְדּוּ.
Ps. 75.4: עַמּוּדֶיהָ ; Origen: עַמּוּדֶיהָ.

Ps. 76.10: עָנְוִי; cf. paragraph XVIII.

Ps. 89.31: וּבְמִשְׁפָּטַי; Origen: וּבְמִשְׁפָּטִי.

Ps. 89.31: יְלֵכוּן; Origen: יְהַלֵּכוּן.

Ps. 89.36: בְּקָדְשִׁי; cf. paragraph XVIII.

Ps. 89.45: מִנֶּזְרָתֹה; Origen: מִנַּרְתָּה.

Ps. 89.47: תַּסְתֵּר; cf. paragraph XVIII.

Ps. 89.51: זְכֹר; Origen: אֶזְכֹּר.

Ps. 92.7: יָדַע; Origen: יֵדַע.

Ps. 110.3: מִשְׁחָר; Origen: מִשַּׁחַר.

Ps. 127.2: הָעֲצָבִים; Origen: עֲצָבִים.

When I had, then assistant editor for the Ancient Bible Versions of Rudolf Kittel's *Biblia Hebraica* (third edition), to revise Frants Buhls manuscript on the book of Psalms for this edition, I embodied in it the variants from Origen's Hexapla, as far as they seemed to me to fit into the plans of the *Biblia Hebraica*; as a siglum I chose the sign "𐤄O," which means: the Hebrew of Origen. By an oversight, due to the death of Professor Rudolf Kittel and my subsequent resignation from the Biblia Hebraica, this sign is not contained in the explanatory list of that edition. The same is true of the siglum "𐤕P," which I had chosen for variants from the Palestinian Targum on the Pentateuch; cf. *MdW* I, p. 11*, note 1.

XXIII. The Pronunciation of the Hebrew Alphabet

In the fall of 1927 I began to study the Greek transliterations of Hebrew proper names contained in the Septuagint, which served as the starting point for this investigation. I soon realized the necessity to extend my investigation also to the material from the Second Column of the Hexapla of Origen. In my paper "Das Alphabet der Septuaginta-Vorlage" (*OLZ* 1929, p. 533–40) I summed up the results which I had arrived at then in the following sentences: "Zwischen der Abfassungszeit der Septuaginta und der der Hexapla des Origenes liegen vier bis fünf Jahrhunderte; trotzdem glaube ich im Rechte zu sein, wenn ich die Transkriptionen der Septuaginta und die der zweiten Kolumne der Hexapla *zusammen* behandelt wissen möchte. Denn weder ist—

wie schon Wutz richtig erkannt hat—die zweite Kolumne eine
erst ad hoc angefertigte Transkription, noch können wir in den
Transkriptionen der frühestens aus dem vierten nachchristlichen
Jahrhundert stammenden ältesten Septuaginta-Handschrift
die Aussprache des Hebräischen im 3.–2. vorchristlichen Jahrhundert wiedererkennen. Hier wie dort ist das Material verschied-
ener Epochen in buntem Durcheinander und man kann eben-
sowenig eine Grammatik des Hebräischen im 2. nachchristlichen
Jahrhundert auf Grund der Transkriptionen der 2. Kolumne
schreiben, wie eine Grammatik des Hebräischen im 3.–2. vorchristlichen Jahrhundert auf Grund der Transkriptionen der
Septuaginta; denn es handelt sich dabei nicht um einheitliche
Formen, die sich in *eine* Grammatik zusammenfassen lassen.
Dagegen ist es unter Benutzung des gesamten Transkriptions-
materials, das aus diesen zwei Quellen stammt, bis zu einem
gewissen Grade wohl möglich, den *Wandel* in der Aussprache
des Hebräischen vom 3. vorchristlichen bis zum 2. nachchristlichen Jahrhundert zu verfolgen." The subsequent years of study
since the publication of the paper cited here, and the inclusion
of Jerome's transliterations in this monograph, only confirmed
me in my conviction of the correctness of that statement. Consequently, only inner criteria were used in the arrangement of
the material, and the relatively higher or lower age of the respective sources has been entirely disregarded; cf. ¶ XXXII and
¶ XXXIII.

Originally I had in mind to write only an essay on the pronunciation of the Hebrew consonants in the period of the Septuagint. By means of the alphabetical arrangement of source material in the third part of this study, this problem is for the most
part solved of its own accord and I can limit myself to brief
explanatory notes:

א has no consonantal value of its own, but serves only to
carry a vowel sign; cf. paragraph XI.

ב is always β.

ג is γ; the gemination of ג is transliterated by $\gamma\gamma$, f. i. חגי
$\alpha\gamma\gamma\epsilon\iota$; at the end of the word ג is sometimes rendered by κ, as
f. i. in דאג $\delta\omega\eta\kappa$, פלג $\varphi\alpha\lambda\epsilon\kappa$; (cf. Mayser, §36 I, 1).

ד is δ; at the end of the word it is not infrequently ϑ, f. i. זבוד

ζαβουϑ, כבוד χαβωϑ, עובד obeth; see also: היגיד αιεγγιϑ and פחד
faath; cf. Mayser, §36 III, 1).

ה is without consonantal value, like א; at the beginning of
the word Jerome nevertheless often transliterates it by h; cf.,
f. i., הוד hod, המה homa, as compared with הבל abal, הרים arim;
cf. also in his Onomastica: הוא hu. Since the Onomastica go back
to a *Vorlage* in Greek characters (see paragraph VII), which have
no equivalent for an h in their alphabet and considered the ה
merely as the bearer of the respective vowel (see Jerome's general
statement in paragraph XI), we are lead to the conclusion that
Jerome added here the h upon his own responsibility, probably
after having consulted the Hebrew text. It is worth while noting
that this is—as far as I can see—the only case of transliterating
an ה by an h in the Onomastica (cases like Ahihod for אחיהוד in
Num. 34.27 are explained in paragraph X) and it does not con-
cern a real proper name, but the Hebrew phrase מן־הוא in Ex.
16.15.

ו at the beginning of the word is mostly ου; cf. the cases of
waw conjunctivum and waw consecutivum, as dealt with in
§§78 and 79; otherwise it is ου or ω; cf. Jerome's statement
(editio Vallarsi, vol. VI, p. 366C): "vau quippe litera et pro u,
et pro o, eorum lingua accipitur." The same uncertainty as to
whether to vocalize a given word with u or with o can be noted
in BV also, cf., f. i., in Ms. Ec 1 בטוב Ps. 27.13 and בטוב: ib. 65.5;
מותר Prov. 14.23 and ומותר ib. 21.5; בעזך Ps. 21.2 and עזך ib. 63.3;
עלקה Prov. 22.14 and עלקה ib. 23.27; תבואת Prov. 10.16 and
תבואת ib. 18.20. To illustrate Jerome's assertion, cf. f. i., sub
סוד: βασωδ and σουδει; sub צור: σουρ and σωρ; sub המון: αμων
and amun; sub כמר: χωμαρειμ and acchumarim; sub עגור: agor and
agur. This statement of Jerome may also be applied to those
transliterations, where ου and ω are promiscuously used to indicate the vowel, which is represented in Hebrew by another mater
lectionis; f. i. ראש: ρως and rus. B–L §14q has to be corrected
accordingly: it is not so, that the o in מנוח changed into u in
מנוחה; but מנוחה is a further development of the feminine formation to מנוח as manue (with u), cf. the Dictionary s. v. Originally
this form must have been pronounced מנוחה manua, with retention of the first vowel a; cf. paragraph XXVIa; cf. similarly (אבל)

מחולה rendered as μαουλα in 1 Kings 4.12 and μεουλα in Jud. 7.22 (both in Cod. B); for the change of a into ε cf. paragraph XXVIb.

ז in the earlier period corresponds to σ, f. i.: אחז αχας, יזרע ισρα, יזרח ιεσραε, נגרותי νεγρεσϑι, כזב chasab, מזבח μασβηη; later it was transliterated by ζ; cf. in the Dictionary the list of words beginning with ז; cf. Mayser, §46 I.

ח in the earlier period equals χ; cf. the characteristics of codex B and A in paragraph IV and our discussion of Jerome's remark on חם in paragraph VIII. In the later period ח lost its consonantal value and like א served merely for carrying the vowel. We may assume that the transition from the earlier to the later period is marked by those transliterations, where ח is rendered by ε; note f. i. at the beginning of the word: חזו εεζου, החזק εεζεκ, החליק εελικ; in the middle of the word: כחשו chaesu, לחם λαεμ, מחלה μαελα; at the end of the word: זרח ζαραε, יזרח ιεσραε, יפתח ιεφϑαε, זנוח zanoe, מנוח μανωε, מזבח μασβηη. These transliterations can, therefore, not be used as evidence for the existence of a patah furtivum, as B–L. §18j would make us believe. The only cases of patah furtivum in transliterations are קולע colea, רוח rua. In this connection I wish to point out, that B–L. §14f is likewise incorrect: ח was never transliterated as κ; but according to Greek phonetics, χ at the end of a word could phonetically and, consequently graphically, be confused with κ. cf. to כ. The transliteration of טבח as ταβεκ, which B–L. quote as a proof for their assertion, is therefore to be explained as a further inner Greek development of the form tabech (=ταβεχ, cf. paragraph X), as represented by Jerome in his Onomastica; cf. the Dictionary s. v.

ט is τ.

י is ι and its phonetic derivations: ε, η, αι, ει; note f. i. in §55a: תפתיר ϑεσϑερ, with ε, but תפתירם ϑεσϑιρημ with ι; also the transliteration of the suffix in חייתני ιυϑανι as compared with דליתני δελλιϑανη (§73b), and the examples listed in §123 1) 2) 4). Note further בית βαιϑ (§138a) as compared with βηϑ (§138b) and s. v. בן: βαναι as compared with βανη; cf. also the helping vowels (ε, ι, η) in §127.

כ is χ; as exceptions, which are most likely due to the phonetic interchange of χ and κ, I note: כבוד caboth; כבר κεχαρ B; כל κολ A; כליון κελαιων B; כפיה caphir; כפתורים caphthorim; the gemination is indicated in the Septuagint by κχ, in Origen by χχ; cf. f. i.: sub סכה σοκχωϑ (G) and σοχχα (O). At the end of the word it is sometimes rendered by κ; f. i.: סבך σαβεκ, סמך σαμακ, מלך μελεκ.

ל is λ.

מ is μ.

נ is ν.

ס is σ.

y is not a consonant, but a vowel; cf. on א, and Jerome's assertions in paragraph VIII. In the middle and at the end of the word it was sometimes transliterated by ε (cf. on ה); f. i. in the middle of the word: נעם νεεμ, רעם reem; see also Jerome's statement on בעלי in paragraph IX; at the end of the word: שמע σαμαε, ידע ιαδαε, יפיע ιαφιε, רע ρηε, שוע sue; cf. similar forms in BV: Job 15.8: תשמֹע, ib. 13.19: ואנֹע; see MTK, p. 31. Against the assumption in B–L. §18j, cf. on ה.—In the Septuagint and accordingly in Jerome's Onomastica cases are still recorded, where an y, corresponding to an Arabic غ, is transliterated by γ; cf. f. i. Jerome's statements on עמרה and on צער in paragraph VIII.

פ is rendered in almost all the instances by φ. Jerome even makes a general statement to the effect that no equivalent for the Latin character P can be found in the Hebrew alphabet (editio Vallarsi, vol. V, p. 724 C): "אפדנו APEDNO. Notandum autem, quod P literam Hebraeus sermo non habet, sed pro ipsa utatur PHE, cuius vim Graecum φ sonat. In isto tantum loco apud Hebraeos scribatur quidem PHE, sed legatur P." As exceptions I would like to note: פחד πααδ and פתח παϑα; the spelling iepte for יפתח and neptalti for נפתלתי may originate in printers (or even copists) mistakes, instead of iephthe and nephthalthi. The gemination of פ is indicated in the Septuagint by πφ and in Origen by φφ; cf. f. i.: s. v. תפוח ϑαπφουε (A) and thaffue, s. v. צפור σεπφωρ (G), s. v. אף βααφφω (O), s. v. נפל: ιεφφολου (O). Forms like חפה χοφφα (B) would prove the late date, when this transliteration originated; but on the other hand, the rendering of ח by χ is old, cf. on ה.

צ is σ; cf. Jerome's statements in paragraph XIII.

ק is κ.

ר is ρ.

שׁ and שׂ are σ; cf. Jerome's assertions in paragraph XIII and our conclusions in paragraph XIV.

ת is ϑ; gemination: τϑ (in the Septuagint) and ϑϑ (in Origen); cf. f. i.: מתן ματϑαν (G), אתה αϑϑα (o), s. v. נתן: ουιεϑϑεν (o).

This list together with the list given in paragraph X will be sufficient to clarify the problem of the phonetic value of the letters of the Greek and Latin alphabets respectively, too. Only one letter remains, which requires a special discussion: ε (e). Does this letter indicate a full vowel or only a murmuring vowel? We are anxious not to introduce into this monograph the terminology of the Tiberian grammar; otherwise we would formulate our problem thus: does ε stand for a vowel or for a שוא? The cases dealt with in §19b as differentiated from c might suggest an answer that ε could very well be thought of as indicating a mere murmuring vowel. But these three instances are, as far as I can see, the only possible proofs for such an assumption, since elsewhere ε stands for a short i sound; cf. f. i. §23α and β. On the other hand it seems to me that the murmuring vowel or שוא of the Tiberian grammar has no equivalent in the pronunciation underlying the transliterations; cf. §22: זכר ζχορ, שמע σμα; §23: לכו λχου. It is practically impossible to pronounce these words, without inserting some kind of a helping vowel between the two subsequent consonants. And yet the transliterator saw no need to indicate it. Consequently, if we find an ε, we have to consider it as representing a full vowel. But how then can we account for the cases listed in §19b? The form נחושה νεουσα can be eliminated, since ε may be considered as the consonantal equivalent of ה (cf. above sub ה) and not as a vowel; thus this form belongs to the subdivision c, being like דרושה drusa. Otherwise §19b corresponds exactly to the nominative forms listed in §103 (as compared with §102). The close phonetic relationship between ε and ι may also be realized from the transliterations in §55α, where ε and ι are used promiscuously; cf. especially the change of ε into ι from the absolute form תסתיר ϑεσϑερ to the corresponding conjugated form תסתירם ϑεσϑιρημ, while תשפיל ϑεσφιλ has the ι even in the absolute form.

XXIV. Sigla

As for the scheme and the arrangement of this study, I trust that I have been sufficiently successful in the systematic ordering and classifying of the transliterations, so that a few short notes of explanation will suffice to make the use of it a relatively simple matter.

The following abbreviations have been employed: A stands for Codex A of the Septuagint; B for Codex B; where both codices agree in their reading, I put G.—O indicates the Second Column of Origen's Hexapla.—H–R refers to the Septuagint Concordance by Hatch and Redpath; cf. ¶ V.—Quotations in Latin alphabet originate from Jerome: On after such a citation indicates, that it is taken from his Onomastica Sacra; J gives his commentaries as the source.—MT = the Hebrew Masoretic Text, according to Kittel's *Biblia Hebraica*, Leipzig 1905.—MdO = P. Kahle: *Masoreten des Ostens*, Leipzig 1913.—The sigla used in connection with Hebrew words in Babylonian vocalization (f. i. Ec 1) refer to Professor Kahle's "Catalogue of Hebrew Bible Mss. from Babylon," published in the *ZAW* 1928, pp. 113–137. A continuation of this Catalogue appeared in a leaflet headed: "Sigla für die hebräischen Bibelhandschriften aus Babylonien," which is included in the edition of Numeri et Deuteronomium of Kittel's *Biblia Hebraica*, Stuttgart 1935.—MTK = Paul Kahle, *Der masoretische Text des Alten Testaments nach der Überlieferung der babylonischen Juden*, Leipzig 1902. The basis of this monograph is the Ms. or. qu. 680 of the Berlin State Library, which is called "Ec 1" in the above cited Catalogue.—MdWI = Paul Kahle, *Masoreten des Westens* I. Stuttgart 1927.—MdWII = id., II. Stuttgart 1930.— Bar = Falk Bar, *Liturgische Dichtungen von Jannai und Samuel*, Bonn 1936.—Edelmann = Raphael Edelmann, *Zur Frühgeschichte des Maḥzor*, Stuttgart 1934.—Ms. 105 JThS = A Bible Ms. with the Babylonian vocalization containing most of the former prophets with Targum, in the Library of the Jewish Theological Seminary of America.—B-L = Hans Bauer und Pontus Leander, *Historische Grammatik der hebräischen Sprache des Alten Testaments*. Halle (Saale) 1918seq. —ZAW = *Zeitschrift für die alttestamentliche Wissenschaft*.—BV = Babylonian vocalization.—PV = Palestinian vocalization.—Sam. = Hebrew Pentateuch of the

Samaritans (not to be identified with von Gall's edition! Cf.paragraph XXVI f.).—Mayser = E. Mayser, *Grammatik der griechischen Papyri aus der Ptolemaerzeit*, Leipzig 1906.—Thompson = E. M. Thompson, *An Introduction to Greek and Latin Palaeography*, Oxford 1912.

XXV. METHOD APPLIED

I put myself to pains to explain every form in transliteration from the standpoint of the text as it is found, without attempting to make arbitrary corrections in conformity with the Masoretic text. The temptation to such a procedure was frequently very great, particularly in those passages, where the different reading of Origen's Hexapla, as compared with the corresponding Hebrew word, did not seem to fit in the context; cf. f. i. Mal. 2.13: MT: פָּנוֹת (Ḳal), Origen: פַּנּוֹת (Pi'el). According to the usage of biblical Hebrew, the verb פנה in the Ḳal means "to turn somewhere," and in the Pi'el "to remove something." It is obvious that Origen, although he read here the verb in the Pi'el, must have connected with it the meaning of the Ḳal; for otherwise the sentence is senseless. A similar case is Ps. 36.2: MT: לָרָשָׁע, Origen: לְרֶשַׁע. The Masoretic vocalization indicates a person who sins, whilst the transliteration would mean the abstractum, the sin. But the personal suffix in the following word לִבִּי clearly refers to a person. Whether Origen has been misled by the rhythm: φεσα . . . ρεσα, or whether in his days רָשָׁע and רֶשַׁע could be used promiscuously to indicate the same meaning, is hard to decide; cf. also Isa. 26.10, where Jerome reads רֶשַׁע for the Masoretic רָשָׁע.

I was saved from any such treatment of the transliterations as based upon subjective corrections by the methodology indicated by Bergsträsser as fundamental to all scholarly activity of this type (*Hebräische Grammatik*, II. Teil. I. C. Hinrichs. Leipzig 1929, p. v): "Zu beachten ist, dass ein in seinem Aufbau gestörter, im ganzen sinnloser Satz sehr wohl einwandfreie Einzelworte und -formen enthalten, dass umgekehrt aus zum Teil unmöglichen Einzelformen ein syntaktisch möglicher Satz aufgebaut sein, ja dass innerhalb des Einzelwortes Sinnvolles und Sinnloses sich mischen kann, dass also die Frage der grammatischen Verwertbarkeit von Fall zu Fall mit Rücksicht auf die zur Erörterung stehende grammatische Erscheinung erwogen werden muss." As an example of the possibilities last referred to by Bergsträsser I should like to cite the word בְּחַסְדְּךָ in Ps. 31.8 which according to Wutz is rendered by Origen: βεεζδαχ, and according to H–R: βεελδαχ. Both transliterations are open to suspicion. Even the rendering of a ס by ζ (according to Wutz) would constitute a ἅπαξ λεγόμενον; but its transliteration into λ (according to H–R) is completely inexplicable. Yet in §118a I have included the word, since there the prepositions are discussed and in that connection the rendering of בְּ in בחסדך is a matter not open to doubt.

XXVI. General Results: the Noun

a)   I am inclined to consider as the most characteristic feature of the pronunciation of Hebrew, as reflected in the transliterations, the fact that the vocalization of the noun does not undergo any changes—except in the latter period—when suffixa are added to it (as for instance: the personal pronoun, the feminine ending), or when the noun is being put in the plural. To illustrate this fact, I bring a selection of examples in the same order as they are listed in the Grammar, always referring to the paragraph, where they can be found: §15a; the singular-forms, which have to be presupposed, can be seen in §13. It will be noted that the second vowel in the singular-forms is an η (f. i. בטח βωτη), whilst in the plural-forms the spelling is with an ε (f. i. בטחים βωτεειμ). Whether this is only accidental, since ε and η were at the time of the transliterations no longer differentiated (cf. f. i. אמת ημεθ and אמתך εμεθϑαχ; נדר γαδερ and נדרה γαδηρα), or whether this change in spelling was meant to indicate that the accent does not rest any longer on this syllable, I must leave open.— §19a; in §20a note לטושים latusim. — §82b: כל χωλ and chollo. — §91a: לבנה λαβανα; נבלה nabala; נדבה nadaboth; נקמה νακαμωϑ; נשמה nasama, nasamoth; צדקה sadaca.—§94a: נדרה γαδηρα and קדשה cadesa, as compared with the corresponding forms in §94: נדר γαδερ and קדש καδης.—§123: יצרי ιεσερει; חלקי χελεκι; מעוזי μαοζι; בשרי basari.—§126: מקומה macoma.—§131: דבריך dabarach.-§133: שכניו σαχηναυ.-§136a: קדש καδης, καδησειμ; שריד

σαριδ, saridim; תמר θαμαρ, thamarim.— §137b: נבעה γαβαα, γαβαωθ; נדרה γαδηρα, γαδηρωθ; נלילה γαλιλα, γαλιλωθ. This grammatical rule can be traced even in the Babylonian and Palestinian systems; cf. לְבִּקְדִ֫ים Lam. 3.23; Ps. 101.8; Job 7.18 in Ms. Ec 1 (MTK, p. 71) בֹרֹאשִׁינוּ 1 Ki. 20.32 in Ms. 105 JThS; cf. also paragraph XXIXB subdivision 6.—In this connection I wish to point out that originally even the Construct State did not imply a change or a dropping of a vowel; cf. f. i. §138a and §139; also in §140b forms like: אמרה εμαραθ; אשמה asamath; נבעה γαβααθ; in §141: ארמון armanoth and שדמה σαδημωθ; cf. ¶ XXIX B 8.

Consequently, if we find the following forms in transliteration for the Hebrew root מלך: מלך μελεχ; המלך ammelech; מלכי μελχει, malchi; מלכם melchechem; מלכם μελχαμ; למלכי λαμαλχη—they go back to the following different ways of pronouncing this triconsonantal noun, and have to be arranged accordingly: מלך: a) (cf. §84): מלכי malchi, למלכי λαμαλχη; b) (cf. §85): מלכי μελχει, מלכם melchechem, מלכם μελχαμ; c) (cf. §95): מלך μελεχ, המלך ammelech. Similarly, שְׂרָפִים seraphim must not be regarded as a pluralis fractus to שְׂרָף saraph—to which the plural could only be saraphim, cf. תמר θαμαρ, plur. thamarim—, but is the regularly built plural to שרף seraph.

b) Generally speaking, all nouns can be divided into three main groups according to their characteristic vowel: the a-class, the i-class and the o-class. Further phonetic development results in the partition of the i-class into an ε-group and an ι-group (cf. paragraph XXIII sub י), and similarly in a subdivision of the o-class into an o-group and an ου-group (cf. ib. sub ו). This observation furnished us with the key for the systematical arrangement of the various nominal formations. While applying this system to the Bisyllabic Triconsonantal Nouns (chapter XIII) we noticed, much to our own surprise, that it was the *second* syllable that mostly had the characteristic vowel, the first syllable varying in every group between α and ε. This would suggest a supposition that in these cases the second syllable had the stressed vowel, a rather startling assertion; for these nouns generally coincide with nominal formations called in the Tiberian grammar nomina segolata, whose characteristic feature it is that their second vowel is grammatically considered as a mere helping vowel, the first vowel being the stressed one. We confine ourselves here to merely noting this amazing fact without commenting upon it; cf. the explanation of this attitude of ours in paragraph XXVIII. The variation between a and ϵ as first vowel we would attribute to dialectical differences; cf. paragraph XXXIII. The same variation occurs also in §19a compared with b, and in §117 compared with §118; cf. subdivision e near the end.

c) Nearly all the cases of nominal formations with prefixed מ, which can be found in transliteration, have the vowel a in the first syllable; they are listed and classified in chapter XIV. But still the following few forms remain to be mentioned, where the prefix has the vowel i: s. v. מזרח: mimizra; s. v. מצהלה: mesaloth; s. v. משגב $\mu\iota\sigma\gamma\alpha\beta$ O; s. v. משכן: $\mu\epsilon\sigma\chi\nu\eta$ O; s. v. משפט: mesphat, $\mu\epsilon\sigma\varphi\alpha\tau\iota$ O; s. v. משרה mesra.

In this connection I wish to call the attention to a similar fact: According to §139, the formation of the stat. constr. masc. plur. does not involve any change of a vowel in the transliteration. The only exception I am aware of is: s. v. בן $\beta\nu\eta$ O (as compared with $\beta\alpha\nu\eta$ in codex A).

d) Chapter XV proves that the article has always been pronounced as "a", even — if we be permitted to point to a differentiation in the Tiberian Grammar — before a ח, (cf. B–L. §31k); cf. in §114: החפץ $\alpha\alpha\varphi\eta s$ and החגב aagab.—It seems that only from the period of the Second Column on, which coincides, as we said in paragraph V, with Codex A of the Septuagint, the article was followed by gemination of the immediately subsequent consonant; cf. f. i. הקוץ $\alpha\kappa\omega s$, הלחש $\alpha\lambda\omega\eta s$, and הקטן $\alpha\kappa\alpha\tau\alpha\nu$, all three in codex B (§115), as compared with their spelling $\alpha\kappa\kappa\omega s$, $\alpha\lambda\lambda\omega\eta s$, and $\alpha\kappa\kappa\alpha\tau\alpha\nu$ in codex A (§116). The period of the Second Column marks the beginning, and not the final accomplishment of this development. So it is explicable that in even as late a period as Jerome's days this rule was not yet strictly observed; note f. i. forms like: הדגים adagim, הצדק asedec (§115), taken from his Commentaries.

e) A careful examination of the examples listed and arranged in Chapter XVI will prove that the transliteration of the Inseparable Prepositions בכל as $\beta\alpha$, $\chi\alpha$, $\lambda\alpha$ respectively (in §117), does not coincide with the cases, when according to the Tiberian grammar (cf. B–L. §25w), they carry this vowel to indicate the article; note f. i. cases like בְּיָה βαια, בְּכַּס βαχας, בְּלְכָּם βαλβαβαμ; the context (construct state or noun with personal suffixes) excludes any possibility of vocalizing these words as with an article; cf. paragraph XXIXB 5.

f) 1) The pronunciation of the nominal suffix of the 2. pers. sing. masc. as αχ, as expounded in §124 subdivision 1, is upheld by the spelling יחידאך in Sam. Gen. 22.2, 13, 16 for יְחִידְךָ of the Masoretic Text. The א is in these cases mater lectionis for "a"; cf. in Sam. forms like Gen. 42.38; 44.32: ביאגון (MT: בִּינוֹן); Ex. 23.31: ושאתי (MT: וְשַׁתִּי); Num. 5.18: המארים (MT: הַמָּרִים); Deut. 28.7: הקאמים (MT: הַקָּמִים); cf. also paragraph XXIXB1.— 2) According to §128, between the noun in the singular and the suffix of the 2. pers. plur. masc. χεμ, a helping vowel ε is inserted; cf. corresponding forms in the Sam. Lev. 26.19: עזיכם (MT: עָזְּכָם); Ex. 12.11: ומקליכם (MT: וּמַקֶּלְכָם); Lev. 1.2: קרבניכם (MT: קָרְבֻּנְכָם). In these instances the noun is undoubtedly in the sing; for the plural formations of the cited nouns would be ומקלותיכם and קרבנותיכם respectively; cf. also Sam. Gen. 45.20: ועיניכם (MT: וְעֵינְכָם), which is a sing. form, according to the verb תחוס; cf. also paragraph XXIX B16.—3) The vocalization of the suffix of the 2. pers. sing. masc. with verbal forms as ach (cf. §74β) has its parallel in the spelling with Sam. Num. 11.23: היקראך (MT: הֲיִקָּרְךָ).

It is very regrettable that we could not rely on the text of the Samaritan Pentateuch, which Gall used as the basis for his edition (*Der hebräische Pentateuch der Samaritaner*, Giessen 1914–18), but had to consult his apparatus criticus in nearly all the instances, where reference is made throughout this monograph to Sam.

XXVII. The Verb

1) Verbal forms (and nominal forms just the same) I have arranged according to the criterion of similar vocalization in the spelling of the transliteration, without paying too much attention as to whether this treatment is justified by their place in the Hebrew conjugations. Take for instance §54: The common element in

the forms discussed there is their vocalization *a-ι*. For this reason I have listed the forms of Imperfect Ḳal of the verba mediae ˀ together with the Imperfect Hiph'il forms of the verba mediae ו, since they belong to that category by virtue of their vocalization (*a–ι*).

2) The verb is dealt with in the Grammar exhaustively; at least I endeavoured, and I may hope that I succeeded in listing there every form which occurs in transliteration. I originally tried to reach the same degree of completeness even in the second part of the Grammar, dealing with the nominal forms: but experience taught me the impossibility of attaining that goal, and practical considerations proved that it may not even be desirable to overload the lists, which are sometimes long enough anyhow.

3) Chapter IX shows that in the earlier period the waw, both as waw conjunctivum and as waw consecutivum, was similarly transliterated merely as *ου*; cf. paragraph XXXIII subdivision 3; cf. also in the MT forms like: וְאָכְרֵת and וְאָבוֹא (Isa. 37.24), וְאָחְרֵב (ib., 25), וּתְהִי (ib., 26). There can be no doubt at all, that the waws in these verbal forms are consecutive waws; note the perfect עָלִיתִי in verse 24, marking the beginning of this poem. B.–L. §24d is therefore wrong in stating that "die ursprüngliche Form dieser Konjunktion (scil. the waw consecutivum) ist *ɐa* (mit kurzem freiem *ă*)''; similarly, the *Biblia Hebraica* editio R. Kittel (Liber Jesaiae, Stuttgart 1929) had no right to emend these forms into: וְאָכרת, וְאָבוֹא, וְאחרב and וּתהי. Here again, as in the case of the article (cf. paragraphs XXVId and XXVIII subdivision 4), the Second Column marks the beginning of a new method; cf. §79. But forms like וַתֵּחֶן *ουϑεϑϑεν* (§78a), וַיִּקְרָא *ουικρα* (§78b), וַיִּזְהַר *ουιεγαρ* (78c) prove that here, too, this development had just begun and the goal was still far from being reached.

XXVIII. Relation to the Tiberian System

I purposely avoided referring to the rules of Hebrew Grammar according to the Tiberian School. The problem as to whether the Tiberian system can be linked to the non-Masoretic systems (I emphasize the plural!), has to be investigated very carefully, and I would consider it poor method, if I were to pick out the raisins from the cake, instead of paying similar attention to all the grammatical and lexical phenomena. Nevertheless, here and there I pointed out a few striking proofs of divergencies in the development of the two systems in question (i. e. the Tiberian system and the transliterations),—cf. f. i. our remarks on וַתְּאָזְרֵנִי (s. v. אזר), אָכַב (s. v. כוב), אוֹן, דְּבָרִיךְ (s. v. דבר), as well as §5a, §15—by merely citing the corresponding paragraph in B-L.

By this procedure I merely wish to indicate what a new approach to so many problems of Hebrew grammar we may arrive at by freeing ourselves of the traditional grammatical conception. Instead of fixing rules and noting exceptions to these rules, a practice adopted by all Hebrew grammars, we do better to realize that the cases listed as mere exceptions form also rules, and are evidence of an otherwise forgotten different pronunciation of certain grammatical formations. To this conclusion we are lead by projecting the results of this monograph upon the Tiberian vocalization. I would rather have any more detailed discussion of these problems postponed until my researches in this field are advanced enough to permit the formulation of more or less definite conclusions. Only this I wish to make clear right now that instead of speaking of the Tiberian system (in the singular!) I would consider it more appropriate to differentiate between the *various ways of pronouncing Hebrew, by the combination of which the so-called Tiberian system arose.* To substantiate this statement, which if proven to be correct, will result, I am sure, in an essentially new explanation of very many grammatical phenomena, thus leading towards the establishment of dialectical differences in the pronunciation of Hebrew between the two kingdoms of Israel and Judah, cf. paragraph XXXIII, I wish to bring a few instances of rather general importance: 1) In the Tiberian grammar the gutturals are treated sometimes as full and sometimes as weak consonants; cf. s. v. אסר the forms: וַיָּאְסֹר Gen. 46.29 and וַיֶּאְסֹר ib. 42.24; לֶאְסֹר Ps. 105.22 and לֶאְסֹר Num. 30.3.—s. v. חבל the forms: תַּחְבֹּל Ex. 22.25 and יַחֲבֹל Deut. 24.6.—s. v. הפך the forms: נֶהְפְּכוּ Ps. 78.57 and נֶהְפְּכוּ 1 Sam. 4.19.—s. v. חזק the forms: יֶחְזְקוּ Isa. 28.22 and יֶחֱזְקוּ 2 Sam. 10.11.—s. v. חרד the forms: יֶחְרְדוּ Ezek. 26.18 and יֶחֱרְדוּ

Hos. 11.11. — 2) The current Hebrew grammar invented the term "virtual lengthening," to explain away some of the cases, where a guttural is treated as a full consonant; cf. s. v. בער the forms: לְבְעֵר Neh. 10.35 and לְבָעֵר Isa. 44.15. — 3) We leave the question open as to whether nominal and verbal forms in pausa represent a lengthening of the context forms or the original forms; but there can be no doubt about it that both, the context form and its pausal form, belong to the same respective grammatical scheme (qatl, qitl, qutl or with a, i, u in the perfect respectively, to give an instance); how can we now account for instance for the following pausal forms: s. v. בטן: Num. 5.21: בִּטְנֵך a qitl-form, but in pausa: Gen. 30.2: בָּטֶן a qatl-form; s. v. שבט: Prov. 13.24: שִׁבְטוֹ a qitl-form, but in pausa: Ex. 28.21: שָׁבֶט a qatl-form; s. v. שמש: Jer. 15.9: שִׁמְשָׁה a qitl-form, but in pausa: Eccl. 1.3: הַשָּׁמֶשׁ a qatl-form. Or verbal forms: Gen. 37.3: אָהַב and ib. 27.14: אָהֵב; Gen. 2.24: דָּבַק and 2 Kings 3.3: דָּבֵק. The usual explanation that these pausal forms are built on the analogy of the other respective group of nominal or verbal forms, does not suffice at all; for, strangely enough, the three nouns cited here are vocalized with an *a* (i. e., as qatl-forms, to use the Tiberian terminology) in the Babylonian vocalization, and in the transliterations, and even their equivalent in Arabic is vocalized with an *a*. Consequently, instead of considering the Tiberian pausal forms as exceptions which require explanation, we find that the respective context-forms fall out of the regular qatl-scheme and belong to a different tradition, which served as one of the basic sources for the Tiberian vocalization. — 4) A similar development we can notice with certain forms with waw consecutivum, like: s. v. בנה the forms: Gen. 2.22: וַיִּבֶן and Josh. 19.50: וַיִּבְנֶה; s. v. נכה the forms: Jer. 52.27: וַיַּכֶּה and 2 Kings 25.21: וַיַּךְ; s. v. אוה the forms: 2 Sam. 23.15: וַיִּתְאַוֶּה and 1 Chron. 14.17: וַיִּתְאָו; further s. v. אסף the forms: Num. 11.30: וַיֵּאָסֵף and Gen. 49.33: וַיֶּאֱסֹף; s. v. בער the forms: Jud. 15.5: וַיַּבְעֵר and וַיִּבְעַר; s. v. ישב the forms: Gen. 47.11: וַיּוֹשֵׁב and Ps. 107.36: וַיּוֹשֶׁב. — 5) To explain away the inconsistency in applying the dagesh lene to the בגדכפת, the grammarians invented the term "שוא medium," the apparent fallacy of which may be demonstrated by a few instances: s. v. ברכה the forms: Gen. 49.26: בִּרְכַת and ib. 28.4:

בְּרְכַּת; further Jer. 17.2: בְּזֹכֵר and 2 Sam. 17.9: בְּנָפֹל; s. v. הפך the forms: Gen. 19.21: הָפְכִּי and 2 Sam. 10.3: וּלְהָפְכָהּ. These and many other similar observations induced me to refrain as far as possible from referring to any parallel phenomena as might otherwise have been pointed out in the course of this study.

XXIX. RELATION TO THE BABYLONIAN AND PALESTINIAN SYSTEM

Entirely different is my attitude in this monograph towards the non-Masoretic systems of vocalization, namely the Babylonian and the Palestinian system. I went carefully through all the material I could get hold of (cf. the list of abbreviations in paragraph XXIV) and made as profuse a use of it as possible. The references to words with the Babylonian vocalization in most cases go back to manuscripts and Geniza fragments, which have not been published until now anywhere else; these texts have been made available to me by the curtesy of Professor Kahle and Professor Marx (cf. paragraph XXXIV). But although the references with the Palestinian vocalization appeared already in print in various text publications, I still venture to say that *my evaluation* of these cited forms is *entirely new*, since I abandon the prevalent standpoint, as adopted in the text publications from which I derived my references, namely not to consider these forms as units in themselves, but always to discuss merely their single vowel points in connection with and as equivalents of the corresponding Tiberian punctuation; cf. f. i. MdW II, p. 17*: "Dies Zeichen (i. e. ʾ) steht auch da, wo in tiberischer Punktation ein defektiv geschriebenes kurzes u steht . . . . . Von den beiden Zeichen für e (ʿ und ʾ) entspricht im allgemeinen das erstere tiberischem Ṣere, das letztere tiberischen Segol und Šwa mobile; jedoch findet sich das erstere Zeichen häufig auch da, wo wir Šwa mobile erwarten würden . . . . ; das Zeichen entspricht auch öfters tiberischem Segol . . . . Andererseits entspricht das Zeichen ʿ gelegentlich auch tiberischem Ṣere," etc. Bar p. 19: "Ein Schwa kennt die Handschrift nicht. Stets ist ein bei uns mit שׁוא versehener Buchstabe mit Vokal versehen. Am häufigsten mit einem a Vokal."

By these explanations the learned editors of the texts referred to presuppose—though perhaps without being aware of it themselves—that the Palestinian vocalization represents merely a new possibility of expressing Tiberian Hebrew vowels. To disprove any assumption of this kind, we wish to point out two examples: In the forms בֹּמְקָה (for במלקחים, cf. further down sub B 11), and יִלֵי (cf. ib. 8) we would have to explain the first ' as corresponding to a שׁוא, and the immediately following same vowel sign as a Ṣere or Segol respectively. The aim of the vocalization was surely not to confuse the reader, who would thus be at a perfect loss in his endeavors to identify the ' with one of the corresponding Tiberian vowels. Similarly we would consider it utterly illogical to state that "in the PV the שׁוא is replaced by a vowel, mostly by a." We are entitled to expect an explanation as to when this שׁוא is replaced by an a and when and under what phonetic conditions by another vowel; furthermore: how do we know that a שׁוא was originally there; and why was a full vowel substituted for it? Cf. our refutation of O. Pretzl in paragraph III.—Pontus Leander's "Bemerkungen zur palastinischen Überlieferung des Hebräischen" (*ZAW* 1936, pp. 91–99) deal with the subject from an entirely different angle.

In dealing with these non-Masoretic texts, I on the other hand paid no attention whatsoever to the Tiberian system, but was anxious to *explain* every *grammatical phenomenon* apart from any outside consideration, startling though the results may have seemed at first to a man who has been thoroughly trained in the Masoretic Grammar. I thus hope to have paved the way also for a real grammatical appreciation of Hebrew according to these two non-Masoretic vocalization systems.

A. 1) As a parallel phenomenon to the cases of preservation of the second vowel in verbal forms, as dealt with in §5a and elsewhere (f. i. in §10ba the forms: יחרגו ιερογου, יפלו ιεφφολου, ישמרו ιεσμωρου), I should like to mention the Babylonian vocalization, where we meet similar forms, like: Job 6.17: יִדֹּוֹ; ib. 6.25: נֹמְרֹ־צֹ; Ps. 106.28: וִיצְמֹדֹ; all these instances are taken from the Ms. Ec 1; cf. also sub B 7.—2) The formations discussed in the §§7a, 31a and 49a have parallels in the Babylonian system, too, in forms like: יֹּבֹרֹכְךָ, יְחֹלוֹן and others, cf. MdO, p. 165. — 3) The

114

preservation of the second vowel in verbal forms with personal suffixes, as f. i. תָּאזֹרֵנִי *θεξoρηνι*, תְּסוֹבְבֵנִי *θσωβαβηνι*, יְסוֹבְבֵנוּ *ισωβa-βεννου* (cf. §73 sq.), can be proved in the Babylonian system as well, cf. forms like: Prov. 29.4: יֶהֶרְסֶֽנָּה; ib. 1.32: תַּהַרְגֵם; Job 29. 16: אֶחְקְרֵהוּ; Ps. 37.33: יַעַזְבֶנּוּ; ib. 27.9: תְּעַזְבֵנִי; Job 21.15: נַעַבְדֶנּוּ; all these examples originate in the Ms. Ec 1; cf. also MdO, p. 185, and similarly here sub B 10. — 4) To the transliteration of the imperative of the pi'el with ϵ in the first syllable (§38a) cf. כַּבְּדֵֽהוּ. Ps. 22.24 in Ms. Ec 1 (MTK, p. 79); עַנֵּ֫הוּ Jud. 19.24 in Ms. 105 JThS. — 5) To the transliteration of the imperative of the hiph'il with ϵ in the first syllable (§63a) cf. הֹסִירוּ 1 Sam. 7.3; הַצִּילֵֽהוּ 2 Sam. 14.30; הַכּוּ 2 Sam. 13.28; all three instances in Ms. 105 JThS. — 6) Parallel forms to §59, cf. the Dictionary s. v. שבת.

B. In his *Masoreten des Westens* I. p. 46, Paul Kahle notes as a result of an evaluation of the Hebrew texts with the Palestinian vocalization, which he published there, three major deviations of general importance from the established rules of the Tiberian Hebrew Grammar; two of them have their parallel phenomena in the transliterations: 1) The nominal suffix of the 2. pers. sing. masc. is *–ak* (and not *–ka*), cf. §124 subdivision 1; under subdivision 2 only two cases could be listed of an ending in *–ka*; cf. also ¶ XXVI f 1). — 2) The verbal forms of the 2. pers. sing. masc. of the perfect are vocalized according to a pronunciation *qatalt* (and not *qatalta*); cf. the §§3a, 27a, 42, 53a and 66. — At this occasion I wish to point out some more parallel developments of general importance between these two systems, which have not been noticed until now in the respective publications of Hebrew texts with PV. — 3) To the cases dealt with in the §§2a and 5a, namely: the retention of the second vowel in verbal formations, cf. וְנִיבְנְתָה Jer. 30.18 (MdWI, p. א), וְיִפְרְחוּ Hos. 14.8 (ib. p. ט); נֹקֵל, abbreviated for וְנוּקְשׁוּ Isa. 8.15 (Kahle in ZAW 1901, p. 281). — 4) To the respective §§ in chapter XIX: the noun remains unchanged in the construct state, cf. שְׁבוּת Jer. 30.18 (ib., p. א), דְּבַר Isa. 44.26 (ib. p. ד), וּמְקוֹם Ps. 26.8 (ib., p. ז) and בְּמַחְשַׁבֹּת (ib., p. ג, line 2). — 5) To §117 (cf. also paragraph XXVIe), cf. forms like: בְּבוֹא (ib., p. יח, line 16), בַּטֵּל and בְּשִׁיר (Bar, p. 19); לְ, abbreviated for לְמַשְׁלַח Isa. 7.25 (Kahle in ZAW 1901, p. 280). — 6) To the cases dealt with in paragraph XXVIa: retention of the original vowels in derived nominal forms, cf. וּתְמֹמֹה (MdWI, p. ר, line 12); גְּלוּיִם (Edelmann, p. אי, line 23; three times!). — 7) To §10ba (and similarly in the Babylonian system, cf. above under subdivision A1),cf. יְעֻמֹדֵה Dan. 11.14 (MdWII, p. 75). — 8) To §15a (cf. also ¶ XXVIa), cf. forms like: יֽדֵעֽי Dan. 11.32 (ib., p. 76), עֹמְדֵים Dan. 12.5 (ib., p. 77), הַצָּא (= הַמְצַפְצְפִים) Isa. 8.19 (Kahle in ZAW 1901, p. 281). — 9) To §35: the prefix מ vocalized with a, cf. מֹא, an abbreviation for מֵאַחֲרֵי, Isa. 5.11 (Kahle in ZAW 1901, p. 277). — 10) To §73 seq. (and similarly in the Babylonian system, cf. above under subdivision A 3), cf. נֹתְחֵיךְ Jer. 1.5 (MdWII, p. 78). — 11) To §118 cf. forms like כֹּב, an abbreviation for כַּדְבַרֹם, Isa. 5.17; בַּמְקֹם, an abbreviation for בַּמְלְקֹחֵים, Isa. 6.6; לֹל, an abbreviation for לֵמֹר, Isa. 5.20; all three instances from Kahle, ZAW 1901. — 12) The forms listed in §79a need not necessarily be considered as waw consecutivum; cf. וְרֹיב Ps. 55.10 (MdWII, p. 84), וּבֹאָן Ps. 55.4 (ib., p. 83), וְצֹהֹרֹים Ps. 55.18 (ib., p. 84). — 13) To §23a: impv. forms with ϵ in the first syllable, cf. חֹשֹׁב (Edelmann, ᛫p. ח, line 1). — 14) To §55a, δ and §57: imperfect forms of the hiph'il with ϵ in the first syllable, cf. וֹיֹסֹב Ex. 13.18 (Edelmann, p. ר, line 6).—15) To §7bδ_3: 3. pers. sing. masc. of the imperfect of verba primae gutturalis, with ϵ in the first syllable, cf. יֹעֹזֹוב Isa. 55.7 (Edelmann, p. רי, line 4). — 16) To §128: the suffix of the 2. pers. plur. masc. as $\epsilon\chi\epsilon\mu$, cf. הֹל, abbreviated for מֶעֲרֹיצְכֹם Isa. 8.13 (Kahle in ZAW 1901, p. 281); cf. also paragraph XXVI f 2.

The parallels to the transliterations of *single words* in their various derivations, that can be found in Hebrew Bible texts with Babylonian or Palestinian vocalization, as differing from the Tiberian way of vocalizing these words, I have noted at the proper places in the Dictionary.

XXX. FORMATION OF THE NOUN

Nouns I have treated separately according to their masculine or feminine formation; not according to their grammatical gender, but rather according to the external criterion of their endings. Thus for instance שׁם $\sigma\eta\omega$ ($\sigma\epsilon\mu\alpha\chi$, $\sigma\epsilon\mu\omega$)—the derivatives of a noun I bring in parenthesis—in §81 is listed as a masculine, where-as שם (semoth, σεμωθαμ) in §81a is given as a feminine *form* (not feminine noun!). This classification has a pragmatic sanction and may also be theoretically justified by the generalization of Jerome (editio Vallarsi, vol. IV., p. 10C): "Estque Hebraici characteris idioma, ut omnia, quae in syllabam finiuntur IM masculina sint, et pluralia, ut CHERUBIM et SERAPHIM. Et quae in OTH, feminina et pluralia, ut SABAOTH;" cf. similarly paragraph XIV.

XXXI. Transliterations and Rabbinic Statements

In paragraph XXIX we believe to have established beyond any doubt the interrelation between the various non-Masoretic systems of pronunciation of Hebrew words. By applying the term "non-Masoretic" to these systems, we are afraid we might create the impression that they are thus discriminated against, denying them, so to say, the right of existence as compared with the authorised Masoretic system. We, therefore, wish to emphasize that the traditional terminology is wrong in both directions: The term Tiberian or Masoretic system is misleading, since it repre-sents a combination of at least two different systems, as we have shown in paragraph XXVIII; and the classification of the non-Tiberian systems as non-Masoretic is incorrect, too; for there are quite a number of Rabbinic passages which can not be understood unless we refer to these non-Tiberian systems as the basic pronunciation of Hebrew of their days. I wish to illustrate this thesis by one example for each: the transliteration system and the Babylonian system: 1) In מדרש בראשית רבה editio Theodor (Berlin 1903 seq.) p. 70 on the verse: וירא אלהים את כל אשר עשה בתורתו של רבי מאיר מצאו כתוב: we read (Gen. 1.31) והנה טוב מאד והנה טוב מאד והנה טוב מות. This statement requires such a pronun-ciation of the two words מאד and מות, that they could phonetically be misunderstood for each other; the Tiberian vocalization as מְאֹד and מָוֶת excludes any such chance. But in the transliteration of the Second Column of the Hexapla מאד is rendered μωδ (Ps. 46.2) and מות μωϑ (Ps. 49.15). The only difference between μωδ and $\mu\omega\vartheta$, namely δ–ϑ, does not count; cf. paragraph XXIII sub ר, where 5 instances are brought to prove that ד at the end of the word was sometimes rendered by ϑ, so that even מאד could very likely have been pronounced as: $\mu\omega\vartheta$; cf. A. Marx in *JQR*, *N. S.* XIII (1923) p. 358. — 2) In the Babylonian Talmud, Sanhedrin fol. 5b we read: פעם אחת הלך רבי למקום אחד וראה בני אדם שמגבלים עיסותיהם בטומאה: אמר להם: מפני מה אתם מגבלים עיסותיכם בטומאה? אמרו לו: תלמיד אחד בא לכאן והורה לנו: מי בצעים אין מכשירין: והוא מי ביצים דרש להו, ואינהו סבור מי בצעים קאמר: "Once Rabbi came to a certain place and saw people kneading their dough in a state of impurity. Said he to them: Wherefore do ye knead your dough in impurity? They replied: A certain scholar came here and taught us: Water of the pond (מי בצעים) does not make fit for impurity. But he had really taught them: the liquid of eggs (מי ביצים) and they misunderstood him to say: water of the pond." On this passage Tossafoth remark: תוספות ד"ה ואינהו סבור מי בצעים, תימא: דהיאך טעו בין ביצים לבצעים? ואר"ת דאינהו סבור דטי ביצים דקאמר. דהיינו מי בצים. דכתיב (Job 8.11) היגאה גמא בלי בצה. וטעו בן בצים לביצים: "It is surprising that they could err between מי ביצים and מי בצעים? Said R. Tam: They thought that by saying מי ביצים he meant water of the pond, referring to the verse Job 8.11; they thus confused בצים (ponds) and ביצים (eggs)." R. Tam thus deviates from the wording of the Talmud by declaring a confusion of ביצים (eggs) and בצעים (ponds) too far fetched; he therefore substitutes the Hebrew words בצים for its Aramaic equivalent בצעים and finds a confusion between ביצים (eggs) and בצים (ponds) quite possible. According to the Tiberian system, they are vocalized בֵּיצִים (eggs) and בִּצִּים (ponds); there does, therefore, still exist a difference in the pronunciation of these two words. Fortunately, the verse Job 8.11 referred to by R. Tam is preserved in the Babylonian vocalization in Ms. Ec 1 and the word in question is vocalized here as בִּצָּה (MTK, p. 71), which corresponds exactly to the pronunciation of this word in the meaning: eggs. We now interpret the Talmudical passage thus: The scholar had taught: מי ביצים meaning: the liquid of eggs; his audience heard him very well, but misunderstood the etymology of his decision מי ביצים as meaning: water of the pond, having in mind the verse Job 8.11; cf. paragraph XX.

118

XXXII. Transliterations and the Septuagint

In paragraph IV I alluded to the fact that this monograph represents a continuation of a series of studies on the Septuagint, which I had begun by publishing my *Septuagintaprobleme* I. By applying the results of this study, as worked out especially in paragraph XXIII, to the Septuagint, we are in a position to differentiate between the various sources, by the combination of which an apparently uniform Septuagint text arose. Since this criterion has entirely been overlooked until now, I wish to substantiate my assertion by pointing out a few instances: Codex A of the Septuagint is composed of different portions, each of them belonging to different periods; cf. f. i. the transliteration of חבר in 1 Chron. 7.31 as χαβερ and ib. 4.18 as αβερ; the explanation may be found in paragraph XXIII sub ח. — עזר is rendered in 1 Chron. 7.21 as εζερ (cf. §95) and ib. 12.9 as αζερ (cf. §94) — חרן is in Gen. 29.4: χαρραν and ib. 11.27: αρραν (cf. paragraph XXIII sub ח). These examples are sufficient to prove that codex A, not only when considered as an entity covering the entire Bible, but even on the single Biblical books, goes back to different sources. The same is true of Codex B also, as may be seen from these examples: the word מחולה (in the connection אבל מחולה) is transliterated in 1 Kings 4.12 as μαωλα; ib. 19.16 as μαουλα and Jud. 7.22 as μεουλα. For explanation cf. paragraph XXIII sub ו (ω–ου) and sub ח (rendered as ε). — 2 Chron. 8.18: אופירה is rendered: εἰς Σωφειρα (read: εἰς Ωφειρα) and ib. 9.10: מֵאוֹפִיר: ἐκ Σουφειρ (read: ἐξ Ουφειρ); cf. paragraph XXIII sub ו. It may be of interest to refer here to the similar conclusions we arrived at concerning the Hexapla of Origen (cf. paragraph V near the end) and the transliterations of Jerome (cf. paragraph IX). We thus realize that *one of the most significant criteria of the works of those early centuries is their mixed type.* And why should we blame those pious compilers or copyists for having overlooked apparent discrepancies, if these inner contradictions escaped the attention of the scholars until to-day, as is the case with the transliterations of the Septuagint and Origen; and as to Jerome, all we have until now is the general statement, unaccompanied by any evidence at all, which Franz X. Wutz makes in his book: *Die*

Transkriptionen ,von der Septuaginta bis zu Hieronymus (Kohl-hammer, Stuttgart 1925, p. 3): "Hieronymus ist nur mit grösster Vorsicht zu benützen, da er ein gewaltiges Sammelsurium von Formen aus allen Jahrhunderten eines Zeitraumes von 7–800 Jahren bot. Da Hieronymus trotz aller Gelehrsamkeit der historisch-kritische Blick für die Divergenz seiner Materialien fehlte, so häufte er Material auf Material ohne zu ahnen, um was es ging; ja er nahm oft Stellung gegen alte Formen, ohne zu wissen, wie sehr sie durch die alte Orthographie berechtigt waren." I do hope that the scholarly reader of this study will not find himself at a loss as Dr. Wutz does; but I am not so sure of it that it is entirely the fault of Jerome that Dr. Wutz could not find the key to an understanding of the systems under-lying his transliterations. And as to Jerome's lack of a historical-critical sense—what an absurdity to expect it from an author of the beginning of the fifth century!

The mixed type as a characteristic feature we could also see, though in general outline only, in the Tiberian system; cf. para-graph XXVIII; the non-Masoretic systems represent it likewise, as became clear to me while going through the entire material to look out for parallel grammatical developments. In future, the *Hebrew Grammar* and the *Hebrew dictionary* will have to take these facts into account and to broaden their basis so as to *include all the material available*, without discriminating between Ma-soretic forms as authoritative and non-Masoretic forms merely to frame the work up scientifically; cf. the statement made in *OLZ* 1929, quoted at the beginning of paragraph XXIII.

XXXIII. Two Dialects of Biblical Hebrew

1) Throughout this study we laid the main emphasis upon re-cording grammatical facts as preserved in these non-Masoretic evidences of pronunciation, and upon arranging and classifying them according to their own laws, the basis for which had to be found through inner criteria. No serious attempt has been made to explain the phenomena; the limited material at our disposal does not seem to be encouraging for any attempt of this kind. But there is even another consideration, which has to be taken

into account and which directly excludes the possibility of phonetic connections and interdependance of the variously pronounced grammatical forms.

While merely noting facts, we had to record a great many nominal and verbal forms, which belong to different formations according to the different systems of vocalization; f. i. שבט and שמש are qitl-forms in the Tiberian system, but qatl-forms in the transliteration; vice versa דרך and נפש are qatl-forms in the Tiberian system, but qitl-forms in the transliteration; the imperative to לחם is in the Tiberian system לְחָם (i. e. an imperfect with a), but λοομ in the transliteration (i. e. imperfect with o); the participle plur. of חפץ is חָפְצֵי in the Tiberian system, but ωφση in the transliteration. These and similar observations suggest the explanation that the two systems involved can not be considered as directly connected with each other, or one to be a later phonetic development of the other, but that they most definitely reflect a twofold way of pronouncing Hebrew. Both of them may go back to a common ancestor, which we would call *Original Hebrew* (Urhebraeisch); they represent two separate branches of this original, each one of them with a further phonetic development of its own.

And now the problem arises: can we account, in the historical development of Hebrew during the biblical period, for such an assumption of two independent pronunciations or dialects? I am inclined to answer this question in the affirmative and to regard the kingdoms of Israel and Judah respectively as the homelands of these dialectical differences.

2) In paragraph XIV we saw that the practice of the transliterations to make no differentiation between שׁ and שׂ (note especially the citations from Jerome referred to: Quaestiones on Gen. 26.12; 41.29) agrees with what we know as an Ephraimitic peculiarity of pronunciation; cf. Jud. 12.6. We, therefore, believe we are justified in ascribing the Tiberian way of differentiating between שׁ and שׂ to the Judaean dialect. We hereby do not mean to generalize, stating that the transliterations as an entirety reflect the Israelitish pronunciation, while the Tiberian system in the same way follows the Judaean dialect. Neither of these systems can be regarded as a whole, since they are lacking in

the first prerequisite: consistency; cf. paragraphs IV, V, IX, XV on the one hand, and paragraph XXVIII on the other. My assertion, therefore, is that by collecting all available evidences for the pronunciation of Hebrew, from Tiberian as well as from non-Tiberian sources, and by systematically arranging them according to the lines set up in this monograph, we may be able to arrive at conclusions concerning the most important characteristic features of the two dialects of Hebrew as a spoken language, namely the Israelitish and the Judaean dialect.

3) To meet a possible argument that the mere fact that שׂ and שׁ were or were not differentiated can not be considered a solid basis for the assumption of dialectical differences between Israel and Judah in general, we wish to avail ourselves of this opportunity to point out that a comparison between the Hebrew Pentateuch in its Masoretic form with Sam. will furnish us with a great many further differences of general importance. A few instances will suffice: To the inconsistency of the Tiberian system as discussed in paragraph XXVIII subdivision 4, cf. the following similar differences between MT and Sam.: Gen. 31.10: MT: וָאֵרָא Sam: ואראה; Deut. 2.33: MT: וַנַּךְ Sam: ונכה; ib. 3.18: MT: וָאֲצַו Sam. ואצוה. Similarly without shortening of the last syllable: Gen. 5.3: MT: וַיּוֹלֶד Sam. ויוליד; ib. 24.28: MT: וַתַּגֵּד Sam. ותגיד; ib. 31.42: MT: וַיּוֹכַח Sam. ויוכיח. Formulating a rule based upon these facts we will say that according to the Samaritan usage the waw consecutivum does not at all affect the structure of the respective verbal form. At the very same conclusion we arrived while discussing the transliterations; cf. §78 and paragraph XXVII subdivision 3. We are thus led to the assumption that, generally speaking, the Samaritan Pentateuch represents the Hebrew Pentateuch in the Israelitish or *Samaritan recension*, while in the Masoretic text the Judaean recension is mainly preserved.

We wish to emphasize that we are far from *identifying* the MT with the Judaean, or Sam. with the Israelitish recension of the Hebrew Bible. Neither of them can be regarded now as representing its prototype in its original dialectical purity; the textual changes which they underwent in the various stages of their redaction may have been instrumental, too, in eliminating here and there characteristic dialectic idioms. We can not even tell, when this process was finished; apparently at a somewhat late century; for we can prove that at least in one important passage Sam. offered as late as in the days of Jerome an entirely different reading from what we now have in all the manuscripts of this text. We discussed this problem in an article "The Targum Onkelos in its Relation to the Masoretic Hebrew text" (*PAAJR* VI, 1934–5, p. 312 seq.).

Keeping this in mind, we realize to what an extent the original text of Sam. may have been changed and modelled; a glimpse into the critical apparatus of Kennicott's *Vetus Testamentum Hebraicum cum variis lectionibus* (Oxford 1776–80) will convince us that the MT shared the same fate. And still I venture to say that by carefully comparing these two textual forms of the Heberw Pentateuch we may arrive at definite conclusions as to the characteristic features of the two Hebrew dialects which they mainly represent. I should like to demonstrate this with a few examples; for the practical benefit of the reader I vocalize some of the Samaritan readings, too, according to the Tiberian system: 1) Gen. 8.3: MT: הָיוּ . . . , Sam.: וָשׁוֹב . . . הָלוֹךְ וָשׁוֹב, ib., 5: הָלוֹךְ וְחָסוֹר, Sam.: הָלְכוּ וְשָׁבוּ; ib., 7: יָצוֹא וָשׁוֹב . . . , Sam. ויצא: יָצָא וְשָׁב; ib. 12.9: הָלוֹךְ . . . ויסע, Sam.: הָלְכוּ וְחָסְרוּ; וְנָסוֹעַ, Sam.: הָלַךְ וְנָסַע In MT a verbum finitum is continued by an infinitivus absolutus, while in the Samaritan Pentateuch it is followed by a verb in the very same tempus. — 2) Gen. 3.13: MT: עָשִׂית, Sam.: עָשִׂיתִי; ib. 12.11: אַתְּ, Sam.: אַתִּי; ib. 16.8: בָּאת, Sam.: בָּאתִי; ib. 16.11: וְיָלַדְתְּ . . . וְקָרֵאת, Sam.: וְקָרֵאתִי . . . וְיָלַדְתִּי; ib. 18.15: צָחַקְתְּ, Sam.: צָחַקְתִּי. The suffix of the 2. pers. fem. of the perfect is in MT: תְּ, but תִי according to the Sam. — 3) Gen. 12.5: MT: אַרְצָה, Sam.: אֶרֶץ; ib. 24.16: הָעַיְנָה, Sam.: הָעַיִן; ib. 28.2: בֵּיתָה, Sam.: בַּיִת; Deut. 4.19: הַשָּׁמַיְמָה, Sam.: הַשָּׁמַיִם. The MT has a locative with the ending in הָ, while in the Sam. the absolute form is used in this meaning. — 4) Gen. 6.17: MT: לְשַׁחֵת, Sam.: לְהַשְׁחִית; cf. 9.11, 15; ib. 19.13: MT: לְשַׁחֲתָהּ, Sam.: לְהַשְׁחִיתה; ib. 19.29: MT: בְּשַׁחֵת, Sam. לְהַשְׁחִית; ib. 7.3: MT: לְחַיּוֹת, Sam.: לְהַחֲיוֹת; Deut. 6.19: לַהֲדֹף, Sam.: לְהַדְרִיף; ib. 9.4: בַּהֲדֹף, Sam.: בְּהַדְרִיף. The Sam. shows a preference for the respective hiph'il forms of the verb.

We hope that we will be able to present the scholarly world in not too remote a future with a detailed evaluation of the Sam. from this point of view, and this approach will result—we are sure—in a new appreciation of the philology of the Bible in its various aspects.

Just a few instances to indicate what we have in mind: In paragraph XIV we could show the influence of the Israelitish dialect upon the language of Jeremiah; in addition to the proof of the pronunciation of שׁ and שׂ, which we discussed there, cf. forms like: לְמַּדְתִּי Jer. 2.33; קְרָאתִי ib. 3.4; דִּבַּרְתִּי. ib. 3.5, which belong to the group of verbal formations listed above under subdivision 2 as a characteristic of Sam. The same holds true of verbal forms with waw consecutivum like וָאַשְׁקֶה Jer. 25.17; וַיִּבֶּה ib. 20.2; cf. above sub 3, near the beginning of the paragraph.

XXXIV. Acknowledgements

I am under the most pleasant obligation to once again publicly acknowledge my deepest indebtedness to my teacher and friend Professor Paul Kahle for having taught me a free and unprejudiced approach to the problems of Hebrew Grammar, unhampered by the rules of the Masorites of Tiberias. I shall never forget those extended Sunday hikes in his company in the glorious surroundings of Bonn, a welcome opportunity for learned conversation, by which I profited more than I can say.

To Professor Kahle I also owe thanks for his suggestion to compare my material with Hebrew Bible texts with the Babylonian vocalization, which like the transliterations represents a system, independent of that of the Tiberians. For this purpose he put at my disposal his unique collection, containing copies of a large number of fragments of Hebrew Bible Mss. with BV covering a very considerable part of the Bible which come from the Geniza of Cairo and are now scattered over various libraries; cf. his Catalogue, cited in paragraph XXIV. I went very carefully through this collection, and after having examined all the fragments I was happy to find there many parallel forms.

My friend Professor Alexander Marx was kind enough to read large parts of this monograph in manuscript form. He also called

my attention to the Ms. 105 of the Library of the Jewish Theological Seminary, which proved to be very useful.

I am further indebted to Professors Eugen Mittwoch and
Ismar Elbogen, through whose recommendation this monograph
of mine was awarded the Zunz-Prize for 1933. Likewise I wish to
thank the Board of Editors of the Hebrew Union College Annual
who, acting on the suggestion of President Dr Julian Morgen-
stern, consented to include this study in their publications. Dr.
Sheldon H. Blank has put me under great obligation by assisting
me in reading the proofs.

ADDENDA

P. 3, 1. 1, after the word "material": (after E. A. Speiser in *JQR, NS* XVI
[1926], pp. 343–382 and XXIII [1933], pp. 233–265 had dealt with the
subject from the point of view of Comparative Semitic Phonetics).

P. 13, last line: cf. similarly paragraph XXX.

P. 26, 1. 5 from end: For the later Greek confusion with ου cf. Dictionary
s. v. און.

P. 29, 1. 1, after "χ and κ": Cf. Mayser, §36, I, 2).

P. 29, 1. 10 fr. bot., after "παθα": Cf. Mayser, §36, II, 1).

P. 30, 1. 19, after "sound": Cf. Mayser, §11, I.

A HEBREW GRAMMAR

The subdivisions (*a*, *β*, *γ* or 1, 2, 3 respectively) separate the sound roots from the various types of weak stems, where one consonant of the stem is apparently missing in the transliteration, as expounded in the Introduction, paragraph XXIII, sub. א, ה, ח and ע.

THE VERB

I. ḲAL

A. PERFECT

§1: *3. pers. sing. masc.:*

a) Sound Verbs:

בְּרַךְ	$\beta\alpha\rho\alpha\chi$ G	נָתַן	$\nu\alpha\vartheta\alpha\nu$ G
זָכַר	$\zeta\alpha\chi\alpha\rho$ A	סָמַךְ	$\sigma\alpha\mu\alpha\chi$ A,
יָשַׁב	$\iota\alpha\sigma\alpha\beta$ O		$\sigma\alpha\mu\alpha\kappa$ B
נָדַב	$\nu\alpha\delta\alpha\beta$ G	צָפַן	$\sigma\alpha\varphi\alpha\nu$ G
	שָׁפַט	$\sigma\alpha\varphi\alpha\tau$ G	

b) Verbs with a Guttural:

a)	אָחַז	$\alpha\chi as$ B, $\alpha\chi\alpha\zeta$ G,		עָזַר	$\alpha\zeta\alpha\rho$ G
		$\alpha\alpha\zeta$ A	*β)*	יָצָא	jasa
	אָמַר	$\alpha\mu\alpha\rho$ G		פָּדָה	$\varphi\alpha\delta\alpha$ G
	אָסַף	$\alpha\sigma\alpha\varphi$ G		קָנָה	$\kappa\alpha\nu\alpha$ G
	אָשַׁם	asam		קָנָנִי	canani
	הָלַךְ	$\alpha\lambda\alpha\chi$ O	*γ)*	פָּעַל	$\varphi\alpha\alpha\lambda$ A
	חָנַן	$\alpha\nu\alpha\nu$ G	*δ)*	הָיָה	$\alpha\epsilon\alpha$ O, haja
	חָשַׁב	$\alpha\sigma\alpha\beta$ G		חָזָה	$\alpha\zeta a$ G

155

126

חָנָה	hana		עָנָם	$ava\mu$ O
חָרָה	ara		עָשָׂה	$a\sigma a$ G
עָנָה	$av a$ A		רָאֹה	raha

c) Verba med. ו and י:

בָּא	βa O		קָם	$\kappa a\mu$ G
דִּו	δav A		רָד	rad
		שָׁם	$\sigma a\mu$ O	

d) Verba tertiae ח and ע:

a)	בָּלַע	$\beta a\lambda a$ A	β)	זְרַח	$\zeta apa\epsilon$ A
	בִּלְעָם	$\beta a\lambda aa\mu$ G		יָדַע	$\iota\delta a\epsilon$ B
	זְרַח	ζapa A		שָׁמַע	$\sigma a\mu a\epsilon$ B
	פָּתַח	$\pi a\vartheta a$ B, $\varphi a\vartheta a$ A	γ)	בָּטַח	$\beta a\tau\epsilon$ O
	יָדַע	$\iota\delta a$ A		זְרַח	$\zeta ap\epsilon$ B
	שָׁמַע	$\sigma a\mu a$ G		שָׁמַע	same

§2: 3. pers. sing. fem.:

a) With retention of the second vowel:

נָחֲתָה	$va a\vartheta a$ O	עָנְתָה	anatha
	רָאֲתָה	$\rho aa\vartheta a$ O	

b) With loss of the second vowel:

עָשְׂשָׂה	$a\sigma\sigma a$ O

§3: 2. pers. sing. masc.:

a) Ending in a Consonant:

a_1)	הָפַכְתָּ	$a\varphi a\chi\vartheta$ O	a_2)	זָנַחְתָּ	$\zeta av a\vartheta$ O
	מָנַרְתָּה	$\mu a\gamma ap\vartheta$ O		יָדַעְתָּ	$\iota\delta a\vartheta$ O
	נָחַתָּה	$va\vartheta a\vartheta$ O		קָרָאתָ	carath
	פָּרַצְתָּ	$\varphi apa\sigma\vartheta$ O		שָׁמַעְתָּ	$\sigma a\mu a\vartheta$ O

127

β_1) פָּדִיתָ   φαδιϑ o β_2) רָאִיתָ   ραιϑ o
      שָׂרִיתָ   sarith γ) שָׂמְתָ   σαμϑ o
              δ) קָלוֹתָ   calloth

b) Ending in a Vowel:

a) בְּרָאתָ   βαραϑα o   צָפַנְתָ   σαφανϑα o
    פָּעַלְתָ   φααλϑα o β) רָאִיתָה   ραειϑα o

§4: 1. pers. sing.:

a) אָמַרְתִּי   αμαρϑι o   חָסִיתִי   ασιϑι o
   בָּטַחְתִּי   βαταϑι o   קָנִיתִי   canithi
   עָבַרְתִּי   abarthi   רָאִיתִי   raithi
   פָּקַדְתִּי   φακαδϑι o γ) שָׂנֵאתִי   σανηϑι o
   קָרָאתִי   καραϑι o δ) שָׁחוֹתִי   σεωϑι o
β) הָיִיתִי   αιϑι o ϵ) שָׂמְתִּי   σαμϑι o

§5: 3. pers. plur.:

a) With retention of the second vowel (cf. B-L. §2w):

דָּקְרוּ   dacaru   יָדְעוּ   jadau
          מָעֲדוּ   μααδου o

b) With loss of the second vowel:

אָמְרוּ   αμρου o   כָּחֲשׁוּ   chaesu
שָׁמְנוּ   ταμνου o   עָזְבוּ   αζβου o

c) Defective verbs:

a) בָּאוּ   bau   שָׂמְחוּ   σαμου o
   הָמוּ   αμου o   שָׁתוּ   σαϑου o
   מָטוּ   ματου o β) דַּמּוּ   δαμμου o
   רָאוּ   rau γ) שָׂסֵהוּ   σασουου o

§6: 2. pers. plur. masc.:

חֲרַשְׁתֶּם   arasthem

B. Imperfect

§7: *3. pers. sing. masc.:*

a) With vocalic prefix:

α) יִזְרַע ισρα B, ιζρα A   יִצְהַר ισααρ A
    יִמְנַע ιμνα G   יִצְחַק ισαακ G
    יִקְרָא ικρα O   יִשְׂחַק isaac
    יִקְרָאֵנִי ικραηνι O   γ) יַקֹר ικαρ O
    יִשְׁמַע ισμα A   יַשֵׂר isar
β) יִבְחַר ιβααρ B   δ) יִשְׂרֹף ισροφ O
    יִנְאַל ιγααλ B   יְסוֹבְבֶנּוּ ισωβαβεννου O

b) With consonantal prefix:

α) יִבְלַע ιεβλα G   δ₄) יַעֲקֹב ιακωβ G
    יִגְדַל iegdal   ε) יָנוּר ιαγουρ A
    יִדְלַף ιεδλαφ A   יָנוּם ιανουμ A
    יִזְרַע ιεζρα A   יָקוּם jaccum
    יִמְלָא ιεμλα A   יָרוּם ιαρουμ O
    יִמְנֶה ιεμνα A   יָשׁוּב ιασουβ G
    יִפְתַּח ιεφθα A   ζ) יָבוֹא ιαβω O
    יִקְבַּע jecba   יָדוֹם ιαδομ O
    יִרְפָּא ιερφα A   יָכוֹן ιεχχον O
    יִתְלֶה ιεθλα A   η₁) יִהְיֶה ιειε O
β) יַחְבֵּל ιεβαλ O   יִחְיֶה ιειε O
    יַחְדֵּל ιεδαλ O   יִרְאֶה ιερε O
γ₁) יִנְאַל iegal   יִרְעָם ιερημ O
    יִנְהַר ιεγαρ O   η₂) יִפְתַּח iepte
    יִשָּׁאֵג jesag   יִפְדֶה ιεφδε O
γ₂) יִבְחַר ιεβααρ A   η₃) יֵרֶד jered
    יִצְהַר iessaar   יֵשֵׁב ιησηβ O
δ₁) יִשְׂבַּק ιεσβοκ A   η₄) יִגְדַּל ιεγδελ O
δ₂) יִזְבְּלֵנִי iezbuleni   יִתֵּן ιεθθεν O
δ₃) יַחֲרֹשׁ jeros   ϑ) יִזְרַח ιεσραε B

           יִפְתַּח ιεφϑαε G

§8: *3. pers. sing. fem. = 2. pers. sing. masc.:*

a) With α in the first syllable:

α) תִּמְנֶה *θαμνα* A   β) תִּרְחַק *θαρακ* O

   תִּמְנַע *θαμνα* A   γ) תָּמוּג *θαμουγ* O

   תִּפְסַח *θαψα* A   תָּשׁוּב *θασουβ* O

   תִּרְצֶה *θαρσα* B   δ) תֶּהְנֶה *θααγε* O

b) With ε in the first syllable:

α) תִּרְצֶה *θερσα* G   תֵּלֵךְ *θηληχ* O

β) תִּבְעַר *θεβαρ* O   δ) תִּתֵּן *θεθθεν* O

   תִּמְאָס *θεμας* O   תִּצְרְנִי *θεσσερηνι* Q

   תִּסְעָדְנִי *θεσαδηνι* O   ε) תֵּפֶל thephphol

β₁) תֵּצֵר *θεσαρ* O   תְּאָזְרֵנִי *θεζορηνι* O

γ) תִּרְאֶה *θερε* O   ε₁) תָּמוֹט *θεμμουτ* O

      ε₂) תִּצְפְּנֵם *θισφνημ* O

c) Miscellaneous forms:

וַתֵּט *ουθετ* O   תְּסוֹבְבֵנִי *θσωβαβηνι* O

§9: *1. pers. sing.:*

α) אֶמְצָא emsa   γ₁) אֶעֱבֹר eebor

   אֶפְתַּח *εφθα* O   אֶמְחָצָם *εμωσημ* O

   אֶקְרָא *εκρα* O   אַשְׁחָקֵם *εσοκημ* O

   אֶשְׁמָּה *εσμα* O   δ) אָרוּם *αρουμ* O

β) אֶשְׁעַן *εσαν* A   אָרֶץ *αρους* O

   אֲהַבְהוּ *εαβηου* O   אָשׁוּב *ασουβ* O

γ) אֶזְכֹּר *ηζχορ* O   ε) אִירָא *ιρα* O

   אֶרְדּוֹף *ερδοφ* O   אָגִילָה *αγιλα* O

   אֶשְׁמֹר *εσμωρ* O   ζ) אֲרוֹמִמְךָ *ερωμεμεχ* O

   אֶשְׁפּוֹךְ esphoch   אַתְנֵהוּ *εθνηου* O

§10: *3. pers. plur. masc.:*

a) With vocalic prefix:

יַחְפְּרוּ *ιφρου* O   יְסַבְּנִי *ισαββουνι* O

יַחְרְדוּ *ιχαρδου* O   יְקַרְצוּ *ικερσου* O

130

b) With consonantal prefix:

α)	יַבְשׁוּ	$\iota\eta\beta\omega\sigma\sigma\nu$ o		יַחְמְרוּ	$\iota\epsilon\mu\rho\sigma\nu$ o
	יַחְרְגוּ	$\iota\epsilon\rho\sigma\gamma\sigma\nu$ o		יַבְלוּ	$\iota\epsilon\beta\lambda\sigma\nu$ o
	יִפְלוּ	$\iota\epsilon\varphi\varphi\sigma\lambda\sigma\nu$ o		יִשְׁמְחוּ	$\iota\epsilon\sigma\mu\sigma\nu$ o
	יִשְׁמְרוּ	$\iota\epsilon\sigma\mu\omega\rho\sigma\nu$ o	δ)	יַעַזְבוּ	$\iota\epsilon\zeta\epsilon\beta\sigma\nu$ o
β)	יְמוּתוּ	$\iota\alpha\mu\omega\vartheta\sigma\nu$ o		יִשְׁמְחוּ	$\iota\epsilon\sigma\epsilon\mu\sigma\nu$ o
	יָרְצוּ	$\iota\alpha\rho\sigma\sigma\sigma\nu$ o		יֶהֱמוּ	$\iota\epsilon\epsilon\mu\sigma\nu$ o
	יָרְנּוּ	$\iota\alpha\rho\sigma\nu\nu\sigma\nu$ o	ε)	יִרְעֲשׁוּ	$\iota\epsilon\rho\alpha\sigma\sigma\nu\iota$ o
β₁)	יָשׁוּבוּ	jasubu		יִתְמָהוּ	jethmau
γ)	יִחְיוּ	jeju	ζ)	יֹאבְדוּ	$\iota\sigma\beta\alpha\delta\sigma\nu$ o
		ζ₁)	יֹאמְרוּ	$\iota\omega\mu\rho\sigma\nu$ o	

§11: *2. pers. plur. masc.*:

תִּהְיוּ	$\vartheta\sigma\nu$ o		תָּמֹדוּ	thamoddu
תַּעֲשׂוּ	$\vartheta\epsilon\sigma\sigma\nu$ o			

§12: *1. pers. plur.*:

נִירָא $\nu\iota\rho\alpha$ o

C. PARTICIPLE

§13: *ptc. act. sing. masc.*:

α)	בּוֹטֵחַ	$\beta\omega\tau\eta$ o		נֹצֵר	$\nu\omega\sigma\eta\rho$ o
	בּוֹקֵר	bocer		נוֹחֵן	$\nu\omega\vartheta\eta\nu$ o
	גּוֹאֵל	goel		סֹפֵר	sopher
	גֹדֵר	goder		עֹזֵר	$\omega\zeta\eta\rho$ o
	דֹּאֵג	$\delta\omega\eta\gamma$ A, $\delta\omega\eta\kappa$ B		עֹשֵׂה	$\omega\sigma\eta$ o
	חֹרֵב	$\chi\omega\rho\eta\beta$ G, oreb		קֹלֵעַ	colea
	יֹעֵץ	ioes		קוֹרֵא	$\kappa\omega\rho\eta$ G
	יֹצֵר	joser		רֹגֵל	$\rho\omega\gamma\eta\lambda$ G
	לוֹחֵשׁ	$\lambda\omega\eta s$ G		רֹעֶה	roe
	נוֹגֵשׂ	noges		שֹׁאֵף	soeph
	עֹבֵד	$\omega\beta\eta\delta$ G, obeth		שׁוֹבֵק	$\sigma\omega\beta\eta\kappa$ G
	עֹדֵד	$\omega\delta\eta\delta$ B		שֹׁמֵר	$\sigma\omega\mu\eta\rho$ G

131

שֹׁקֵד soced   שָׁלֵם σαλημ o

β) חָפֵץ αφης o   γ) גֵּר gar

יָרֵא ιαρη o   רָם ραμ G

§14: ptc. act. sing. fem.:

a) זֹחֶלֶת ζωελεθ A   קֹהֶלֶת coeleth

יוֹשֶׁבֶת josebeth   β) הֹמָה homa

γ) רֹפָה ραμα G

§15: ptc. act. plur. masc. (cf. B-L. §26t):

a) With retention of the second vowel (cf. B-L. §14f'):

בֹּטְחִים βωτεειμ o   נֹקְדִים nocedim

חֹלְמִים ωλεμιμ o   פֹּחֲזִים phoezim

מֹשְׁכִים mosechim   רֹגְלִים ρωγελειμ A

b) With loss of the second vowel (cf. B-L. §26t):

a) אֹרְגִים ωργειμ G   צֹפִים σωφιμ A

שֹׁמְרִים σωμριμ o   רֹעִים roim

β) חֹסִים ωσιμ o   γ) רָצִים ρασειμ A

§16: ptc. act. plur. fem.:

רָמוֹת ραμωθ A

§17: Inflected forms of the act. ptc.:

a) גֹּזִי gozi   מֹשְׁכִי mosche

רֹעִי roi   חֹפְצִי ωφση o

β) לֹחֲמִי λωαμαι o   עֹבְרִי ωβρη o

קָמַי καμαι o   שֹׂנְאִי σωνη o

γ) יוֹרְדִי ιωρδη o   δ) בֹּנַיִךְ bonaich

לִירֵאָיִךְ λιριαχ o

§18: pass. ptc. sing. masc.:

בָּרוּךְ βαρουχ G   זָבוּד ζαβουθ B

נָמוּל γαμουλ B   חָמוּל amul

חָנוּן	ανουν G	פָּקוּד	phacud
הָרוּץ	αρους G	פָּרוּחַ	φαρρου A
סָמוּךְ	samuch	צָפוּן	σαφουν O
סָתוּר	σαθουρ G	רָפוּא	ραφου G
עָזוּר	azur	שָׁאוּל	σαουλ A
עָצוּם	ασουμ O	שָׂדוּד	sadud

§19: *pass. ptc. sing. fem.:*

a) With retention of the vowel after the first radical:

בְּרוּרָה	barura	עֲזוּבָה	αζουβα A
חֲשֻׁבָה	ασουβε B	צְרוּעָה	σαρουα A
סְנֻאָה	σανουα A	שְׁלֻחָה	salua

b) With ε after the first radical:

נְחוּשָׁה	νεουσα O	צְרוּפָה	σερουφα O
		שְׁלֻחָה	selua

c) With elision of the first vowel:

בְּעוּלָה	bula	דְּרוּשָׁה	drusa

§20: *pass. ptc. plur. masc.:*

a) With retention of the vowel after the first radical:

אֲסוּרִים	assurim	לְטוּשִׁים	latusim

b) With ε after the first radical:

אֲמֻנִים	εμουνιμ O

§21: *Inflected forms of the pass. ptc.:*

a)	חֲלָצַי	eluse	β)	עֲקֻבֵּי	ακοββαι O
	נְצוּרֵי	nesure		זְרוּעֹתַי	ζερουωθαι O

133

D. IMPERATIVE

§22: *impv. sing. masc.:*

a) זְכֹר ζχορ ο   שְׁמַע σμα ο, σμαε ο
   לְחֹם λοομ ο   γ) קוּם κουμ ο
β) חֲזַק εζακ ο   δ) רִיבָה ριβα ο
     ε) הֱיֵה αιη ο

§23: *impv. plur. masc.:*

a) בִּטְחוּ βετου ο   γ) אֱהָבוּ αβου ο
   חֲזוּ εεζου ο   הָבוּ αβου ο
   קִרְאוּ κερου ο   δ) לְכוּ λχου ο
   שִׂמְחוּ σεμου ο   רְאוּ ρου A
   שִׁמְעוּ semu   דְּעוּ δου ο
β) גִּילוּ γιλου ο   ε) רְעוּ rou
   שִׁמְעוּ σιμου ο   ζ) חִדְלוּ hedalu

E. INFINITIVE

§24: *inf. abs.:*

a) זָנוֹחַ ζανω A, zanoe   קָרֹב καρωβ ο
   חָבוֹר αβωρ G   β) בּוֹז buz
   חָרֹק αρωκ ο   חוּל ουλ A
   פָּדֹה φαδω ο   צוּד sud
     קוּם κουμ ο

§25: *inf. constr:*

a) With prefix:

a) לִבְלוּם λαβλωμ ο   לִפְנוֹת λαφνωθ ο
   לִמְצֹא λαμσω ο   β) לָבוֹא λαβω B
     בְּמֹט βαμωτ ο

b) With suffix:

a) בּוּזִי βουζει G   בְּחָפְזִי βααφζι ο
   שְׂאֵתִי σαθι ο   בְּרִדְתִּי βρεδεθι ο
β) בְּשׁוּרִי basori   γ) בַּחֲלוֹתָם βααλωθαμ ο

II. PI'EL

A. Perfect

§26: *3. pers. sing. masc.:*

אָמַר εμμηρ G   עִקֵּשׁ εκκης A
גִּדֵּל γεδδηλ A   קִצֵּץ κεσσης O
הִלֵּל ελληλ B   שִׁלַּם σελλημ A

§27: *2. pers. sing. masc.:*

a) Ending in a consonant:

חִלַּלְתָּ ελλελϑ O   נֵאַרְתָּה νηερϑ O
                          שִׂמַּחְתָּ σεμεϑ O

b) Ending in a vowel:

פִּתַּחְתָּ φεϑεϑα O   דְּלִיתָנִי δελλιϑανη O
                          חִיִּיתָנִי uϑανι O

§28: *1. pers. sing.:*

גִּדַּלְתִּי γεδδελϑι A   מִלֵּיתִי μελληϑι A
                          עִנִּיתִי εννηϑι O

§29: *3. pers. plur.:*

חֵרְפוּ ηρφου O

§30: *1. pers. plur.:*

דִּמִּינוּ δεμμηνου O   בִּלַּעֲנוּהוּ βελλενουου O

B. Imperfect

§31: *3. pers. sing. masc.:*

a) With vocalic prefix:

יְדַבֵּר ιδαββερ O   יְוַסְּרֵךְ ιζαμμερεχ O
                          יְמַלֵּט ιμαλλετ O

135

b) With consonantal prefix:

יְדַבֵּר   ιεδαββερ ο   יְהַלֵּל   ιαλλελ Α

§32: 2. pers. sing. masc.:

α) וַתְּאַזְּרֵנִי   ουεθαζερηνι ο   וַתַּנְחֵלְנִי   ουθνεελνι ο

β) תְּשַׁבֵּר   θεσσαβερ ο

§33: 1. pers. sing.:

α) אֶדְלַג   εδαλλεγ ο   γ) אֲהַלְלָךְ   εελλελεχ ο

אֲנַסֶּה   enasse   δ) אַשֶּׁה   ασσανε ο

β) אֲחַלֵּל   ααλλελ ο   אֲשַׁקֵּר   ασσακερ ο

אֲמַגֶּנְךָ   amaggenach   ε) אֲכַזֵּב   εχαζεβ ο

§34: 3. pers. plur. masc.:

a) With vocalic prefix:

יְדַבְּרוּ   ιδαββηρου ο

b) With consonantal prefix:

יְהַלְכוּן   ιαλληχουν ο   יְחַלְּלוּ   ιαλληλου ο

יְשַׁוֵּעוּ   ιεσανου ο

C. PARTICIPLE

§35: ptc. act. sing. masc.:

α) מְלַמֵּד   μαλαμμεδ ο   β) מְנַחֵם   μαναημ G

מְנַצֵּחַ   μανασση ο   מְפַתֶּה   maphate

מְנַשֶּׁה   μανασση Β;   הַמְאַזְּרֵנִי   αμμααζερηνι ο

μανΝασση Α   γ) מְשַׁוֶּה   μοσανε ο

מְעוֹפֵף   mopheph

§36: ptc. act. sing. fem.:

מְרַחֶפֶת   marahaefeth

§37: *ptc. act. plur. masc.*:

הַמְיַחֲלִים $\alpha\mu\mu\eta\alpha\lambda\iota\mu$ o   וּמְשַׁנְּאֵי $ov\mu\alpha\sigma\sigma\alpha\nu\epsilon\alpha\iota$ o

D. Imperative

§38: *impv. sing. masc.*:

a) נְשָׂאֵם $\nu\epsilon\sigma\sigma\eta\mu$ o   β) בְּרֵךְ $\beta\alpha\rho\epsilon\chi$ o
פַּלְּטֵנִי $\varphi\epsilon\lambda\lambda\epsilon\tau\eta\nu\iota$ o   צַדְּקֵנוּ sadecenu
γ) חַיֵּיהוּ heieu

§39: *impv. plur. masc.*:

הַלְלוּ allelu   זַמְּרוּ $\zeta\omega\eta\mu\epsilon\rho ov$ o

E. Infinitive

§40: *inf. constr.*:

a) פְּנוֹת $\varphi\epsilon\nu\nu\omega\vartheta$ o   γ) פַּלֵּט $\varphi\alpha\lambda\eta\tau$ o
כַּלּוֹתָם $\chi\epsilon\lambda\lambda\omega\vartheta\alpha\mu$ o   לְבַלּוֹת $\lambda\alpha\beta\alpha\lambda\omega\vartheta$ o
β) כַּסּוֹת $\chi\epsilon\sigma\sigma ov\vartheta$ o   בְּשׁוּעִי $\beta\alpha\sigma\alpha v\epsilon\iota$ o

III. NIPH'AL

A. Perfect

§41: *3. pers. sing. masc.*:

נִמְשַׁל $\nu\epsilon\mu\sigma\alpha\lambda$ o   נוֹעַד $\nu\omega\alpha\delta$ A

§42: *2. pers. sing. masc.*:

נִשְׁבַּעְתָּ $\nu\epsilon\sigma\beta\alpha\vartheta$ o

§43: *1. pers. sing.*:

a) נֶעֱזַרְתִּי $\nu\epsilon\zeta\alpha\rho\vartheta\iota$ o   נִשְׁבַּעְתִּי $\nu\epsilon\sigma\beta\alpha\vartheta\iota$ o
נִפְתַּלְתִּי neptalti   β) נִגְרַזְתִּי $\nu\epsilon\gamma\rho\epsilon\sigma\vartheta\iota$ o

§44: *3. pers. plur.:*

נֶאֶסְפוּ νεεσαφου o   נִדְמוּ νεδμου o

B. IMPERFECT

§45: *3. pers. sing. masc.:*

יְלָוֶה illaue

C. PARTICIPLE

§46: *ptc. sing. masc.:*

a) נִבְהָל νεβαλ o   β) נֶאֱמָן νεεμαν o

נֶחְשָׁב nesab   γ) נִמְצָא νεμσα o

נִתְעָב nethab   δ) נִשְׁפֶּה nesphe

§47: *ptc. sing. fem.:*

נֶאֱמָנָת νεεμαναϑ o   נֶעְלָמָה naalma

נִמְרָצָת nimrezeth

§48: *ptc. plur. masc.:*

נֶאֱמָנִים neemanim

IV. PU‘AL

A. IMPERFECT

§49: *3. pers. sing. masc.:*

a) With vocalic prefix:

יְשֻׁבַּר ισουβερ o

b) With consonantal prefix:

יְרֻחַם ιεροαμ A   יְפֻנֶּה ιεφοννη G

B. Participle

§50: *ptc. sing. masc.:*

מְהוֹלֵל molal   מְשֻׁלָּם $\mu\epsilon\sigma\sigma\nu\lambda\alpha\mu$ G

הַמְּסֻכָּן amsuchan

§51: *ptc. plur. masc.:*

מְעוֹנְנִים $\mu\sigma\sigma\nu\nu\epsilon\iota\mu$ A

V. HIPH'IL

A. Perfect

§52: *3. pers. sing. masc.:*

a) הֵכִין hechin   הִרְעִים $\epsilon\rho\iota\mu$ O

הִפְלִיא $\epsilon\varphi\lambda\iota$ O   *β)* הֶחֱלִיק $\epsilon\epsilon\lambda\iota\kappa$ O

הֶעֱלִים eelim

§53: *2. pers. sing. masc.:*

a) Ending in a consonant:

a) הִקְצַרְתָּ $\epsilon\kappa\sigma\epsilon\rho\vartheta$ O   *β₁)* הֶעֱלִיתָ $\epsilon\epsilon\lambda\vartheta$ O

הֵשֵׁבְתָּ $\epsilon\sigma\beta\epsilon\vartheta$ O   *β₂)* הֶעֱמַדְתָּ $\epsilon\epsilon\mu\epsilon\delta\epsilon\vartheta$ O

הִשְׂמַחְתָּ $\epsilon\sigma\mu\epsilon\vartheta$ O   *γ)* הֲרִימֹתָ $\alpha\rho\eta\mu\omega\vartheta$ O

β) הֶעֱטִיתָ $\epsilon\epsilon\tau\eta\vartheta$ O   *γ₁)* הֲקִמֹתוֹ $\alpha\kappa\iota\mu\omega\vartheta\omega$ O

b) Ending in a vowel:

הִסְתַּרְתָּ $\epsilon\sigma\vartheta\epsilon\rho\vartheta\alpha$ O   הִקְנַרְתַּנִי $\epsilon\sigma\gamma\epsilon\rho\vartheta\alpha\nu\iota$

B. Imperfect

§54: *3. pers. sing. masc.:*

a) Verba mediae ו and י:

a) יָאִיר $\iota\alpha\epsilon\iota\rho$ G   יָכִין $\iota\alpha\chi\epsilon\iota\nu$ G

יָבִין $\iota\alpha\beta\epsilon\iota\nu$ B   יָקִים $\iota\alpha\kappa\epsilon\iota\mu$ G

יָזִיז $\iota\alpha\zeta\epsilon\iota\zeta$ B   יָרִיב $\iota\alpha\rho\epsilon\iota\beta$ A

	יָשִׁיב	ιασειβ A	יָרִיב	ιαριβ A
β)	יָבִין	ιαβιν O	γ) יָאִיר	iair
	יָלִין	ιαλιν O	יָכִין	iachin
	יָפִיעַ	ιαφιε A	יָקִים	iacim

יָשִׁיר jasir

b) Miscellaneous forms:

a)	יוֹאֵל	ιωηλ G	β)	יַגִּיד	ιεγγιθ O
	יוֹסֵף	ιωσηφ G	β₁)	יַעֲמִידְנִי	ιεμιδηνι O
a₁)	יוֹדְךָ	ιωδεχχα O	γ)	יִגְיֶה	ιαγι O

§55: *2. pers. sing. masc.:*

a)	תַּשְׁפִּיל	θεσφιλ O	γ)	תָּאִיר	θαειρ O
	תַּסְתִּיר	θεσθερ O		תָּשִׁיב	θασιβ O
	תַּסְתִּירֵם	θεσθιρημ O	δ)	תַּנְחַנִי	θενηνι O
a₁)	תַּרְחִיב	θεριβ O		תַּרְבֵּנִי	θερβηνι O
β)	תּוֹשִׁיעַ	θωσι O	ε)	תַּחֲרֵשׁ	θαρεs O
	תּוֹצִיאֵנִי	θωσιηνι O	ζ)	תּוֹתַר	θωθαρ O

§56: *1. pers. sing.:*

a)	אָפִיר	αφιρ O	γ)	אוֹדְךָ	ωδεχ O
	אַצְמִיתֵם	ασμιθαυμ O		אוֹרְךָ	ωρεχ O
β)	אַשְׂכִּילְךָ	εσχιλεχ O	δ)	אֱהוֹדֶנּוּ	αωδεννου O
	אַשֵּׁינָם	εσιγημ O	ε)	אַטֶּה	αττε O

§57: *3. pers. plur. masc.:*

יַגִּיעוּ	ιγγιου O	יַרְחִיבוּ	ιεριβου O
		יַשְׂפִּיקוּ	jesphicu

§58: *2. pers. plur. masc.:*

תָּלִינוּ thalinu

140

C. Participle

§59: *ptc. sing. masc.*:

מַשְׁמִים masmim   מַשְׁבִּית $\mu\iota\sigma\beta\iota\vartheta$ o

                             מוֹשִׁיע $\mu\omega\sigma\iota$ o

§60: *ptc. sing. fem.*:

מֵינִיקָה meneca   מֵינֶקֶת meneceth

§61: *ptc. plur. masc.*:

מַנְדִּילִים $\mu\alpha\gamma\delta\iota\lambda\iota\mu$ o   מוֹשִׁיעִים mosim

D. Imperative

§62: *impv. sing. masc.*:

a) הַקִּיצָה $\alpha\kappa\iota\sigma\alpha$ o   β) הַטֵּה $\epsilon\tau\tau\eta$ o

    הָשִׁיבָה $\alpha\sigma\iota\beta\alpha$ o   הַחֲזֵק $\epsilon\epsilon\zeta\epsilon\kappa$ o

הַצְלִיחָה נָא $\alpha\sigma\lambda\iota\alpha\nu\nu\alpha$ o   β₁) הַצִּילֵנִי $\epsilon\sigma\iota\lambda\eta\nu\iota$ o

    הָעִירָה $\alpha\iota\rho\alpha$ o   γ) הוֹשִׁיעָה $\omega\sigma\iota\alpha$ o

a₁) הָרֵם $\alpha\rho\eta\mu$ o   γ₁) הוֹשִׁיעָה נָא $\omega\sigma\iota\epsilon\nu\nu\alpha$ o

§63: *impv. plur. masc.*:

a) הַרְנִינוּ $\epsilon\rho\nu\iota\nu ou$ o   β) הַרְפּוּ $\alpha\rho\varphi ou$ o

    הַאֲזִינוּ eezinu   γ) הוֹדוּ $\omega\delta ou$ o

E. Infinitive

§64: a) *inf. abs.*:

הָבֵין $\alpha\beta\iota\nu$ o   הַצְנֵעַ esne

b) *inf. constr.*:

בְּהָמִיר $\beta\alpha\alpha\mu\iota\rho$ o   לְהוֹשִׁיעֵנִי $\lambda\omega\sigma\iota\eta\nu\iota$ o

VI. HOPH'AL

Imperfect

§65: *3. pers. sing. masc.:*

יוּבַל   ιουβαλ   A

VII. HITHPA'EL

A. Perfect

§66: *2. pers. sing. masc.:*

הִתְעַבְּרְתָ   εϑαββαρϑ   o

§67: *1. pers. sing.:*

הִתְהַלָּכְתִּי   εϑαλλαχϑι   o

B. Imperfect

§68: *2. pers. sing. masc.:*

תִּתְבָּרָר   ϑεϑβαραρ   o   תִּתְפַּתָּל   ϑεϑφαϑϑαλ   o

תִּתַּמָּם   ϑεϑαμμαμ   o

§69: *1. pers. sing.:*

אֶתְחַנָּן   εϑανναν   o

§70: *3. pers. plur. masc.:*

יִתְהַלְלוּ   ιϑαλλαλου   o

C. Participle

§71: *ptc. plur. fem.:*

מְתְנוֹסְסוֹת   methnosasoth

ALEXANDER SPERBER

D. Imperative

§72: *impv. plur. masc.:*

הִשְׁתַּחֲווּ   εσϑαυου   o

VIII. VERBAL FORMS WITH SUFFIXES

§73: *suffix of the 1. pers. sing.: νι:*

a) With helping vowel η:

α) זֻבְלֵנִי   iezbuleni   פִּלְּטֵנִי   φελλετηνι   o
   תִּסְעָדֵנִי   ϑεσαδηνι   o   יַעֲמִידֵנִי   ιεμιδηνι   o
   תִּצְרֵנִי   ϑεσσερηνι   o   תַּנְחֵנִי   ϑενηνι   o
   תַּאַזְרֵנִי   ϑεζορηνι   o   תִּרְבֵּנִי   ϑερβηνι   o
   תְּסוֹבְבֵנִי   ϑσωβαβηνι   o   הַצִּילֵנִי   εσιληνι   o
   נִתָּאַזְרֵנִי   ουεϑαζερηνι   o   β) יִקְרָאֵנִי   ικραηνι   o
   הַמְאַזְרֵנִי   αμμααζερηνι   o   תּוֹצִיאֵנִי   ϑωσιηνι   o
              לְהוֹשִׁיעֵנִי   λωσιηνι   o

b) Without a helping vowel:

α) יְסֻבְּנִי   ισαββουνι   o   β) חִיְּיתַנִי   ιυϑανι   o
   קָנָנִי   canani   הִסְגַּרְתַּנִי   εσγερϑανι   o
   β₁) דְּלִיתָנִי   δελλιϑανη   o

§74: *suffix of the 2. pers. sing. masc.:*

εχ, ach (cf. ¶ XXVI f 3), χα:

α) אֲרוֹמִמְךָ   ερωμεμεχ   o   אוֹדְךָ   ωδεχ   o
   יֹסְרְךָ   ιζαμμερεχ   o   אוֹרְךָ   ωρεχ   o
   אֲהַלְלֶךָ   εελλελεχ   o   β) אֲמַגֶּנְךָ   amaggenach
   אַשְׂכִּילֶךָ   εσχιλεχ   o   γ) יוֹדְךָ   ιωδεχχα   o

§75: *suffix of the 3. pers. sing. masc.: ου, ω:*

α) יְסוֹבְבֶנּוּ   ισωβαβεννου   o   חַיֵּהוּ   heieu
   אֲהוֹדֶנּוּ   αωδεννου   o   γ) שָׂטֵהוּ   σασουου   o
   β) אֶתְּנֵהוּ   ευϑηου   o   בִּלְעֲנוּהוּ   βελλενουου   o
   אֲהַבֵּהוּ   εαβηου   o   δ) הֲקֵמֹתוֹ   ακιμωϑω

143

§76: *suffix of the 1. pers. plur.:* ενου:

צִדְקֵנוּ   sadecenu

§77: *suffix of the 3. pers. plur. masc.:* ημ, αμ:

a) אָמְחָצָם   εμωσημ o   נְשָׁאָם   νεσσημ o

אֶשְׁחָקֵם   εσοκημ o   אַשִׁינָם   εσιγημ o

תַּסְתִּירֵם   θεσθιρημ o   β) עָנָם   αναμ o

תִּצְפְּנֵם   θισφνημ o   בִּלְעָם   βαλααμ G

יֵרְעֵם   ιερημ o   אָצְמִיתֵם   ασμιθαυμ o

IX. WAW CONJUNCTIVUM AND WAW CONSECUTIVUM

§78: *Transliterated as* ου (cf. ¶ XXVII 3):

a) Before a consonant:

וְנֶחָתָה   ουνααθα o   וְנִילוּ   ουγιλου o

וּפָקַדְתִּי   ουφακαδθι o   וְקָצָץ   ουκεσσης o

וְרָאִיתִי   uraithi   וּתְנַחֲלָנִי   ουθνεελνι o

וְשָׂמְתִּי   ουσαμθι o   וּבְרָךְ   ουβαρεχ o

וַתִּתֵּן   ουθεθθεν o   וְנָשָׁאם   ουνεσσημ o

וְהָאָזַרְנִי   ουθεζορηνι o   וְנֶעְזָרְתִּי   ουνεζαρθι o

וְקוּם   ουκουμ o   וְנָאָסְפוּ   ουνεεσαφου o

b) Before a vowel:

וְאֶשְׁחָקֵם   ουεσοκημ o   וְהָרֵם   ουαρημ o

וְאֶשְׂמַח   ουεσμα o   וְהוֹדוּ   ουωδου o

וְאַשִׁינָם   ουεσιγημ o   וְאוֹרֵךְ   ουωρεχ o

וְהָרְנִינוּ   ουερνινου o   וַיִּקֹר   ουικαρ o

וְאֶהְבְּהוּ   ουεαβηου o   וַיִּקְרָא   ουικρα o

וְעָזְבוּ   ουαζβου o   וַיֶּחֱרְדוּ   ουιχαρδου o

וְהָקִיצָה   ουακισα o   וַיְחַפְּרוּ   ουιφρου o

c) Before a consonantal ι:

וַיִּתֵּן   ουιεθθεν o   וְיַחְרְנוּ   ουιερογου o

וַיִּזְהַר   ουιεγαρ o   וְיָרוּם   ουιαρουμ o

וַיְדַבֵּר   ουιεδαββερ o   וְיָבֹא   ουιαβω o

§79: *Transliterated as* ου *plus helping vowel:*

α) וַתְּאָזְרֵנִי ουεϑαζερηνι ο   β) וִדְעוּ ουαδου ο

וַיִּרְחִיבוּ ουειεριβου ο   וַתְּמָאֵס ουαϑϑεμας ο

וַתֵּט ουαϑετ ο

THE NOUN

(Derived Forms are given in Parentheses)

X. MONOSYLLABIC BICONSONANTAL NOUNS

§80: *The a–class* (a, a):

1)	בר	bar		רב	ραβ A (ραβιμ ο)
	בת	bath		רם	ραμ G
	גב	gab		שי	σαι A
	גל	gal (γαλειμ B)		שר	σαρ A (sarim, sare)
	דג	dag (dagim)	2)	אב	αβ G (αβει B)
	דם	(δαμι ο; dame)		אח	αχ G (αχει B)
	יד	(ιαδαχ, ιαδω,		הד	ad
		ιαδαι ο)		הר	αρ A (αριμ ο)
	ים	iam (ιαμιμ ο)		עז	as B
	פז	φας B		עם	αμ ο (αμει B,
	פר	phar (pharim)			αμιμ ο)
	צל	σαλ G		שע	as
	צר	σαρ ο (σαραυι ο)		רע	ρα ο (raim)

a) feminine forms:

1)	במה	βαμα G (βαμωϑ G)	2)	אב	(abotham)
	פרה	φαρα B		דעה	(daath)
	צרה	(σαρωϑ ο)		מאה	(maath)
	רמה	ραμα G (ραμαϑ A;		פחה	(φααϑ A)
		ramathaim;		רעה	(raath; ρααϑι ο)
		ραμωϑ G)		חמה	(αμαϑι A)

145

b) With geminated 2nd radical:

1) בד bad (baddim,   רב ραβ A (ραββιμ O)
         baddau)   2) אף (αφφω O)
  גל gal (γαλλειμ A)   חג (αγγει B)
  גן γαν A (γαννιμ A)   עם αμ O (ammi;
                                    αμμαχ, αμμιμ O)

c) feminine forms:

1) רבה ραββα A (rabbath,   2) אמה αμμα G
            rabboth)

§81: *The i–class* (ε, η, e):

1) בל bel   צל σελ G (sela)
  בן βεν A   שם σημ A (σεμαχ,
  בת beth   σεμω O)
  גב (gebim)   תל θελ G
  גר γηρ G   2) אל ηλ G (ηλει B)
  גת γεθ G   אם εμ O
  חן hen   אש εs O
  יד ιεδ O   חך (echcha)
  לץ (λησιμ O)   עד ηδ O
  נכים (νηχιμ O)   עד ηρ A
  נר νηρ G   רע ρε G (reim)
  סף seph   תא (theim)

a) feminine forms:

1) שם (semoth;   2) דעה dea
        σεμωθαμ O)   חמה (εμαθαχ O)
            עצה (ησαθ O)

b) With geminated 2nd radical:

1) לב λεβ O (λεββι,   שק σεκ O (σεκκι O)
        λεββαυ O)   2) איש ιs A (issi)
  צל σελ G (σελλα A)   עד (eddim)

c) feminine form:

זמה ζεμμα B

d) Reduplicated form:

נלגל γελγελ G   צלצל selsel

§82: *The o–class (o, ω, o):*

1)   גב gob   רב ροβ o
     דק doc   שד sod
     כר χορ G   2)   אח oiim)
     עז οζ o (οζει o)

a) feminine form:

אב (ωβωϑ G)

b) With geminated 2nd radical:

כל χωλ A (chollo)

c) feminine forms:

חפה χοφφα B   סכה σοχχα o

d) Reduplicated forms:

בקבוק bocboc   כדכד chodchod

§83: *Nouns with varying vocalization:*

1) change of a and ε (cf. B.–L. §14 z):

בת bath—beth   צל σαλ G—σελ G
יד (ιαδαχ o)—ιεδ o   חמה (αμαϑι A)—
                            (εμαϑαχ o)

2) change of a and o:

גב gab—gob

147

XI. MONOSYLLABIC TRICONSONANTAL NOUNS

§84: *The a–class* (a, a):

1) גבר γαβρ o (γαβρι G)   קרן (καρναιν A)
    דרך (δαρχαμ o)   קשת κασϑ o
    זבד (ζαβδει G)   שבט σαβτ o
    זמר (ζαμβρει B)   שמש σαμς o
    כרם χαρμ o (χαρμει,   2) ארץ aρs o
         χαρμειμ B)   חפץ (αψει B)
    מלך (malchi; μαλχη o)   חצר aσρ B
    פרד φαρδ o   עבד aβδ G (aβδει B;
    קרב (καρβαμ o)   aβδαχ, aβδω o)
                        ערב aρβ o

a) feminine forms:

חרפה aρφa o (aρφaϑ o)   עגלה aγλa A
                  עלמה alma ·

b) With weak 2nd radical:

בער βaρ o   מעט μaτ o
יער ιaρ A (ιaρειμ B)   פעל (phalach)
כעס χas o   שאר sar
לען (λaγη o)   שחק σaκ o
                  תחש thas

c) feminine forms:

בהלה bala   בעלה (βaλωϑ A)
                  נהר (ναρωϑ o)

§85: *The i–class:*

A. WITH THE VOWEL ε OR η:

1) בקר βεκρ o   זבד (zebdi)
    דרך δερχ o (δερχι,   זכר ζεχρ o (ζεχρει B)
         δερχω o)   יצר (ιεσρι A; ιεσρο o)

148

יתר	(iethro)	רגל	(ρεγλαι o; reglau)
כסל	χεσλ o	רסן	ρεσν o
לתך	λευθχ o	רשת	ρεσθ o
מלך	(μελχει B; melche-chem; μελχαμ A)	שטף	σετφ o
		שמש	(semsi)
נגד	νεγδ o (νεγδι o)	שקר	σεκρ o
נזר	(νεζρω o)	2) אבל	εβλ o
נפש	(νεφσι, νεφσω, νεφσινου o)	חסד	εσδ A (εσδι, εσδω, εσδαχ o)
סתר	σευθρ o (σευθρει A)	חפץ	(ephsi)
צדק	(σεδκι, σεδκαχ o)	חשק	(esci)
קרב	(κερβα o)	עזר	εζρ o (εζρι A; εζρα o)
קשת	κεσθ o		

שמע (σεμει A)

a) feminine forms:

1) חלקה	(χελκαθ A)	עברה	(ebrath) ·
צדקה	(σεδκαθαχ o)	עזרה	(εζραθι o)
רצפה	ρεσφα G	עגלה	egla
2) דמעה	δεμα o	עקב	(εκβωθ o)

שמחה σεμα o

b) With weak 2nd radical:

איל	el (elim, ele, elau)	כאב	cheb
באר	βηρ G	נער	νερ o
זאב	ζηβ G	רחם	ρεμ o
זעיר	zer	תחת	θεθ o

c) feminine forms:

באר	(βηρωθ G)	בהמה	(βημωθ o)

B. WITH THE VOWEL ι:

With weak 2nd radical:

זיז	ziz ·	סיג	sig (sigim)
חיץ	his	סיס	sis

עיר   ειρ o   קיר   cir
ציר   sir   שיר   σιρ o (σιρι o)
                    שעיר (sirim)

a) feminine form:

קינה   κινα A

§86:   *The o–class:*

A. WITH THE VOWEL O OR ω:

1) בקר   βοκρ o   חדש   (odsi)
    גלם   (γολμη o)   חלד   ολδ o
    כפר   (χοφρω o)   חמר   ομρ o
    קדש   κοδs o (κοδσω o;   חפץ   (οφσι A)
             codsa)   חשך   (οσχι o)
    קרב   κορβ o   ערף   ορφ o
2) אזן   (οϛνι, οϛναχ o)   עשר   (οσραμ o)

a) With weak 2nd radical:

און   ων G (oni; ωνω, G;   מאד   μωδ o
        ωναμ, ωναν A)   מות   μωϑ B
אור   or   סוד   σωδ A (sodi)
בור   βωρ o   צאן   σων o
דוד   (dodi, dodach)   צום   σωμ o
דור   δωρ G   צור   σωρ o (sori)
הוד   ωδ A   קול   κωλ A (κωλω o)
זהר   zor   קרץ   κωs G
טוב   τωβ G (tobim)   ראש   ρωs G
יאר   ior   רחב   rob
יום   iom   שאול σωλ o
                    שוט sot

b) feminine forms:

אור   (oroth)   חומה homa
בושה βωσα o   יונה ιωνα G
חובה choba   מוטה mota
                    פותה photha

150

B. WITH THE VOWEL ου:

With weak 2nd radical:

אור	ουρ G (ουρει B)	סוס	sus (σουσει B)
באש	(busim)	צוף	σουφ G
בוץ	bus	צור	σουρ G (σουρει B;
טוב	(τουβαχ O)		σουραμ O)
נאם	νουμ O	ראש	rus
סוד	(σουδει B)	שור	(surim)

שור   σουρ G

a) feminine forms:

טור	(turoth)	פארה	phura
סופה	supha	פורה	phura

§87: *Monosyllabic Nouns with affixed helping vowel:*

בטן	βατνε A	כרם	χαρμα B
בשת	βοσθε β	מתנ	μεθγε O

§88: *Nouns with varying vocalization:*

1) change of α and ε:

דרך	(δαρχαμ O)—	קרב	(καρβαμ O)—
	δερχ O		(κερβα O)
זבד	(ζαβδει G)—(zebdi)	קשת	κασθ O—κεσθ O
חפץ	(αψει B)—(ephsi)	שמש	σαμs O—(semsi)
מלך	(malchi)—	עגלה	αγλα A—egla
	(μελχει B)		

2) change of α and o:

חפץ	(αψει B)—(οφσι A)	קרב	(καρβαμ O)—
			κορβ O

With weak 2nd radical:

3) change of *o* and *ον* (cf. paragraph XXIII sub. ן):

סוד (sodi)—(σουδι A)   צור σωρ˙ o—σουρ G

ראש ρωs G—rus

XII. TRICONSONANTAL NOUNS, WHICH APPEAR AS MONOSYLLABIC OR BISYLLABIC FORMS

§89: *Insertion of ε as second vowel:*

1) Nouns of the a–class:

גבר γαβρ o—γαβερ G   עבד αβδ G—αβεδ A

חצר ασρ B——aser   שמש σαμs o—σαμεs A

2) Nouns of the i–class:

חפץ (ephsi)—(ephesi)   עזר εζρ o—εζερ G

לתך λευχ o——lethech   קשת κεσϑ o—ceseth

רסן ρεσν o—resen

3) Nouns of the o–class

בשת βοσϑε B—boseth   חמר oμρ o—homer

חלד oλδ o—holed   קדש κοδs o—codes

§90: *Rëiteration of the vowel:*

Nouns with weak 2nd radical

1) Nouns of the a-class

בער βαρ o—βααρ o   יער ιαρ A—ιααρ B

נהר (ναρωϑ o)—νααρ o

a) feminine form:

בעלה (βαλωϑ A)—(baaloth)

2) Nouns of the i-class:

באר $\beta\eta\rho$ G—$\beta\epsilon\eta\rho$ B   רחם $\rho\epsilon\mu$ o—rehem

תחת $\vartheta\epsilon\vartheta$ o—theeth

a) feminine form:

בהמה ($\beta\eta\mu\omega\vartheta$ o)—(beemoth)

3) Nouns of the o-class

אהל ($o\lambda\iota$ A)—($oo\lambda\iota$ B)

XIII. BISYLLABIC TRICONSONANTAL NOUNS

1. WITH THE CHARACTERISTIC VOWEL IN
THE SECOND SYLLABLE (cf. paragraph XXVI b)

A. THE A–CLASS:

§91: *With a in the first syllable:*

1) ברד $\beta\alpha\rho\alpha\delta$ A   נבר $\nu\alpha\beta\alpha\rho$ o
   ברק $\beta\alpha\rho\alpha\kappa$ B   סבך sabac
   בשר basar (basari)   פגר (phagarim)
   גמל ($\gamma\alpha\mu\alpha\lambda\iota$ A)   פרץ ($\varphi\alpha\rho\alpha\sigma\epsilon\iota\mu$ A)
   דבר $\delta\alpha\beta\alpha\rho$ G (dabarach)   קטן $\kappa\alpha\tau\alpha\nu$ G
   ישן $\iota\alpha\sigma\alpha\nu$ G   שטן $\sigma\alpha\tau\alpha\nu$ G
   כזב chasab   שכר $\sigma\alpha\chi\alpha\rho$ A
   ככר chachar   שפן $\sigma\alpha\varphi\alpha\nu$ G
   כסמים (chasamim)   שרף $\sigma\alpha\rho\alpha\varphi$ A
   לבן $\lambda\alpha\beta\alpha\nu$ A   תמר $\vartheta\alpha\mu\alpha\rho$ G
   משל $\mu\alpha\sigma\alpha\lambda$ A   (thamarim)
   נבל $\nu\alpha\beta\alpha\lambda$ G   2) אבן (abanim)

אדם	αδαμ A	חצר	ασαρ A
אדם	(adamim)	עבר	(αβαρειμ G)
אטד	αταδ G	ענק	anacim
אמץ	(amasim)	עפר	αφαρ O (afara)
ארז	araz	ערב	arab
הבל	(abal, abalim)	עשן	ασαν A
המסים	(amasim)	3) זרח	ʒαρα G (ʒαραει B)
חגב	αγαβ G	פרא	phara
חכם	(αχαμιμ O)	רפאים	(raphaim)
חלק	αλακ A	שלח	σαλα A

a) feminine forms:

1) לבנה	λαβανα G	חכמה	(αχαμωθ O)
מקל	(macaloth)	חרדה	arada
נבלה	nabala	עגלה	(αγαλωθ O)
נדבה	(nadaboth)	עזרה	azara
נקמה	(νακαμωθ O)	עטרה	αταρα B
נשמה	nasama (nasamoth)		(αταρωθ G)
צדקה	sadaca	עלמה	(alamoth)
שלמה	σαλαμα G	עצרה	asara
2) אדמה	αδαμα G	ערבה	αραβα G
	(αδαμωθ O)		(αραβωθ G)
אילה	aiala (αιαλωθ O)	3) גבעה	γαβαα G (γαβααθ A; γαβαωθ B)
אנקה	ανακα O		
אשמה	(asamath)	לביא	(labaoth)
חדשה	αδασα A	צבאות	(σαβαωθ G)

b) With weak 2nd radical:

אחד	aad	יחד	ιααδ O
בעל	βααλ G (baali; βααλειμ G)	יער	ιααρ B
		להב	(laabim)
בער	βααρ O	נהר	νααρ O
דעת	daath	נחש	ναας G
זהב	zaab	נחת	naath

154

פחד‎ $\pi\alpha\alpha\delta$ G   שחר‎ $\sigma\alpha\alpha\rho$ A
צער‎ $(\sigma\alpha\alpha\delta\alpha\iota$ O)   שחת‎ $\sigma\alpha\alpha\vartheta$ O
קהל‎ $\kappa\alpha\alpha\lambda$ O   שער‎ $(\sigma\alpha\alpha\rho\epsilon\iota\mu$ O)

תחת‎ $\vartheta\alpha\alpha\vartheta$ G

c) feminine forms:

בעלה‎ $\beta\alpha\alpha\lambda\alpha$ A (baaloth)   נחמה‎ (naamathi)
צעקה‎ saaca

d) With geminated 2nd radical:

חגא‎ agga   חטא‎ $(\alpha\tau\tau\alpha\epsilon\iota\mu$ O)
כשף‎ (cassaphe)

§92: *With ϵ in the first syllable:*

1) ככר‎ $\kappa\epsilon\chi\alpha\rho$ B   שלמים‎ (selamim)
    כנף‎ chenaph   שמנים‎ (semanim)
    נכר‎ $\nu\eta\chi\alpha\rho$ O   שרף‎ seraph (seraphim)
    קסת‎ cesath   2) אנך‎ enach
        ענק‎ $\epsilon\nu\alpha\kappa$ A $(\epsilon\nu\alpha\kappa\epsilon\iota\mu$ G)

a) feminine forms:

אלם‎ (elamoth)   אמרה‎ $(\epsilon\mu\alpha\rho\alpha\vartheta$ O)
            שגגה‎ segaga

b) Tertiae ‎ח‎ and ‎ע‎:

גזע‎ geza   פשע‎ $\varphi\epsilon\sigma\alpha$ O $(\varphi\epsilon\sigma\alpha\mu$ O)
זבח‎ zeba   צמח‎ sema
זרע‎ zera   רשע‎ $\rho\epsilon\sigma\alpha$ O

§93: *With α and ϵ respectively in the first syllable:*

זרע‎ zara—zera   ככר‎ chachar—$\kappa\epsilon\chi\alpha\rho$ B
        שרף‎ saraph—seraph

B. THE I–CLASS:

1) With the vowel ε:

§94: *With a in the first syllable:*

1) גבר γαβερ G   אבן αβεν G
    גדר γαδερ A   און aven
    גור γαζερ G   אחר αερ B (αηριμ Ο)
    זבד ζαβεδ G   אצל asel
    חבר χαβερ B   הבל αβελ A
    טבח tabech   הרס ares
    יתד jathed   חצר ασερ A
    משק masec   חרב areb
    נקב νακεβ A   חרס αρες G
    סבך σαβεκ A   חרש ares
    פלג φαλεκ A   עבד αβεδ A
    פרץ φαρες A   עדר ader
    פרש phares   עצבים (ασεβειν Ο)
    קדש καδης A   ערש ares
         (καδησειμ B) 3) בקע bace
    שבר σαβερ B   זרח zare
    שכן (σαχηναυ Ο)   ירח ιαρη Ο
    שמש σαμες A   קצה κασε Ο
2) אבל αβελ G   שלח sale

a) feminine forms:

1) גדרה γαδηρα G   קדשה cadesa (cadesoth)
        (γαδηρωϑ A)   שדמה (σαδημωϑ A)
   גזרה gazera   2) אטם (atemoth)
   פליטה phaleta   חצר (ασηρωϑ G)
              מלא malea

§95: *With ε in the first syllable:*

1) בזק βεζεκ B   נזם gezem
   בטן beten   נשם gesem
   גבר geber   דבר deber

156

הרס	heres		שבר	σεβερ A
זמר	(zemeri)		שכם	σεχεμ A
חלום	helem		שמש	semes
חלק	χελεκ A (χελεκι A)		שקד	seced
חרם	herem		שקל	secel
יצר	ιεσερ B (ιεσερει B)		תבל	thebel
יתר	ιεθερ O	2)	אבל	εβελ B
לתך	lethech		אמת	ημεθ O
מלך	μελεχ B			(εμεθθαχ O)
משק	mesec		אפר	εφηρ O
נבל	nebel		חפץ	(ephesi)
נגב	negeb		חדל	edel
נזם	nezem		חלד	eled
נמר	nemer		עבר	εβερ A
נצר	neser		עדן	εδεν A
נשף	neseph		עדר	εδερ A
פרץ	pheres		עזר	εζερ G
פרק	pherec		עמק	εμεκ A
צדק	σεδεκ A		עקב	eceb
קדם	cedem	3)	בטה	bete
קרב	cereb		בצע	βεσε O
קשת	ceseth		זבח	ζεβεε G
רמש	remes		יזע	jeze
רסן	resen		מלח	μελε B
רשף	reseph		פלא	phele
	שמע	(σεμεει B)		

a) feminine forms:

לבנה	lebena	נשפה	nesepha

b) With weak 2nd radical:

באר	βεηρ B (beeri)	נעם	νεεμ G
בעל	βεελ G	רהב	reeb
לחם	λεεμ G (λεεμει A)	רחם	rehem
נחל	nehel	רעם	reem

157

c) feminine forms:

בהמה‎ (beemoth)   נחלה‎ nehela
                  (νεελαϑαχ O)

§96: *With a and ε respectively in the first syllable:*

גבר‎ γαβερ G—geber   עדר‎ ader—εδερ A
הרס‎ ares—heres   פרץ‎ φαρες A—pheres
משׁק‎ masec—mesec   שבר‎ σαβερ B—σεβερ A
         שׁמשׁ‎ σαμες A—semes

2) With the vowel ι:

§97: *With a in the first syllable:*

1) דביר‎ δαβειρ G   שׂריד‎ σαριδ A (saridim)
   חסיל‎ hasil   תמיד‎ ϑαμιδ O
   יבשׁ‎ ιαβεις G   תמים‎ ϑαμιμ O
   ימין‎ ιαμειν A   2) אביב‎ abib
   כסיל‎ chasil   אמיר‎ amir
   כפיס‎ chaphis   אסיר‎ ασειρ B
   כפיר‎ chapir   אשׁישׁי‎ (asise)
   נפילים‎ (naphilim)   חזיז‎ (azizim)
   נציב‎ νασειβ B   חסיד‎ ασιδ O (ασιδαυ O)
   נתינים‎ (ναϑινειμ A)   חריף‎ αρειφ B
   סריס‎ σαρεις A   עליל‎ αλιλ O
   פריץ‎ pharis   עמית‎ (amithi)
   צניף‎ saniph   עשׁיר‎ ασιρ O
   קדים‎ cadim   3) בריח‎ bari
   קצין‎ κασιν A   נשׂיא‎ nasi
   רכיל‎ rachil   4) יחיד‎ jaid
   שׁלישׁ‎ salis   ליש‎ λαεις B
   שׁמיר‎ σαμειρ B   מעיל‎ mail

a) feminine forms:

גלילה‎ galila (γαλιλωϑ A)   קריה‎ caria (καριαϑ G;
חסידה‎ asida   καριαϑαιμ A;
לפידות‎ (λαφειδωϑ B)   καριωϑ A)

158

§98: *With ε in the first syllable:*

1) ברית βεριϑ B   רתיק rethic
   נסיך (nesiche)   2) בכי βεχι O
   נציב νεσιβ A   חצי εσει A
                פרי pheri

a) feminine form:

גבירה gebira

§99: *With a and ε respectively in the first syllable:*

נציב νασειβ B—νεσειβ A

C. THE O–CLASS:

1) With the vowel o:

§100: *With a in the first syllable:*

1) גדול gadol   ששון σασων O
   חזון hazon   2) אדון (αδωνει B;
   כבוד χαβωδ O   αδωναι O)
   נכון ναχων A   המון αμων G (amona,
   ציון saion   amonim)
   צפון σαφων B   עגור agor
      (σαφωνει B)   ערום arom
   רזון ραζων A   עשור ασωρ O
   רצון ρασων O   3) גאון (gaon)
   שלום σαλωμ G   שאון σαων G

§101: *With ε in the first syllable:*

1) בכור bechor   אפוד ephod
   דרור deror   חמור emor
   כפור χεφορ O   3) אלוה ελω O
2) אנוש ενως A   מלוא μελω A

a) feminine forms:

בכורה   (βεχωραϑ A)   לבונה   λεβωνα G

b) With geminated 2nd radical:

חמור   εμμωρ G   מלוא   mello
כנור   χεννωρ O   רמון   ρεμμων G

c) feminine forms:

בכורה   bechchora   דבורה   δεββωρα G

2) With the vowel ου:

§102: *With a in the first syllable:*

1) זנונים (zanunim)   עגור agur
   כרוב χαρουβ B   עלומים (αλουμαυ O)
   רכוש rachus   עמוד (αμουδα O)
2) אנוש anus   3) תפוח ϑαφου B
   אשור (ασουρενου O)   4) בחור (βαουρειμ G)
   המון amun   רחום ραουμ A

a) feminine form:

ישועה   (ιασουαϑι O)

§103: *With ε in the first syllable:*

אמון (εμουνιμ O)   זבול ζεβουλ G
גבול gebul (gebulaic)   כלוב chelub
גדוד γεδουδ O   כרוב χερουβ A
גלולים (gelule)   (χερουβειμ G)
זבוב zebub   לבוש (λεβουσι O)
         שקרץ (secuse)

a) feminine forms:

אמונה emuna (εμουναϑαχ   נבורה (geburoth;
      o; emunatho)   .   γεβουρουϑαυ o)

בתולה bethula   ירושה ιερουσα A

          ישועה jesua

§104: *With a and ε respectively in the first syllable:*

כרוב   χαρουβ B—χερουβ A

2: WITH THE CHARACTERISTIC VOWEL IN THE FIRST SYLLABLE:

D. THE A–CLASS:

§105: *With a and ε respectively in the second syllable:*

חצר   ασαρ A—ασερ A   פרץ (pharasim)—
סבך   sabac—σαβεκ A   φαρες A

E. THE O-CLASS:

§106: *With a in the second syllable:*

1)   חותם   χωϑαμ A   2)   אצר   ωσαρ B
     כמר   (χωμαρειμ G)   עולם   ωλαμ o
     שופר   sophar   3)   מוטה   mota

         מוצא   μωσα o

§107: *With ε in the second syllable:*

1)   בשת   boseth   סכן   socen
    חדש   hodes   קדש   codes
    חלד   holed   שחל   sohel
    חמר   homer   תפת   thophet
    חרש   hores   2)   ארך   ορεχ A

         חנף   oneph

a) feminine form:

        עננה   onena

§108: *With o in the second syllable:*

Nouns with weak 2nd radical:

אהל	ooλ A (ooλι B)	צהר	soor
זהב	ʓooβ A	רעות	rooth
	שחל	sohol	

a) feminine forms:

גאלה	(goolathach)	רחוב	(rooboth)

3. Nouns With Varying Vocalization:

§109: *Change of o and ου (cf. paragraph XXIII sub ו):*

המן	αμων G—amun	כמר	(χωμαρειμ G)—(chumarim)
	ענור	agor—agur	

§110: *nomina tertiae* ח:

זבח	ʓεβεε G—zeba	זרח	zare—zara

XIV. NOUNS WITH PREFIXED מ

VOCALIZED AS μα (cf. ¶ XXVI c):

§111: *The a–class:*

1) מבצר	μαβσαρ A		2) מאכל	machal
	(μαβσαραυι O)		מחמד	mamad
מבשם	μαβσαμ A		3) מלקחים	(malcaim)
מגדל	μαγδαλ A		משמע	μασμα A
מגרש	magras		4) מבחר	μαβαρ A
מדבר	μαδβαρ B		מרחב	μαραβ O
מכתב	machthab		מלאך	malach, (malachi,
מספר	μασφαρ G			malache)

162

a) feminine forms:

1) ממלכה (μαμλαχωϑ o)   (μαλαμωϑ o)
   מרכבת (μαρχαβωϑ A)   מפעל (μαφαλωϑ o)
2) מחלה μαλα G   4) מרמה μαρμα A
3) מלחמה μαλαμα o   (μαρμωϑ o)
            5) מנחה μανα o

§112: *The i–class:*

With the vowel e, η:

מזבח μασβηη o   מקנה macne
מכתש machthes   מרפא marphe
ממזר mamzer   משא μασση A

a) feminine form:

מקהלה (μακηλωϑ G)

§113: *The o–class:*

1) With the vowel o, ω:

מזמור μαζμωρ o   מכאוב (μαχωβιμ o)

a) mediae ו:

מאור maor   מעוג μαωγ o
מדון μαδων A   מעוז μαοζ o (μαοζι o)
מחול μαωλ o   מעון μαων A
מנוח μανωε G   מצור μασωρ o
            מקום (macoma)

2) With the vowel ου: nomina mediae ו:

מגור magur   מנוד μανουδ o
מחול μαουλ A   מנוח manue
            מצור masur

a) feminine form:

מבוכה mabucha

XV. THE ARTICLE

THE ARTICLE IS ALWAYS TRANSLITERATED AS α (cf. ¶ XXVI d):

§114: *Before a vowel:*

1) האדם aadam   2) החגב aagab
האיש αεις O   החפץ ααφης O
האל αηλ O   החסים αωσιμ O
הארץ ααρs O   3) העיר αειρ O
העמק αεμεκ A

§115: *Before a consonant:*

הגן agan   הקטן ακαταν B
הדגים adagim   הראש αρωs A
היום αιωμ O   הרדידים ardidim
הלוחש αλωηs B   הרשעים αρσαειμ O
הסנאה ασανουα A   השדמות asademoth
הצדק asedec   השמינית ασεμινιϑ O
הקוץ ακωs B   השפתים asephathaim

§116: *With gemination of the following consonant:*

הבא αββα O   המיחלים αμμηαλιμ O
הבוטח αββωτη O   המים αμμαιμ O
הבוטחים αββωτεειμ O   המלך ammelech
הבית αββαιϑ O   המנחה αμμανα O
הגוי aggoi   הנותן αννωϑην O
הכבוד αχχαβωδ O   הנתינים ανναϑινιμ A
הכמרים acchumarim   הפרה affara
הכרובים accherubim   הקוץ ακκωs A
הלוחש αλλωηs A   הקטן ακκαταν A
הלחות alluoth   הקריות ακκαριωϑ A
המאזרני αμμααζερηνι O   השחת ασσααϑ O
השמרים ασσωμριμ O

XVI. THE INSEPARABLE PREPOSITIONS בכלם.

A. The Prepositions בכל:

§117: *Transliterated as* βα, χα, λα *respectively:*

a) Before a consonant:

1)	בבן	baben		בשמות	basemoth
	ביה	βαια o	2)	כבהמות	χαβημωϑ o
	בכעס	βαχας o		כנצר	chaneser
	בלבבם	βαλβαβαμ o		כצאן	χασων o
	בנגעים	βανγαιμ o		כשמש	χασαμς o
	בנהרות	βαναρωϑ o	3)	לבקר	λαβεκρ o
	בסוד	βασωδ A		לכל	λαχολ o
	בסופה	basupha		למלחמה	λαμαλαμα o
	בפיהם	βαφιεμ o		למשל	λαμασαλ o
	בפתחיה	baphethee		למשפטי	λαμεσφατι o
	בצום	βασωμ o		לנגד	λανεγδ o
	בציון	basaion		לצו	lasau
	בקרב	bacereb		לקו	lacau
	ברוח	barua		לרשע	λαρασα o
	ברצונך	βαρσωναχ o		לרשע	λαρεσα o
	ברצונו	βαρσωνω o		לשאול	λασωλ o

b) Before the vowel α:

1)	באפו	βααφφω o		בערב	βααρβ
	בארץ	βααρς o	2)	כאח	χαα o
	בהדרת	βααδαρεϑ o		כעפר	χααφαρ o
	בחנפי	βαανφη o	3)	לארץ	λααρς o
	בעליל	βααλιλ o		להרדי	λααραρι o
	בעם	βααμ o		לעבד	λααβδ o

c) Before the vowel ε:

באמונתך	βαεμουναϑαχ o		באש	βαες o
באמונתו	baemunatho		בעזרתי	βαεζραϑι o
		לעד	laed	

§118: *Transliterated as* βε, χε, λε *respectively:*

a) Before the vowel ε:

בחיקי   βηηκι ο   בעיר   βεειρ ο

בחסדך   βεεζδαχ ο   כאבל   χεεβλ ο

b) Before a consonant:

בגבורתו   βεγεβουροϑαυ ο   בעברות   βεγαβρωϑ ο

לבני   λεβνη ο

§119: *Transliterated merely as* β, χ, λ *respectively:*

a) Before a consonant:

בנאותו (1	βγηουαϑω ο		בקרבה	βκερβα ο
בדמי	βδαμι ο		בראשית	βρησιϑ ο
בדרך	βδερχ ο		ברב	βροβ ο
ביד	βιεδ ο		בשבט	βσαβτ ο
בידך	βιαδαχ ο		בשחק	βσακ ο
ביום	biom		בשלוי	βσαλουι ο
בכנור	βχεννωρ ο		בשמותם	βσεμωϑαμ ο
בלב	βλεβ ο		בתורת	βϑωραϑ ο
במשפטי	βμεσφατι ο		כירה (2	χιαρη ο
בסכה	βσοχχα ο		כפדד	χφαρδ ο
בסתר	βσεϑρ ο		כצדקך	χσεδκαχ ο
בצדקתך	βσεδκαϑαχ ο		כרע	χρηε ο
בצלעי	βσαλη ο		לבית (3	λβηϑ ο
בצרות	βσαρωϑ ο		למחול	λμαωλ ο
בקולו	βκωλω ο		לשטף	λσετφ ο

לשכניו   λσαχηναυ ο

b) Before a vowel:

באלהי (1	βελωαι ο		בעצת	βησαϑ ο
באלהיו	βελοαυ ο		כאילות (2	χαιαλωϑ ο
ביהוה	βαδωναι ο		כימי	χιμη ο
בימי	βιμη ο		לאחרים (3	λαηριμ ο

לעולם   λωλαμ ο

166

§120: *Transliterated as βα, with gemination of the following consonant:*

בנוים	baggoim	במרחב	βαμμαραβ o
במלחמה	βαμμαλαμα o	בפוך	baphphuch

B. The Preposition מ:

§121: *Transliterated as μ plus helping vowel ε:*

a) Before a consonant:

מבטן	mebeten	מנגד	μενεγδ o
מיד	μειεδ o	מקדם	mecedem
מים	mejam	מרחם	μηρεμ o
מכפירים	μεχφεριμ o	מרכסי	μερυχση o
ממסגרותיהם	μεμασγρωϑεειμ o	מרשת	μερεσϑ o

b) Before a vowel:

מאין	μηην o	מידיכם	μειδηχεμ o
		מעברים	meabarim

§122: *With gemination of the following consonant:*

מבית	mebbeth	ממשקה	memmasce
מבלעדי	μεββελαδη o	משאול	μεσσωλ o
מכנף	mecchenaph	משחר	μεσσααρ o
ממצרים	μεμμισραιμ o	משירי	μεσσιρι o

XVII. NOUNS WITH PERSONAL SUFFIXES

A. The Singular Noun

§123: *The suffix of the 1. pers. sing.: ει, ι, η:*

1)	אבי	αβει B		אדוני	αδωνει B
	אחי	αχει B		חני	αγγει B
	אלי	ηλει B		לחמי	λεεμει A
	אורי	ουρει B		יצרי	ιεσερει B

2) אהלי $ooλι$ B   לבושי $λεβουσι$ o

חשכי $oσχι$ o   משפטי $μεσφατι$ o

אזני $oζνι$ o   לבי $λεββι$ o

דרכי $δερχι$ o   מנני $μαγεννι$ o

יצרי $ιεσρι$ A   3) אוני oni

מלכי $μελχι$ A   חדשי odsi

נגדי $νεγδι$ o   חשקי esci

כרמי $χαρμι$ A   בשרי basari

מעוזי $μαοζι$ o   אישי issi

גמלי $γαμαλι$ G   4) נלמי $γολμη$ o

חלקי $χελεκι$ A   צלעי $σαλη$ o

רוחי $ρουη$ o

§124: The suffix of the 2. pers. sing. masc.: $αχ$
(cf. ¶ XXIX B 1), $χα$:

1) אזנך $oζναχ$ o   נחלתך $νεελαϑαχ$ o

ארחך $oραχ$ o   אמתך $εμεϑϑαχ$ o

דודך dodach   אמונתך $εμουναϑαχ$ o

עבדך $αβδαχ$ o   נאלתך goolathach

טובך $τουβαχ$ o   משיחך $μεσιαχ$ o

היכלך $ηχαλαχ$ o   2) ישעך $ιεσαχα$ o

חמתך $εμαϑαχ$ o   חכך echcha

§125: The suffix of the 3. pers. sing. masc.: $ω$, o:

אונו $ωνω$ G   כפרו $χοφρω$ o

ידו jado   אפו $αφφω$ o

דרכו $δερχω$ o   כסאו $χεσσω$ o

חסדו $εσδω$ o   ימינו $ιμινω$ o

יצרו $ιεσρο$ o   משיחו $μεσιω$ o

יתרו iethro   מנוחתו mnuatho

נזרו $νεζρω$ o   אמונתו emunatho

§126: The suffix of the 3. pers. sing. fem.: $α$:

עזרה $εζρα$ o   מקומה macoma

קדשה codsa   עמודה $αμουδα$ o

המונה amona   עפרה afara

§127: *The suffix of the 1. pers. sing.:*
ενου, ινου, ηνου:

אשורנו ασουρενου O   נפשנו νεφσινου O
                          עינגו ηνηνου O

§128: *The suffix of the 2. pers. plur. masc.:* εχεμ (cf. ¶ XXVI f 2):

לבבכם λεββαβεχεμ O   מלככם melchechem

§129: *The suffix of the 3. pers. plur. masc.:* αμ, εμ:

1) דרכם δαρχαμ O   עשרם οσραμ O
   חילם αιλαμ G   לבבם λβαβαμ O
   מלכם μελχαμ A   אונם ωναμ A
   עינם enam   פשעם φεσαμ O
              2) פיהם φιεμ O

B. THE PLURAL NOUN:

§130: *The suffix of the 1. pers. sing.:* αι:

אדוני αδωναι O   צעדי σααδαι O
אלהי ελωαι O   מצותי μσωϑαι O
איבי οιεβαι O   שפתי σφωϑαι O
ידי ιαδαι O   תחנוני ϑανουναι O

§131: *The suffix of the 2. pers. sing. masc.:* αχ (cf. on §128), cha:

1) איביך οιβαχ O   חסדיך εσδαχ O
   אלהיך ελωαχ O   עבדיך αβδαχ O
   דבריך dabarach   עיניך ηναχ O
              2) מתיך methecha

§132: *The suffix of the 2. pers. sing. fem.:* aich:

בניך benaich   גבוליך gebulaich

§133: *The suffix of the 3. pers. sing. masc.:* αυ, αυι:

1) איביו	οιβαυ ο	עלומיו	αλουμαυ ο
איליו	elau	שכניו	σαχηναυ ο
אלהיו	ελοαυ ο	גבורתיו	γεβουροθαυ ο
בניו	βαναυ ο	בדיו	baddau
עיניו	ηναυ ο	2) מבצריו	μαβσαραυι ο
מימיו	μημαυ ο	צריו	σαραυι ο
חסידיו	ασιδαυ ο	עליו	αλαυι ο

§134: *The suffix of the 2. pers. plur. masc.:* χεμ:

ידיכם ιδηχεμ ο

§135: *The suffix of the 3. pers. plur. masc.:* εμ, αμ, ημω:

1) אחריהם	αρηεμ ο	2) משכנותם	μισχνωθαμ ο
כסיליהם	chisileem	אבותם	abotham
		3) שנימו	σεννημω ο

XVIII. THE FORMATION OF THE PLURAL

§136: *Masculine forms:*

a) By adding ειμ, ιμ to the noun:

אביון	ebion—ebionim	סיג	sig—sigim
איתן	ethan—ethanim	עם	αμ G—αμιμ ο
אחר	αερ B—αηριμ ο	פר	phar—pharim
איל	el—elim	כרם	χαρμ ο—
אל	ηλ G—ηλιμ ο		χαρμειμ B
בעל	βααλ G—	קדש	καδης A—
	βααλειμ G		καδησειμ B
בריח	bari—barihim	רע	ρα ο—raim
גל	gal—γαλειμ B	שועל	σουαλ A—sualim
המון	αμων G—amonim	שטה	setta—settim
הר	αρ ο—αριμ ο	שריד	σαριδ A—saridim
טוב	τωβ G—tobim	שרף	seraph—seraphim
ים	iam—ιαμιμ ο	תמר	θαμαρ G—
כרוב	χερουβ A—χερουβειμ G		thamarim

170

ALEXANDER SPERBER

b) With gemination of the 2nd radical:

נל   gal—γαλλειμ A   נן   γαν A—γαννιμ A
      עם   αμ G—αμμιμ O

§137:   *Feminine forms: By adding* ωϑ*:*

a) The noun ending in a consonant:

אור   or—oroth   באר   βηρ G—βηρωϑ G
                      חצר   ασερ A—ασηρωϑ G

b) The noun ending in a vowel (*a*, *ε*),
      and dropping it:

אדמה	αδαμα G—	נשמה	nasama—nasamoth
	αδαμωϑ O	סכה	σοχχα O—
אילה	aiala—αιαλωϑ O		σοκχωϑ G
במה	βαμα G—βαμωϑ G	עטרה	αταρα B—
בעלה	βααλα A—baaloth		αταρωϑ G
נבעה	γαβαα G—	קדשה	cadesa—cadesoth
	γαβαωϑ B	קריה	caria—carioth
גדרה	γαδηρα G—	רמה	ραμα G—ραμωϑ G
	γαδηρωϑ A	שבועה	sabaa—sabaoth
גלילה	galila—γαλιλωϑ A	שדה	sade—sadoth
מלחמה	μαλαμα O—	שדה	sadda—saddoth
	μαλαμωϑ O	שמה	σαμα B—σαμωϑ A
מרמה	μαρμα A—	שמה	σαμμα A—
	μαρμωϑ O		σαμμωϑ B

XIX. THE CONSTRUCT STATE

A. MASCULINE FORMS:

§138:   *stat. constr. masc. sing.:*

a) Equals the absolute state:

בית	βαιϑ B	מזבח	μασβηη O
כבוד	χαβωϑ O	שלום	σαλωμ O
גאון	gaon	הבל	abal
	מנוד	μανουδ O	

171

b) With a change in the vowel:

אין $\eta\nu$ o   בית $\beta\eta\vartheta$ o

עין $\eta\nu$ A   ניא ge

§139: *stat. constr. masc. plur.* (cf. ¶ XXVI c):

1) בן $\beta\alpha\nu\eta$ A   לען $\lambda\alpha\gamma\eta$ o

   דם dame   מלך $\mu\alpha\lambda\chi\eta$ o

   פנים $\varphi\alpha\nu\eta$ o   עבד $\alpha\beta\delta\eta$ A

   שנים sane   3) ישר $\iota\sigma\rho\eta$ o

   שר sare   רנע $\rho\epsilon\gamma\eta$ o

2) דבר $\delta\alpha\beta\rho\eta$ o   4) גלולים gelule

   הבל $\alpha\beta\lambda\eta$ o   מלאך malache

   חנף $\alpha\nu\varphi\eta$ o   נסיך nesiche

                 תעלולים thalule

B. FEMININE FORMS

§140: *stat. constr. fem. sing:*

a) Monosyllabic nouns:

1) חלקה $\chi\epsilon\lambda\kappa\alpha\vartheta$ A   רמה $\rho\alpha\mu\alpha\vartheta$ A

  חרפה $\alpha\rho\varphi\alpha\vartheta$ o   תורה $\vartheta\omega\rho\alpha\vartheta$ o

  עברה ebrath   2) מאה maath

  עצה $\eta\sigma\alpha\vartheta$ o   פחה $\varphi\alpha\alpha\vartheta$ A

  רבה rabbath   רעה raath

b) Bisyllabic nouns:

אמרה $\epsilon\mu\alpha\rho\alpha\vartheta$ o   נבעה $\gamma\alpha\beta\alpha\alpha\vartheta$ A

אשמה asamath   קריה $\kappa\alpha\rho\iota\alpha\vartheta$ G

בכורה $\beta\epsilon\chi\omega\rho\alpha\vartheta$ A   הדרה $\alpha\delta\alpha\rho\epsilon\vartheta$ o

§141: *stat. constr. fem. plur:*

ארמון armanoth   ערבה $\alpha\rho\alpha\beta\omega\vartheta$ G

מפעל $\mu\alpha\varphi\alpha\lambda\omega\vartheta$ o   שדמה $\sigma\alpha\delta\eta\mu\omega\vartheta$ A

משרפת $\mu\alpha\sigma\rho\epsilon\varphi\omega\vartheta$ A   שם semoth

§142· *Dual-forms:*

מחנה manaim   קריה καριαϑαιμ A
מלקחים malcaim   קרן καρναιμ A
עין enaim   רמה ramathaim

שפה asephathaim

A HEBREW DICTIONARY

The subdivisions (a, b, c) indicate that these transliterations are evidence of different pronunciations, as dealt with in the respective paragraphs of the Grammar; for nominal forms cf. the Introduction paragraph XXVIa (classifications of מֶלֶךְ). As a rule, differences in the rendering of Hebrew consonants (cf. Introduction, paragraph XXIII) are hereby *not* considered.

א

אַב $\alpha\beta$ G in Ελιαβ, Ex. 31.6;   a b   On in Eliab ib.

אֲבִי $\alpha\beta\epsilon\iota$ B in Αβειηλ, 1 Sam. 9.1;

   $\alpha\beta\iota$ A in Αβιηλ, ib.; o Ps. 89.27;

   a b i   J in Abimelech, Gen. 20.2.

אֲבוֹתָם   a b o t h a m   J Isa. 14.21.

אב   אבת $\omega\beta\omega\vartheta$ G Num. 21.10.

אבד   יֹאבְדוּ $\iota o\beta\alpha\delta o\upsilon$ o Ps. 49.11; cf. BV Prov. 19.9: יֹאבֵד in Ms. Ec 1 for MT יֹאבַד.

אָבִיב   a b i b   J Ezek. 3.15.

אֶבְיוֹן   e b i o n   J Isa. 25.4.

   וְאֶבְיוֹן $o\upsilon\epsilon\beta\iota\omega\nu$ o Ps. 49.3.

אֶבְיוֹנִים   e b i o n i m   J Jer. 5.28.

אֲבִיּוֹנָה   a b i o n a   J Eccl. 12.5.

אָבֵל $\alpha\beta\epsilon\lambda$ G 2 Sam. 20.14;   a b e l   On in Abelsattim, Num. 33.49.

אָבַל   a) כָּאָבֵל $\chi\epsilon\epsilon\beta\lambda$ o Ps. 35.14; MT: כַּאֲבֵל; cf. BV ib. אֹבֵל in Ms. Ec l.

   b) אָבֵל $\epsilon\beta\epsilon\lambda$ B in Εβελχαρμειν, Ju. 11.33; MT: אָבֵל.

אֶבֶן   a) אֲבָנִים   a b a n i m   J Jer. 18.3; MT: אֲבָנִים.

   b) אֶבֶן $\alpha\beta\epsilon\nu$ G in Αβενεζερ, 1 Sam. 7.12;   a b e n   J Zech. 5.7.

אַבְרֵךְ   a b r e c h   J Gen. 41.43.

אַגְמוֹן   a g m o n   J Isa. 19.15.

אגן   אַגָּנוֹת   a g a n o t h   J Isa. 22.24.

אדון   אֲדֹנִי $a\delta\omega\nu\epsilon\iota$ B in $A\delta\omega\nu\epsilon\iota\rho\alpha\mu$, 1 Ki. 4.6;

     $a\delta\omega\nu\iota$ A in $A\delta\omega\nu\iota\rho\alpha\mu$, ib.; a d o n i On in Adoni-
ram, ib.

     אֲדֹנָי $a\delta\omega\nu\alpha\iota$ o Ps. 30.9.

אָדָם $a\delta a\mu$ A Gen. 3.21; o Ps. 31.20; a d a m On Gen. 3.21.

     הָאָדָם   aadam J Isa. 2.22.

אדם   אֲדָמִים   adamim J Zech. 6.2; cf. s. v. אמר.

אֲדָמָה $a\delta a\mu a$ G Deut. 29.23; MT: אֲדָמָה; a d a m a On ib.

     אֲדָמוֹת $a\delta a\mu\omega\vartheta$ o Ps. 49.12.

אהב   וָאֹהֲבֵהוּ $o\upsilon\epsilon a\beta\eta o\upsilon$ o Hos. 11.1; MT: וָאֹהֲבֵהוּ; cf. אָהֵב
Prov. 8.17; cf. B-L. §53r, u.

     אָהֲבוּ $a\beta o\upsilon$ o Ps. 31.24.

אהל   a) אָהֳלִי $o\lambda\iota$ A in $O\lambda\iota\beta a$, Ezek. 23.4; o l i On in
Olibama, Gen. 36.2; cf. in BV monosyllabic nominal
forms like: כָּאֹהֶל Cant. 1.5; בָּאֹהֶל Ps. 91.10;
בְּאָהֳלֵיהֶם Ps. 106.25 (Ms. Ecl).

     b) אֹהֶל $o o\lambda$ A 1 Chron. 3.20: OOA lege: OOΛ.

     אָהֳלִי $o o\lambda\iota$ B in $Oo\lambda\iota\beta a$, Ezek. 23.4; o o l i On in
Ooliba, ib.

אוֹי   o i J Isa. 24.16.

אוֹיֵב   a) $\omega\iota\eta\beta$ o Ps. 31.9.

     אֹיְבַי $\omega\iota\eta\beta\eta$ o Ps. 35.19: ΩHBH lege: ΩIHBH;
H-R; $\omega\epsilon\beta\eta$ cf. Thompson Face. 6 (I—E); MT: אֹיְבַי.

     אֹיְבַי $o\iota\epsilon\beta a\iota$ o Ps. 18.38; $o\iota\epsilon\beta\beta a\iota$ o Ps. 30.2.

     b) אֹיְבֶיךָ $o\iota\beta a\chi$ o Ps. 89.52.

     אֹיְבָיו $o\iota\beta a\upsilon$ o Ps. 89.43.

אוּלָם $o\upsilon\lambda a\mu$ G 1 Chron. 7.16; u l a m J Ezek. 40.24; MT:
אֵילָם.

אָוֶן   a v e n J Amos 1.5; a b e n On in Bethaben, Hos. 4.15;
for the interchange of v and b, cf. Josh. 3.10.
הַחִוִּי Codex B: $\epsilon\upsilon a\iota o\upsilon$, Codex n: $\epsilon\beta a\iota o\upsilon$ (the
Hebrew ו rendered as: υ—β); the reverse cf. ib:
וְהַיְבוּסִי Codex B: $\iota\epsilon\beta o\upsilon\sigma a\iota o\upsilon$, Codex b: $\iota\epsilon\upsilon o\upsilon\sigma a\iota o\upsilon$
(the Hebrew ב rendered as: β—υ); cf. *The Old
Testament in Greek*, edited by A. E. Brooke and
N. McLean, Vol. I, Part IV, Cambridge 1917.

אוֹן   a) $a\upsilon\nu$ B Num. 16.1; a u n On Ezek. 30.17; MT: אָוֶן;
cf. B-L., §17b'; cf. s. v. מות sub a).

אוֹנָן *a υ ν a ν* A Gen. 38.9.

b) אוֹן *ω ν* G Hos. 4.15; MT: אָן; o n On, ib.; cf. in the
PV הָאוֹן, (MdWI, p. ז, line 5), וּמֹאוֹן (ib., line 6).
אוֹנִי o n i On in Benoni, Gen 35.18.
אֹנוֹ *ω ν ω* G Neh. 7.37.
אוֹנָם *ω ν a μ* A 1 Chron. 1.40.
אוֹנָן *ω ν a ν* B 1 Chron. 1.40; MT: אוֹנָם; o n a n
On Gen. 38.9.

אוֹר o r J Isa. 31.9.
אוֹרֹת o r o t h J Isa. 26.19.

אוּר *o υ ρ* G in Cεδιουρ, Num. 1.5; u r J Isa. 31.9.
אוּרִי *o υ ρ ε ι* B 1 Chron. 2.20; *o υ ρ ι* A, ib.

אוּר יָאִיר *ι a ε ι ρ* G Deut. 3.14; i a i r On Num. 32.41.
הַאִיר *ϑ a ε ι ρ* O Ps. 18.29.

אוּן אָזְנִי *o ζ ν ι* O Ps. 49.5; o z n i On Num. 26.16.
אָזְנֶךָ *o ζ ν a χ* O Ps. 31.3.

אוֹן הַאֲזִינוּ e e z i n u J Joel 1.2.

אוּר וְתָאְזְרֵנִי *o υ ϑ ε ζ o ρ η ν ι* O Ps. 18.40; MT: וַתְּאַזְּרֵנִי.
וַתְּאַזְּרֵנִי *o υ ε ϑ a ζ ε ρ η ν ι* O Ps. 30.12; without gemination of the 2nd radical; cf. on אֲזָב.
הַמְאַזְּרֵנִי *a μ μ a a ζ ε ρ η ν ι* O Ps. 18.33; MT: הַמְא'.

אָח a) *a χ* G in Αχααβ, 2 Ki. 1.1.
אָחִי *a χ ε ι* B in Αχεινααν, 1 Sam. 25.43; *a χ ι* A in
Αχιναaμ, ib.; a c h i On in Achisamech, Ex. 31.6.

b) אָח *a* O Ps. 49.8; cf. paragraph XXIII sub ה.
בְּאָח *χ a a* O Ps. 35.14.
אָחִי a h i On in Ahihod, Num. 34.27; for the insertion
of the h between a and i, cf. paragraph X.

אָח אֹחִים o i i m J Isa. 13.21; p. 245c; o h i m J ib., p. 174E;
for the insertion of h between o and i, cf. paragraph X.

אָחַד a a d J Gen. 48.22.

אָחוּ a h u J Gen. 41.2; cf. paragraph X, and paragraph
XXIII sub ה.

אָחָז *a χ a s* B in Ιωαχαs, 2 Ki. 10.35; cf. paragraph XXIII
sub ז and ה.
a χ a ζ A in Ιωαχαζ, ib.; a c h a z On Mic. 1.1.
a a ζ A in Ααζια, 2 Ki. 14.13; a a z On 2 Ki. 15.38.

אַחַר   α ε ρ   B 1 Chron. 7.12; aher J Isa. 42.8; cf. paragraph X and XXIII sub ה.

לָאַחֲרִים   λ α η ρ ι μ   o Ps. 49.11; for the change of ε in the singular to η in the plural, see our remarks in paragraph XXVIa.

אחרי   וְאַחֲרֵיהֶם   o υ α α ρ η ε μ   o Ps. 49.14: ΟΥΔΑΡΗΕΜ, lege A pro Δ; cf. Thompson Facs. 4 and 5.

אָחַח   α α ϑ   o Ps. 89.36.

אָטָד   α τ α δ   G Gen. 50.10; a t a d   On, ib.

אטם   אֲטֻמוֹת   a t e m o t h   J Ezek. 40.16; MT: אֲטֻמוֹת.

אִי   אִיִּים   i i m   J Isa. 13.22.

אַיֵּה   α ι η   o Ps. 89.50.

אֵיל   e l   J Ezek. 40.14.

אֵלִים   e l i m   J Ezek. 40.14.

אֵלֵי   e l e   J Isa. 61.3.

אֵלוֹ   e l a u   J Ezek. 40.21.

אַיָּלָה   a i a l a   J Gen. 49.21.

כְּאַיָּלוֹת   χ α ι α λ ω ϑ   o Ps. 18.34.

אֵין   אֵין   η ν   o Ps. 32.9.

וְאֵין   o υ η ν   o Ps. 18.42.

מֵאֵין   μ η η ν   o Mal. 2.13.

אֵיפָה   e p h a   J Isa. 5.10.

אִישׁ   ε ι s   B in Ειστωβ, 2 Sam. 10.6; o Ps. 31.21; e i s   J Gen. 32.29.

ι s   A in Ιστωβ, 2 Sam. 10.6; o Ps. 92.7; i s   J Jer. 1.11. h i s   On in Histob, 2 Sam. 10.6.

הָאִישׁ   α ε ι s   o Ps. 1.1.

אִישִׁי   i s s i   J Hos. 2.18; cf. in the BV אִשִׁי 2 Sam. 14.5 in Ms. 105 JThS; the omission of the י after א necessitates a gemination of the שׁ according to the rules of the Tiberian Grammar.

אֵיתָן   a)   α ι ϑ α ν   G 1 Chron. 15.17; cf. s. v. בית and חיל sub a). b)   e t h a n   J Jer. 5.15.

אֵתָנִים   e t h a n i m   J Mic. 6.2.

אַךְ   a c h   J Jer. 32.30.

אָכֵן   α χ η ν   o Ps. 31.23.

אַל   ε λ   o Gen. 49.4; Ps. 31.2; cf. in the BV אַל 2 Sam. 1.21 in Ms. 105 JThS.

אֵל a) a l J in alechcha: אֶל־חִכְּךָ Hos. 8.1; cf. in the BV
אֵל 2 Sam. 14.8 in Ms. 105 JThS.

b) ε λ o Mal. 2.13.

וְאֶל o υ ε λ o Ps. 30.9.

אֵלַי η λ a ι o Gen. 43.23; e l a i J Isa. 21.11.

ι λ ε ι o Ps. 31.3; cf. in the BV אֵל 2 Sam. 3.8 in Ms.
105 JThS.

אֵלֶיךָ η λ a χ o Ps. 30.9.

אֵלָיו η λ a υ o Ps. 32.6.

אֵל η λ G in Αβειηλ, 1 Sam. 9.1; o Ps. 29.3; ε λ G in
Ελκανα, Ex. 6.24; e l J Isa. 9.15.

הָאֵל a η λ o Ps. 18.31.

אֵלִי η λ ε ι B in Μελλιηλει, Num. 26.45; η λ ι o Ps.
89.27; ε λ ι G in Ελιαβ, Num. 1.9; e l i On in
Eliezer, Ex. 18.4.

אֵלִים η λ ι μ o Ps. 29.1.

אֱלֹהִים ε λ ω ε ι μ o Ps. 36.2; e l o i m J Gen. 6.2.

מֵאֱלֹהִים μ η ε λ ω ε ι μ o Ps. 8.6.

אֱלֹהַי ε λ ω η o Ps. 18.47; ε λ ω ε ι o Ps. 72.15; ε λ ω ι
o Ps. 47.10; to the Hebrew ending in ־ַי, rendered
by η, ει and ι respectively, cf. paragraph XXIII
sub י.

אֱלֹהֵי ε λ ω a ι o Ps. 18.29.

וּבֵאלֹהֵי o υ β ε λ ω a ι o Ps. 18.30.

אֱלֹהֶיךָ ε λ ω a χ o Ps. 45.8; e l o a c h J Amos 4.12:
ELOAH is a misprint for: ELOACH.

בֵּאלֹהָיו β ε λ o a υ o Isa. 8.21; MT: וּבֵאלֹהָיו.

אֱלֹהֵינוּ ε λ ω η ν o υ o Ps. 18.32: ΕΛΩΝΝΟΥ lege
ΕΛΩΗΝΟΥ; cf. Thompson Facs. 5 (N—H).

אֱלוֹהַ ε λ ω o Ps. 18.32; cf. in the BV אֱלוֹהַ Job 3.23: in Ms.
Ec 1.

אֵלֶּה e l l a J Jer. 2.34.

אֵלֶּה e l a On Gen. 36.41.

אֵלָמוֹת אלם e l a m o t h J Ezek. 40.16.

אָם ε μ o Ps. 35.14.

אָם ε μ o Ps. 89.31.

אַמָּה a μ μ a G 2 Sam. 2.24 (B: AMMAN is a scribe's mistake); a m m a On ib.

אמון   אֲמוּנִים a) ε μ ο υ ν ι μ o Ps. 31.24.

        b) ε μ μ ο υ ν ε ι μ o Isa. 26.2; e m m u n i m J ib.

אֱמוּנָה   e m u n a J Jer. 5.3.

בָּאֱמוּנָתִי   β α ε μ ο υ ν ν α ϑ ι o Ps. 89.34: BAMOTNAΘI

        lege BAEMOTNAΘI.

בָּאֱמוּנָתָךְ   β α ε μ ο υ ν ν α ϑ α χ o Ps. 89.50.

בָּאֱמוּנָתוֹ   b a e m u n a t h o J Hab. 2.4.

אָמִיר   a m i r J Isa. 17.9.

אָמֵן   α μ η ν o Ps. 89.53; a m e n J Isa. 65.16.

וְאָמֵן   ο υ α μ η ν o Ps. 89.53.

אמן   נֶאֱמָן ν ε ε μ α ν o Ps. 89.38.

נֶאֱמָנָת   ν ε ε μ α ν α ϑ o Ps. 89.29.

נֶאֱמָנִים   n e e m a n i m J Isa. 17.11.

אמץ   אֲמָצִים a m a s i m J Zech. 6.3; cf. s. v. אדם.

אָמַר   α μ α ρ G in Αμαρεια, 1 Chron. 5.33.

אָמַרְתִּי   α μ α ρ ϑ ι o Ps. 30.7.

אָמְרוּ   α μ ρ ο υ o Ps. 35.21.

יֹאמְרוּ   ι ω μ ρ ο υ o Ps. 35.25.

אֹמֶר   ε μ μ η ρ G Jer. 20.1; e m m e r J ib.

אמרה   אִמְרָת ε μ α ρ α ϑ o Ps. 18.31.

אֱמָת   η μ ε ϑ o Ps. 31.6; cf. in the BV אֹמֶא Prov. 11.18 in

        Ms. Ec 1, and in the PV אֹמֶת Prov. 22.21 (MdWI,

        p. יה).

אֲמִתָּךְ   ε μ ε ϑ ϑ α χ o Ps. 30.10; on the change of η in

        ημεϑ to ε in εμεϑϑαχ, see our remarks in paragraph

        XXVIa.

אָנָּא   α ν ν α o Ps. 118.25.

אָנָּה   a n n a J Jon. 4.2.

אֱנוֹשׁ   ε ν ω s A Gen. 4.26; e n o s On ib.

אֱנוֹשׁ   a n u s J Isa. 17.11.

אֲנִי   α ν ι o Ps. 89.48.

וַאֲנִי   ο υ α ν ι o Ps. 30.7.

אֲנָךְ   e n a c h J Amos 7.7.

אָנֹכִי   α ν ω χ o Ps. 46.11.

אנקה   וַאֲנָקָה ο υ α ν α κ α o Mal. 2.13.

אָסִיר   α σ ε ι ρ B Ex. 6.4; MT: אַסִּיר; α σ η ρ A ib.; a s i r On

        ib.; cf. our note on אֱלֹהַי.

אָסָף   α σ α φ G Isa. 36.3; a s a f On ib.

וְנֶאֶסְפוּ   ο υ ν ε ε σ α φ ο υ   o Ps. 35.15: ΟΤΝЄϹϹΑΦΟΤ
      lege Є for first Ϲ; cf. s. v. אמן; cf. Thompson Facs.
      5 (Є—Ϲ).

אסר   אֲסוּרִים   a s s u r i m   J Eccl. 7.26.

אַף   α φ   o Ps. 89.28.

אַף   אַפּוֹ   a p h p h o   J Amos 1.11.
     בְּאַפּוֹ   β α α φ φ ω   o Ps. 30.6;   baaphpho   J Isa. 2.22.

אֵפוֹד   e p h o d   J Zech. 12.10.

אֶפְעֶה   e p h e e   J Isa. 59.5; the second e is probably the trans-
     literation of the ע; cf. paragraph XXIII sub ע.

אפר   בָּאֵפֶר   χ α ε φ η ρ   o Ps. 147.16.

אָצֵל   a s e l   J Zech. 14.5; cf. MT אָצַל 1 Chron. 8.37.

אָצֵל   a s e l   J Mic. 1.11.

אֹצֶר   ω σ α ρ   B 1 Chron. 1.42; MT: אֵצֶר.

אֶקְדָּח   e c d a   J Isa. 54.11.

אַרְבֶּה   a r b e   J Hos. 13.3.

אַרְבֶּה   a) o r o b b a   J Hos. 13.3.
     b) אֲרֻבּוֹת   a r o b b o t h   On 1 Ki. 4.10.

אַרְבַּע   a r b e e   On Gen. 23.2; on the second e cf. paragraph
     XXIII sub ע.

אַרְבָּעִים   α ρ β α ε ι μ   o 1 Sam. 4.18;   a r b a i m   J Jon. 3.4.

ארג   אֹרְגִים   ω ρ γ ε ι μ   G 2 Sam. 21.19.

אַרְגָּמָן   a r g a m a n   J Ezek. 27.16.

אָרֶז   a r a z   J Jer. 22.15.

ארח   אָרְחֲךָ   ο ρ α χ   o Ps. 44.19.

אֲרִי   α ρ ι   G in Αριηλ, Isa. 29.1;   a r i   J in ariel, ib.

אַרְיֵה   a) α ρ ε ι α   B 2 Ki. 15.25;   a r i a   J Isa. 21.8 (IV.,
     p. 216 A).
     b) α ρ ι ε   A 2 Ki. 15.25;   a r i e   J Isa. 21.8 (IV., p.
     305 A).

אֶרֶךְ   ο ρ ε χ   A Gen. 10.10; MT: אֶרֶךְ;   o r e c h   On ib.

אַרְמוֹן   אַרְמְנוֹת   a r m a n o t h   J Jer. 17.27; cf. B-L.§67f and
     §260'.

אֶרֶץ   α ρ s   o Ps. 35.20.
     הָאָרֶץ   a a ρ s   o Ps. 46.3; MT: אָרֶץ.
     בָּאָרֶץ   β a a ρ s   o Ps. 46.9, 11.
     לָאָרֶץ   λ a a ρ s   o Ps. 89.40, 45.

אֵשׁ   ε s   o Ps. 89.47.

בְּאֵשׁ $\beta a \epsilon \varsigma$ o Ps. 46.10.

אִשָּׁה   issa J Jer. 1.11; hissa J Gen. 2.23; cf. s. v. אִישׁ.

     נָשִׁים nasim J Isa. 3.12.

     נְשֵׁי nese J Zech. 12.12.

אשור   אֲשׁוּרֵינוּ $a \sigma o \upsilon \rho \epsilon \nu o \upsilon$ o Ps. 44.19.

אשם   וְאָשֵׁם vasam J Hab. 1.11; MT: וְאָשֵׁם; cf. in the BV
     כָּאֹשֶׁם 2 Sam. 14.13 in Ms. 105 JThS for MT כָּאֵשׁ;
     וִיבֵשׁ Job 14.11 in Ms. Ec 1 for MT וְיָבֵשׁ; כֹּבֵד Gen.
     13.2 and שֹׁלֵם ib. 15.16, both instances in Ms. Ka 2,
     for MT כָּבֵד and שָׁלֵם respectively. The spelling of
     the transliteration has to be corrected to: uasam;
     cf. paragraph XXIII sub ו.

אשמה   אֲשָׁמַת asamath J Amos 8.14.

אֲשֶׁר   a) $a \sigma \epsilon \rho$ o Ps. 1.1; aser J Isa. 2.22.
     b) $\epsilon \sigma \epsilon \rho$ o Ps. 31.8; eser J Ezek. 40.49.

אֲשֶׁר $a \sigma \eta \rho$ G Ex. 1.4; aser On ib.

אֹשְׁרֵי $\epsilon \sigma \rho \eta$ o Ps. 1.1.

אֲשִׁישֵׁי   asise J Hos. 3.1.

אֵת $\epsilon \vartheta$ o Mal. 2.13; Ps. 28.9; eth J Hab. 3.13.

     אוֹתִי $\omega \vartheta \iota$ o Ps. 31.6.

אַתָּה   a) $a \vartheta \vartheta a$ o Ps. 18.28.
     b) וְאַתָּה $o \upsilon a \vartheta$ o Ps. 89.39.

ב

בְּךָ $\beta a \chi$ o Isa. 26.3.

   בוֹ $\beta \omega$ o Ps. 18.31.

   בָּהּ βa G in Οψειβα, 2 Ki. 21.1; ba On in Ooliba,
     Ezek. 23.4.

   בָּהֶם bahem J Gen. 14.5; MT: בְּהֶם.

   בָּם $\beta a \mu$ o Ps. 49.15.

בְּאֵר   a) בְּאֵר $\beta \eta \rho$ G in Βηρσαβεε, 1 Chron. 21.2; cf. Sam.
     Gen. 24.20: הביר (MT: הבאר). ber On in Bersabee,
     ib.

   בְּאֵרֹת $\beta \eta \rho \omega \vartheta$ G Deut. 10.6; beroth On ib.

   b) בְּאֵר $\beta \epsilon \eta \rho$ B in Βεηρσαβεε, 2 Chron. 19.4.

   בְּאֵרִי beeri On Gen. 26.34.

באש   בְּאֻשִׁים busim J Isa. 5.2.

181

בַּד b a d J Zech. 12.12.

בַּדִּים b a d d i m J Ezek. 9.2.

בַּדָּיו b a d d a u J Hos. 11.6.

בהל נִבְהָל $\nu \epsilon \beta \alpha \lambda$ O Ps. 30.8.

בהלה לַבְּהָלָה l a b a l a J Isa. 65.23.

בהמה a) כַּבְּהֵמוֹת $\chi \alpha \beta \eta \mu \omega \vartheta$ O Ps. 49.13.

b) בְּהֵמוֹת b e e m o t h J Isa. 30.6.

בוא בָּא $\beta \alpha$ O Gen. 43.23.

בָּאוּ b a u J Jer. 32.29.

וְיָבוֹא $o \upsilon \iota \alpha \beta \omega$ O Isa. 26.2.

לְבוֹא $\lambda \alpha \beta \omega$ B Ju. 3.3; cf. MT Jer. 46.13: לָבוֹא.

הַבָּא $\alpha \beta \beta \alpha$ O Ps. 118.26.

בוז b u z On Gen. 22.21.

בֻּזִי $\beta o \upsilon \zeta \epsilon \iota$ G Ezek. 1.3; b u z i On ib.

בוץ b u s J Ezek. 27.16.

בּוֹר $\beta \omega \rho$ O Ps. 30.4; b o r J Jer. 6.7.

בוש וְיֵבֹשׁוּ $\iota \eta \beta \omega \sigma o \upsilon$ O Ps. 35.26.

בוּשָׁה $\beta \omega \sigma \alpha$ O Ps. 89.46.

בָּזָק $\beta \epsilon \zeta \epsilon \kappa$ B Ju. 1.4; b e z e c J Ezek. 1.14; MT: בָּזֶק.

בחור בְּחוּרִים $\beta \alpha o \upsilon \rho \epsilon \iota \mu$ G 2 Sam. 19.17; b a u r i m On ib.

בחר יִבְחַר a) $\iota \beta \alpha \alpha \rho$ B 1 Chron. 3.6: $\beta \alpha \alpha \rho$ lege $\iota \beta \alpha \alpha \rho$; haplography.

b) $\iota \epsilon \beta \alpha \alpha \rho$ A ib.

בֶּטַח b e t e J Gen. 34.25.

בֶּטַח $\beta \alpha \tau \epsilon$ O Ps. 28.7.

בָּטַחְתִּי $\beta \alpha \tau \alpha \vartheta \iota$ O Ps. 31.7.

וְהַבּוֹטֵחַ $o \upsilon \alpha \beta \beta \omega \tau \eta$ O Ps. 32.10.

הַבֹּטְחִים $\alpha \beta \beta \omega \tau \epsilon \epsilon \iota \mu$ O Ps. 49.7.

בִּטְחוּ $\beta \epsilon \tau o \upsilon$ O Isa. 26.4.

בֶּטֶן a) בֶּטֶן $\beta \alpha \tau \nu \epsilon$ A Josh. 19.25; cf. in the BV בֹּטֽנִי Prov. 31.2; בֹּטְנֵךְ Cant. 7.3 in Ms. Ec 1.

b) בֶּטֶן b e t e n On Josh. 19.25.

מִבֶּטֶן m e b e t e n J Isa. 46.3; MT: מִנִּי־בָטֶן.

בין יָבִין $\iota \alpha \beta \epsilon \iota \nu$ B Ju. 4.2; $\iota \alpha \beta \iota \nu$ O Ps. 92.7; i a b i n On Ju. 4.2.

הָבִין $\alpha \beta \iota \nu$ O Ps. 32.9.

בֵית   a) הַבַּיִת   α β β α ι ϑ   o Ps. 30.1.

בֵית   β α ι ϑ   B in Βαιϑηλ, Josh. 7.2; cf. s. v. חיל sub a).

b) בֵית   β η ϑ   A in Βηϑαυν Josh. 7.2; β ε ϑ   A in Βεϑϑ-
απφουε, Josh. 15.53; b e t h   On in Bethel, Gen. 12.8.

לְבֵית   λ β η ϑ   o Ps. 31.3.

מִבֵּית   m e b b e t h   J Amos 1.5.

בֵיתִי   b e t h i   J Gen. 15.2.

בֵיתָמוֹ   β η ϑ α μ ο υ   o Ps. 49.12; MT: בְּתֵימוֹ.

בְּכוֹר   a) β χ ω ρ   o Ps. 89.28.

b) b e c h o r   On Gen. 46.21; MT: בְּכָר.

בכורה   בְּכֹרַת   β ε χ ω ρ α ϑ   A 1 Sam. 9.1.

בְּכוּרָה   b e c h c h o r a   J Mic. 7.1.

בְּכִי   β ε χ ι   o Mal. 2.13; Ps. 30.6.

בֵּל   b e l   J Hos. 2.18.

בַּל   β α λ   o Ps. 30.7.

בלה   יִבְלוּ   ι ε β λ ο υ   o Ps. 18.46: ΙΕΒΑΟΤ lege Λ for Α.

לְבָלוֹת   λ α β α λ ω ϑ   o Ps. 49.15.

בְּלִיַּעַל   β ε λ ι α λ   o Prov. 16.27; cf. in the BV בְּלִיַּעַל ib. 6.12:
in Ms. Ec 1; b e l i a l   J Isa. 27.1.

בלם   לְבְלוֹם   λ α β λ ω μ   o Ps. 32.9.

בָּלַע   β α λ α   A Gen. 46.21; MT: בָּלַע.

בְּלְעָם   βαλααμ   G Num. 22.5; MT: בִּלְעָם;   b a l a a m
On ib.

יִבְלַע   ι ε β λ α   G in Ιεβλααμ, Ju. 1.27; i e b l a   On in
Ieblaam, 2 Ki. 9.27.

בְּלַעֲנוּהוּ   β ε λ λ ε ν ο υ ο υ   o Ps. 35.25.

בלעדי   מִבַּלְעֲדֵי   μ ε β β ε λ α δ η   o Ps. 18.32; MT: מִבַּלְעֲדֵי.

בָּמָה   β α μ α   G 1 Sam. 9.12; b a m a   On ib.

בָּמוֹת   β α μ ω ϑ   G Num. 21.19; b a m o t h   On ib.

בֵּן   a) β ε ν   A 1 Ki. 4.8; o Ps. 9.1; MT: בֵּן;   b e n   On in
Ruben, Gen. 29.32.

וּבֵן   u b e n   J Gen. 15.2.

בְּבֵן   b a b e n   J Gen. 1.1.

בָּנַיִך   b e n a i c h   J Ezek. 27.4; cf. in the PV בֹּנִי (Edelmann, p. ד, line 15); בֹּנִי Ex. 13.18 (ib., line 7).

b) לְבְנִי   λ α β α ν ι   o Hos. 11.1.

בְּנִי β α ν α ι B in Βαναιβακατ, Josh. 19.45.

β α ν η A in Βανηβαρακ, ib.; O Ps. 18.46; b a n e
On in Banebarac, Josh. 19.45.

בְּנָיו β α ν α υ O Ps. 89.31.

c) בְּנִי β ν η O Ps. 29.1.

לִבְנִי λ α β ν η O Ps. 49.1; Ps. 46.1 : ABNH lege ΛΑBNH;
λ ε β ν η O Ps. 12.9.

בנה בָּנַיִךְ ˙ b o n a i c h J Ezek. 27.4.

בַּעַל β α α λ G in Βααλβεριϑ, Ju. 9.4; b a a l On in Baal-
berith, Num. 33.7.

בַּעֲלִי b a a l i J Hos. 2.18.

בְּעָלִים β α α λ ε ι μ G 1 Sam. 7.4; b a a l i m On ib.

בעל בְּעוּלָה b u l a J Isa. 62.4.

בַּעֲלָה a) בְּעָלוֹת β α λ ω ϑ A Josh. 15.24.

b) בַּעֲלָה β α α λ α A Josh. 15.29; b a a l a On ib.

בְּעָלוֹת b a a l o t h On Josh. 15.24.

בַּעַר a) בַּעַר β α ρ O Ps. 92.7.

b) וַבָּעַר o υ β α α ρ O Ps. 49.11.

בער תִּבְעַר ϑ ε β α ρ O Ps. 89.47.

בָּצַע β ε σ ε O in μεββεσε, Ps. 30.10.

בַּקְבּוּק a) b o c b o c J Jer. 19.1.

b) β α κ β ο υ κ A Ezra 2.51.

בָּקַע b a c e J Gen. 24.22.

בֹּקֶר a) לַבֹּקֶר λ α β ε κ ρ O Ps. 49.15.

b) בֹּקֶר β ο κ ρ O Ps. 46.6.

בקר בּוֹקֵר b o c e r J Amos 7.14.

בָּר b a r J Zech. 12.12.

ברא בָּרָאתָ β α ρ α ϑ α O Ps. 89.48.

בָּרָד β α ρ α δ A Gen. 16.14; MT: בָּרָד; b a r a d On ib.

ברד בְּרָדִים b o r o d i m J Zech. 6.3.

בָּרִיחַ b a r i J Isa. 27.1.

בְּרִיחִים b a r i h i m J Isa. 43.14; cf. paragraph X and
XXIII sub ח.

בְּרִית a) β ε ρ ι ϑ B in Βααλβεριϑ, Ju. 9.4; b e r i t h On
Ju. 9.46.

b) β ρ ι ϑ O Ps. 89.40; b r i t h J Mal. 2.4.

בְּרִיתִי β ρ ι ϑ ι O Ps. 89.35.

וּברִיתִי o υ β ρ ι ϑ ι O Ps. 89.29.

בְּרִית   b o r i t h   J Jer. 2.22.

בְּרַךְ $\beta \alpha \rho \alpha \chi$ G in $B\alpha\rho\alpha\chi\iota\eta\lambda$, Job 32.2;   b a r a c h   On in Barachel, ib.

בָּרוּךְ $\beta \alpha \rho o \upsilon \chi$ G Jer. 32.12; o Ps. 118.26;   b a r u c h On Jer. 32.12.

וּבָרַךְ $o \upsilon \beta \alpha \rho \epsilon \chi$ o Ps. 28.9.

בָּרָק $\beta \alpha \rho \alpha \kappa$ B Ju. 4.6;   b a r a c   On ib.

ברר   בְּרוּרָה   b a r u r a   J Zeph. 3.9.

תִּתְבָּרָר $\vartheta \epsilon \vartheta \beta \alpha \rho \alpha \rho$ o Ps. 18.27: ΘΕΘΒΑΡΑΒ lege P for second B.

בָּשָׂר   a) b a s a r   J Ezek. 10.12.

בְּשָׂרִי   b a s a r i   J Hos. 9.12; cf. B-L. §26s'.

      b) בָּשָׂר   b o s o r   J Isa. 34.6; cf. s. v. זָכַר; cf. also the following spellings in Sam: Gen. 11.31: כלוחו (MT: בָּלָחו); ib. 18.33: שוב (MT: שָׁב); Ex. 32.25: בקומיהם (MT: בְּקָמֵיהֶם); Lev. 26.26: במשקול (MT: בְּמִשְׁקָל).

בּשֶׁת   a) $\beta o \sigma \vartheta \epsilon$ B in $I\sigma\beta o\sigma\vartheta\epsilon$, 2 Sam. 2.8.

      b) b o s e t h   On in Hisboseth, ib.

בַּת   a) b a t h   J Ezek. 45.11; Mic. 4.14.

      b) b e t h   J Isa. 5.10.

בְּתוּלָה   b e t h u l a   J Isa. 7.14.

ג

גַּאֲוָה   a) $\gamma \alpha \upsilon \alpha$ o Ps. 31.24: $\rho \alpha \upsilon \alpha$ lege γ for ρ; phonetic mistake: γ before an α and o sounded like ρ.

      b) בְּגַאֲוָתוֹ $\beta \gamma \eta o \upsilon \alpha \vartheta \omega$ o Ps. 46.4.

גאון   גָּאוֹן   g a o n   J Hos. 5.5.

נאל   יִגְאַל   a) $\iota \gamma \alpha \alpha \lambda$ B Num. 13.7: ΙΛΑΑΛ lege: ΙΓΑΑΛ; cf. Thompson Facs. 6 (Λ—Γ).

      b) $\iota \gamma \alpha \lambda$ A ib.

      c) i e g a l   On ib.

      גּוֹאֵל   g o e l   J Isa. 59.20.

נאלה   גְּאֻלָּתְךָ   g o o l a t h a c h   J Ezek. 11.15.

גַּב   a) g a b   J Ezek. 43.13.

      b) g o b   J Ezek. 16.24.

גב   גַּבִּים   g e b i m   J Isa. 10.31.

גְּבוּל   g e b u l   J Obad. 20.

גְּבוּלָיִךְ g e b u l a i c h J Ezek. 27.4: gebulaic lege -aich;
cf. paragraph XXIII sub כ.

גִּבּוֹר a) γιββωρ o Isa. 9.5; gibbor J ib.

b) גִּבּוֹרִים g e b o r i m J Isa. 13.3.

גְבוּרה גְּבוּרוֹת g e b u r o t h J Jer. 13.18; cf. in the PV נְבֹוּלֹתֲךָ
Ps. 71.18 (MdWII, p. 86).

בִּגְבוּרֹתָיו βεγεβουροθαυ o Ps. 150.2.

גְּבִירָה g e b i r a J Jer. 13.18.

גִּבְעָה γαβαα G Josh. 15.57; gabaa On 1 Sam. 10.26.

גִּבְעַת γαβααθ A Josh. 18.28; gabaath On Josh.
24.33.

גִּבְעוֹת γαβαωθ B Josh. 18.28; MT: גִּבְעָת.

גֶּבֶר a) גֶּבֶר γαβρ o Ps. 89.49.

גַּבְרִי‎ γαβρι G in Γαβριηλ, Dan. 8.16.

b) גֶּבֶר g e b e r J Isa. 22.17.

c) גֶּבֶר γαβερ G Num. 33.35.

גֶּבֶר γαβρ o Ps. 18.26.

גְּדוּד γεδουδ o Ps. 18.30; g e d u d J Mic. 4.14.

גָּדוֹל g a d o l J Jon. 2.1.

גְּדוּפָה g e d d u p h a J Ezek. 5.15.

גדל יְגַדֵּל ιεγδελ o Ps. 35.27.

גַּדֵּל γεδδηλ A Ezra 2.47.

גְּדַלְתִּי γεδδελθι A 1 Chron. 25.29.

הַמַּגְדִּילִים [αμ]μαγδιλιμ o Ps. 35.26.

גָּדֵר γαδερ A Josh. 12.13; MT: גָּדֵר; g a d e r J Ezek. 42.7.

גדר גָּדֵר g o d e r J Isa. 58.12.

גְּדֵרָה a) γαδηρα G Josh. 15.36; g a d e r a On ib.

גְּדֵרוֹת γαδηρωθ A Josh. 15.41; gaderoth On ib.

b) גְּדֵרֹתָיו γαδρωθαυ o Ps. 89.41: ΓΑΔΡΩΘΑC,
lege Υ for C.

גהר וַיִּגְהַר ουιεγαρ o 2 Ki. 4.35.

גּוֹי γωι o Isa. 26.2; g o i J Zeph. 2.5.

הַגּוֹי aggoi J Mal. 3.9.

גּוֹיִם γωειμ A Josh. 12.23; γωιμ o Ps. 46.7.

בַּגּוֹיִם b a g g o i m J Hab. 1.5.

גור יָגוּר ιαγουρ A Josh. 15.21; i a g u r On ib.

גָּר g a r J Zeph. 2.5.

גזז גֹּזִי g o z i J Amos 7.1; MT: גִּזִּי; cf. Ps. 71.6.

186

גֶּזֶם g e z e m ʝ Joel 1.4; MT: גֶּזָם.

גֵּזַע g e z a ʝ Isa. 11.1.

גֶּזֶר γ α ζ ε ρ G Josh. 12.12; g a z e r On ib.

גְּזֵרָה g a z e r a ʝ Ezek. 42.10.

גַּיְא γ α ι G Deut. 34.6; g a i On ib.

גֵּיְא g e ʝ Isa. 28.1.

גִיל אֲגִילָה α γ ι λ α o Ps. 31.8.

וְגִילוּ o υ γ ι λ o υ o Ps. 32.11.

גַּל g a l ʝ Gen. 31.46.

גַּלִּים a) γ α λ ε ι μ B Isa. 10.30.

b) γ α λ λ ε ι μ A ib.; g a l l i m ʝ ib.

גַּלְגַּל γ ε λ γ ε λ G Ezek. 10.13; g e l g e l ʝ ib.; cf. MT: גַּלְגַּל
Isa. 28.28 and וְגִלְגָּלָיו ib. 5.28.

גלולים גִּלּוּלַי g e l u l e ʝ Ezek. 20.7.

גְּלִילָה g a l i l a ʝ Ezek. 47.8; cf. MT: גְּלִילָה 2 Ki. 15.29.

גְּלִילוֹת γ α λ ι λ ω ϑ A Josh. 22.10; B Josh. 18.17:
ΓΑΛΙΑΩΘ lege Λ for the second A; g a l i l o t h
ʝ Joel 4.4.

גלם גָּלְמִי γ o λ μ η o Ps. 92.7.

גַּם γ α μ o Ps. 49.3.

גמל גְּמַלִּי γ α μ α λ ι A Num. 13.12; cf. B-L. §24g; B ib.:
ΓΑΜΑΙ lege ΓΑΜΑΛΙ.

גמל גָּמוּל γ α μ o υ λ B 1 Chron. 24.17.

גַּן γ α ν A in Βαιατγαν, 2 Ki. 9.27; g a n ʝ Gen. 2.2.
הַגַּן a g a n On in Bethagan, 2 Ki. 9.27.

גַּנִּים γ α ν ν ι μ A in Ηγαννιμ, Josh. 19.21; g a n n i m
On in Engannim, ib.

גֵּר γ η ρ G in Γηρσαμ, Ex. 2.22; g e r On in Gersom, ib.

גרז נִגְרַזְתִּי ν ε γ ρ ε σ ϑ ι o Ps. 31.23.

גֶּשֶׁם g e s e m ʝ Zech. 14.17.

גַּת γ ε ϑ G 1 Sam. 6.17; g e t h On Josh. 11.22; cf. B-L.
§14c'.

ד

דֹּאֵג רֹאֶג δ ω η γ A 1 Sam. 22.9; δ ω η κ B ib.; d o e c On ib.

דְּבִיר δ α β ε ι ρ G Josh. 11.21; δ α β ι ρ o Ps. 28.2; d a b i r
On Josh. 11.21.

דְּבוֹרָה δ ε β β ω ρ α G Ju. 4.4; d e b b o r a On ib.

דְּבָר a) דִּבְרִי δαβρη ο Ps. 35.20; d a b r e J in Dabre-
jamim, 1 Chron. 1.1.

b) דְּבָר δαβαρ G in Λωδαβαρ, 2 Sam. 17.27; d a b a r
On in Lodabar, ib.

דְּבָרִיךְ d a b a r a c h J Hos. 13.14; cf. B-L. §2 w and
§26 c'.

דבר יְדַבֵּר ιδαββερ ο Ps. 49.4; i d a b b e r J Isa. 32.6.

וַיְדַבֵּר ουιεδαββερ ο Ps. 18.48; MT: וַיְדַבֵּר.

יְדַבְּרוּ ιδαββηρου ο Ps. 35.20.

דֶּבֶר d e b e r J Hab. 3.4.

דַּבָּשֶׁת d a b b a s t h On Josh. 19.11; cf. similarly in the PV
וּדְבַשׁ Deut. 26.15 (MdWI, p. ז); cf. also s. v. חרשת.

דָּג d a g J Jon. 2.1.

הַדָּגִים a d a g i m J Zeph. 1.10.

דּדִים d o d i m J Ezek. 16.8.

דוד דּוֹדִי d o d i J Jer. 32.8.

דֹּדְךָ d o d a c h J Jer. 32.7.

דון דָּן δαν A Gen. 14.14; d a n On ib.

דוֹר δωρ G in Αελδωρ, 1 Sam. 28.7; d o r On in Aendor, ib.

לְדוֹר λδωρ ο Ps. 49.12: ΑΔΩΡ lege ΛΔΩΡ (Λ for A)
or ΛΑΔΩΡ (Λ before A, haplography).

וְדוֹר ουαδωρ ο Ps. 49.12; cf. in the PV זְדוֹר (Bar,
p. 22).

דיה דִּיּוֹת d a j o t h J Isa. 34.15.

דלנ אֶדְלָנ εδαλλεγ ο Ps. 18.30.

דלה דְּלִיתָנִי δελλιθανη ο Ps. 30.2.

דלף יִדְלֹף ιεδλαφ A Gen. 22.22: ΙΕΛΔΑΦ lege: ΙΕΔΛΑΦ;
cf. in the BV יִדְלֹף Eccl. 10.18 in Ms. Ec 1; i e d l a f
On Gen. 22.22.

דם בְּדָמִי βδαμι ο Ps. 30.10.

דְּמִי d a m e J Isa. 38.10; MT: דְּמִי.

דמה דְּמִּינוּ δεμμηνου ο Ps. 48.10.

נִדְמוּ νεδμου ο Ps. 49.13.

דמם דַּמּוּ δαμμου ο Ps. 35.15.

יֵדֹם ιαδομ ο Ps. 30.13; MT: יִדֹּם.

דִּקְעָה δεμα ο Mal. 2.13.

דֵּעָה d e a J Isa. 28.9.

דַּעַת d a a t h J Eccl. 8.6.

דק   d o c ɪ Isa. 40.22.

דקר   דָּקְרוּ d a c a r u ɪ Zech. 12.10.

דְּרוֹר   d e r o r ɪ Ezek. 46.17.

דֶּרֶךְ   a) דֶּרֶךְ δ ϵ ρ χ o Ps. 89.42.

        בְּדֶרֶךְ β δ ϵ ρ χ o Ps. 32.8.

        דַּרְכִּי δ ϵ ρ χ ι o ·Ps. 18.33; cf. in the BV דרכם Prov. 1.31; דרכֹּי ib. 3.17: in Ms. Ec 1.

        דַּרְכּוֹ δ ϵ ρ χ ω o Ps. 18.31; cf. in the BV דרכֹו Prov. 11.5: in Ms. Ec 1.

        b) דַּרְכָּם δ α ρ χ α μ o Ps. 49.14.

דרש   דְּרוּשָׁה d r u s a ɪ Isa. 62.12.

ה

הָאָח   α α o Ps. 35.21.

הבל   a) הַבְלִי α β λ η o Ps. 31.7.

        b) הֶבֶל a b a l ɪ Eccl. 1.2; cf. in the BV הֶבֶל ib. in Ms. Ec 1.

        הֲבָלִים a b a l i m ɪ Eccl. 1.2.

        c) הֶבֶל α β ϵ λ A Gen. 4.2; a b e l On ib.

הגה   תֶּהְגֶּה ϑ α α γ ϵ o Ps. 35.28: ΘΑΑΓϹ, lege Є for C.

הגיון   a) ϵ γ α ω ν o Ps. 92.4: ΕΙΑΩΝ lege Γ for I; cf. Thompson Facs. 3.

        b) ϵ γ γ α ω ν o Ps. 9.17.

הגית   וְהָגִית o υ α γ ι ϑ o Ps. 49.4; ᴍᴛ: וְהָגוּת.

הד   a d ɪ in adarim, Ezek. 7.7.

הדרה   בְּהַדְרַת β α α δ α ρ ϵ ϑ o Ps. 29.2.

הוא   o υ o Ps. 18.31; h u On Ex. 16.15 s. v. man.

הוד   ω δ A 1 Chron. 8.6; ᴍᴛ: אֵחוּד; h o d ɪ Zech. 6.13.

הוי   o i ɪ Isa. 29.1.

הָיָה   α ϵ α o Ps. 89.42; h a j a ɪ Zeph. 3.18.

        הָיִיתִי α ι ϑ ι o Ps. 30.8.

        יִהְיֶה ι ϵ ι ϵ o Ps. 89.37; cf. in the PV יהׂ: Ps. 69.23; חהׂי ib., 26 (MdWII, p. 84).

        תֶּהֱיוּ ϑ o υ o Ps. 32.9.

        הָיָה α ι η o Ps. 30.11.

היכל   הֵיכָלֶךָ η χ α λ α χ o Ps. 48.10.

הילל   e l i l ɪ Isa. 14.12.

הִין   h i n ɪ Ezek. 4.11.

189

הָלַךְ α λ α χ o Ps. 1.1.

תֵּלֵךְ ϑ η λ η χ o Ps. 32.8.

לְכוּ λ χ ο υ o Ps. 46.9.

יְהַלְכוּן ι α λ λ η χ ο υ ν o Ps. 89.31; MT: יְלַכוּן.

הִתְהַלָּכְתִּי ε ϑ α λ λ α χ ϑ ι o Ps. 35.14.

הלל הַלֵּל ε λ λ η λ B Ju. 12.13.

יְהַלֵּל ι α λ λ ε λ A in Ιαλλελ ηλ, 1 Chron. 4.16.

אֲהַלְלָה ε ε λ λ ε λ ε χ o Ps. 35.18: ϹΕΛΛΕΛΕΧ, lege Ε for Ϲ; cf. Thompson Facs. 5.

הַלְלוּ a l l e l u J in alleluia, Isa. 26.4.

מְהוֹלָל m o l a l J Eccl. 2.2.

יְתְהַלְלוּ ι ϑ α λ λ α λ ο υ o Ps. 49.7.

הֵם ε μ o Ps. 9.7; MT: הֵמָּה.

המה הָמוּ α μ ο υ o Ps. 46.7.

יֶהֱמוּ ι ε ε μ ο υ o Ps. 46.6.

הֹמָה h o m a J Jer. 4.19; MT: הֹמֶה.

הָמוֹן a) a m u n J Isa. 33.3.

b) α μ ω ν G in Βεεϑλαμων, Cant. 8.11.

הֲמוֹנָהּ a m o n a J Ezek. 7.13.

הֲמֹנִים a m o n i m J Joel 4.14.

הַמָּסִים a m a s i m J Isa. 64.1.

הֲפֵךְ הָפַכְתָּ α φ α χ ϑ o Ps. 30.12.

הר α ρ A in Αρσαφαρ, Num. 33.23; o Ps. 48.3.

הָרִים α ρ ι μ o Ps. 46.3; a r i m J Amos 4.13.

לְהַרְרֵי λ α α ρ α ρ ι o Ps. 30.8.

הָרֵס a) a r e s J Isa. 19.18.

b) h e r e s J Isa. 24.23.

ז

וְאֵב ζ η β G Ju. 7.25; z e b On ib.

זֹאת ζ ω ϑ o Ps. 49. 2.

וְזֹאת ο υ ζ ω ϑ o Mal. 2.13.

זבד a) וַבְדִּי ζ α β δ ε ι. G 1 Chron. 8.19; z a b d i On Josh. 7.1.

b) וַבְדִּי z e b d i On Josh. 7.1.

c) וָבָד ζ α β ε δ G 1 Chron. 2.36; MT: וְבָד.

זבד זְבוּד a) ζαβουϑ B 1 Ki. 4.5.

    b) ζαββουϑ A ib.

זבוב z e b u b On in Baalzebub, 2·Ki. 1.2.

זבול ζεβουλ G Ju. 9.28; z e b u l On ib.

זבח a) ζεβεε G Ju. 8.5; the last ε is the transliteration
    of the ח; cf. paragraph XXIII sub ח; cf. in the
    PV זֹבֵח (Bar. p. 20).

    b) z e b a J Ezek. 46.20.

זבל יִזְבְּלֵנִי i e z b u l e n i J Gen. 30.20.

זה ζε o Ps. 49.14.

זהב a) ζοοβ A in Μεζοοβ, Gen. 36.39.

    b) z a a b On in Mezaab, ib.

זהר z o r J Ezek. 8.2.

זו a) ζου o Ps. 32.8.

    b) z o J Hag. 1.1.

זיז יִזְ ιαζειζ B 1 Chron. 27.31.

זולתי ζουλαϑι o Ps. 18.32.

זחל זֹחֶלֶת ζωελεϑ A 1 Ki. 1.9; z o e l e t h On ib.

זיז z i z J Isa. 66.11.

זכר z o c h o r J Isa. 26.14; cf. s. v. בָּשָׂר sub b).

זכר a) לְזַכֶּר λζεχρ o Ps. 30.5: ΑΖΕΧΡ lege ΛΖΕΧΡ or
    ΛΑΖΕΧΡ.

    זִכְרִי ζεχρει B Ex. 6.21; z e c h r i On ib.

    b) זָכַר z a c h a r J Isa. 26.14.

זכר ζαχαρ A in Ιωζαχαρ, 2 Ki. 12.22; zachar On in
    Iozachar, ib.

    אֶזְכֹּר ηζχορ o Ps. 89.51; MT: זְכֹר.

    זְכֹר ζχορ o Ps. 89.48.

זמה ζεμμα B 1 Chron. 6.5; z e m m a J Ezek. 16.27.

זמר a) זִמְרִי ζαμβρει B Num. 25.14; the Septuagint
    frequently renders the letters מר by μβρ; f. i.:
    Gen. 46.13: שמרן ζαμβραμ; Ex. 6.18: עמרם αμβραμ;
    Num. 32.3: נמרה ναμβρα.

    ζαμβρι A Num. 25.14.

    z a m r i On ib.

    b) זְמְרִי z e m e r i On Num. 25.14.

זמר זַמְּרָךְ ιζαμμερεχ o Ps. 30.13.

    זַמְּרוּ ζωημερου o Ps. 30.5.

זמרה   זְמְרת z e m r o t h J Isa. 24.16; MT: זִמְרָת; cf. the relation
of MT בְּנִקְרַת in Ex. 33.22 to the form בנקירות in
the Sam; Gen 4.23; MT: אָמְרָתִי and Sam. אמירתי.

זְנוּנִים   z a n u n i m J Hos 1.2.

זנח   זָנַחְתָּ ζ a ν a ϑ O Ps. 89.39.

זָנוֹחַ ζ a ν ω A Josh 15.34; z a n o e On ib.; cf. paragraph XXIII sub ה.

זְעֵיר   z e r J Isa. 28.10.

זרח   a) ζ a ρ a G Num. 26.20.

זַרְחִי ζ a ρ a ε ι B Num. 26.20; ζ a ρ a ι A ib.

b) זְרַח z a r e On Num. 26.20.

זרח   ζ a ρ a A 1 Chron. 6.6; z a r a On Gen. 36.13.

ζ a ρ a ε A 1 Chron. 4.24; cf. paragraph XXIII sub ה.

ζ a ρ ε B in Ζαρεια, Ezra 8.4.

יִזְרַח ι ε σ ρ α ε B 1 Chron. 27.8: ECPAE lege IECPAE,
haplo.; cf. Thompson Facs. 6 (I—E); also ¶ XXIII
sub ה.

זַרְע   a) z e r a J Isa. 1.4.

b) z a r a J Ezek. 31.17.

זַרְעוֹ ζ a ρ ω O Ps. 89.30.

זרע   יִזְרַע a) ι σ ρ a B in Ισραηλ, 1 Sam. 29.1.

ι ζ ρ a A in Ιζραηλ A, ib.

b) ι ε ζ ρ a A in Ιεζραελ, Josh. 17.16; i e z r a On
in Iezrahel, ib.

•   זְרוּעֹתָי ζ ε ρ ο υ ω ϑ a ι O Ps. 18.35; MT: זְרוֹעֹתַי.

ח

חבל   יַחְבָּל ι ε β a λ O Ps. 7.15; MT: יְחַבָּל.

חָבֶר   χ a β ε ρ B Ju. 4.11; c h a b e r On Gen. 46.17.

a β ε ρ A 1 Chron. 4.18; a b e r On Num. 26.45; MT: חֶבֶר.

חבר   חָבוֹר a β ω ρ G 2 Ki. 17.6.

חג   חַגִּי a γ γ ε ι B Num. 26.15; a γ γ ι A ib.; a g g i On ib.

חָנָא   a g g a J Isa. 19.17.

חָנָב   a γ a β G Ezra 2.46.

הֶחָנָב a a g a b J Eccl. 12.5.

חד   חַדָּה a δ δ a A in Ηναδδα, Josh. 19.21; a d d a On in
Enadda, ib.

חָדֵל   e d e l ʝ Isa. 38.11.

חדל   יֶחְדָּל $\iota \epsilon \delta a \lambda$ o Ps. 49.9; мт: וְחָדָל.

     חֶדְלוּ h e d a l u ʝ Isa. 2.22; with retention of the 2nd vowel (against B-L. §26 d'').

חדש   חֲדָשָׁה $a \delta a \sigma a$ A Josh. 15.37; a d a s a On ib.

חֹדֶשׁ   a) h o d e s ʝ Hos. 4.6.

     b) חָדְשֵׁי o d s i On 2 Sam. 24.6.

חוֹבָה   c h o b a On Gen. 14.15.

חוּל $o \upsilon \lambda$ A Gen. 10.23; u l On ib.

חוֹמָה   h o m a ʝ Isa. 24.23.

חוֹתָם $\chi \omega \vartheta a \mu$ A 1 Chron. 7.32.

חָזֶה $a \zeta a$ G in Aζαηλ, 1 Ki. 19.15; a z a On in Azahel, ib.

     חֲזוּ $\epsilon \epsilon \zeta o \upsilon$ o Ps. 46.9; cf. paragraph XXIII sub ח.

חָזוֹן   h a z o n ʝ Hab. 2.2.

חִזָּיוֹן   e z z a h o n On 1 Ki. 15.18; мт: חֶזְיוֹן.

חזיי   חָזִיזִים a z i z i m ʝ Zech. 10.1.

חזק   חֲזַק $\epsilon \zeta a \kappa$ o Ps. 31.25: εζαχ lege εζακ; мт: חִזְקוּ. The ϵ may be considered as a transliteration of the ח; cf. paragraph XXIII sub ח; or otherwise cf. in the BV the corresponding vocalization with א in forms like אֵזֹר Job 38.3 in Ms. Ec 5; אֹמֹר Ezek. 33.10 in Ms. Eb 10.

     הֶחָזָק $\epsilon \epsilon \zeta \epsilon \kappa$ o Ps. 35.2.

חטא   חַטָּאִים $a \tau \tau a \epsilon \iota \mu$ o Ps. 1.1.

חַטָּאת   a t t a t h ʝ Gen. 4.7; h a t a t h ʝ ib. (editio Lagarde).

חַי $a \iota$ o Ps. 18.47.

חידה   חִידָתִי $\iota \delta a \vartheta \iota$ o Ps. 49.5.

חיה   יְחָיֶה $\iota \epsilon \iota \epsilon$ o Ps. 89.37.

     יִחְיוּ j e j u ʝ Isa. 26.19.

     חִיתָנִי $\iota \iota \vartheta a \nu \iota$ o Ps. 30.4: ιϑανι lege ιιϑανι.

     חָיֵיהוּ h e i e u ʝ Hab. 3.2.

חַיִל   a) $\chi a \iota \lambda$ G in Aβειχαιλ, Num. 3.35.

     $a \iota \lambda$ o Ps. 18.40.

     חֵילָם $a \iota \lambda a \mu$ G 2 Sam. 10.16; cf. s. v. איתן sub a).

     b) חֵילָם $\eta \lambda a \mu$ o Ps. 49.7; cf. мт: בְּחֵיל 2 Ki. 18.17.

חַיִּים $a \iota \iota \mu$ o Ps. 30.6.

חַיִץ   h i s ʝ Ezek. 13.10.

חֵיק   חֵיקִי $\eta \kappa \iota$ o Ps. 35.13.

בְּחֻקָּי $\beta \eta \eta \kappa \iota$ o Ps. 89.51.

חך חִכְּךְ echcha J in alechcha, Hos. 8.1.

חכם חֲכָמִים $\alpha \chi \alpha \mu \iota \mu$ o Ps. 49.11.

חכמה חָכְמוֹת $\alpha \chi \alpha \mu \omega \vartheta$ o Ps. 49.4; MT: חָכְמוֹת.

חָלֶד eled J Isa. 38.11.

חֶלֶד a) o $\lambda \delta$ o Ps. 49.2; MT: חָלֶד.
b) holed J Isa. 38.11.

חלה בַּחֲלוֹתָם $\beta \alpha \alpha \lambda \omega \vartheta \alpha \mu$ o Ps. 35.13.

חָלוֹם helem J Zech. 6.10.

חָלְי oli On Josh. 19.25; MT: חָלִי.

חלל חִלַּלְתָּ $\epsilon \lambda \lambda \epsilon \lambda \vartheta$ o Ps. 89.40.
אֲחַלֵּל $\alpha \alpha \lambda \lambda \epsilon \lambda$ o Ps. 89.35.
יְחַלְּלוּ $\iota \alpha \lambda \lambda \eta \lambda o \upsilon$ o Ps. 89.32.

חלם בְּחֲלֹמִים $\chi \alpha \omega \lambda \epsilon \mu \iota \mu$ o Ps. 126.1.

חלץ חֲלָצָי eluse J Isa. 15.4.

חָלָק $\alpha \lambda \alpha \kappa$ A Josh. 11.17; alac On ib.

חֵלֶק $\chi \epsilon \lambda \epsilon \kappa$ A Num. 26.30.
חֶלְקִי $\chi \epsilon \lambda \epsilon \kappa \iota$ A ib.
חֵלֶק elec On Josh. 17.2.

חלק הַחֲלִיק $\epsilon \epsilon \lambda \iota \kappa$ o Ps. 36.3; cf. paragraph XXIII sub ח.

חלקה חֶלְקַת $\chi \epsilon \lambda \kappa \alpha \vartheta$ A Josh. 19.25.
elcath On ib.

חָם $\chi \alpha \mu$ A Gen. 10.1; cham On ib.

חַמָּה hamma J Isa. 24.23.

חמה a) חֲמָתְךָ $\epsilon \mu \alpha \vartheta \alpha \chi$ o Ps. 89.47.
b) חֲמָתִי $\alpha \mu \alpha \vartheta \iota$ A Gen. 10.18; amathi On ib.

חָמוֹר $\epsilon \mu \mu \omega \rho$ G Ju. 9.28; cf. in the BV לַחֲמֹרֹינוּ Ju. 19.19; וַחֲמֹרִים 1 Sam. 27.9 in Ms. 105 JThS; this vocalization (ﬣ) would imply a gemination of the following מ according to the rules of the Masoretic Grammar; cf. MTK, p. 27.
emor On Gen. 33.19.

חמל חָמוּל amul On Gen. 46.12.

חֹמֶר a) וְחֹמֶר $o \upsilon o \mu \rho$ o Hos. 3.2.
חמר b) חֹמֶר omer J Hos. 3.2.
homer J Ezek. 45.13.

חמר יַחְמְרוּ $\iota \epsilon \mu \rho o \upsilon$ o Ps. 46.6.

חֵן hen J Jer. 31.2.

חָנָה   h a n a   J Isa. 29.1.

חֲנִית $a\,\nu\,\iota\,\vartheta$ o Ps. 46.10.

חִנָּם $\epsilon\,\nu\,\nu\,a\,\mu$ o Ps. 35.19.

חָנָן $a\,\nu\,a\,\nu$ G in $E\lambda\epsilon a\nu a\nu$, 2 Sam. 21.19; a n a n On in Elianan, ib.

חָנוּן $a\,\nu\,o\,\upsilon\,\nu$ G Neh. 3.13.

אֶתְחַנָּן $\epsilon\,\vartheta\,a\,\nu\,\nu\,a\,\nu$ o Ps. 30.9.

בְּחַנְפֵּי $\beta\,a\,a\,\nu\,\varphi\,\eta$ o Ps. 35.16.   חנף

o n e p h   J Isa. 32.6.   חֹנֶף

חֶסֶד $\epsilon\,\sigma\,\delta$ A 1 Ki. 4.10; o Ps. 32.10.

חַסְדִּי $\epsilon\,\sigma\,\delta\,\iota$ o Ps. 89.29; cf. in the BV חֹסְדִי Ps. 107.43 in Ms. Ec 1.

בְּחַסְדְּךָ $\beta\,\epsilon\,\epsilon\,\zeta\,\delta\,a\,\chi$ o Ps. 31.8; H-R: $\beta\epsilon\epsilon\lambda\delta a\chi$.

חַסְדּוֹ $\epsilon\,\sigma\,\delta\,\omega$ o Ps. 31.22; cf. in the BV חֹסְדוֹ Ps. 100.5 in Ms. Ec 1.

חֲסָדֶיךָ $\epsilon\,\sigma\,\delta\,a\,\chi$ o Ps. 89.50.

חָסִיתִי $a\,\sigma\,\iota\,\vartheta\,\iota$ o Ps. 31.2.   חסה

הַחֹסִים $a\,\omega\,\sigma\,\iota\,\mu$ o Ps. 18.31.

לַחֹסִים $\lambda\,a\,\omega\,\sigma\,\iota\,\mu$ o Ps. 31.20.

חָסִיד $a\,\sigma\,\iota\,\delta$ o Ps. 18.26.

חֲסִידָיו $a\,\sigma\,\iota\,\delta\,a\,\nu$ o Ps. 31.24.

חֲסִידָה   a s i d a   J Jer. 8.7.

חָסִיל   h a s i l   J Joel 1 .4.

חֻפָּה $\chi\,o\,\varphi\,\varphi\,a$ B in $O\chi\chi o\varphi\varphi a$, 1 Chron. 24.13.

$o\,\varphi\,\varphi\,a$ A ib.

בְּחָפְזִי $\beta\,a\,a\,\varphi\,\zeta\,\iota$ o Ps. 31.23.   חפז

חָפְצִי   a) $a\,\psi\,\epsilon\,\iota$ B in $A\psi\epsilon\iota\beta a$, 2 Ki. 21.1.   חפץ

b) $o\,\varphi\,\sigma\,\iota$ A in $O\varphi\sigma\iota\beta a$ ib.

c) e p h s i   J Isa. 62.4; e b s i On in Ebsiba, 2 Ki. 21.1.

d) e p h e s i   J in epesiba lege ephesiba, Isa. 62.4.

הֶחָפֵץ $a\,a\,\varphi\,\eta\,s$ o Ps. 35.27: $A\Lambda\Phi HC$ lege A for Λ חפץ

הֹפְצֵי $\omega\,\varphi\,\sigma\,\eta$ o Ps. 35.27; MT: חֲפֵצֵי.

וְיַחְפְּרוּ $o\,\upsilon\,\iota\,\varphi\,\rho\,o\,\upsilon$ o Ps. 35.26; cf. in the BV וִיחֹפְרוּ   חפר Ps. 35.4 in Ms. Ec 1.

חֲפַרְפָּרוֹת   p h a r p h a r o t h   J Isa. 2.20.   חפר

חָצִי $\epsilon\,\sigma\,\epsilon\,\iota$ A 1 Chron. 2.52.   חצי

חָצֵר a) α σ ρ B in Αρσεναειμ lege Ασρεναειμ, Num. 34.9.

b) α σ α ρ A in Ασαρμωϑ, Gen. 10.26; a s a r On in
Asarmoth, ib.

c) α σ ε ρ A in Ασερναιν, Num. 34.9; a s e r On in
Asergadda, Josh. 15.27.

חֲצֵרוֹת α σ η ρ ω ϑ G Num. 11.35; a s e r o t h On ib.

חָרֵב a r e b J Zech. 13.7.

h a r e b J Zeph. 2.14; Hag.1.11; MT: חֹרֶב.

חרב חוֹרֵב χ ω ρ η β G Ex. 3.1.

o r e b On ib.

חרבה חָרְבוֹת α ρ β ω ϑ O Ps. 9.7; MT: חֳרָבוֹת.

חרג וַיַּחְרְגוּ ο υ ι ε ρ ο γ ο υ O Ps. 18.46.

חרד וַיֶּחֶרְדוּ ο υ ι χ α ρ δ ο υ O Ps. 49.15; MT: וַיִּרְדוּ.

חֲרָדָה a r a d a On Num. 33.24.

חָרָה a r a J Jon. 4.4.

חָרִיף α ρ ε ι φ B Neh. 7.24.

חֵרֶם h e r e m J Ezek. 44.29.

חֶרֶס α ρ ε ς G Ju. 8.13; MT: חֶרֶס; a r e s On ib.

חַרְסִית h a r s i t h J Jer. 19.2.

חֶרֶף η ρ φ ο υ O Ps. 89.52.

חֶרְפָּה α ρ φ α O Ps. 89.42: ΑΡΦ lege ΑΡΦΑ, haplography
before a Λ.

חֶרְפַּת α ρ φ α ϑ O Ps. 89.51.

חרץ חָרוּץ α ρ ο υ ς G 2 Ki. 21.19; a r u s On ib.

h a r u s On Joel 4.14.

חֲרָצוֹת a r s o t h J Amos 1.3.

חרק חָרֹק α ρ ω κ O Ps. 35.16.

חָרֵשׁ a r e s J Isa. 19.18.

חָרָשׁ α ρ ε ς A 1 Chron. 9.15.

חוֹרֵשׁ h o r e s J Isa. 17.9.

חרש חֲרַשְׁתֶּם a r a s t h e m J Hos. 10.13.

יַחֲרֹשׁ j e r o s J Hos. 10.11; cf. in the BV יֹחֲרֹשׁ Prov.
20.4 in Ms. Ec 1.

תֶּחֱרַשׁ ϑ α ρ ε ς O Ps. 35.22; MT: תֶּחֱרַשׁ.

חֲרֹשֶׁת a r a s t h On Ju. 4.2; MT: חֲרֹשֶׁת; cf. s. v. דַּבָּשֶׁת dabbasth.

חָשַׁב α σ α β G in Ασαβια, 1 Chron. 9.14.

חֲשֻׁבָה α σ ο υ β ε B 1 Chron. 3.20.

נֶחְשָׁב n e s a b J Isa. 2.22.

חֶשְׁבּוֹן $\epsilon \sigma \epsilon \beta \omega \nu$ G Num. 21.25; e s e b o n On ib.
חשך חָשְׁכִּי $o \sigma \chi \iota$ o Ps. 18.29.
חשק חִשְׁקִי e s c i J Isa. 21.4.

ט

טָבַח t a b e c h On Gen. 22.24; cf. MT in pausa טָבַח: Isa. 34.2.
טַבָּעַת טַבָּעוֹת a) $\tau a \beta a \omega \vartheta$ B Neh. 7.46: ΓΑΒΑΩΘ lege T
for Γ; cf. Thompson Facs. 3.
b) $\tau a \beta \beta a \omega \vartheta$ A ib.
טֶבַח t e b e t h J Ezek. 29.1; cf. Esth. 2.16.
טוֹב $\tau \omega \beta$ G Ju. 11.3; t o b On in Achitob, 1 Sam. 14.3.
טוֹבִים t o b i m J Zech. 8.19.
טוב טוּבְךָ $\tau o \upsilon \beta a \chi$ o Ps. 31.20.
טור טוּרֹת t u r o t h J Ezek. 46.23; MT: טִירוֹת.
טמן טָמְנוּ $\tau a \mu \nu o \upsilon$ o Ps. 31.5.

י

יאל יוֹאֵל $\iota \omega \eta \lambda$ G 1 Sam. 8.2; i o h e l On ib.; cf. paragraph
X (insertion of h).
יְאֹר i o r J Isa. 23.10.
יבל יוּבָל $\iota o \upsilon \beta a \lambda'$ A Gen. 4.21; i u b a l On ib.
יָבֵשׁ $\iota a \beta \epsilon \iota s$ G Ju. 21.8; i a b e s On ib.; elsewhere $\epsilon \iota$
and ι of the Septuagint correspond to i in the
Onomastica.
יד a) בְּיָדְךָ $\beta \iota a \delta a \chi$ o Ps. 31.6: ΒΙΑΔΑΘ lege ΒΙΑΔΑΧ.
יָדוֹ $\iota a \delta \omega$ o Ps. 89.26; j a d o J Hab. 3.4.
יָדִי $\iota a \delta a \iota$ o Ps. 18.35.
b) בְּיַד $\beta \iota \epsilon \delta$ o Ps. 31.9.
מְיָד $\mu \epsilon \iota \epsilon \delta$ o Ps. 89.49.
c) מִידֵיהֶם $\mu \epsilon \iota \delta \eta \chi \epsilon \mu$ o Mal. 2.13; MT: מִיֶּדְכֶם; cf. in
the BV יְדֵיהֹם Lev. 8.18 in Ms. Ea 11.
ידה הַיּוֹדְךָ $a \iota \omega \delta \epsilon \chi \chi a$ o Ps. 30.10.
אוֹדְךָ $\omega \delta \epsilon \chi$ o Ps. 35.18; 30.13; MT: אוֹדְךָ.
אֲהוֹדֶנּוּ $a \omega \delta \epsilon \nu \nu o \upsilon$ o Ps. 28.7.
וְהוֹדוּ $o \upsilon \omega \delta o \upsilon$ o Ps. 30.5.
יָדִיד $\iota \delta \epsilon \delta$ B in Ιδεδει, 2 Sam. 12.25; i d i d On in Ididia, ib.

יְדִידֹת ιδιδωϑ o Ps. 45.1.

יָדַע ιαδα A in Βαλλιαδα, 1 Chron. 14.7.

ιαδαε B in Ελιαδαε, 1 Ki. 11.14; o Ps. 92.7; MT: יָֽדְעוּ;
cf. paragraph XXIII sub ע; i a d a h e On in
Ioiadahe, 2 Sam. 23.20; cf. paragraph X.

יָדַעְתָּ ιαδαϑ o Ps. 31.8.

יָדְעוּ j a d a u J Hos. 9.7; MT: יָֽדְעוּ; cf. B-L. §2w.

וּדְעוּ ουαδου o Ps. 46.11.

יָהּ i a J Isa. 26.4.

בְּיָהּ βαια o Isa. 26.4.

יָהב הָבוּ αβου o Ps. 29.1.

יהוה αδωναι o Ps. 118.25; a d o n a i J Isa. 7.12.

בְּיהוה βαδωναι o Isa. 26.4.

יוֹם בְּיוֹם biom J Isa. 17.11.

הַיּוֹם αιωμ o Ps. 35.28.

יָמִים i a m i m J Gen. 35.18.

יְמֵי ιμη o Ps. 89.46.

בִּימֵי βιμη o Ps. 49.6.

כִּימֵי χιμη o Ps. 89.30.

יוֹנָה ιωνα G 2 Ki. 14.25; i o n a On ib.

יֵזַע j e z e J Ezek. 44.18.

יַחַד ιααδ o Ps. 49.3; ιααδε o Ps. 49.11; I find this form
inexplicable, unless by assuming that ε is the
scribe's suggestion for the second α: ιαεδ; cf. paragraph XXIII sub ח.

יַחְדּוּ ιαδαυ o Ps. 35.26: IΔΑΥ lege IAΔAΥ, haplography
A before Δ.

יָחִיד j a i d J Jer. 6.26.

יְחִידָתִי ιιδαϑι o Ps. 35.17; cf. in the BV יְחִידְךָ Gen.
22.2 in Ms. Ea 1.

יחל הַמְּיַחֲלִים αμμηαλιμ o Ps. 31.25; MT: הַם.

יָם i a m J Isa. 2.16.

מְיָם m e j a m J Hos. 11.10.

יַמִּים ιαμιμ o Ps. 46.3.

יָמִין a) ιαμειν A Gen. 46.10; i a m i n On ib.

b) יָמִין ιμιν o Ps. 89.43.

וִימִינְךָ ουιμιναχ o Ps. 18.36: OΥΕΜΙΝΑΧ, lege I
for E; cf. Thompson Facs. 6.

יְמִינוֹ $\iota \mu \iota \nu \omega$ O Ps. 89.26.

c) יְמִינִי $\iota \epsilon \mu \epsilon \nu \epsilon \iota$ B Ps. 7.1; $\iota \epsilon \mu \epsilon \nu \iota$ A ib.; iemini On ib.

ינק   מֵינִיקָה m e n e c a J Gen. 35.8 (editio Lagarde): mene-cha is a misprint; MT: מֵינֶקֶת.

מֵינֶקֶת m e n e c e t h J Gen. 35.8.

יסף   יוֹסֵף $\iota \omega \sigma \eta \varphi$ G Gen. 30.24; i o s e p h On ib.

יעד   נוֹעַד $\nu \omega a \delta$ A in N$\omega a \delta a$, Ezra 8.33.

יעץ   יוֹעֵץ i o e s J Isa. 9.5.

יַעַר   a) יַעַר $\iota a \rho$ A 1 Sam. 14.25; j a r J Hos. 2.15; cf. in the PV לִיעֵר Isa. 32.15 (MdWI, p. יב).

יְעָרִים $\iota a \rho \epsilon \iota \mu$ B Josh. 15.9; $\iota a \rho \iota \mu$ A ib.; i a r i m On in Cariathiarim, ib.

b) יַעַר $\iota a a \rho$ B 1 Sam. 14.25: Iaaλ lege ρ for λ.

יָצָא   j a s a J Zech. 2.7; MT: יְצָא.

תּוֹצִיאֵנִי $\vartheta \omega \sigma \iota \eta \nu \iota$ O Ps. 31.5: ΘΟΩϹΙΗΝΙ dele O; dittography; cf. Thompson Facs. 3 and 5 (Θ—O).

יצר   a) יִצְרִי $\iota \epsilon \sigma \rho \iota$ A Num. 26.49.

יִצְרוֹ $\iota \epsilon \sigma \rho o$ O Isa. 26.3; MT: יֵצֶר.

b) יֵצֶר $\iota \epsilon \sigma \epsilon \rho$ B Num. 26.49; i e s e r On ib.

יִצְרִי $\iota \epsilon \sigma \epsilon \rho \epsilon \iota$ B ib.

יצר   יוֹצֵר j o s e r J Zech. 11.12.

יקר   בִּיקָר $\beta \iota a \kappa a \rho$ O Ps. 49.13: BAKAP lege BIAKAP; cf. in the PV יְקָר (MdWI, p. י, line 3).

יקר   וַיַּקָּר $o \upsilon \iota \kappa a \rho$ O Ps. 49.9; cf. MT וַיֵּיקַר 1 Sam. 18.30.

ירא   אִירָא $\iota \rho a$ O Ps. 49.7.

נִירָא $\nu \iota \rho a$ O Ps. 46.3.

יָרֵא $\iota a \rho \eta$ O Ps. 112.1: APH lege IAPH.

לִירָאֶיךָ $\lambda \iota \rho \iota a \chi$ O Ps. 31.20.

ירד   יֶרֶד j e r e d J Jon. 1 .3.

מְיוֹרְדִי $\mu \epsilon \iota \omega \rho \delta \eta$ O Ps. 30.4.

בְּרִדְתִּי $\beta \rho \epsilon \delta \epsilon \vartheta \iota$ O Ps. 30.10; the addition of the suffix does thus not result in a change of the vocali-zation of the verb; cf. in the Sam. Ex. 32.34: פקודי as compared with the Masoretic form פָּקְדִי.

ירה   וְאוֹרְךָ $o \upsilon \omega \rho \epsilon \chi$ O Ps. 32.8.

יְרוּשָׁה $\iota \epsilon \rho o \upsilon \sigma a$ A 2 Chron. 27.1.

$\iota \epsilon \rho o \upsilon \sigma \sigma a$ B ib.

יֶרַח i a r e J Amos 4.7; i a r e e On Gen. 10.26; MT: יֶרַח;
cf. paragraph XXIII sub ה.

בְּיֶרַח χ ι α ρ η o Ps. 89.38.

יריב יְרִיבִי ι ρ ι β ι α ι o Ps. 35.1; perhaps to be explained as
an amalgamation of the two readings: יְרִיבִי ι ρ ι β ι
and יְרִיבַי ι ρ ι β α ι: cf. on מֶעְמוֹ.

ירכה יַרְכְּתִי ι ε ρ χ ϑ η o Ps. 48.3; cf. in the BV יֹרכֹתֹי Ju. 19.18
in Ms. 105 JThS.

יֵשׁ i s J Gen. 30.18.

יָשַׁב ι α σ α β o Ps. 29.10.

יָשַׁב ι η σ η β o Ps. 9.8.

יוֹשֶׁבֶת j o s e b e t h J Mic. 1.11.

ישועה a) יְשׁוּעָתִי ι α σ ο υ α ϑ ι o Ps. 89.27.

b) לִישׁוּעָה l a j e s u a J Hab. 3.13; MT: לְיֵשַׁע; cf. in the
PV יְשׁוּעָתְךָ Ps. 69.30 (MdWII, p. 85).

c) יְשׁוּעוֹת ι σ ο υ ω ϑ o Ps. 28.8.

יָשֵׁן ι α σ α ν G 2 Sam. 23.32: ασαν lege ιασαν, haplography;
MT: יָשֵׁן; i a s a n On ib.

הַיְשָׁנָה α ι σ α ν α G Neh. 3.6.

ישע יִשְׁעִי ι ε σ ε ι A 1 Chron. 2.31; o Ps. 18.47: IЄCCI is to
be emended in IЄCЄI, the second ε corresponding
to the ע, cf. paragraph XXIII sub ע, or in IЄCI;
dittography.

יִשְׁעֲךָ ι ε σ α χ α o Ps. 18.36.

ישע תּוֹשִׁיעַ ϑ ω σ ι o Ps. 18.28: ΘΩЄI lege C for Є.

מוֹשִׁיעַ μ ω σ ι o Ps. 18.42.

מוֹשִׁיעִים m o s i m J Obad. 21.

הוֹשִׁיעָה ω σ ι α o Ps. 28.9: IΩCIA lege ΩCIA.

הוֹשִׁיעָה נָּא ω σ ι ε ν ν α o Ps. 118.25.

לְהוֹשִׁיעֵנִי λ ω σ ι η ν ι o Ps. 31.3.

ישר יִשְׁרֵי ι σ ρ η o Ps. 32.11.

ישר יָשָׁר i s a r J Hos. 12.5; cf. וַיַּקֵּר s. v. יקר; MT: וַיִּשָׁר.

יָתֵד j a t h e d J Isa. 22.25.

יתר a) יִתְרוֹ i e t h r o On Ex. 3.1.

b) יָתַר ι ε ϑ ε ρ o Ps. 31.24

יתר תּוֹתַר ϑ ω ϑ α ρ o Gen. 49.4.

כ

כְּאָב c h e b J Isa. 29.4; MT: כְּאוֹב.

כְּבוֹד χ a β ω δ o Ps. 29.1; c h a b o d J Isa. 11.10.

χ a β ω ϑ G in Βαρχαβωϑ, 1 Sam. 4.21.

c a b o t h On in Escaboth, 1 Sam. 14.3.

הַכָּבוֹד a χ χ a β ω δ O Ps. 29.3.

כְּבוֹד χ a β ω δ O Ps. 29.2.

כברה כְּבְרַת c h a b r a t h a On 2 Ki. 5.19.

כַּדְכֹּד c h o d c h o d J Isa. 54.12.

כּוֹכָב c h o c a b J Amos 5.26.

כון יִכּוֹן ι ε χ χ o ν o Ps. 89.38.

הָכִין h e c h i n J Amos 4.12; MT: הֵכִּון.

יָכִין ι a χ ε ι ν G Num. 26.12; i a c h i n On Gen. 46.10.

כַּוָּנִים c h a u o n i m J Jer. 7.18.

כָּזָב c h a s a b J Isa. 28.17.

כוב אֶכְזָב ε χ a ζ ε β o Ps. 89.36; without gemination of the
second radical; cf. וַתְּאַזְרֵנִי, פַּלֵּט, פִּתַּחְתָּ, שִׂמַּחְתָּ, under
their respective headings.

כחש כְּחַשׁוּ c h a e s u J Zech. 13.4; the e = ח, cf. paragraph
XXIII.

כִּי χ ι o Ps. 18.28; c h i J Isa. 2.22.

כִּידוֹן c h i d o n On Josh. 8.18.

כִּיּוּן c h i o n J Amos 5.26.

כִּימָה c h i m a J Amos 5.8.

כִּכָּר c h a c h a r J Zech. 5.7; cf. in the BV כֹּכַרֹי 2 Chron.
9.13 in Ms. Ec 1.

κ ε χ a ρ B 2 Sam. 18.23.

כָּל a) χ ω λ A in Εσχωλ, Gen. 14.24; χ o λ o Ps. 31.24;
c h o l On in Fichol, Gen. 21.22.

κ o λ A in Φικολ, Gen. 21.22.

לְכֹל λ a χ o λ o Ps. 18.31.

כְּלֹה c h o l l o J Ezek. 11.15; cf. in the BV כֹּולֹה Berakot
6, 2 (Kahle, "The Mishna Text in Babylonia",
HUCA, Cincinnati, 1935).

b) c h u l l o J ib.

כלה כְּלוֹתָם χ ε λ λ ω ϑ a μ o Ps. 18.38.

כָּלוּב c h e l u b J Amos 8.2.

כִּלְיוֹן   κ ε λ α ι ω ν   B Ruth 1.2;   MT: כִּלְיוֹן; cf. in the PV כֹלי
      (= כליון) Isa. 10.22 (Kahle in *ZAW* 1901, p. 282).

כַּמָּה   χ α μ μ α   o Ps. 35.17.

כְּמוֹ   χ α μ ω   o Ps. 89.47.

כמר   a) כְּמָרִים   χ ω μ α ρ ε ι μ   G 2 Ki. 23.5; c h o m a r i m
      On ib.

      b) הַכְּמָרִים   a c c h u m a r i m   J Zeph. 1.4.

כֵּן   χ ε ν   o Ps. 46.3; c h e n   J Zech. 11.11.

כִּנּוֹר   c h e n n o r   On Ezek. 26.13.

בְּכִנּוֹר   β χ ε ν ν ω ρ   o Ps. 49.5.

כְּנַעֲנִי   c h a n a n i   On Ex. 3.8.

כנף   מִכְּנַף   m e c c h e n a p h   J Isa. 24.16; cf. in the PV
      כֹנְפִי Ezek. 16.12 (MdWII, p. 70).

כסא   וְכִסְאוֹ   o υ χ ε σ σ ω   o Ps. 89.30.

כסה   כָּסוֹת   χ ε σ σ ο υ ϑ   o Mal. 2.13.

כְּסִיל   a) c h a s i l   J Amos 5.8.

      b) כְּסִילְי   c h i s i l e   J Isa. 13.10.

      כְּסִילֵיהֶם   c h i s i l e e m   J Isa. 13.10.

      c) כְּסִיל   χ σ ι λ   o Ps. 49.11: ΧϵΙΛ lege Ϲ for ϵ.

      וּכְסִיל   o υ χ σ ι λ   o Ps. 92.7.

כָּסָל   χ ε σ λ   o Ps. 49.14.

כִּסְלֵו   c h a s l e u   J Zech. 7.1.

כְּסָמִים   c h a s a m i m   J Isa. 28.17.

כעס   בְּכַעַס   β α χ α s   o Ps. 31.10.

כִּפָּה   c h a p h p h e   J Isa. 19.25.

כְּפוֹר   χ ε φ ο ρ   o Ps. 147.16.

כָּפִיס   c h a p h i s   J Hab. 2.11.

כְּפִיר   a) c h a p h i r   J Ezek. 38.13.
      c a p h i r   J ib.

      b) מִכְּפִירִים   μ ε χ φ ε ρ ι μ   o Ps. 35.17.

כפר   כָּפְרוּ   χ ο φ ρ ω   o Ps. 49.8.

כפתור   כַּפְתּוֹרִים   c a p h t h o r i m   J Amos 9.1,7.

כֹּר   χ ο ρ   G in Βαιϑχορ, 1 Sam. 7.11.

כְּרוּב   a) χ α ρ ο υ β   B Neh. 7.61.

      b) χ ε ρ ο υ β   A Neh. 7.61; c h e r u b   J Ezek. 9.3.

      כְּרוּבִים   χ ε ρ ο υ β ε ι μ   G Ex. 25.18; c h e r u b i m
      Ezek. 9.3.

הַכְּרוּבִים a c c h e r u b i m   On Ex. 25.20: accherubin
lege m for n.

כָּרֶם   χ α ρ μ   o Ps. 12.9; MT: כֶּרֶם.

χ α ρ μ α   B in Βαιϑϑαχαρμα, Jer. 6.1;   c h a r m a
On in Bethacharma, ib.

כַּרְמִי   χ α ρ μ ε ι   B Ex. 6.14;   χ α ρ μ ι A ib.;   c h a r m i
On ib.

כַּרְמִים   χ α ρ μ ε ι μ   B in Εβελχαρμειν lege–ειμ, Ju.
11.33.

כָּשַׁף   בַּשָּׁפִי   c a s s a p h e   J Jer. 27.9.

ל

ל-   לִי   λ ι   o Ps. 18.36; l i   J Isa. 24.16.

לָךְ   λ α χ   o Ps. 110.3; l a c   J Jon. 4.4.

לוֹ   λ ω   o Ps. 89.29.

לָנוּ   λ α ν ο υ   o Ps. 46.8; l a n u   J Isa. 6.8.

לָכֶם   l a c h e m   J Isa. 2.22.

לָהֶם   l a e m   J Mic. 7.13;   l a h e m   J Isa. 33.7; cf.
paragraph X and XXIII sub ה.

לָמוֹ   λ α μ ο υ   o Ps. 28.8.

לא   λ ω   G in Λωδαβαρ, 2 Sam. 17.27; o Ps. 32.6;   l o   On
in Lodabar, 2 Sam. 9.4.

וְלֹא   u l o   J Isa. 7.12.

לב   λ ε β   o Ps. 32.11.

בְּלֵב   β λ ε β   o Ps. 46.3.

לִבִּי   λ ε β β ι   o Ps. 28.7.

לִבּוֹ   λ ε β β α υ   o Ps. 36.2; MT: לִבִּי.

לבב   a) לְבָבָם   λ ε β β α β ε χ ε μ   o Ps. 31.25.

b) בִּלְבָבָם   β α λ β α β α μ   o Ps. 35.25; MT: בִּלְבָּם; cf.
Gen. 18.5: MT: לְבָּם Sam. לבבכם.

לְבוֹנָה   λ ε β ω ν α   G Ju. 21.19.

לבוש   לְבוּשִׁי   λ ε β ο υ σ ι   o Ps. 35.13.

לביא   לְבָאוֹת   l a b a o t h   On in Bethlabaoth, Josh. 19.6.

לָבָן   λ α β α ν   A Gen. 24.29; l a b a n   On ib.

לְבָנָה   λ α β α ν α   G Neh. 7.48; MT: לְבָנָא;   l a b a n a   J
Isa. 24.23.

לְבֶנָה   l e b e n a   J Isa. 24.23.

לַהַב   לְהָבִים   l a a b i m   On Gen. 10.13.

לוה   יִלְוָה   i l l a u e   J Gen. 30.34 (editio Lagarde).

לִוְיָתָן   l e v i a t h a n   J Isa. 27.1.

לוח   הַלְחוֹת   a l l u o t h   J Hab. 2.2.

לָחָם   a) לָחֶם   λ α ε μ   B in Βαιθαλαεμ, 1 Chron. 2.51; the ε is
=ח, cf. paragraph XXIII sub ח.

     b) לָחָם   λ ε ε μ   G in Βαιθλεεμ, Ju. 12.10; the second
ε=ח; cf. paragraph XXIII sub ח.

     לְחָמִי   λ ε ε μ ε ι   A 1 Chron. 20.5; see the note on לחם

לחם   לְחָמִי   λ ω α μ α ι   O Ps. 35.1.

     לָחֹם   λ ο ο μ   O Ps. 35.1; MT: לָחֶם; cf. in the BV לִלְחֹמוֹ.
Prov. 9.5 in Ms. Ec 1, for MT לַחֲמוּ.

לחש   הַלּוֹחֵשׁ   a) a λ ω η s   B Neh. 10.25.

     b) a λ λ ω η s   A Neh. 3.12.

לטש   לְטוּשִׁים   λ α τ ο υ σ ι ε ι μ   A Gen. 25.3.
l a t u s i m   On ib.

לִילִית   l i l i t h   J Isa. 34.14.

לִין   יָלִין   ι α λ ι ν   O Ps. 30.6.

     תָּלִינוּ   t h a l i n u   J Isa. 21.13.

לַיִשׁ   a) λ α ε ι s   B 1 Sam. 25.44: ΛΜΕΙC lege ΛΑΕΙC;
cf. Thompson Facs. 3; λ α ι s   A ib.

     b) l e i s   J Isa. 30.6.

למד   מְלַמֵּד   μ α λ α μ μ ε δ   O Ps. 18.35.

לָמָה   λ α μ α   O Ps. 49.6.

לְמַעַן   λαμαν   O Ps. 30.13.

     וּלְמַעַן   ο υ λ μ α ν   O Ps. 31.4.

לעג   לְעֲנֵי   λ α γ η   O Ps. 35.16.

לַפִּידוֹת   λ α φ ε ι δ ω θ   B Ju. 4.4; λ α φ ι δ ω θ   A ib.; l a p i d o t h
On ib.

לץ   לֵצִים   λ η σ ι μ   O Ps. 1.1.

לִקְרַאת   l a c e r a t h   J Amos 4.12.

לשון   וּלְשׁוֹנִי   ο υ α λ σ ω ν ι   O Ps. 35.28.

     לִשְׁנוֹת   λ σ ω ν ω θ   O Ps. 31.21.

לֶתֶךְ   a) וְלֶתֶךְ   ο υ λ ε θ χ   O Hos. 3.2.

     b) לֶתֶךְ   l e t h e c h   J Hos. 3.2.

מ

מְאֹד $\mu \omega \delta$ o Ps. 46.2.

מאה מְאַת maath J Eccl. 8.12.

מָאוֹר maor J Isa. 24.23.

מאזנים מֹאזְנֵי mozene J Ezek. 45.10.

מַאֲכָל machal J Ezek. 47.12; cf. in the BV מֹאכל Ps.44.12 in Ms. Ec 1.

מאס וַתִּמְאָס $o \upsilon a \vartheta \vartheta \epsilon \mu a s$ o Ps. 89.39.

מְבוּכָה mabucha J Mic. 7.4.

מִבְחָר $\mu a \beta a \rho$ A 1 Chron. 11.38.

מִבְצָר $\mu a \psi a \rho$ G 2 Sam. 24.7; $\mu a \beta \sigma a \rho$ A 1 Chron.1.53; mabsar On Gen. 36.42; cf. in the BV הֹמִבְצָר 2 Chron. 17.19 in Ms. Ec 1.

מִבְצָרָיו $\mu a \beta \sigma a \rho a \upsilon \iota$ o Ps. 89.41.

מִבְשָׂם $\mu a \beta \sigma a \mu$ A 1 Chron. 1.29: $\mathrm{Ma}\beta\sigma\alpha\nu$ lege μ for ν; cf. in the BV מבשם 1 Chron. 4.25 in Ms. Ec 1; mabsam On Gen. 25.13.

מָג mag On in Rabmag, Jer. 39.3.

$\mu a \kappa$ A in $\mathrm{Pa}\beta\mu\alpha\kappa$, ib.

מִגְדָּל $\mu a \gamma \delta a \lambda$ A Josh. 15.37; cf. in the BV מֹגדל Prov. 18.10 in Ms. Ec 1; magdal On in Magdalgad, Josh. 15.37; J Ezek. 29.10; MT: מִגְדָּל.

מָגוֹר magur J Jer. 20.3.

מְגִלָּה megella J Zech. 5.1.

מָגֵן $\mu a \gamma \epsilon \nu$ o Ps. 18.31.

וּמָגִנִּי $o \upsilon \mu a \gamma \epsilon \nu \nu \iota$ o Ps. 28.7; H-R: $o \upsilon \mu a \gamma \epsilon \nu \nu \eta$; cf. in the BV מֹגניו Job 15.26 in Ms. Ec 1.

מגן אֲמַגֶּנְךָ amaggenach J Hos. 11.8.

מגר מְגָרְתָה $\mu a \gamma a \rho \vartheta$ o Ps. 89.45; MT: מְגָרְתָה.

מִגְרָשׁ magras J Ezek. 48.17; cf. in the BV מֹגרשׁה 1 Chron. 6.43 in Ms. Ec 1.

מִדְבָּר $\mu a \delta \beta a \rho$ B in $\mathrm{Ma}\delta\beta\alpha\rho\epsilon\iota\tau\iota\delta\iota$, Josh. 5.5; cf. in the BV מֹדבר Prov. 21.19 in Ms. Ec 1.

מדד תָּמֹדּו thamoddu J Ezek. 47.18.

מָדוֹן $\mu a \delta \omega \nu$ A Josh. 11.1; madon On ib.

מָה a) $\mu\,a$ o Ps. 89.47; MT: מָה; m a J Amos 4.13.

בַּמָּה b a m a J Isa. 2.22; b a m m a J ib.

b) מָה $\mu\,\epsilon$ o in $\mu\epsilon\beta\beta\epsilon\sigma\epsilon$, Ps. 30.10.

מָה $\mu\,\eta$ o Ps. 89.48.

מְהֵרָה $\mu\,\eta\,\eta\,\rho\,a$ o Ps. 31.3.

מוג תָּמוּג $\vartheta\,a\,\mu\,o\,v\,\gamma$ o Ps. 46.7.

מוט מָטוּ $\mu\,a\,\tau\,o\,v$ o Ps. 46.7.

תָּמוֹט $\vartheta\,\epsilon\,\mu\,\mu\,o\,v\,\tau$ o Ps. 46.6: ΘEMMOT lege ΘEMMOTT;
cf. Thompson Facs. 5 and 6 (Y—T).

וּבְמוֹט $o\,v\,\beta\,a\,\mu\,\omega\,\tau$ o Ps. 46.3.

מוֹטָה a) m o t a J Isa. 58.6.

b) מוֹטֺת m u t o t h J Jer. 28.13.

מוּל m u l J Mic. 2.8.

מוֹצָא וּמוֹצָא $o\,v\,\mu\,\omega\,\sigma\,a$ o Ps. 89.35.

מוֹקֵשׁ m o c e s J Amos 8.2.

מוֹר בְּהָמִיר $\beta\,a\,a\,\mu\,\iota\,\rho$ o Ps. 46.3.

מוֹרֶשֶׁת מֹרֶשֶׁת m a r a s e t h J Mic. 1.14.

מָוֶת a) $\mu\,a\,v\,\vartheta$ o Ps. 89.49; cf. B.-L. §17b'.; cf. s. v. אוֹן sub a).

b) $\mu\,\omega\,\vartheta$ B in $B\eta\vartheta a\sigma\mu\omega\vartheta$, Neh. 7.28; A in $A\sigma a\rho\mu\omega\vartheta$.
Gen. 10.26; o Ps. 49.15; m o t h On in Asarmoth
Gen. 10.26.

מוֹת יְמוּתוּ $\iota\,a\,\mu\,\omega\,\vartheta\,o\,v$ o Ps. 49.11: $\iota a\mu o v\vartheta\omega$ lege $\iota a\mu\omega\vartheta o v$

מזבח מִזְבֵּחַ $\mu\,a\,\sigma\,\beta\,\eta\,\eta$ o Mal. 2.13; cf. in the BV מֹזְבֹּח 2 Sam.
24.21 in Ms. Eb 12; stat. constr. מֹזְבֹּח Ps. 43.4 in
Ms. Ec 1.

מָזוֹר a) m e z u r J Hos. 5.13.

b) m e z o r J ib.

מִזְמוֹר $\mu\,a\,\zeta\,\mu\,\omega\,\rho$ o Ps. 29.1.

מזרח מִמְּזְרָח m i m i z r a J Gen. 2.8.

מָחוֹל a) $\mu\,a\,o\,v\,\lambda$ A 1 Ki. 5.11.

b) m a o l On ib.

לְמָחוֹל $\lambda\,\mu\,a\,\omega\,\lambda$ o Ps. 30.12.

מַחֲלָה a) $\mu\,a\,\lambda\,a$ G Num. 26.33; MT: מַחְלָה, here and in the following instances.

$\mu\,a\,\epsilon\,\lambda\,a$ B 1 Chron. 7.18; ϵ corresponds ח, cf. paragraph XXIII sub ח.

b) $\mu\,a\,a\,\lambda\,a$ G Num. 36.11; m a a l a On Num. 26.33.

מַחְמָד m a m a d J Hos. 9.6.

מחנה   מַחֲנַיִם   m a n a i m   On Josh. 13.26.

מחסה   מַחֲסֶה $\mu\,a\,\sigma\,\epsilon$ o Ps. 46.2.

מחץ   אֶמְחָצֵם $\epsilon\,\mu\,\omega\,\sigma\,\eta\,\mu$ o Ps. 18.39.

מְחִתָּה $\mu\,\epsilon\,\epsilon\,\vartheta\,\vartheta\,a$ o Ps. 89.41.

מַטֶּה   a) m e t a   J Gen. 48.2.

       b) m e t t a   J ib., editio Lagarde.

מַטֶּה   m a t e   J Ezek. 4.16.

מִי $\mu\,\iota$ o Ps. 18.32.

מַיִם $\mu\,a\,\epsilon\,\iota\,\mu$ A in $\mathrm{M}a\sigma\rho\epsilon\varphi\omega\vartheta\mu a\epsilon\iota\mu$, Josh. 11.8; $\mu\,a\,\iota\,\mu$ A in
       $\mathrm{A}\beta\epsilon\lambda\mu a\iota\nu$, lege μ for ν, 2 Chron. 16.4; m a i m
       J Hos. 11.10.

       הַמַּיִם $a\,\mu\,\mu\,a\,\iota\,\mu$ o Ps. 29.3.

       מֵימָיו $\mu\,\eta\,\mu\,a\,\upsilon$ o Ps. 46.4.

מִישׁוֹר $\mu\,\epsilon\,\iota\,\sigma\,\omega\,\rho$ G Deut. 3.10; m i s o r   On ib.

מישר   מֵישָׁרִים   m e s s a r i m   J Isa. 26.7.

מכאוב   מַכְאוֹבִים $\mu\,a\,\chi\,\omega\,\beta\,\iota\,\mu$ o Ps. 32.10.

מכונה   מְכֹנוֹת $\mu\,\epsilon\,\chi\,\omega\,\nu\,\omega\,\vartheta$ G 1 Ki. 7.27; m e c h o n o t h   On ib.

מִכְתָּב   m a c h t h a b   J Isa. 38.9; cf. in the BV מִכְתָּב Deut.
       10.4 in Ms. Ka 19.

מִכְתָּשׁ   m a c h t h e s   J Zeph. 1.11.

מלא   מְלֵאָה   m a l e a   J Nah. 3.1.

מלא   יִמָּלֵא $\iota\,\epsilon\,\mu\,\lambda\,a$ A 2 Chron. 18.7; i e m l a   On 1 Ki. 22.8;
       MT: יִמָּלֵה.

       מְלֵיתִי $\mu\,\epsilon\,\lambda\,\lambda\,\eta\,\vartheta\,\iota$ A 1 Chron. 25.26; MT: מָלּוֹתִי.

מַלְאָךְ   m a l a c h   J Hag. 1.13.

       מַלְאָכִי   m a l a c h i   J Mal. 1.1.

       מַלְאָכִי   m a l a c h e   J Isa. 14.32.

מִלּוֹא   a) $\mu\,\epsilon\,\lambda\,\omega$ A 1 Ki. 9.15.

       b) m e l l o   J Isa. 38.8.

מֶלַח   a) $\mu\,\epsilon\,\lambda\,\epsilon$ B in $\mathrm{P}\epsilon\mu\epsilon\lambda\epsilon$, 2 Ki. 14.7; the second ϵ is the
       transliteration of the ח, cf. paragraph XXIII
       sub ח; this is, therefore, a qitl-form; cf. in the PV
       מֶּלַח (MdWI, p. ט׳, line 13).

       b) $\mu\,\epsilon\,\lambda\,a$ A in $\Gamma a\iota\mu\epsilon\lambda a$, 2 Ki. 14.7.

מלחמה   וּמִלְחָמָה $o\,\upsilon\,\mu\,a\,\lambda\,a\,\mu\,a$ o Ps. 76.4; cf. in the BV מִלְחֹמָה
       Prov. 20.18 in Ms. Ec 1.

       בְּמִלְחָמָה $\beta\,a\,\mu\,\mu\,a\,\lambda\,a\,\mu\,a$ o Ps. 89.44; cf. in the BV
       בְּמִלְחֹמֹה 1 Chron. 7.40 in Ms. Ec 1.

לַמִּלְחָמָה λαμαλαμα o Ps. 18.35.

מִלְחָמוֹת μαλαμωϑ o Ps. 46.10; cf. in the BV מֹלְחֹמוֹ
  1 Chron. 16.9 in Ms. Ec 1.

מלט   יְמַלֵּט ιμαλλετ o Ps. 89.49.

מלך   a) מַלְכִּי m a l c h i On in Malchihel, Num. 26.45.
      לְמַלְכִּי λαμαλχη o Ps. 89.28.

      b) מַלְכִּי μελχει B in Μελχειηλ, Num. 26.45; cf. in
         the BV מלכיה 1 Chron. 9.12 in Ms. Ec 1 for MT
         מִלְכִּיָה; μελχι A in Μελχιηλ, Num. 26.45;
         m e l c h i On in Melchisedec, Gen. 14.18; cf.
         B-L. §14c'.

      מַלְכְּכֶם m e l c h e c h e m j Amos 5.26.
      מַלְכָּם μελχαμ A 1 Chron. 8.9.

      c) מֶלֶךְ μελεχ B in Αδραμελεχ, 2 Ki. 17.31; m e l e c h
         On in Adramelech, ib.

      μελεκ A in Αδραμελεκ, ib.
      הַמֶּלֶךְ a m m e l e c h j Zech. 14.10.

מַלְכֹּם   m e l c h o m j Zeph. 1.5; MT: מַלְכָּם.
מַלְקֹחַיִם   m a l c a i m j Isa. 6.6.
מַמְזֵר   m a m z e r j Zech. 9.6.
ממלכה   מַמְלָכוֹת μαμλαχωϑ o Ps. 46.7: ΜΑΛΛΑΧΩΘ lege
         M for first Λ; cf. Thompson Facs. 3.

ממשק   מְמְשַׁק m a m a s a c j Zeph. 2.9.
מָן   m a n On Ex. 16.15.
מִן   m e n j Isa. 2.22.

      מִמֶּנִּי a) μιμμενι o Ps. 35.22.
            b) m e m m e n n i j 2 Ki. 4.27.

מנה   יִמְנָה ιεμνα A Gen. 46.17; MT: יִמְנָה; i e m n a On ib.
      תִּמְנָה ϑαμνα A Josh. 15.57; t h a m n a On ib.

מִנִּי   a) μενι o Ps. 44.19. b) m e n n i j Isa. 46.3.
מנוד   מָנוֹד μανουδ o Ps. 44.15.
מָנוֹחַ   a) m a n u e On Ju. 13.2. b) μανωε G ib.
מנוחה   מְנוּחָתוֹ m n u a t h o j Jer. 11.10.
מִנְחָה   a) הַמִּנְחָה αμμανα o Mal. 2.13.
      b) מִנְחָה m a n a a j Jer. 17.26.

מנע   יִמְנַע ιμνα G 1 Chron. 7.35: IMANA lege IMNA;
      cf. Thompson Facs. 3 (M—A).

      תִּמְנַע ϑαμνα A Gen. 36.12; t h a m n a On ib.

מסנרת   מְמַסְגְּרוֹתֵיהֶם $\mu\epsilon\mu\alpha\sigma\gamma\omega\rho\omega\vartheta\epsilon\epsilon\iota\mu$ o   Ps. 18.46:
MEMACTΩPΩΘEEIM lege Γ for T; cf. Thompson
Facs. 3.

מִסְפָּר $\mu\alpha\sigma\varphi\alpha\rho$ G Neh. 7.7; cf. in the BV מִסֽפָּר Job 5.9 in
Ms. Ec 1.

מֶעָד   מָעֲדוּ $\mu\alpha\alpha\delta o\upsilon$ o Ps. 18.37.

מָעוּג $\mu\alpha\omega\gamma$ o Ps. 35.16.

מָעוֹז $\mu\alpha o \zeta$ o Ps. 31.3; m a o z J Isa. 30.3.

     מָעוּזִּי $\mu\alpha o \zeta \iota$ o Ps. 31.5; cf. in the BV מָעוֹזִי ib.; מָעוֹזֹם
ib. 37.39 in Ms. Ec 1; cf. B-L. §14q.

מָעוֹן $\mu\alpha\omega\nu$ A 1 Chron. 2.45; m a o n On Josh. 15.55.

     $\mu\epsilon\omega\nu$ B 1 Chron. 2.45; the ϵ may be considered as the
rendering of the ע, cf. paragraph XXIII sub ע;
m e o n On in Bahalmeon, Num. 32.38.

מְעַט $\mu\alpha\tau$ o Ps. 8.6; cf. the bisyllabic form in the PV מֹעַט
and מֹעֵט Job 10.20 (MdWI, p. יב); cf. s. v. שאר.

מְעִיל   m a i l J Isa. 61.10.

מִמַּעַל   m e m m a l J Isa. 6.2.

מפעל   מִפְעֲלוֹת $\mu\alpha\varphi\alpha\lambda\omega\vartheta$ o Ps. 46.9; cf. in the BV מִֽפְעָֽלֽיֽ
Prov. 8.22 in Ms. Ec 1.

מִפְקָד $\mu\alpha\varphi\epsilon\kappa\alpha\delta$ G Neh. 3.31.

מצא   אָמְצָא   e m s a J Zech. 12.5; MT: אָמְצָה.

     לִמְצֹא $\lambda\alpha\mu\sigma\omega$ o Ps. 36.3.

     נִמְצָא $\nu\epsilon\mu\sigma\alpha$ o Ps. 46.2.

מַצָּב $\mu\epsilon\sigma\sigma\alpha\beta$ G 1 Sam. 14.1.

מצודה   וּמְצוּדָתִי $o\upsilon\mu\sigma o\upsilon\delta\alpha\vartheta\iota$ o Ps. 31.4.

     מְצוּדוֹת $\mu\sigma o\upsilon\delta\omega\vartheta$ o Ps. 31.3.

מצוה   וּמִצְוֹתִי $o\upsilon\mu\alpha\sigma\omega\vartheta\alpha\iota$ o Ps. 89.32: OYMCΩΘAI lege
OYMACΩΘAI; cf. Thompson Facs. 3 (M—A);
in the BV מִצֽוֹתִי Lev. 26.15 inMs. Ea 13.

מָצוֹר   a) m a s u r J Hab. 2.1.

     b) $\mu\alpha\sigma\omega\rho$ o Ps. 31.22; m a s o r J Mic. 7.12.

מצהלה   מְצַהֲלוֹת   m e s a l o t h J Zech. 14.20; MT: מְצִלּוֹת.

מצולה   מְצוּלוֹת   m e s u l o t h J Zech. 14.20; MT: מְצֻלּוֹת.

מִצְרַיִם   m e z r a i m J Isa. 19.1.

     וּמִמִּצְרַיִם $o\upsilon\mu\epsilon\mu\mu\iota\sigma\rho\alpha\iota\mu$ o Hos. 11.1.

מקהלה   מַקְהֵלֹת $\mu\alpha\kappa\eta\lambda\omega\vartheta$ G Num. 33.25; m a c e l o t h On
ib.

מקום   מְקוֹמָה   m a c o m a   J Nah. 1.8.

מקל   מְקָלוֹת   m a c a l o t h   J Zech. 11.7.; cf. B.–L. §14a'.

מִקְנֶה   m a c n e   J Jer. 9.9; cf. in the BV מִקְנֹה Eccl. 2.7 in Ms. Ec 1.

מר   מָרָה   m a r a   On Ex. 15.23.

    מָרוֹת   m a r o t h   J Mic. 1.12.

מרחב   בְּמֶרְחָב $\beta\alpha\mu\mu\alpha\rho[\alpha\beta]$ o Ps. 31.9.

מרכבת   מַרְכָּבוֹת $\mu\alpha\rho\chi\alpha\beta\omega\vartheta$ A in $B\alpha\iota\vartheta\mu\alpha\rho\chi\alpha\beta\omega\vartheta$, 1 Chron. 4.31; m a r c h a b o t h   On Josh. 19.5.

מִרְמָה $\mu\alpha\rho\mu\alpha$ A 1 Chron. 8.10; cf. in the BV מִרְמֹה Prov.11.1 in Ms. Ec 1.

    מִרְמוֹת $\mu\alpha\rho\mu\omega\vartheta$ o Ps. 35.20; cf. in the BV וּמִרְמוֹת Ps. 38.13 in Ms. Ec 1.

מְרֵעִים   m r i m   J Isa. 1.4.

    m e r e i m   J ib.

מַרְפֵּא   m a r p h e   J Eccl. 10.4.

מרץ   נִמְרָצֶת   n i m r e z e t h   J 1 Ki. 2.8.

מַשָּׂא $\mu\alpha\sigma\sigma\eta$ A Gen. 25.14.

    m a s s a   On ib.; J Isa. 19.1.

    m e s s a   J Isa. 13.1.

מִשְׁאָל $\mu\alpha\sigma\alpha\alpha\lambda$ A Josh. 21.30.

מִשְׂגָּב $\mu\iota\sigma\gamma\alpha\beta$ o Ps. 46.8.

מְשִׁי   a) m e s i   J Ezek. 16.13.

    b) m e s s e   J Ezek. 16.10.

משיח   a) מְשִׁיחֲךָ $\mu\sigma\iota\alpha\chi$ o Ps. 89.52; but perhaps should MCIAX be corrected to MЄCIAX? haplography: Є before C; cf. Thompson Facs. 9.

    $\mu\epsilon\sigma\iota\alpha\chi$ o Ps. 89.39.

    מְשִׁיחוֹ $\mu\epsilon\sigma\iota\omega$ o Ps. 28.8.

    b) מְשִׁיחֲךָ   m e s s i a c h   J Hab. 3.13.

    מְשִׁיחוֹ   m e s s i o   J Amos 4.13.

משך   מֹשְׁכִים   m o s e c h i m   J Jer. 5.8; MT: מֹשְׁכִים.

    מֹשְׁכֵי   m o s c h e   J Isa. 66.19.

משכן   מִשְׁכָּנִי $\mu\epsilon\sigma\chi\nu\eta$ o Ps. 46.5: MCXNH lege MЄCXNH.

    מִשְׁכְּנֹתָם $\mu\iota\sigma\chi\nu\omega\vartheta\alpha\mu$ o Ps. 49.12.

מָשָׁל $\mu\alpha\sigma\alpha\lambda$ A 1 Chron. 6.59; m a s a l   J Isa. 14.4.

לְמָשָׁל $\lambda\alpha\mu\alpha\sigma\alpha\lambda$ o Ps. 49.5; so according to H-R: Wutz has the spelling: $\lambda\alpha\mu\epsilon\sigma\alpha\lambda$.

מָשָׁל נִמְשַׁל ‎ $\nu\epsilon\mu\sigma\alpha\lambda$ o Ps. 49.13.

מִשְׁמָע ‎ $\mu\alpha\sigma\mu\alpha$ A Gen. 25.14; cf. in the BV מִשְׁמָע 1 Chron. 4.25 in Ms. Ec 1; m a s m a On Gen. 25.14.

מִשְׁפָּח m e s p h a a J Isa. 5.7.

מִשְׁפָּט m e s p h a t J Isa. 5.7.

לְמִשְׁפָּטִי ‎ $\lambda\alpha\mu\epsilon\sigma\varphi\alpha\tau\iota$ o Ps. 35.23.

וּבְמִשְׁפָּטִי ‎ $o\upsilon\beta\mu\epsilon\sigma\varphi\alpha\tau\iota$ o Ps. 89.31: ΟΥΒΜCΦΑΤΙ lege ΟΥΒΜЄCΦΑΤΙ; MT: וּבְמִשְׁפָּטִי.

מָשָׁק m a s e c On Gen. 15.2.

m e s e c J ib.; mesech is a mistake, dele h; cf. paragraph XXIII sub ק.

מַשְׁקֶה מַמְשָׁקֶה m e m m a s c e J Ezek. 45.15.

מִשְׁרָה m e s r a J Isa. 9.6.

משרפת מִשְׂרְפוֹת ‎ $\mu\alpha\sigma\rho\epsilon\varphi\omega\vartheta$ A in $M\alpha\sigma\rho\epsilon\varphi\omega\vartheta\mu\alpha\epsilon\iota\mu$, Josh. 11.8.

m a s a r f o t h On ib.

מת מָתָיךְ m e t h e c h a J Isa. 26.19: metheca is a mistake cf. paragraph XXIII sub כ.

מֹתֶג בְּמָתֶג ‎ $\beta\alpha\mu\epsilon\vartheta\gamma\epsilon$ o Ps. 32.9.

מַתָּן ‎ $\mu\alpha\vartheta\vartheta\alpha\nu$ B 2 Ki. 24.17; MT: מַתַּנְיָה; ‎ $\mu\alpha\tau\vartheta\alpha\nu$ A 2 Chron. 23.17; m a t t h a n On 2 Ki. 11.18.

מַתָּנָה m a t h a n a On Num. 21.18.

m a t t h a n a J Eccl. 7.7.

נ

נָאוֹת n a o t h J Joel 1.20.

נְאָם ‎ $\nu o\upsilon\mu$ o Ps. 36.2.

נֹאר נֵאַרְתָּה ‎ $\nu\eta\epsilon\rho\vartheta$ o Ps. 89.40.

נְבִיא n e b i a J Jer. 28.1.

נְבִיאִים n e b i m J Zech. 13.2.

n e b e i m J Jer. 28.1.

נֶבֶל a) ‎ $\nu\epsilon\beta\lambda$ o Ps. 92.4; MT: נֵבֶל.

b) n e b e l J Jer. 13.12.

נָבָל ‎ $\nu\alpha\beta\alpha\lambda$ G 1 Sam. 25.3; n a b a l On ib.

נְבָלָה n a b a l a J Isa. 32.6.

נֵכֶר ‎ $\nu\alpha\beta\alpha\rho$ o Ps. 18.26.

נֶגֶב n e g e b T Isa. 30.6.

נֶגֶד   ν ε γ δ o Ps. 31.20.

לְנֶגֶד λ α ν ε γ δ o Ps. 36.2.

מִנֶּגֶד μ ε ν ε γ δ o Ps. 31.23.

נֶגְדִּי ν ε γ δ ι o Ps. 89.37.

נגד   הַגִּיד α ι ε γ γ ι ϑ o Ps. 30.10: ΑΙΕΓΓΙΘΙ lege ΑΙΕΓΓΙΘ.

נגה   a) ν α γ α ι B 1 Chron. 3.7.   b) ν α γ ε A ib.

נגה   יַגִּיהַ [ι] α γ ι o Ps. 18.29.

נגע   וּבְנְגָעִים o υ β α ν γ α ι μ o Ps. 89.33.

נגע   יַגִּיעוּ ι γ γ ι ο υ o Ps. 32.6.

נגש   נוֹגֵשׂ noges J Zech. 10.4.

נָדָב   ν α δ α β G Ex. 6.23; MT: נָדָב; n a d a b On ib.

נדבה   נְדָבוֹת nadaboth J Amos 4.5.

נהל   וּתְנַהֲלֵנִי o υ ϑ ν ε ε λ η ν ι o Ps. 31.4: ΟΤΘΝΕΕΛΝΙ lege
ΟΤΘΝΕΕΛΗΝΙ; cf. §73a; cf. Thompson Facs. 5
(N—H).

נהר   a) וּבַנְּהָרוֹת o υ β α ν α ρ ω ϑ o Ps. 89.26.

b) נָהָר ν α α ρ o Ps. 46.5.

נום   יָנוּם ι α ν ο υ μ A Josh. 15.53; i a n u m On ib.

נֶזֶם   nezem J Ezek. 16.12.

נזר   נִזְרוֹ ν ε ζ ρ ω o Ps. 89.40.

נחה   תַּנְחֵנִי ϑ ε ν η ν ι o Ps. 31.4.

נַחַל   n e h e l J Ezek. 47.7; cf. paragraph X and XXIII
sub ח.

נַחֲלָה   n e h e l a J Isa. 17.11; see the note on נַחַל.

נַחֲלָתְךָ ν ε ε λ α ϑ α χ o Ps. 28.9.

נחם   מְנַחֵם μ α ν α η μ G 2 Ki. 15.17; m a n a e m On ib.

נחמה   נִחָמְתִּי naamathi J Zech. 8.14; MT: נִחָמְתִּי.

נָחָשׁ   ν α α s G 2 Sam. 17.25; n a a s On ib.

נחש   נְחוּשָׁה ν ε ο υ σ α o Ps. 18.35.

נַחַת   n a a t h On Gen. 36.13.

נחת   וְנָחֲתָה o υ ν α α ϑ α o Ps. 18.35; MT: וְנִחֲתָה.

נטה   וַתֵּט o υ α ϑ ε τ o Ps. 44.19.

אַטֶּה α τ τ ε o Ps. 49.5.

הַטֵּה ε τ τ η o Ps. 31.3.

נְכֹאת   nechotha J Gen. 43.11.

נְכֹתֹה nechotha J Isa. 39.2.

נָכוֹן   ν α χ ω ν A 2 Sam. 6.6.

נָכִים   ν η χ ι μ o Ps. 35.15.

נֵכָר $\nu\,\eta\,\chi\,a\,\rho$ o Ps. 18.46.

נָמֵר n e m e r J Jer. 5.6.

נסה אֲנַסָּה e n a s s e J Isa. 7.12.

נסיך נְסִיכֵי n e s i c h e J Mic. 5.4.

נסס מְתְנוֹסָסוֹת m e t h n o s a s o t h J Zech. 9.16.

נעמן נַעֲמָנִים n e a m e n i m J Isa. 17.10.

נעם a) $\nu\,\epsilon\,\epsilon\,\mu$ G in $A\beta\epsilon\iota\nu\epsilon\epsilon\mu$, Ju. 4.6; the second ϵ is a
transliteration of the ע; cf. paragraph XXIII sub ע.

b) n o e m On in Abinoem, ib.; see the preceding note.

נַעֲצוּץ n e s u s J Isa. 55.13.

נַעַר $\nu\,\epsilon\,\rho$ o Hos. 11.4.

נְפִילִים a) n i f i l i m J Gen. 6.4 (editio Lagarde).

b) הַנְּפִילִים a n n a p h i l i m J Gen. 6.4.

נפל תִּפֹּל t h e p h p h o l J Ezek. 8.1.

יִפְּלוּ $\iota\,\epsilon\,\varphi\,o\,\lambda\,v$ o Ps. 18.39.

נפתול נַפְתּוּלֵי n e p h t h u l e J Gen. 30.8; n e p t u l e J ib.
(ed. Lagarde).

נפש נַפְשִׁי $\nu\,\epsilon\,\varphi\,\sigma\,\iota$ o Ps. 30.4.

נַפְשׁוֹ $\nu\,\epsilon\,\varphi\,\sigma\,\omega$ o Ps. 89.49.

נַפְשֵׁנוּ $\nu\,\epsilon\,\varphi\,\sigma\,\iota\,\nu\,o\,v$ o Ps. 35.25.

נצח לָנֶצַח $\lambda\,a\,\nu\,\epsilon s$ o Ps. 49.10.

נצח לַמְנַצֵּח $\lambda\,a\,\mu\,a\,\nu\,a\,\sigma\,\sigma\,\eta$ o Ps. 31.1; l a m a n a s s e J
praefatio in Dan.

נְצִיב a) $\nu\,a\,\sigma\,\epsilon\,\iota\,\beta$ B Josh. 15.43; n a s i b On ib.

b) $\nu\,\epsilon\,\sigma\,\iota\,\beta$ A ib.

נצל הַצִּילֵנִי $\epsilon\,\sigma\,\iota\,\lambda\,\eta\,\nu\,\iota$ o Ps. 31.3.

נֵצֶר n e s e r J Isa. 11.1.

כְּנֵצֶר c h a n e s e r J Isa. 14.19.

נצר תֵּצֹר $\vartheta\,\epsilon\,\sigma\,a\,\rho$ o Isa. 26.3.

תִּצְּרֵנִי $\vartheta\,\epsilon\,\sigma\,\sigma\,\epsilon\,\rho\,\eta\,\nu\,\iota$ o Ps. 32.7.

נֹצֵר $\nu\,\omega\,\sigma\,\eta\,\rho$ o Ps. 31.24.

נְצוּרֵי n e s u r e J Isa. 49.6.

נֶקֶב $\nu\,a\,\kappa\,\epsilon\,\beta$ A Josh. 19.33.

נקד נֹקְדִים n o c e d i m J Amos 1.1.

נקמה נְקָמוֹת $\nu\,a\,\kappa\,a\,\mu\,\omega\,\vartheta$ o Ps. 18.48.

נֵר $\nu\,\eta\,\rho$ G 2 Sam. 14.51; n e r On ib.

נשא שָׂאתִי $\sigma\alpha\vartheta\iota$ o Ps. 89.51.

וְנָשָׂאם $ov\nu\epsilon\sigma\sigma\eta\mu$ o Ps. 28.9.

נשג וְאַשִּׂינֵם $ov\epsilon\sigma\iota\gamma\eta\mu$ o Ps. 18.38.

נשה מְנַשֶּׁה a) $\mu\alpha\nu\alpha\sigma\sigma\eta$ B Gen. 41.51; m a n a s s e On ib.
    b) $\mu\alpha\nu\nu\alpha\sigma\sigma\eta$ A ib.

נָשִׂיא n a s i J Ezek. 46.12.

נְשָׁמָה n a s a m a J Isa. 2.22.

נְשָׁמוֹת n a s a m o t h J Isa. 57.16.

נֶשֶׁף n e s e p h J Isa. 21.4.

נְשָׁפָה n e s e p h a J Jer. 13.16; MT: נָשַׁף.

נְתִינִים $\nu\alpha\vartheta\iota\nu\epsilon\iota\mu$ A Ezra 2.58.

הַנְּתִינִים $\alpha\nu\nu\alpha\vartheta\iota\nu\iota\mu$ A in $B\eta\vartheta\alpha\nu\nu\alpha\vartheta\iota\nu\iota\mu$, Neh. 3.31.

נתן $\nu\alpha\vartheta\alpha\nu$ G Ezra 8.16; o Ps. 46.7; n a t h a n On in Jonathan, Ju. 18.30.

נְתָתָה $\nu\alpha\vartheta\alpha\vartheta$ o Ps. 18.41.

וַיִּתֵּן $ov\iota\epsilon\vartheta\vartheta\epsilon\nu$ o Ps. 18.33.

וַתִּתֵּן $ov\vartheta\epsilon\vartheta\vartheta\epsilon\nu$ o Ps. 18.36.

אָתְּנֵהוּ $\epsilon\vartheta\nu\eta ov$ o Ps. 89.28.

הַנּוֹתֵן $\alpha\nu\nu\omega\vartheta\eta\nu$ o Ps. 18.48.

ס

סבב יְסוֹבְבֶנּוּ $\iota\sigma\omega\beta\alpha\beta\epsilon\nu\nu ov$ o Ps. 32.10.

תְּסוֹבְבֵנִי $\vartheta\sigma\omega\beta\alpha\beta\eta\nu\iota$ o Ps. 32.7.

יְסַבְּנִי $\iota\sigma\alpha\beta\beta ov\nu\iota$ o Ps. 49.6; MT: יְסׇבְּנִי.

סְבָךְ a) s a b a c On Gen. 22.13.
    b) $\sigma\alpha\beta\epsilon\kappa$ A ib.; s a b e c h J ib.

סְגֻלָּה s g o l l a J Mal. 3.17.

סֻנֵּר הִסְגַּרְתַּנִי $\epsilon\sigma\gamma\epsilon\rho\vartheta\alpha\nu\iota$ o Ps. 31.9.

סוד a) בְּסוֹד $\beta\alpha\sigma\omega\delta$ A in $B\alpha\sigma\omega\delta\iota\alpha$, Neh. 3.6; b a s o d J Jer. 23.18.
    סוֹדִי s o d i On Num. 13.10.
    b) $\sigma ov\delta\epsilon\iota$ B ib.; $\sigma ov\delta\iota$ A ib.

סוס s u s J Isa. 38.14.

כְּסוּס $\chi\iota\sigma ov s$ o Ps. 32.9.

סוּסִי $\sigma ov\sigma\epsilon\iota$ B Num. 13.11; $\sigma ov\sigma\iota$ A ib.; s u s i On ib.

סוּפָה בְּסוּפָה b a s u p h a J Nah. 1.3.
סִיג s i g J Ezek. 22.18.
סִינִים s i g i m J Isa. 1.22.
סִינִים s i n i m J Isa. 49.12.
סִיס s i s J Isa. 38.14.
סכה בְּסֻכָּה $\beta \sigma o \chi \chi a$ O Ps. 31.21: BCXXA lege BCOXXA;
    cf. Thompson Facs. 4 and 7 (C—O).
    סֻכֹּת $\sigma o \kappa \chi \omega \vartheta$ G Num. 33.5; s o c c h o t h On
    Ex. 12.37.
    s o c o t h On Gen. 33.17; s o c h o t h J ib.; Amos
    5.26; MT: סֻכּוּת.
סֹכֵן s o c e n J Isa. 22.15.
סֹכֵן הַמְסֻכָּן a m s u c h a n J Isa. 40.20.
סֶלָה a) $\sigma \epsilon \lambda a$ O Ps. 32.7; s e l a J Hab. 3.3.
    b) $\sigma \epsilon \lambda$ O Ps. 3.3.
סלע סַלְעִי $\sigma \epsilon \lambda \epsilon \iota$ O Ps. 31.4; cf. in the BV סלעי ib. 42.10
    in Ms. Ec 1.
סָמַךְ $\sigma a \mu a \chi$ A in $A\chi\iota\sigma a\mu a\chi$, Ex. 35.34; $\sigma a \mu a \kappa$ B
    in $A\chi\iota\sigma a\mu a\kappa$, ib.
    סָמוּךְ s a m u c h J Isa. 26.3.
סנא הַסְּנָאָה $a \sigma a \nu o \upsilon a$ A 1 Chron. 9.7.
סער תִּסְעָדֵנִי $\vartheta \epsilon \sigma a \delta \eta \nu \iota$ O Ps. 18.36: ΘΕCΔΗΝΙ lege
    ΘΕCΑΔΗΝΙ.
סַף s e p h J Ezek. 40.6.
ספר סֹפֵר s o p h e r J Isa. 36.3.
סְפָרַד s a p h a r a d J Obad. 20.
סָרִיס $\sigma a \rho \epsilon \iota s$ A in $P a\beta\sigma a\rho\epsilon\iota s$, 2 Ki. 18.17; s a r i s On in
    Rabsaris, ib.
סַרְפַּד s a r p h o d J Isa. 55.13.
סֵתֶר $\sigma \epsilon \vartheta \rho$ O Ps. 32.7.
    בְּסֵתֶר $\beta \sigma \epsilon \vartheta \rho$ O Ps. 31.21.
    סִתְרִי $\sigma \epsilon \vartheta \rho \iota$ A Ex. 6.22; s e t h r i On ib.
    $\sigma \epsilon \tau \rho \iota$ B ib.: CEΓPI lege T for Γ; cf. Thompson
    Facs. 3.
סתר הִסְתַּרְתָּ $\epsilon \sigma \vartheta \epsilon \rho \vartheta a$ O Ps. 30.8.
    תַּסְתִּיר $\vartheta \epsilon \sigma \vartheta \epsilon \rho$ O Ps. 89.47; MT: תַּסְתֵּר.
    תַּסְתִּירֵם $\vartheta \epsilon \sigma \vartheta \iota \rho \eta \mu$ O Ps. 31.21.
    סָתוּר $\sigma a \vartheta o \upsilon \rho$ G Num. 13.13; MT: סָתוּר.

ע

עָבְד a) $a \beta \delta$ G in Aβδεμελεχ, Jer. 38.7.

לְעֶבֶד $\lambda a a \beta \delta$ o Ps. 36.1.

עַבְדֵי $a \beta \delta \epsilon \iota$ B 1 Chron. 6.29; $a \beta \delta \iota$ A ib.

עַבְדְּךָ $a \beta \delta a \chi$ o Ps. 89.40.

עַבְדוֹ $a \beta \delta \omega$ o Ps. 35.27.

עַבְדֵי $a \beta \delta \eta$ A in Aβδησελμα, Ezra 2.58; o Ps. 113.1.

עֲבָדֶיךָ $a \beta \delta a \chi$ o Ps. 89.51; cf. in the PV עֲבָדִיךְ Ps. 90.13
(MdWI, p. א).

עבד b) עבד $a \beta \epsilon \delta$ A Ju. 9.26; a b e d On ib.; cf. B-L.
§20 m.

עבד עוֹבֵד $\omega \beta \eta \delta$ G Ruth 4.17; o b e t h On ib.

עֶבֶר a) $\epsilon \beta \epsilon \rho$ A Gen. 10.21; e b e r On ib.

b) עֲבָרִים $a \beta a \rho \epsilon \iota \mu$ G Num. 33.47; a b a r i m On ib.

מַעֲבָרִים m e a b a r i m J Jer. 22.20.

עבד עָבַרְתִּי a b a r t h i J Hos. 10.11.

אֶעֱבֹר e e b o r J Amos 5.17.

עֶבְרִי $\omega \beta \rho \eta$ o Ps. 89.42.

הַתְעַבַּרְתָּ $\epsilon \vartheta a \beta \beta a \rho \vartheta$ o Ps. 89.39.

עברה עֶבְרַת e b r a t h J Amos 1.11.

עברה בְּעַבְרוֹת $\beta \epsilon \gamma a \beta \rho \omega \vartheta$ o Ps. 7.7.

עִבְרִי i b r i J Gen. 14.13.

הָעִבְרִים a h e b r i m On Ex. 2.6; on the h see paragraph X.

עִבְרִיּוֹת e b r i o t h On Ex. 1.16.

עָגוּר a) a g o r J Isa. 38.14.

b) a g u r J ib.

עֶגְלָה a) $a \gamma \lambda a$ A 1 Chron. 3.3.

b) e g l a J Hos. 10.11.

עגלה עֲגָלוֹת $a \gamma a \lambda \omega \vartheta$ o Ps. 46.10.

עד a) $a \delta$ o Ps. 89.47.

b) $\epsilon \delta$ o Ps. 18.38.

לָעַד l a e d J Mic. 7.18.

עד וָעַד $o \upsilon \eta \delta$ o Ps. 89.38.

עדד עוֹדֵד $\omega \delta \eta \delta$ B 2 Chron. 15.1.

עדים e d d i m J Isa. 64.5.

עדי עֶדְיוֹ $a \delta \iota \omega$ o Ps. 32.9.

עֵדֶן $\epsilon\delta\epsilon\nu$ A Gen. 2.8; e d e n On ib.

עֵדֶר a) $\epsilon\delta\epsilon\rho$ A 1 Chron. 23.23.

b) a d e r On Gen. 35.21.

עוֹד $\omega\delta$ o Ps. 49.10.

עוֹלם a) לְעוֹלָם $\lambda\omega\lambda\alpha\mu$ o Ps. 30.7; l o l a m J Ezek. 26.21.

הָעוֹלָם $\alpha\omega\lambda\alpha\mu$ o Ps. 28.9.

b) עוֹלָמִים $\omega\lambda\epsilon\mu\epsilon\iota\mu$ o Isa. 26.4.

עוֹן עָוֹן $\alpha\omega\nu$ o Ps. 49.6.

עֲוֹנָם $\alpha\nu\omega\nu\alpha\nu$ o Ps. 89.33; perhaps to be explained as an amalgamation of two readings: $\alpha\nu\nu\alpha\nu$ (cf. אוֹנֶן $\alpha\nu\nu\alpha\nu$)$+\omega\nu\alpha\nu$ cf. on מַעֲמוּ; o n a m J Zech. 5.6.

עוּר הָעִירָה $\alpha\iota\rho\alpha$ o Ps. 35.23.

עוֹרֵב $\omega\rho\eta\beta$ G Ju. 7.25; o r e b On ib.

עוֹרְבִים o r b i m J Isa. 15.7.

עז o ζ o Ps. 28.8.

עָזִי o $\zeta\epsilon\iota$ G in O$\zeta\epsilon\iota\eta\lambda$, Ex. 6.18; o Ps. 28.7; cf. עָז Ex. 15.2; further in the BV: עָזְּךָ Ps. 63.3; עֹז Prov. 10.15 in Ms. Ec 1; o z i On in Ozihel, Ex. 6.18.

עַז α s B in A$\sigma\gamma\alpha\delta$, Ezra 2.12; $\alpha\zeta$ A in A$\zeta\gamma\alpha\delta$, Ezra 8.12.

עָזַב וְעָזְבוּ $o\nu\alpha\zeta\beta o\nu$ o Ps. 49.11.

יַעַזְבוּ $\iota\epsilon\zeta\epsilon\beta o\nu$ o Ps. 89.31.

עֲזוּבָה $\alpha\zeta o\nu\beta\alpha$ A 1 Ki. 22.42; a z u b a On ib.

עֵזֶר a) $\epsilon\zeta\rho$ o Ps. 46.2; MT: עֶזְרָה.

עָזְרִי $\epsilon\zeta\rho\iota$ A Ju. 6.11; e z r i On ib.; $\epsilon\sigma\delta\rho\epsilon\iota$ B ib.

וְעָזְרָה $o\nu\epsilon\zeta\rho\alpha$ o Ps. 46.6; MT: יַעְזְרָה.

b) עֵזֶר $\epsilon\zeta\epsilon\rho$ G in A$\beta\iota\epsilon\zeta\epsilon\rho$, Ju. 6.34.

עָזַר $\alpha\zeta\alpha\rho$ G in E$\lambda\epsilon\alpha\zeta\alpha\rho$, Ex. 6.23; a z a r On in Eleazar, ib.

עֶזֶר $\omega\zeta\eta\rho$ o Ps. 30.11.

עָזוּר a z u r On Ezek. 11.1; MT: עָזֻר.

וְנֶעֱזָרְתִּי $o\nu\nu\epsilon\zeta\alpha\rho\vartheta\iota$ o Ps. 28.7: $o\nu\nu\alpha\zeta\epsilon\rho\vartheta\iota$ lege $o\nu\nu\epsilon\zeta\alpha\rho\vartheta\iota$.

עזרה בְּעָזְרָתִי $\beta\alpha\epsilon\zeta\rho\alpha\vartheta\iota$ o Ps. 35.2.

עֲזָרָה a z a r a J Ezek. 43.17.

עטה הָעֱטִיתָ $\epsilon\epsilon\tau\eta\vartheta$ o Ps. 89.46.

עֲטָרָה $\alpha\tau\alpha\rho\alpha$ B 1 Chron. 2.26.

עֲטָרוֹת $\alpha\tau\alpha\rho\omega\vartheta$ G Num. 32.3; a t a r o t h On ib.

עַיִן   a) $a\iota\nu$ A Josh. 19.7; o Ps. 35.9; a i n On Num. 34.11.

b) עַיִן $\eta\nu$ A in $H\nu a\delta\delta a$, Josh. 19.21; e n On in Enadda, ib.

עֵינִי $\eta\nu\iota$ o Ps. 31.10.

עֵינֵנוּ $\eta\nu\eta\nu ov$ o Ps. 35.21.

עֵינָם e n a m J Zech. 5.6.

עֵינַיִם e n a i m On Gen. 38.21.

וְעֵינַיִם $ov\eta\nu a\iota\mu$ o Ps. 18.28: OTNNAIM lege H for
the first N; cf. Thompson Facs. 5.

עֵינֶיךָ $\eta\nu a\chi$ o Ps. 31.23.

עֵינָיו $\eta\nu av$ o Ps. 36.2.

בְּעֵינָיו $\beta\eta\eta\nu av$ o Ps. 36.3: BHNNAY lege H for the
first N; cf. Thompson Facs. 5.

עִיר $\iota\rho$ o Ps. 46.5; i r J Isa. 26.5.

בְּעִיר $\beta\epsilon\epsilon\iota\rho$ o Ps. 31.22.

הָעִיר $a\epsilon\iota\rho$ o Gen. 28.19.

עִירָם i r a m On Gen. 36.43.

עָרִים a r i m J Isa. 14.21.

עַל $a\lambda$ o Ps. 8.1; a l J Hab. 3.1.

וְעַל $ov a\lambda$ o Ps. 18.34.

עָלַי $a\lambda a\iota$ o Ps. 35.21.

עָלֶיךָ $a\lambda a\chi$ o Ps. 32.28.

עָלָיו $a\lambda av\iota$ o Ps. 89.46.

וְעָלֶיהָ $ov a\lambda\epsilon a$ o Ps. 7.8.

עֲלֵיהֶם a l e h e m J Zech. 14.17.

עֹלֶה   הָעֹלִית $\epsilon\epsilon\lambda\vartheta$ o Ps. 30.4; perhaps to be corrected to
$\epsilon\epsilon\lambda\eta\vartheta$; cf. §53a$\beta$.

עֲלִי $a\lambda\eta$ o Ps. 49.12; $a\lambda\epsilon$ o Ps. 92.4 (1°).

וְעֲלִי $ov a\lambda\epsilon$ o Ps. 92.4.

עֹלֶה   a l e J Ezek. 47.12.

עֲלוּמִים עֲלוּמָיו $a\lambda ov\mu av$ o Ps. 89.46.

עֶלְיוֹן $\epsilon\lambda\iota\omega\nu$ o Ps. 46.5; e l i o n J Isa. 2.22.

עֲלִיל בַּעֲלִיל $\beta a a\lambda\iota\lambda$ o Ps. 12.7.

עֶלֶם נַעְלְמָה n a a l m a J Job 28.21.

הָעֶלִים e e l i m J 2 Ki. 4.27 (vol. IV, p. 109 B).

עַלְמָה a l m a J Isa. 7.14.

עֲלָמוֹת a l a m o t h J Ps. 9.1 (on Isa. 7.14); MT: עַל מוּת.

עֲלָמוֹת $a\lambda\mu\omega\vartheta$ o Ps. 46.1; MT: עֲלָמוֹת.

עַם   ε μ   o Ps. 18.26.

מָעַמּוֹ   μ η ε μ μ ω α υ   o Ps. 89.34; perhaps originating in the combination of two separate readings: μηεμμω+μηεμμαυ; cf. on יְרִיבִי and on עָוֹנָם.

עִמָּנוּ   ε μ μ α ν ο υ   G in Εμμανουηλ, Isa. 7.14; o Ps. 46.8; e m m a n u On in Emmanuhel, Isa. 7.14.

עַם   a) a μ   o Ps. 18.28; a m On in Amram, Ex. 6.18.

בְּעַם   β a a μ   o Ps. 35.18.

עַמִּי   a μ ε ι   B in Αμειναδαβ, Num. 1.7; a μ ι   A in Αμιναδαβ, ib.; a m i On in Aminadab, ib.

עַמִּים   a μ ι μ   o Ps. 89.51.

הָעַמִּים   a a μ ι μ   o Ps. 49.2: AAMIN lege M for N.

b) עַמִּי   a m m i On in Ammiod, 2 Sam. 13.37.

עַמֶּךָ   a μ μ α χ   o Ps. 28.9.

עַמִּים   a μ μ ι μ   o Ps. 18.48: AMIMIM lege AMMIM.

עמד   הֶעֱמַדְתָּ   ε ε μ ε δ ε ϑ   o Ps. 31.9.

    יַעֲמִדֵנִי   ι ε μ ι δ η ν ι   o Ps. 18.34.

עמוד   עַמּוּדֶהָ   a μ ο υ δ a   o Ps. 75.4; MT: עַמּוּדֶיהָ.

עמית   עֲמִיתִי   a m i t h i J Zech. 13.7.

עמק   e m e c On Josh. 17.16.

    הָעֵמֶק   a ε μ ε κ   A in Βηϑαεμεκ, Josh. 19.27.

ענה   a ν a   A Gen. 36.14; MT: עֲנָה; a n a On ib.

    עָנָם   a ν a μ   O Ps. 18.42.

    עֲנָתָה   a n a t h a J Hos. 2.17.

    עִנִּיתִי   ε ν ν η ϑ ι   o Ps. 35.13.

    מְעוֹנִים   μ ο ο υ ν ε ι μ   A Ezra 2.50.

ענוה   וְעַנְוָתְךָ   ο υ a ν a υ a ϑ a χ   o Ps. 18.36; perhaps to be corrected to: ουανουαϑαχ.

עֲנִי   a ν ι   o Ps. 18.28.

    עֲנִיֵי   a ν ι η   o Ps. 76.10; MT: עַנְוֵי; a n i e J Zech. 11.11.

עני   עָנְיִי   ο ν ι   o Ps. 31.8; perhaps to be corrected to ονιι; haplography; the following word ιαδαϑ begins with ι, too.

עִנְיָן   a n i a n J Eccl. 1.13.

עֹנְנָה   o n e n a J Isa. 57.3.

עֲנָק   ε ν a κ   A Num. 13.22; ε ν a χ   B ib.

    עֲנָקִים   ε ν a κ ε ι μ   G Deut. 2.10.

    a n a c i m On ib.: anacin, lege m for the second n.

עפף   מְעוֹפֵף m o p h e p h J Isa. 14.29.

עָפָר   α φ α ρ o Ps. 30.10; a p h a r J Gen. 3.14; a f a r J ib.,
ed. Lagarde.

       בֶּעָפָר χ α α φ α ρ o Ps. 18.43.

       עֶפְרָה a f a r a On Josh. 18.23; MT: עָפְרָה.

עֲצָבִים   α σ ε β ε ι ν o Ps. 127.2; MT: הָעֲצָבִים.

עצה   בַּעֲצַת β η σ α ϑ o Ps. 1.1; cf. in the PV וּעֹצָה Isa. 44.26
(MdWI, p. ד).

עצם   עָצוּם α σ ο υ μ o Ps. 35.18.

עֲצָרָה   a s a r a J Joel 1.14.

עָקֵב   a) עִקְבוֹת ε κ β ω ϑ o Ps. 89.52.
     b) עָקֵב e c e b J Amos 4.12.

עקב   יַעֲקֹב ι α κ ω β G Gen. 25.26; i a c o b On ib.
     עֲקֻבֵּי α κ ο β β α ι o Ps. 49.6; MT: עָקֵבָי; cf. Hos. 6.8.

עקרב   עַקְרַבִּים a) α κ ρ α β ε ι μ B Josh. 15.3: Ακραβειν lege
μ for ν.
     b) α κ ρ α β β ε ι μ A ib.; a c r a b b i m On ib.

עָקֵשׁ   ε κ κ η s o Ps. 18.27.

עקש   עָקֵשׁ ε κ κ η s A 1 Chron. 11.28.

עֵר   η ρ A Gen. 38.3; e r On ib.

ערב   a) בָּעָרָב β α α ρ β o Ps. 30.6.
     b) עָרָב a r a b J Isa. 21.13.

עֲרָבָה   α ρ α β α B in Βαιϑαραβα, Josh. 15.6; a r a b a On
Deut. 1.7.

       עֲרָבוֹת α ρ α β ω ϑ G Num. 26.63; a r a b o t h On ib.

עֲרָבִי   a r a b e J Jer. 3.2.

       עֲרָבִים a r a b i m J Isa. 15.7.

עָרוּם   a r o m J Gen. 3.1.

עֲרִירִי   a r i r i J Jer. 22.29.

עֹרֶף   o ρ φ o Ps. 18.41.

עֶרֶשׂ   a r e s J Amos 3.12.

עָשׁ   a s J Hos. 5.12.

עֲשָׂה   α σ α G in Ασαηλ, 2 Sam. 23.24; a s a On in Asahel, ib.

       תַּעֲשׂוּ ϑ ε σ ο υ o Mal. 2.13.

       עֹשֶׂה ω σ η o Ps. 31.24.

עָשׂוֹר   α σ ω ρ o Ps. 92.4.

עָשִׁיר   α σ ι ρ o Ps. 49.3: CIP lege AC IP; haplography (IAAΔ
CIP; Δ—A).

עָשָׂן‎ α σ α ν A 1 Sam. 30.30; a s a n On Josh. 19.7.

עשר‎ עָשְׂרָם‎ ο σ ρ α μ O Ps. 49.7.

עָשְׂרָה‎ e s r e J Ezek. 40.49.

עשש‎ עָשְׁשָׁה‎ α σ σ α O Ps. 31.10.

עָשְׁתַּי‎ a s t e J Ezek. 40.49.

פ

פאה‎ פֵּאָת‎ f a t h On Lev. 19.9.

פְּאֵרָה‎ p h u r a J Isa. 10.33.

פגר‎ פְּגָרִים‎ p h a g a r i m J Jer. 31.40; cf. in the BV פֹּנֵרֵי‎ Lev. 26.30 in Ms. Ea 13.

פְּדָה‎ φ α δ α G in Φαδαηλ, Num. 34.28; f a d a On in Fadaia, 2 Ki. 23.36.

פְּדִיָת‎ φ α δ ι ϑ O Ps. 31.6: ΦΑΛΙΘ, lege Δ for Λ.

יַפְדֶּה‎ ι ε φ δ ε O Ps. 49.8: ΙΕΦΑΕ, lege Δ for A.

פְּדֹה‎ φ α δ ω O Ps. 49.8.

פִּדְיוֹן‎ φ ε δ ι ω ν O Ps. 49.9.

פה‎ st. constr. פִי‎ φ ι A in Φικολ, Gen. 21.22; f i On in Fichol, ib.

פִי‎ φ ι O Ps. 49.4.

פִּיהֶם‎ φ ι ε μ O Ps. 35.21.

בְּפִיהֶם‎ β α φ ι ε μ O Ps. 49.14.

פוך‎ בְּפוּךְ‎ b a p h p h u c h J Isa. 54.11.

פוע‎ יָפִיעַ‎ ι α φ ι ε A Josh. 10.3; ε is the transliteration of the y, cf. paragraph XXIII sub y; i a f i e On ib.

פור‎ אָפִיר‎ α φ ι ρ O Ps. 89.34.

פוּרָה‎ p h u r a J Isa. 63.3.

פָּז‎ φ α s B in Ελειφας, 1 Chron. 1.35.

φ α ζ A in Ελιφαζ, ib.; p h a z J Isa. 13.12; f a z On in Elifaz, Gen. 36.4.

פַּחַד‎ π α α δ G in Σαλπααδ, Num. 26.33.

φ α α δ O Ps. 36.2; f a a t h On in Salfaath, Num. 26.33.

פחה‎ פַּחַת‎ φ α α ϑ A in Φααϑμωαβ, Ezra 10.30.

φ α α δ B in Φααδμωαβ, ib.

פחז‎ פּוֹחֲזִים‎ p h o e z i m J Zeph. 3.4.

פָּלָא‎ p h e l e J Isa. 9.5.

פלא‎ הִפְלִיא‎ ε φ λ ι O Ps. 31.22.

פֶּלֶג a) f a l e g On Gen. 10.25; φαλεκ A ib.; φαλεχ
B 1 Chron. 1.25.

b) פְּלָנָיו φαλαγαυ vel φλαγαυ o Ps. 46.5 (H-R.).

פֶּלֶט φαλητ o Ps. 32.7; without gemination of the 2nd
radical; cf. on אָכְזָב.

פְּלֵטָנִי φελλετηνι o Ps. 31.2.

פְּלֵיטָה a) p h a l e t a J Joel 3.5.

b) פְּלֵיטִים p h e l e t i m J Obad. 17.

פֶּנַג p h a n a g J Ezek. 27.17.

פנה לִפְנוֹת λαφνωϑ o Ps. 46.6: ΛΦΝΩΘ lege ΛΑΦΝΩΘ.

פָּנוֹת φεʹννωϑ o Mal. 2.13; MT: פָּנוֹת.

יִפְנֶה ιεφοννη G Num. 13.7.

פנים פְּנֵי φανη o Ps. 18.43.

פָּנֶיךָ φαναχ o Ps. 30.8.

פָּנָיו p h a n a u J Isa. 6.2.

פֶּסַח p h a s e J Ezek. 25.15.

תִּפְסַח ϑαψα A 1 Ki. 5.4.

פעל פְּעָלְךָ p h a l a c h J Hab. 3.2.

פָּעַל φααλ A in Ελφααλ, 1 Chron. 8.18.

פָּעַלְתָּ φααλϑα o Ps. 31.20.

פקד וּפְקַדְתִּי ουϑακαδϑι o Ps. 89.33: ουφαδϑι lege ουφακαδϑι.

פָּקוּד p h a c u d J Ezek. 23.23; MT: פָּקוֹד.

פַּר p h a r J Ezek. 43.23.

פָּרִים p h a r i m J Hos. 14.3.

פָּרָא p h a r a J Gen. 16.12; f a r a J ib., ed. Lagarde.

פרד כְּפָרֶד χφαρδ o Ps. 32.9.

פָּרָה φαρα B Josh. 18.23.

הַפָּרָה a f f a r a On ib.

פרח פָּרוּחַ φαρρου A 1 Ki. 4.17.

פְּרִי p h e r i J Hos. 14.3.

פָּרִיץ p h a r i s J Ezek. 18.10.

פֶּרֶץ a) φαρες A Gen. 38.29; f a r e s On ib.

b) p h e r e s J Isa. 58.12.

c) פְּרָצִים φαρασειμ A in Βααλφαρασειν, lege μ for
ν, 1 Chron. 14.11; p h a r a s i m J Isa. 28.27.

פרץ פָּרָצְתָּ φαρασϑ o Ps. 89.41.

פֶּרֶק p h e r e c J Nah. 3.1.

פָּרָשׁ p h a r e s J Mal. 2.3.

פֶּשַׁע   φ ε σ α   o Ps. 36.2.

פְּשָׁעָם   φ ε σ α μ   o Ps. 89.33: ΦϹΑΜ lege ΦΕϹΑΜ.

פּוֹתָה   p h o t h a   J Mic. 7.11.

פתח   בְּפִהָחֶיךָ   b a p h e t h e e   J Mic. 5.5.

פתוח   פְּתוּחָהּ   p h e t e e   J Zech. 3.9.

פתח   π α ϑ α   B in παϑαια, Neh. 11.24.

     φ α ϑ α   A in Φαϑαια, ib.

     יִפְתָּח   ι ε φ ϑ α   A Josh. 15.43;   ι ε φ ϑ α ε   G Ju. 11.14;
     the second ε=ה, cf. paragraph XXIII sub ה;
     i e p t e On Josh. 15.43.

     אֶפְתָּח   ε φ ϑ α   o Ps. 49.5.

     מְפַתֵּהַ   m a p h a t e   J Zech. 3.9.

     פִתֵּחַ   φ ε ϑ ε ϑ α   o Ps. 30.12; without gemination of
     the 2nd radical; cf. on אָכוּב.

פְּתִיגִיל   p h t h i g a l   J Isa. 3.24.

פתל   נִפְתַּלְתִּי   n e p h t h a l e t h i   J Gen. 30.8;   n e p t a l t i
     J ib., ed. Lagarde.

     תִּתְפַּתָּל   ϑ ε ϑ φ α ϑ ϑ α λ   o Ps. 18.27.

צ

צֵאָה   s o a   J in cisoa, Isa. 28.8.

צאן   כַּצֹּאן   χ α σ ω ν   o Ps. 49.15.

צֶאֱצָאִים   s a s a i m   J Isa. 22.24.

צְבָאוֹת   σ α β α ω ϑ   G 1 Sam. 1.3; o Ps. 46.8;   s a b a o t h   On
     1 Sam. 1.3.

צְבִי   s a b a i   J Dan. 11.41.

צֵדָה   s e d a   J Gen. 45.21.

צַדִּיק   a) σ α δ ι κ   o Isa. 26.2.

     b) צַדִּיקִים   σ α δ δ ι κ ι μ   o Ps. 32.11.

צדק   a) צִדְקִי   σ ε δ κ ι   o Ps. 35.27.

     צִדְקֶךָ   σ ε δ κ α χ   o Ps. 35.28.

     כְּצִדְקֶךָ   χ σ ε δ κ α χ   o Ps. 35.24: ΧϹΕΔΚΑΔ lege X for
     second Δ; for some resemblance cf. Thompson
     Facs. 18.

     b) צֶדֶק   σ ε δ ε κ   A in Μελχισεδεκ, Gen. 14.18;   s e d e c
     On in Melchisedec, ib.

     הַצֶּדֶק   a s e d e c   J Isa. 19.18.

צדק   צִדְקֵנוּ s a d e c e n u J Jer. 23.6; MT: צִדְקֵנוּ; but cf. in
the BV צִדְקִי Job 35.2 in Ms. Ec 1, for MT צִדְקִי.

צדקה   a) בְּצִדְקָתֶךָ β σ ε δ κ α ϑ α χ o Ps. 31.2.
b) צְדָקָה s a d a c a J Isa. 5.7.

צהר   יִצְהָר ι σ α α ρ A Ex. 6.18; MT: יִצְהָר; i s a a r J Zech. 4.14.
i e s s a a r On Ex. 6.18.

צו   s a u J Isa. 28.10; cf. B-L. §17z.
לָצָו l a s a u J ib.

צוד   s u d J Hos. 9.13.

צום   בָּצֹום β α σ ω μ o Ps. 35.13.

צוף   σ ο υ φ G 1 Chron. 6.20.

צור   a) σ ο υ ρ G Num. 25.15; o Ps. 18.32; s u r J Isa. 10.26.
צוּרִי σ ο υ ρ ε ι B in Σουρεισαδαι, Num. 1.6; σ ο υ ρ ι
A in Σουρισαδαι, ib.; o Ps. 18.47; s u r i On in
Surisaddai, Num. 1.6.
וְצוּרָם ο υ σ ο υ ρ α μ o Ps. 49.15.
b) צוּר σ ω ρ o Isa. 26.4.
צוּרִי s o r i On in Sorihel, Num. 3.35.

צחק   יִצְחָק ι σ α α κ G Gen. 21.3; i s a a c On ib.; MT: יִצְחָק.

צחר   s o o r J Ezek. 27.18.

צי   צִיִּים s i i m J Isa. 13.21.

ציון   בְּצִיֹּון b a s a i o n J Isa. 25.5.

ציון   צִיֻּנִים s i o n i m J Jer. 31.21.

צינק   s i n a c J Jer. 29.26.

ציר   s i r J Obad. 1.

צל   a) σ α λ G in Σαλπααδ, Num. 26.33; cf. in the BV
צֵל Job 8.9 in Ms. Ec 1; s a l On in Salfaath,
Num. 26.33; cf. B-L. §14z and g'.
b) בְּצֵל β ε σ ε λ G in Βεσελεηλ, Ex. 31.2; b e s e l On
in Beselehel, ib.
צִלָּה s e l a On Gen. 4.19; MT: צִלָּה; cf. Jerome's explanation: umbra e i u s.
σ ε λ λ α A ib.

צלח   הַצְלִיחָה נָא α σ λ ι α ν ν α o Ps. 118.25.

צלע   וּבְצַלְעִי ο υ β σ α λ η o Ps. 35.15.

צלצל   s e l s e l J Isa. 18.1.

צמה   צַמָּתֵךְ s e m m a t h e c h J Isa. 47.2.
s a m t h e c h J ib.

צָמַח   s e m a J Zech. 6.12.

צמת   אַצְמִיתֵם $\alpha\sigma\mu\iota\vartheta\alpha\upsilon\mu$ O Ps. 18.41.

צִנָּה   a) $\sigma\epsilon\nu\alpha$ A Josh. 15.3.

       b) $\sigma\epsilon\nu\nu\alpha$ B ib.: CENNAK dele K, dittography.

       וְצִנָּה $o\upsilon\sigma\epsilon\nu\nu\alpha$ O Ps. 35.2.

       c) צִנּוֹת s a n n o t h J Amos 4.2.

צָנִיף   s a n i p h J Zech. 8.5.

צנע   הַצְנֵעַ e s n e J Mic. 6.8.

צנתר   צַנְתְּרוֹת s i n t h o r o t h J Zech. 4.12.

צעד   צְעָדִי $\sigma\alpha\alpha\delta\alpha\iota$ O Ps. 18.37; MT: צַעֲדִי.

צְעָקָה   s a a c a J Isa. 5.7.

צפה   צוֹפִים $\sigma\omega\varphi\iota\mu$ A 1 Sam. 1.1; s o f i m On ib.

צָפוֹן $\sigma\alpha\varphi\omega\nu$ B Num. 26.15; MT: צְפוֹן; s a p h o n J Jer. 25.26.

צְפוֹנִי $\sigma\alpha\varphi\omega\nu\epsilon\iota$ B Num. 26.15; $\sigma\alpha\varphi\omega\nu\iota$ A ib.

צִפּוֹר $\sigma\epsilon\pi\varphi\omega\rho$ G Num. 22.2; s e f o r On ib.

צְפִיעוֹת   s e p h o t h J Isa. 22.24.

צְפִירָה   s e p h p h i r a J Ezek. 7.10.

צָפַן $\sigma\alpha\varphi\alpha\nu$ G in Ελεισαφαν, Num. 3.30.

       צָפַנְתָּ $\sigma\alpha\varphi\alpha\nu\vartheta\alpha$ O Ps. 31.20.

       תִּצְפְּנֵם $\vartheta\iota\sigma\varphi\nu\eta\mu$ O Ps. 31.21.

       צָפוֹן $\sigma\alpha\varphi o\upsilon\nu$ O Ps. 48.3; MT: צָפוֹן.

צפען   צִפְעֹנִים s a p h p h o n i m J Jer. 8.17.

צַר $\sigma\alpha\rho$ O Ps. 31.10; s a r J Amos 3.11.

       מֵצַר $\mu\epsilon\sigma\sigma\alpha\rho$ O Ps. 32.7.

       צָרָיו $\sigma\alpha\rho\alpha\upsilon\iota$ O Ps. 89.43.

צרה   בְּצָרוֹת $\beta\sigma\alpha\rho\omega\vartheta$ O Ps. 31.8; 46.2.

צרע   צְרוּעָה $\sigma\alpha\rho o\upsilon\alpha$ A 1 Ki. 11.26.

צָרַעַת   s a r a t h J Gen. 17.16.

צרף   צְרוּפָה $\sigma\epsilon\rho o\upsilon\varphi\alpha$ O Ps. 18.31.

ק

קבע   הֲיִקְבַּע h a j e c b a J Mal. 3.8.

קָדִים   c a d i m J Ezek. 27.26.

קֶדֶם $\kappa\epsilon\delta\epsilon\mu$ G Ezek. 25.4; c e d e m J ib.

       מִקֶּדֶם m e c e d e m J Gen. 2.8.

קֵדְמָה $\kappa\epsilon\delta\mu\alpha$ A Gen. 25.15; c e d m a On ib.

קדש   קֹדֶשׁ $\kappa o\delta s$ O Ps. 46.5.

קֹדֶשׁ a) κο δ s ο Ps. 29.2.

בְּקֹדֶשׁ β ε κ ο δ s ο Ps. 89.36; MT: בְּקָדְשִׁי.

קָדְשׁוֹ κ ο δ σ ω ο Ps. 30.5: ΚΟΔΕΩ lege C for Є.

קָדְשָׁה codsa J Isa. 40.13.

b) קֹדֶשׁ codes J Isa. 52.1.

קָדְשׁוֹ cadeso J Isa. 63.10; cf. in the PV קָדְשׁוֹ Ps. 105.42 (Edelmann, p. ד, line 8).

c) הַקְּדֵשִׁים α κ κ ο δ α σ ι μ ο 2 Ki. 23.7; MT: הַקְּדֵשִׁים.

קָדֵשׁ κ α δ η s A Gen. 14.7; c a d e s On ib.

קְדֵשִׁים κ α δ η σ ε ι μ B 2 Ki. 23.7; κ α δ η σ ι μ A ib.: καδησιν lege μ for ν; c a d e s i m On ib.

קָדֵשָׁה c a d e s a J Isa. 27.1.

קְדֵשׁוֹת c a d e s o t h J Hos. 4.14.

קָהָל בְּקָהָל β α κ α α λ ο Ps. 35.18.

קָהָל קֹהֶלֶת c o e l e t h J Eccl. 1.1.

קַו c a u J Isa. 28.10; cf. B-L. §17z.

לְקָו l a c a u J ib.

קוֹל κ ω λ A in Κωλεια, Neh. 11.7; ο Ps. 28.6.

בְּקוֹלוֹ β κ ω λ ω ο Ps. 46.7.

קוּם קָם κ α μ G in Αδανεικαμ, Ezra 8.13; c a m On in Ahicam, 2 Ki. 22.12.

יָקוּם j a c c u m J Nah. 1.6.

קָמַי κ α μ α ι ο Ps. 18.40.

וְקוּם ο υ κ ο υ μ ο Ps. 35.2; MT: וְקוּמָה.

קוּם κ ο υ μ ο Ps. 18.39.

הֲקִמֹתוֹ α κ ι μ ω ϑ ω ο Ps. 89.44.

יָקִים ι α κ ε ι μ G 1 Chron. 8.19; i a c i m On in Eliacim 2 Ki. 18.18.

קוֹץ κ ω s G 1 Chron. 24.10.

הַקּוֹץ a) α κ ω s B Neh. 3.4.

b) α κ κ ω s A ib.

קוּץ וְהָקִיצָה ο υ α κ ι σ α ο Ps. 35.23.

קָטֹן הַקָּטֹן a) α κ α τ α ν B Ezra 8.12.

b) α κ κ α τ α ν A ib.

קִיא c i J in cisoa, Isa. 28.8.

קִיטֹר c i t o r J Gen. 19.28.

קִינָה κ ι ν α A Josh. 15.22.

קִיקָיוֹ c i c e i o n J Jonah 4.6.

קִיר   c i r ɟ Isa. 38.2.

קלל   קְלֹות   c a l l o t h ɟ Nah. 1.14.

קלע   קֹולֵעַ   c o l e a ɟ Jer. 10.18.

קִנְאָה   c e n a ɟ Ezek. 8.3.

קָנֶה   c a n e ɟ Jer. 6.20.

קָנָה $\kappa\alpha\nu\alpha$ G in Ἐλκανα, Ex. 6.24; c a n a On in Elcana, ib.

     קָנָּנִי   c a n a n i ɟ Prov. 8.22.

     קָנִיתִי   c a n i t h i ɟ Gen. 4.1.

קֶסֶת   c e s a t h ɟ Ezek. 9.2.

קצה   קָצֵה $\kappa\alpha\sigma\epsilon$ O Ps. 46.9.

קָצִין $\kappa\alpha\sigma\iota\nu$ A Josh. 19.13: $\kappa\alpha\sigma\iota\mu$ lege ν for μ; c a s i n
     On ib.: casim lege n for m.

קצץ   וְקָצַץ $o\upsilon\kappa\epsilon\sigma\sigma\eta s$ O Ps. 46.10: ΟΤΚ.ϹϹΗϹ lege
     ΟΤΚΕϹϹΗϹ.

קצר   הִקְצַרְתָּ $\epsilon\kappa\sigma\epsilon\rho\vartheta$ O Ps. 89.46.

קרא   קָרָאתָ   c a r a t h ɟ Jer. 3.12.

     קָרָאתִי $\kappa\alpha\rho\alpha\vartheta\iota$ O Hos. 11.1; c a r a t h i ɟ Isa. 7.14;
     MT: קָרָאת.

     וַיִּקְרָא $o\upsilon\iota\kappa\rho\alpha$ O Lev. 1.1.

     יִקְרָאֵנִי $\iota\kappa\rho\alpha\eta\nu\iota$ O Ps. 89.27.

     אֶקְרָא $\epsilon\kappa\rho\alpha$ O Ps. 30.9.

     קֹרֵא $\kappa\omega\rho\eta$ G 2 Chron. 31.14.

     קְראוּ $\kappa\epsilon\rho o\upsilon$ O Ps. 49.12; MT: קָראוּ.

קרב   a) בְּקֶרֶב $\beta\epsilon\kappa o\rho\beta$ O Ps. 36.2.

     b) בְּקִרְבָּהּ $\beta\kappa\epsilon\rho\beta\alpha$ O Ps. 46.6.

     c) קִרְבָּם $\kappa\alpha\rho\beta\alpha\mu$ O Ps. 49.12.

     d) בְּקֶרֶב   b a c e r e b ɟ Hab. 3.2.

קרב   קָרֹב $\kappa\alpha\rho\omega\beta$ O Ps. 32.9: ΚΑΡΩΘ lege B for Θ; MT: רֹב.

קִרְיָה   c a r i a ɟ Isa. 26.5.

     קִרְיַת $\kappa\alpha\rho\iota\alpha\vartheta$ G in Καριαθβααλ, Josh. 15.60; c a r -
     i a t h ɟ Hos. 2.15.

     קִרְיָתַיִם $\kappa\alpha\rho\iota\alpha\vartheta\alpha\iota\mu$ A Jer. 48.1; c a r i a t h a i m
     On Num. 32.37.

     קְרִיֹות   c a r i o t h On Jer. 48.24.

     הַקְּרִיֹות $\alpha\kappa\kappa\alpha\rho\iota\omega\vartheta$ A Jer. 48.41.

קרן   קַרְנַיִם $\kappa\alpha\rho\nu\alpha\iota\mu$ A Gen. 14.5: $\kappa\alpha\rho\nu\alpha\iota\nu$ lege μ for
     second ν; c a r n a i m On ib.

קרסלים קַרְסֻלָּי׳ κορσελαι o Ps. 18.37: XOPCEΛAI lege K
for X; cf. Thompson Facs. 7.

קרץ יְקְרְצוּ ικερσου o Ps. 35.19; cf. in the BV יִשְׁמְעוּ
1 Sam. 13.3; יִקְרָאוּ Jer. 23.6 in MdO, p. 185; cf.
also Sam. Ex. 21.35: יחיצון for MT: יֶחֱצוּן.

קשה קָשָׂה casa J Isa. 27.1.

קָשְׁת a) κασϑ o Ps. 46.10.
b) κεσϑ o Ps. 18.35.
c) ceseth J Isa. 66.19.

ר

רָאָה raa J Gen. 32.29; raha J ib., ed. Lagarde.
רָאֲתָה ρααϑα o Ps. 35.21.
רָאִיתָ ραιϑ o Ps. 31.8.
רָאִיתָה ραειϑα o Ps. 35.22: PACIΘA lege Є for C.
וְרָאִיתִי uraithi J Ezek. 41.8.
רְאוּ rau J Hab. 1.5; MT: רְאוּ.
יִרְאֶה ιερε o Ps. 89.49.
תֵּרֶאה ϑερε o Ps. 35.17: ΘEPC lege Є for C.
רְאוּ ρου A in Ρουβην, Gen. 29.32; ru On in Ruben, ib.
רָאמוֹת ramoth J Ezek. 27.16.
ראש a) ρωs G Ezek. 38.3; ros J ib.
הָרֹאשׁ αρωs A 1 Chron. 24.31.
b) ראש rus On Gen. 46.21.
ראשית בְּרֵאשִׁית βρησιϑ o Gen. 1.1; bresith J ib.
ראשון הָרֵאשׁנִים αρισωνιμ o Ps. 89.50.
רב a) ραβ A in Ραβσαρεις, 2 Ki. 18.17; o Ps. 31.20:
rab On in Rabsaris, 2 Ki. 18.17.
רַבִּים ραβιμ o Ps. 32.6.
b) רַבָּה ραββα A Josh. 13.25.   •
רַבַּת rabbath On Deut. 3.11.
רַבִּים ραββιμ o Ps. 32.10.
רַבּוֹת rabboth On Josh. 19.20; MT: רְבִית.
רב וּבְרֹב ουεβροβ o Ps. 49.7.

רבה   תֵּרְבֵּנִי $\vartheta \epsilon \rho \beta \eta \nu \iota$ O Ps. 18.36: ΘΕΡΒΝΝΙ lege H for
      first N; cf. Thompson Facs. 5.

רגל   רַגְלִי $\rho \epsilon \gamma \lambda a \iota$ O Ps. 18.34; ib. 31.9: $\epsilon \rho \gamma \lambda a \iota$ lege
      $\rho \epsilon \gamma \lambda a \iota$; cf. in the BV רֹגְלֵי Ps. 40.3 in Ms. Ec 1.

      רַגְלָיו   r e g l a u   J Isa. 6.2; cf. in the BV רֹגְלָיו Ex. 25.26
      in Ms. Ea 5.

רגל   רֹגַל $\rho \omega \gamma \eta \lambda$ G Josh. 18.16.

      רֹגְלִים   a) $\rho \omega \gamma \epsilon \lambda \epsilon \iota \mu$ A 2 Sam. 17.27.
            b) $\rho \omega \gamma \epsilon \lambda \lambda \epsilon \iota \mu$ B ib.

רָגַע $\rho \epsilon \gamma \epsilon$ O Ps. 30.6.

רגע   רְגֵעִי $\rho \epsilon \gamma \eta$ O Ps. 35.20.

רדידים   הָרְדִידִים   a r d i d i m   J Isa. 3.23.

רדף   אֶרְדּוֹף $\epsilon \rho \delta o \varphi$ O Ps. 18.38.

רַהַב   r e e b   J Isa. 30.7.

רוד   רָד   r a d   J Hos. 12.1.

רוּחַ   a) r u a   J Isa. 40.13.   r u h a   J Eccl. 6.9.
      בְּרוּחַ   b a r u a   J Gen. 3.8, ed. Lagarde; MT: לְרוּחַ.
      b) לְרוּחַ   l a r u e   J Gen. 3.8; on the e cf. paragraph
      XXIII sub ה.

      רוּחִי $\rho o \upsilon \eta$ O Ps. 31.6.
      r u h i   J Ezek. 39.29.

רום   וְיָרֻם $o \upsilon \iota a \rho o \upsilon \mu$ O Ps. 18.47.

      אָרוּם $a \rho o \upsilon \mu$ O Ps. 46.11.

      רָם $\rho a \mu$ G 1 Chron. 2.9.

      רָמָה $\rho a \mu a$ G Josh. 18.25;   r a m a   On ib.

      רָמוֹת $\rho a \mu \omega \vartheta$ A 1 Ki. 4.13; O Ps. 18.28;   r a m o t h   On
      1 Ki. 4.13.

      הָרִמוֹת $a \rho \eta \mu \omega \vartheta$ O Ps. 89.43.

      וְהָרֵם $o \upsilon a \rho \eta \mu$ O Ps. 28.9; MT: וּרְעֵם.

רוץ   אָרֶץ $a \rho o \upsilon s$ O Ps. 18.30.

      רָצִים $\rho a \sigma \epsilon \iota \mu$ A 2 Ki. 11.4.

רָזוֹן $\rho a \zeta \omega \nu$ A 1 Ki. 11.23; MT: רְזוֹן;   r a z o n   On ib.

רחב   וְרֹחַב   u r o b   J Ezek. 40.49.

רחב   תַּרְחִיב $\vartheta \epsilon \rho \iota \beta$ O Ps. 18.37.

      וַיַּרְחִיבוּ $o \upsilon \epsilon \iota \epsilon \rho \iota \beta o \upsilon$ O Ps. 35.21.

רחוב   רְחֹבֹת   r o o b o t h   On Gen. 10.11.

רָחוּם $\rho\,a\,o\,v\,\mu$ A Neh. 3.17; MT: רְחוּם.

רָחֵל $\rho\,a\,\chi\,\eta\,\lambda$ A Gen. 29.6; r a c h e l On ib.

רחם   a) מֵרָחָם $\mu\,\eta\,\rho\,\epsilon\,\mu$ o Ps. 110.3.

      b) רֶחֶם   r e h e m J Amos 1.11.

      מֵרָחָם   m e r e h e m J Isa. 46.3; MT: מְנִי רָחַם.

רחם   יְרֹחָם $\iota\,\epsilon\,\rho\,o\,a\,\mu$ A 1 Sam. 1.1; i e r o a m On ib.

רחף   מְרַחֶפֶת   m a r a h a e f e t h J Gen. 1.2, ed. Lagarde.
      m e r e f e t h J ib.

רחק   תִּרְחַק $\vartheta\,a\,\rho\,a\,\kappa$ o Ps. 35.22.

ריב   רִיבָה $\rho\,\iota\,\beta\,a$ o Ps. 35.1.

      יָרִיב $\iota\,a\,\rho\,\epsilon\,\iota\,\beta$ A 1 Chron. 4.24; $\iota\,a\,\rho\,\iota\,\beta$ A in Ιωιαριβ,
      Neh. 11.5; j a r i b J Hos. 5.13; MT: יָרֵב.

ריב   לְרִיבִי $\lambda\,\epsilon\,\rho\,\iota\,\beta\,\iota$ o Ps. 35.23: ΛΕΡΒΙ lege ΛΕΡΙΒΙ;
      haplography I—P; cf. Thompson Facs. 6 and 9.

      מְרִיבִי $\mu\,\rho\,\iota\,\beta\,\eta$ o Ps. 31.21; MT: מָרִיב.

רָכִיל   r a c h i l J Ezek. 22.9.

רְכוּשׁ   r a c h u s J Gen. 14.16.

מֶרְכָסַי $\mu\,\epsilon\,\rho\,v\,\chi\,\sigma\,\eta$ o Ps. 31.21.

רֹם $\rho\,a\,\mu$ G 1 Chron. 2.9.

      רָמָה $\rho\,a\,\mu\,a$ G Josh. 18.25; r a m a On ib.

      רָמַת $\rho\,a\,\mu\,a\,\vartheta$ A Josh. 19.21; MT: רָמָת; r a m a t h On ib.

      רָמָתַיִם   r a m a t h a i m On 1 Sam. 1.1.

      רֹמַת $\rho\,a\,\mu\,\omega\,\vartheta$ G Josh. 21.38; o Ps. 18.28; r a m o t h
      On Josh. 21.38.

רִמּוֹן $\rho\,\epsilon\,\mu\,\mu\,\omega\,v$ G in Γεθερεμμων, Josh. 21.24; r e m m o n
      On in Remmonfares, Num. 33.19.

רמם   אֲרוֹמִמְךָ $\epsilon\,\rho\,\omega\,\mu\,\epsilon\,\mu\,\epsilon\,\chi$ o Ps. 30.2.

רֶמֶשׂ   r e m e s J Hab. 1.14.

רֻנִּי $\rho\,a\,v\,v\,\eta$ o Ps. 32.7.

רנן   יָרֹנּוּ $\iota\,a\,\rho\,o\,v\,v\,o\,v$ o Ps. 35.27.

      וְהַרְנִינוּ $o\,v\,\epsilon\,\rho\,v\,\iota\,v\,o\,v$ o Ps. 32.11.

רֶסֶן   a) וְרָסָן $o\,v\,a\,\rho\,\epsilon\,\sigma\,v$ o Ps. 32.9.

      b) רֶסֶן   r e s e n J Zech. 14.20.

רַע $\rho\,\epsilon$ G in Αχειρε, Num. 1.15; r e J Hos. 3.1.
      r e e J Gen. 38.12; on the second e (= ע) cf. paragraph
      XXIII sub ע.

כְּרֵעַ χ ρ η ε o Ps. 35.14.
רֵעִים r e i m J Jer. 3.1.
רע ρ α o Ps. 49.6.
רֵעִים r a i m J Isa. 56.11.
רעה רָעַת r a a t h J Eccl. 8.6.
רָעָתִי ρ α α ϑ ι o Ps. 35.26.
רעה יִרְעָם ι ε ρ η μ o Ps. 49.15.
רֹעֶה r o e J Gen. 38.12.
רֹעִים r o i m J Isa. 56.11.
רֹעִי r o i J Isa. 44.28.
רְעוּת r o o t h J Eccl. 1.14.
רַעַם r e e m J in banereem, Isa. 62.4.
רעם הָרְעִים ε ρ ι μ o Ps. 29.3.
רעע רֹעוּ r o u J Isa. 8.9.
רעש יִרְעֲשׁוּ ι ε ρ α σ ο υ ι o Ps. 46.4.
רפא יִרְפָּא ι ε ρ φ α A in Ιερφαηλ, Josh. 18.27.
רוֹפְאִים r o p h a i m J Isa. 26.19.
רְפוּא ρ α φ ο υ G Num. 13.9.
רְפָאִים r a p h a i m J Isa. 26.19.
רפה הַרְפּוּ α ρ φ ο υ o Ps. 46.11.
רצה תִּרְצָה ϑ α ρ σ α B Josh. 12.24; MT: תִּרְצָה.
תִּרְצָה ϑ ε ρ σ α G Num. 26.33; MT: תִּרְצָה; t h e r s a On ib.
רצון ρ α σ ω ν o Mal. 2.13.
בִּרְצוֹנְךָ β α ρ σ ω ν α χ o Ps. 30.8.
בִּרְצוֹנוֹ β α ρ σ ω ν ω o Ps. 30.6.
רִצְפָּה ρ ε σ φ α G 2 Sam. 3.7; r e s p h a On ib.
רצץ יָרֹצוּ ι α ρ ο σ ο υ o Ps. 49.14; MT: יָרֹצוּ.
רַק ρ ε κ o Ps. 32.6.
רָקָב r e c o b J Hos. 5.12.
רשע לָרָשָׁע λ α ρ α σ α o Ps. 32.10.
הָרְשָׁעִים α ρ σ α ε ι μ o Ps. 1.1; MT: רְשָׁעִים.
רָשָׁע r e s a J Isa. 26.10; MT: רָשָׁע.
לָרָשָׁע λ α ρ ε σ α o Ps. 36.2; MT: לָרָשָׁע.
רֶשֶׁף r e s e p h J Hab. 3.5.
רשת מֶרֶשְׁת μ ε ρ ε σ ϑ o Ps. 31.5.
רחיק הָרָתִּיק a r e t h i c J Ezek. 7.23; MT: הָרָתוּק.
רְחַת r a t h a t h J Hos. 13.1.

שׁ

(cf. Introduction, paragraph XIV)

שאנ יִשָּׁאַנ jesag J Amos 1.2.

שָׁאוֹל σωλ o Ps. 89.49.

לִשְׁאוֹל λασωλ o Ps. 49.15.

מִשְׁאוֹל μεσσωλ o Ps. 30.4; MT: מִן שְׁאוֹל.

שָׁאוֹן σαων G Jer. 46.17; saon J Hos. 10.14.

שאל שָׁאוּל σαουλ A Gen. 36.37; saul On ib.

שאף שׁוֹאֵף soeph J Eccl. 1.5.

שְׁאָר sar J Isa. 10.21; cf. the bisyllabic form in the PV שְׁאֹר
  (MdWI, p. ב, line 15); cf. s. v. מעט.

שְׁבָבִים sababim J Hos. 8.6.

שְׁבוּעָה sabaa J Isa. 65.15.

שְׁבָעַת sabaoth J Jer. 5.24.

שבט בְּשֵׁבֶט βσαβτ o Ps. 89.33.

שְׁבָט sabat J Zech. 1.7.

שֶׁבַע a) sabe On Josh. 19.2.
  σαβεε G in Βηρσαβεε, Josh. 19.2; on the second ε
    (=ע) cf. paragraph XXIII sub ע; sabee On in
    Bersabee, 1 Sam. 3.20.
  b) saba J Isa. 4.1.

שבע נִשְׁבַּעְתָּ νεσβαϑ o Ps. 89.50.
  נִשְׁבַּעְתִּי νεσβαϑ [ι] o Ps. 89.36.

שִׁבְעָה saba J Jer. 15.9; cf. in the BV שִׁבְעָה 1 Chron. 5.13 in
  Ms. Ec 1.

שבק יִשְׁבָּק ιεσβοκ A Gen. 25.2; iesboc On ib.
  שׁוֹבֵק σωβηκ G Neh. 10.24.

שֶׁבֶר a) σεβερ A 1 Chron. 2.48.
  b) σαβερ B ib.

שבר תְּשַׁבֵּר ϑεσσαβερ o Ps. 48.8; with gemination of
  the *first* radical; cf. on וּמִשְׁנֵא.
  יִשְׁבָּר ισουβερ o Ps. 46.10; MT: יְשַׁבֵּר; without gemination, cf. on אָכַב.

שַׁבָּת sabat On 2 Ki. 4.23.

שבת הִשְׁבַּתָּ εσβεϑ o Ps. 89.45.
  מִשְׁבִּית μισβιϑ o Ps. 46.9; cf. in the BV forms like
  מֹצִיל Job 5.4; מֹצִיב 1 Sam. 15.12 in MdO, p. 193.

שְׁגָגָה   s e g a g a J Eccl. 5.5.
שִׁגְיֹנוֹת   s e g i o n o t h J Hab. 3.1.
שׂד   s o d J Isa. 16.4.
שדד   שָׁדוּד s a d u d J Jer. 4.30.
שָׂדֶה   s a d e J Ezek. 21.2.
   שָׂדוֹת s a d o t h J Amos 3.10.
שָׂדַי   s a d a i J Ps. 80.14.
שָׂדָה   s a d d a J Eccl. 2.8.
   שָׂדוֹת s a d d o t h J ib.
שַׁדַּי   σ α δ δ α ι G Ezek. 10.5; s a d d a i J Ezek. 1.24.
שְׁדֵמָה   הַשְּׁדֵמוֹת a s a d e m o t h J Jer. 31.39.
שְׁדֵמ ה   σ α δ η μ ω ϑ A 2 Ki. 23.4; s a d e m o t h On ib.
שָׁוְא   σ α υ o Ps. 31.7; cf. B-L. §17z.
שׁוב   יָשׁוּב ι α σ ο υ β G Num. 26.24; i a s u b On ib.
   תָּשׁוּב ϑ α σ ο υ β o Ps. 35.13.
   אָשׁוּב α σ ο υ β o Ps. 18.38.
   יְשׁוּבוּ j a s u b u J Mic. 5.3; MT: יָשֻׁבוּ.
   יָשִׁיב ι α σ ε ι β A in Ελιασειβ, 1 Chron. 3.24.
   תָּשִׁיב ϑ α σ ι β o Ps. 89.44.
   הָשִׁיבָה α σ ι β α o Ps. 35.17.
שָׁוֵה   σ α υ η A Gen. 14.5; s a u siue s a u h e On ib.
שׁוה   מְשַׁוֶּה μ ο σ α υ ε o Ps. 18.34.
שׁוח   σ ο υ ε A Gen. 25.2: Σωυε lege σουε or σωε cf. paragraph XXIII sub ו; s u e On ib.
שׁוט   s o t J Isa. 28.15.
שׁוע   s u e J Ezek. 23.23.
שׁוע   יְשׁוּעִי ι ε σ α υ ο υ o Ps. 18.42; cf. B.-L. §17z and d'.
   בְּשׁוּעִי β ε σ α υ ε ι o Ps. 31.23.
שׁוּעָל   σ ο υ α λ A 1 Chron. 7.36.
   שׁוּעָלִים s u a l i m On in Asarsualim, Josh. 19.3.
שׁוֹפָר   s o p h a r J Isa. 58.1.
שׁור   שְׁוָרִים s u r i m J Hos. 12.12.
שׁוּר   σ ο υ ρ G Ex. 15.22; o Ps. 18.30; s u r On Gen. 20.1.
שׁור   בְּשׁוּרִי b a s o r i J Hos. 9.12.
   יָשִׁיר j a s i r J Jer. 5.26.
שׁחה   הִשְׁתַּחֲווּ ε σ ϑ α υ ο υ o Ps. 29.2.
שׁחח   שְׁחוֹתִי σ ε ω ϑ ι o Ps. 35.14; ε is possibly the transliteration of ח; cf. paragraph XXIII sub ח.

שְׁחִין   s i i n ﹐J Isa. 38.21.

שַׁחַל   a) s o h o l ﹐J Hos 5.14.

     b) s o h e l ﹐J ib.

שחק   בְּשַׂחֵק   βσακ ﹐o Ps. 89.38.

שחק   יְשְׂחַק   i s a a c ﹐J Amos 7.16; MT: יִשְׂחָק.

שחק   וְאֶשְׁחָקֵם   ουεσοκημ ﹐o Ps. 18.43.

שַׁחַר   σααρ ﹐A in Αχισααρ, 1 Chron. 7.10.

     מְשָׁחָר   μεσσααρ ﹐o Ps. 110.3; MT: מִשְׁחָר.

שַׁחַת   σααϑ ﹐o Ps. 30.10.

     הַשַּׁחַת   ασσααϑ ﹐o Ps. 49.10; MT: הַשָּׁחַת.

שִׁטָּה   s e t t a ﹐J Isa. 41.19.

     שִׁטִּים   s e t t i m ﹐On Ex. 25.5.

שָׂטָן   σαταν ﹐G 1 Ki. 11.14; s a t a n ﹐On ib.

שִׂטְנָה   s a t a n a ﹐J Gen. 26.21.

שֶׁטֶף   לְשֶׁטֶף   λσετφ ﹐o Ps. 32.6.

שִׂי   σαι ﹐A in Αβισαι, 1 Sam. 26.6; s a i ﹐On in Abisai,
     1 Ki. 1.3.

שִׂיחַ   s i a ﹐J Amos 4.13.

     שִׂיחוֹ   s i o ﹐J in masio, Amos 4.13.

שִׂים   שָׂם   σαμ ﹐o Ps. 46.9.

     שָׂמְתָּ   σαμϑ ﹐o Ps. 89.41.

     וְשַׂמְתִּי   ουσαμϑι ﹐o Ps. 89.30.

שִׂימָה   שְׂמוֹת   σιμωϑ ﹐o Ps. 46.9 (from the root שִׂים); MT: שְׂמוֹת.

שִׁיר   σιρ ﹐o Ps. 30.1.

     וּמִשִּׁירִי   ουμεσσιρι ﹐o Ps. 28.7.

שַׁיִת   s a i t h ﹐J Isa. 5.6.

שכל   אַשְׂכִּילְךָ   εσχιλεχ ﹐o Ps. 32.8.

שְׁכֶם   σεχεμ ﹐A Josh. 17.2.

שָׁכֵן   לִשְׁכֵנָיו   λσαχηναυ ﹐o Ps. 89.42.

שָׂכָר   σαχαρ ﹐A in Ισσαχαρ, Gen. 30.18; s a c h a r ﹐On in
     Issachar, ib.

שכור   שְׁכּוֹרֵי   s a c c h o r e ﹐J Isa. 28.3.

שלו   בְּשַׁלְוִי   βσαλουι ﹐o Ps. 30.7.

שָׁלוֹם   σαλωμ ﹐G in Αβεσσαλωμ, 2 Sam. 3.3; o Ps. 35.20.

     שָׁלוֹם   σαλωμ ﹐o Ps. 35.27.

שֶׁלַח   a) s a l e ﹐On in Mathusale, Gen. 5.21; on e (=ח) cf.
     paragraph XXIII sub ח.

     b) σαλα ﹐A Gen. 10.24; s a l a ﹐J Joel 2.8.

שלח   שָׁלְחָה a) s a l u a J Gen. 49.21: sluaa is a misprint.

       b) s e l u a J ib., ed. Lagarde.

שָׁלִישׁ   s a l i s J Isa. 40.12.

שָׁלֵם   a) σ α λ η μ A Gen. 33.18; s a l e m On ib.

       b) שָׁלְמָה s a l m a J Amos 1.9.

       c) שְׁלָמִים s a l a m i m J Gen. 34.21.

שלם   וְשָׁלֵם o υ σ α λ η μ O Ps. 31.24 (cf. s. v. חָפַץ); MT: וּמְשַׁלֵּם.

       שָׁלֵם σ ε λ λ η μ A Num. 26.49.

       מְשֻׁלָּם μ ε σ ο υ λ α μ G Neh. 6.18.

שַׂלְמָה   σ α λ α μ α G Gen. 36.36; s a l a m a On ib; MT:

       שַׂמְלָה; cf. Ex. 22.8: MT: שלמה, Sam. שמלה.

שְׁלָמִים   s a l a m i m J Ezek. 46.12.

שָׁלֹשׁ   s a l o s J Jonah 3.4.

שְׁלִישִׁיָּה   a) σ α λ α σ ε ι α B Jer. 48.34.

       b) σ α λ ι σ ι α A ib.; cf. in the BV שְׁלִשִׁים 1 Sam. 19.21

       in Ms. 105 JThS.

שָׁם   σ α μ O Isa. 28.13; s a m J Isa. 28.10.

       שָׁמָּה s a m a J Ezek. 48.34.

שֵׁם   σ η μ A Gen. 6.10; σ ε μ O Gen. 28.19; s e m On

       Gen. 6.10.

       שִׁמְךָ σ ε μ α χ O Ps. 31.4.

       שְׁמוֹ σ ε μ ω O Ps. 29.2.

       בְּשֵׂמֹת b a s e m o t h On Gen. 26.34; MT: בָּשְׂמַת; cf. our

       remark on שַׂר.

       שֵׁמֹות s e m o t h On Ezek. 48.1.

       בִּשְׁמוֹתָם β σ ε μ ω ϑ α μ O Ps. 49.12: ΒϹΕΒΩΘΑΜ

       lege M for the second B.

שַׁמָּה   a) σ α μ α B 1 Sam. 16.9.

       שַׁמֹּות σ α μ ω ϑ A 1 Chron. 11.27.

       b) שַׁמָּה σ α μ μ α A 1 Sam. 16.9; s a m m a On Gen.

       36.13.

       שַׁמֹּות σ α μ μ ω ϑ B 1 Chron. 11.27: ϹΑΜΑΩΘ lege M

       for the second A.

שמח   שָׂמְחוּ σ α μ ο υ O Ps. 35.15.

       וְאֶשְׂמַח o υ ε σ μ α O Ps. 31.8: ΟΥϹΕΜΑ lege ΟΥΕϹΜΑ;

       MT: וְאֶשְׂמְחָה.

יִשְׂמְחוּ ι ε σ μ ο υ o Ps. 46.5; MT: יִשְׂמָחוּ.

ι ε σ ε μ ο υ o Ps. 35.24; cf. on יְקָרְצוּ.

שְׂמְחוּ σ ε μ ο υ o Ps. 32.11: ΙϹΜΟΥ lege ϹϹΜΟΥ; cf. Thompson Facs. 6 (Ι—Ϲ).

שָׂמַחְתָּ σ ε μ ε ϑ o Ps. 30.2; without gemination of the second radical; cf. on אֱכַב.

הִשְׂמַחְתָּ ε σ μ ε ϑ o Ps. 89.43.

שִׂמְחָה σ ε μ α o Ps. 30.12.

שָׁמַיִם a) s a m a i m J Isa. 1.2.

b) σ α μ μ α ι μ o Ps. 89.30.

c) σ ο υ μ η ν o Gen. 1.8.

שְׁמִינִי הַשְּׁמִינִית α σ ε μ ι ν ι ϑ o Ps. 12.1.

שָׁמִיר σ α μ ε ι ρ B Josh. 15.48; s a m i r On Ju. 10.1.

שמם שְׁמָמָה s e m e m a J Isa. 62.4; MT: שְׁמָמָה.

שמם מַשַּׁמִּים m a s m i m J Ezek. 3.15.

שְׁמָנִים s e m a n i m J Isa. 28.1.

שמע שְׁמְעִי σ ε μ ε ε ι B Ex. 6.17; on the second ε (=ע) cf. ¶ XXIII sub ע; σ ε μ ε ι A ib.; s e m e i On ib.

שָׁמַע σ α μ α G in Ελεισαμα, Num. 1.10; o Ps. 28.6.

σ α μ α ε B in Ελεισαμαε, 1 Chron. 14.7; cf. paragraph XXIII sub ע.

s a m e On in Elisame, Num. 1.10; ε=ע; cf. paragraph XXIII sub ע.

שָׁמַעְתָּ σ α μ α ϑ o Ps. 31.23.

יִשְׁמַע ι σ μ α A in Ισμαηλ, Gen. 16.11; i s m a On in Ismahel, ib.

שְׁמַע σ μ α o Ps. 30.11.

σ μ α ε o Ps. 28.6: ϹΜΑϹ lege ϹΜΑϹ; MT: שָׁמַע.

שִׁמְעוּ σ ι μ ο υ o Ps. 49.2; s e m u J Isa. 1.2.

שמר אֶשְׁמוֹר ε σ μ ω ρ o Ps. 89.29.

יִשְׁמְרוּ ι ε σ μ ω ρ ο υ o Ps. 89.32.

שׁוֹמֵר σ ω μ η ρ G 1 Chron. 7.32; o Isa. 26.2; s o m e r On 1 Ki. 16.24; MT: שֹׁמֵר.

הַשֹּׁמְרִים α σ σ ω μ ρ ι μ o Ps. 31.7.

שמש a) כַּשֶּׁמֶשׁ χ α σ α μ s o Ps. 89.37.

b) שִׁמְשִׁי s e m s i On 1 Sam. 6.18.

ALEXANDER SPERBER

c) שָׁמָשׁ σαμες A Josh. 19.41; s a m e s On ib.

d) s e m e s J Isa. 24.23.

שן שְׁנֵּימוֹ. σεννημω o Ps. 35.16.

שנא שְׁנֵאתִי σανηϑι o Ps. 31.7.

שֹׂנְאַי σωνη o Ps. 35.19; MT: שֹׂנְאָי.

וּמְשַׂנְאַי ουμασσανεαι o Ps. 18.41; MT: וּמשׂנ'; with gemination of the *first* radical; cf. §32β and §33δ.

שנה אֲשַׁנֶּה ασσανε o Ps. 89.35; cf. on וּמְשַׂנְאַי.

שני שֵׁנִית σηνιϑ o Mal. 2.13.

שנים שְׁנֵי s e n e J Ezek. 15.4.

שָׁנִים s a n i m J Hab. 3.2.

שְׁנֵי s a n e J Ezek. 15.4.

שסס שְׁסָהוּ σασουου o Ps. 89.42.

שְׂעִירִים s i r i m J Isa. 13.21.

שען אָשְׁעַן εσαν A Josh. 15.52.

שער שְׁעָרִים σααρειμ o Isa. 26.2; s a a r i m On Josh. 15.36; MT: שְׁעָרִים; cf. in PV שֹׁעֲרִ'ם (MdWI, p. י', 22).

שערה שְׁעָרִים a) σεωρειμ B 1 Chron. 24.8; σεωριμ A ib: σεωριν lege μ for ν; o Hos. 3.2; s e o r i m J ib.

b) s o r i m J Gen. 26.12; MT: שְׂעָרִים.

שְׂעָרִים s u a r i m J Jer. 29.17.

שפה הַשְּׁפַתָּיִם a s e p h a t h a i m J Ezek. 40.43.

שְׂפָתַי σφωϑαι o Ps. 89.35; MT: שְׂפָתַי.

שפה נְשָׁפָּה n e s p h e J Isa. 13.2.

שפט σαφατ G Num. 13.5; s a f a t On ib.; s a p h a t On in Josaphat, 1 Ki. 22.2.

שפך אֶשְׁפּוֹךְ e s p h o c h J Joel 3.1.

שפל תַּשְׁפִּיל ϑεσφιλ o Ps. 18.30: ΘΕΟΦΙΛ lege C for O; cf. Thompson Facs. 4 and 7.

שְׁפֵלָה σεφηλα G Jer. 33.13; s e f e l a On ib.; s e p h e l a J Jer. 17.26.

שָׁפָן σαφαν G Jer. 39.14; s a f a n On ib.

שפק יַשְׂפִּיקוּ j e s p h i c u J Isa. 2.6.

שק שֵׂק σεκ o Ps. 35.13.

שַׂקִּי σεκκι o Ps. 30.12.

שקד שָׁקֵד s e c e d J Jer. 1.11.

שקד שָׁקַד s o c e d J Eccl. 12.5.

שקוץ שִׁקוּצֵי s e c u s e J Ezek. 20.7.

שָׁקֶל s e c e l J Gen. 23.15.

שֶׁקֶר σ ε κ ρ O Ps. 35.19.

שקר אֲשַׁקֵּר α σ σ α κ ε ρ O Ps. 89.34; cf. our note on וּמְשַׂנְּאַי.

שר σ α ρ A in Αχισαρ, 1 Ki. 4.6; s a r On in Ahisar, ib.;
ט for Masoretic שׂ; cf. the reverse case s. v. שם
בְּשָׂמוֹת for Masoretic בְּשָׂמָה (שׂ for ט).

שָׂרִים s a r i m J Hos. 12.12.

שָׂרֵי s a r e J Ezek. 21.2.

שרה שָׂרִיתָ s a r i t h J Gen. 32.29.

שָׂרִינִים a) s a r i g i m J Gen. 4.10.
b) s a r i a g i m J ib., ed. Lagarde.

שָׂרִיד σ α ρ ι δ A Josh. 19.12; s a r i d J Obad. 18; s a r i t h
On Josh. 19.12.

שְׂרִידִים s a r i d i m J Joel 3.5.

שָׂרָף a) σ α ρ α φ A 1 Chron. 4.22; s a r a p h J Isa. 14.29.
b) s e r a p h J Isa. 6.6.

שְׂרָפִים s e r a p h i m J Isa. 6.6.

שרף יִשְׂרֹף ι σ ρ ο φ O Ps. 46.10.

שרק σ ω ρ η κ G Isa. 5.2; s o r e c On ib.

שׂשׂון σ α σ ω ν O Ps. 45.9.

שֹׁשַׁנִים σ ω σ α ν ε ι μ O Ps. 45.1.

שתת שַׁתּוּ σ α ϑ ο υ O Ps. 49.15.

ת

תא תָּאִים t h e i m J Ezek. 40.16.
תָּאֵי t h e e J Ezek. 40.21; MT: תָּאָו.

תבונה תְּבוּנוֹת ϑ β ο υ ν ω ϑ O Ps. 49.4.

תֵּבֵל t h e b e l J Isa. 13.11.

תהלה תְּהִלָּתְךָ ϑ ε λ α ϑ α χ O Ps. 35.28.

תָּו t h a v J Isa. 59.20.

תֹּא t h o J Isa. 51.20.

תּוֹדָה t h o d a J Jer. 17.26.

תּוֹלַעַת t h o l a t h J Isa. 41.14.

תּוֹרָה t h o r a J Ezek. 9.4.

בְּתוֹרַת   β ϑ ω ρ α ϑ   o   Ps. 1.2: BOΩPAΘ lege Θ for O;
cf. Thompson Facs. 1–5.

תּוֹרָתִי   ϑ ω ρ α ϑ ι   o   Ps. 89.31.

תחנון   תַּחֲנוּנִי   ϑ α ν ο υ ν α ι   o   Ps. 28.6.

תַּחַשׁ   t h a s   j   Ezek. 16.10.

תַּחַת   a)   ϑ ε ϑ   o   Ps. 18.39.

          תַּחְתֵּי   ϑ ε ϑ ι   o   Ps. 18.37; MT: תַּחְתֵּי.
          תַּחְתֵּי   ϑ ε ϑ α ι   o   Ps. 18.48.

          b)   תַּחַת   t h e e t h   On Num. 33.26.

          c)   ϑ α α ϑ   G 1 Chron. 6.22.

תחתי   תַּחְתִּים   t h e e t h i m   On 2 Sam. 24.6.

תֵּימָן   t h e m a n   j   Hab. 3.3.

תִּירוֹשׁ   t h i r o s   j   Zech. 9.17.

תֵּל   ϑ ε λ   G in Θελμελεϑ, Neh. 7.61.

תלה   יִתְלָה   ι ε ϑ λ α   A Josh. 19.42; MT: יִתְלָה.

תמה   יִתְמָהוּ   j e t h m a u   j   Jer. 4.9.

תַּמּוּז   t h a m u z   j   Ezek. 8.14.

תָּמִיד   ϑ α μ ι δ   o   Ps. 35.27.

תָּמִים   a)   ϑ α μ ι μ   o   Ps. 18.26;   t h a m i m   j   Ezek. 46.13.

          b)   ϑ α μ μ ι μ   o   Ps. 18.33; ib. 18.31: ΘAMMIN lege
          M for N.

תמם   תֻּתַּמּוּ   ϑ ε ϑ α μ μ α μ   o   Ps. 18.26: ΘEMAMMAM lege
          Θ for the first M.

תָּמָר   ϑ α μ α ρ   G Ruth 4.12;   t h a m a r   On Gen. 14.7.

          תְּמָרִים   t h a m a r i m   j   Ezek. 40.16; MT: תְּמֹרִים.

תַּמְרוּרִים   t h e m r u r i m   j   Jer. 31.21.

תַּנִּים   a)   t h e n n i n   j   Jer. 13.22.   b)   t h a n n i m   j ib.

תַּנִּין   t h a n n i n   j   Isa. 27.1.

תֹעֵב   נִתְעָב   n e t h a b   j   Isa. 14.19.

תַּעֲלוּלִים   t h a l u l i m   j   Isa. 3.4.

          תַּעֲלֻלַי   t h a l u l e   j   Isa. 66.4.

תִּפְאָרָת   t h o p h e r t   j   Ezek. 16.12.

תַּפּוּחַ   a)   ϑ α φ ο υ   B in Βαιϑαχου lege Βαιϑϑαφου, Josh.
          15.53;   τ α φ ο υ   B Josh. 16.8.
          t h a f u e   On in Beththafue, Josh. 15.53.

          b)   ϑ α π φ ο υ ε   A in Βεϑϑαπφουε, Josh. 15.53; cf. para-
          graph XXIII sub ח;   t h a f f u e   On Josh. 12.17:
          cf. paragraph XXIII sub פ.

תָּפֵל .t h a p h e l ɟ Ezek. 13.10.

תפלה תְּפִלַּת t h e p h e l l a t h ɟ Isa. 38.5.

וּתְפִלָּתִי $o\, v\, \vartheta\, \varphi\, \epsilon\, \lambda\, \lambda\, a\, \vartheta\, \iota$ o Ps. 35.13.

תֹּפֶת t h o p h e t ɟ Jer. 19.6; t o p h e t ɟ Jer. 7.31.

תַּרְדֵּמָה thardema ɟ Isa. 29.10; tardema ɟ Gen. 15.12.

תְּרוּעָה therua ɟ Amos 2.2.

תְּרָפִים therafim ɟ Gen. 31.19.

ALPHABETICAL INDEX OF HEBREW PROPER NAMES OCCURING IN THE DICTIONARY IN THE TRANSLITERATION OF THE SEPTUAGINT OR OF THE ONOMASTICA

(Only the consonants matter; the matres lectionis and the Masoretic vocalization are immaterial; cf. paragraph I)

Name	Root	Name	Root	Name	Root
אֲבִיאֵל	אב, אל	אוֹנָן	און	אֶלְיָדָע	ידע
אֲבִיחַיִל	חיל	אוּרִי	אור	אֱלִיעֶזֶר	אל
אֲבִימֶלֶךְ	אב	אָזְנִי	אזן	אֱלִיפַז	פז
אֲבִינֹעַם	נעם	אֶחְאָב	אח	אֱלִיצָפָן	צפן
אֲבִיעֶזֶר	עזר	אֵחוּד	הוד	אֶלְיָקִים	קום
אֲבִישַׁי	שי	אָחָז	אחז	אֶלְיָשִׁיב	שוב
אָבֵל		אֲחַזְיָהוּ		אֱלִישָׁמָע	שמע
אָבֵל הַשִּׁטִּים	אבל	אֲחִטוּב	טוב	אֶלְעָזָר	עזר
אָבֵל כְּרָמִים	אבל, כרם	אֲחִיהוּד	אח	אֶלְפַּעַל	פעל
אָבֵל מָיִם	מים	אֲחִינֹעַם	אח	אֶלְקָנָה	אל, קנה
אֶבֶן הָעֵזֶר	אבן	אֲחִיסָמָךְ	אח, סמך	אִמָּה	
אַבְשָׁלוֹם	שלום	אֲחִיקָם	קום	אָמָר	
אֵבֶת	אב	אֲחִירַע	רע	אֲמַרְיָה	אמר
אָדָם		אֲחִישַׁחַר	שחר	אֱנוֹשׁ	
אֲדָמָה		אֲחִישָׁר	שר	אַסִּיר	
אֲדֹנִיקָם	קום	אַחֵר		אָסָף	
אֲדֹנִירָם	אדון	אֶטָד		אָצָר	
אֲדַרְמֶלֶךְ	מלך	אִי כָבוֹד	כבוד	אַרְבּוֹת	ארבה
אֹהֶל		אֵילָם	אולם	אַרְגִּים	ארג
אָהֳלִיבָה	אהל, ב-	אִישׁ בֹּשֶׁת	בשת	אֲרִיאֵל	ארי
אָהֳלִיבָמָה	אהל	אִישׁ טוֹב	איש	אֲרָיָה	
אוֹן		אֵיתָן		אַרְדְּ	
אָנוּ		אֵלָה	אלה	אֶשְׁכֹּל	כל
אוֹנוֹ	און	אֶלְחָנָן	חנן	אֶשְׁעָן	שען
אוֹנָם	און	אֱלִיאָב	אב, אל	אָשֵׁר	

270

בְּאֵרוֹת	באר	בְּעָלִים	בַּעַל	דּוֹן	דון
בְּאֵרִי	באר	בַּעַל מְעוֹן	מעון	הֶבֶל	
בְּאֵר שֶׁבַע	באר, שבע	בַּעַל פְּרָצִים	פרץ	הוֹד	
בּוּז		בְּצַלְאֵל	צל		
בּוּזִי	בוז	בַּקְבּוּק		הַיְשָׁנָה	ישן
בָּנַק		בֶּרֶד		הַכְּרֻבִים	כרוב
בַּחוּרִים	בחור	בָּרוּךְ		הַלּוֹחֵשׁ	לחש
בָּטֶן		בְּרִית		הַלֵּל	
בֵּית אָוֶן	און, בית	בַּרְכְּאֵל	ברך	הַשְּׂנוּאָה	סנא
בֵּית אֵל	בית	בָּרָק		הָעִבְרִים	עברי
בֵּית הַגָּן	גן	בָּשְׂמַת	שם	הַפָּרָה	פרה
בֵּית הַכָּרֶם	כרם			הַקּוֹץ	קוץ
בֵּית הַנְּתִינִים	נתינים	גֻּבְעָה		הַקָּטָן	קטן
בֵּית הָעֵמֶק	עמק	גֻּבְעַת	גבעה	הַקְּרִיּוֹת	קריה
בֵּית הָעֲרָבָה	ערבה	גֻּבֶּר		הָרֹאשׁ	ראש
בֵּית כָּר	כר	גַּבְרִיאֵל	גבר	הַר שָׁפֵר	הר
בֵּית לְבָאוֹת	לביא	גַּדִּל		הַשִּׁמְשִׁי	שמש
בֵּית לָחֶם	לחם	גֻּדַּלְתִּי	נדל		
בֵּית מַרְכָּבוֹת	מרכבת	גֻּדֵּר		זְאֵב	
בֵּית עַזְמָוֶת	מות	גְּדֵרָה		זָבָד	
בֵּית תַּפּוּחַ	בית, תפוח	גְּדֵרוֹת	גדרה	זַבְדִּי	זבד
בְּכוֹרַת	בכורה	גּוֹיִם	גוי	זָבוּד	זבד
בָּכָר	בכור	גֶּזֶר		זָבַח	
בָּלַע		גֵּיא		זָכָל	
בִּלְעָם	בלע	גֵּיא סָלַח	מלח	זָחָלַת	זחל
בָּמָה		גַּלְגַּל		זִכְרִי	זכר
בָּמוֹת	במה	גְּלִילוֹת	נלילה	זִמָּה	
בֵּן		גֻּלִים	נל	זִמְרִי	זמר
בֶּן אוֹנִי	און	גָּמוּל	נמל	זָנוֹחַ	זנח
בְּנֵי בְּרַק	בן	גְּמַלִי	נמל	זֶרַח	
בְּסוֹדְיָה	סוד	גֵּרְשֹׁם	נר	זַרְחִי	זרח
בַּעַל בְּרִית	בעל, ברית	גַּת		זַרְחְיָה	זרח
בַּעֲלָה		גַּת רִמּוֹן	רמון	סָבוּר	חבר
בַּעַל הָמוֹן	המון	דָּאַג		סָבָר	
בְּעָלוֹת	בעלה	דְּבוֹרָה		סַבָּר	
בַּעַל זְבוּב	זבוב	דְּבִיר		חָנָב	
בְּעַלְיָדָע	ידע	דַּבֶּשֶׁת		חַנִּי	חג
				חֲדָשָׁה	חדש

242

פתח	יִפְתָּח		טָבַח	חדש	חָדְשִׁי
צהר	יִצְהָר	טבעת	טַבָּעוֹת		חוֹבָה
צחק	יִצְחָק	טוב	טוֹב		חוֹל
	יָצָר			חרב	חוֹרֶב
יצר	יְצָרִי	אור	יָאִיר		חוֹתָם
קום	יָקִים	בחר	יִבְחָר	חזה	חֲזָאֵל
	יְרוּשָׁה	בלע	יִבְלְעָם		חִזָּיוֹן
	יְרַח	בין	יָבִין	חיל	חַיִלָם
רחם	יְרַחָם		יָבֵשׁ		חֲלִי
ריב	יָרִיב	נאל	יֻאֵל		חָלָק
רפא	יְרַפְאֵל	גור	יָנוּר		חָלָק
שבק	יִשְׁבָּק	ידיד	יְדִידְיָה	חלק	חֶלְקִי
שוב	יָשׁוּב	דלף	יִדְלָף	חלקה	חֶלְקַת
שמע	יִשְׁמָעֵאל	ידע	יְהוֹיָדָע		חָם
	יָשֵׁן	נתן	יְהוֹנָתָן	חמל	חָמוּל
	יִשְׁעִי	שפט	יְהוֹשָׁפָט		חָמוֹר
שכר	יִשָּׂשכָר	הלל	יְהַלַלְאֵל	חמה	חֲמָתִי
תלה	יִתְלָה	יאל	יוֹאֵל	חנן	חָנוּן
יתר	יִתְרוֹ	יבל	יוּבָל		חֶסֶד
כברה	כְּבְרָת	זכר	יוֹכָר		חָפָּה
	כִּידוֹן	ריב	יוֹיָרִיב	ב–, חפץ	חֶפְצִי בָהּ
	כִּכָּר		יוֹנָה		חֲצִי
	כִּלְיוֹן	יסף	יוֹסֵף	חצר	חֲצַר גַּדָּה
כמר	כְּפָרִים	זוז	יָזִיז	חצר	חֲצֵרוֹת
	כְּנוֹר	זרח	יִזְרָח	חצר, מות	חֲצַר מָוֶת
	כְּנַעֲנִי	זרע	יִזְרְעֶאל	חצר	חֲצַר עֵינָן
	כָּרוּב	כון	יָכִין	שועל	חֲצַר שׁוּעָל
כרוב	כְּרֻבִים		יָמִין		חֶרְדָּה
כרם	כַּרְמִי	ימין	יְמִינִי		חָרוּץ
		מלא	יִמְלָא	חרץ	חָרִיף
		מנה	יִקְנָה		חֶרֶס
דבר, לא	לֹא דָבָר	מנע	יִמְנַע		חֶרֶשׁ
בוא	לָבוֹא	נום	יָנוּם		חֲרֶשֶׁת
	לְבוֹנָה	עקב	יַעֲקֹב		מַחֲשָׁבָה
	לָבָן		יַעַר	חשב	חֶשְׁבּוֹן
לבן	לִקְנָא	יער	יָעָרִים		מַחֲשָׁבִיָה
להב	לְהָבִים	פוע	יָפִיעַ		
לחם	לַחְמִי	פנה	יַעֲנָה	חשב	

עבד	עוֹבֵד		מִשְׁמָע	לטש	לְטוּשִׁים
עדד	עוֹדֵד		מָשָׁק		לַיְשׁ
	עוֹרֵב	מים, משרפת	מִשְׂרְפוֹת מַיִם		לַפִּידוֹת
עז	עֻזֵּד	שלח	מְתוּשֶׁלַח		
עזב	עֲזוּבָה		מַתָּן		מִבְחָר
עזר	עַזּוּר		מַתָּנָה		מִבְצָר
עז	עֻזִּיאֵל	מתן	מַתַּנְיָה		מִבְשָׂם
עזר	עֶזְרִי			מנדל	מִגְדָּל גָּד
	עֲטָרָה		נָבָל		מִדְבָּר
עטרה	עֲטָרוֹת		נֹנָה		מָדוֹן
	עַיִן		נֶרֶב		מָחוֹל
נן	עֵין גַּנִּים	יעד	נוֹעַדְיָה		מִחָלָה
דור	עֵין דּוֹר		נָחָשׁ	מחנה	מַחֲנַיִם
חד, עין	עֵין חַדָּה		נַחַת	זהב	מֵי זָהָב
עין	עֵינַיִם		נָכוֹן		מִישׁוֹר
עיר	עִירָם		נְצִיב	מכונה	מְכֻנוֹת
עם	עַמִּיהוּד		נָקָב	מלא	מִלּוֹא
עם	עַמִּינָדָב		נֵר		מַלּוֹתִי
עם	עִמָּנוּאֵל		נְתִינִים	מלך	מַלְכִּיאֵל
	עֵמֶק		נָתָן	אל	מַלְכִּיאֵלִי
עם	עָמְרָם			מלך, צדק	מַלְכִּי צֶדֶק
	עֲנָה		סָבָךְ	מלך	מַלְכָּם
ענק	עֲנָק	סוד	סוֹדִי		מֵן
ענק	עֲנָקִים	סוס	סוּסִי		מָנוֹחַ
עפר	עֶפְרָה	סכה	סֻכּוֹת	נחם	מְנַחֵם
עקרב	עַקְרַבִּים	סתר	סָתוּר	נשה	מְנַשֶּׁה
	עֶקֶשׁ	סתר	סִתְרִי		מִסְפָּר
	עֵר				מְעוֹן
ערבה	עֲרָבוֹת		עָבָד	ענה	מְעוֹנִים
עשה	עֲשָׂהאֵל	עבד	עַבְדִּי		מִפְקָד
	עֵשָׂו	עבד	עֶבֶד מֶלֶךְ		מַצָּב
		עבד	עַבְדֵי שְׁלֹמֹה	מקהלה	מַקְהֵלָת
פאה	פֵּאַת		עֵבֶר	מר	מָרָה
פדה	פְּדַהְאֵל	עבר	עֲבָרִים		מִרְקָה
פדה	פְּדָיָה	עברי	עֲבָרִיּוֹת		מַשָּׂא
פחה	פַּחַת מוֹאָב		עֶגְלָה		מִישָׁאֵל
כל, פה	פִּיכֹל		עֵדֶן		מָשָׁל
	פֶּלֶג		עֶדֶר	שלם	מְשֻׁלָּם

	(Group A)		(Group B)		(Group C)
פקד	פָּקוֹד	בן, ראה	רְאוּבֵן		שֻׁעָל
	פָּרָה		רֹאשׁ		שׁוֹר
פרח	פָּרוּחַ	רב	רַבָּה	שטה	שִׁטִּים
	פֶּרֶץ	רב	רַבּוֹת		שָׁטָן
פתח	פְּתַחְיָה	רב	רַבִּית		שְׁכֶם
	צְבָאוֹת	מג	רַב מָג		שָׁלַח
	צוּף	סריס, רב	רַב סָרִיס		שְׁלִישִׁיָּה
צפה	צוֹפִים	רב	רַבַּת		שָׁלֵם
	צוּר		רֶגֶל		שַׁלֵּם
צור	צוּרִיאֵל	רגל	רַגְלַיִם		שֵׁם
צור	צוּרִישַׁדָּי		רָצוֹן		שָׁמָּה
צל	צָלָה	רחוב	רְחֹבֹת	שם	שֵׁמוֹת
פחד, צל	צְלָפְחָד		רָחוּם	שמה	שְׁמוֹת
	צִנָּה		רָחֵל		שָׁמִיר
	צָפוֹן	רום, רם	רָם	שלמה	שִׂמְלָה
צפון	צְפוֹנִי	רום, רם	רָמָה	שמע	שִׁמְעִי
	צִפּוֹר	רום, רם	רָמוֹת		שָׁמַר
צרע	צְרוּעָה	רם	רָמַת		שֶׁמֶשׁ
	קֶדֶם	רם	רָמָתַיִם	שער	שְׁעָרִים
	קִדְמָה	רמון	רִמּוֹן פֶּרֶץ	שערה	שְׁעָרִים
	קָדֵשׁ	רפא	רָפוּא		שָׁפָט
קדש	קֳדָשִׁים	רוץ	רָצִים		שִׁפְלָה
קהל	קֹהֶלֶת		רִצְפָּה		שָׁפָן
קול	קוֹלָיָה	שאל	שָׁאוּל		שָׂרִיד
	קוֹץ		שָׁאוֹן		שָׂרָף
קרא	קוֹרֵא		שֶׁבַע		שֶׂרֶק
	קִינָה		שֶׁבֶר		תַּחַת
	קִיצוֹן		שַׁבָּת	תחתי	תַּחְתִּים
ארבע	קִרְיַת אַרְבַּע		שַׁדַּי	תל	תֵּל מֶלַח
קריה	קִרְיַת בַּעַל	אור	שְׁדֵיאוּר	מנה	תִּמְנָה
קריה	קִרְיָתַיִם	שדמה	שְׂדֵמוֹת	מנע	תִּמְנָע
יער	קִרְיַת יְעָרִים	שבק	שׁוֹבָק		תָּמָר
קרן	קַרְנַיִם		שָׁוֵה		תַּפּוּחַ
			שׁוּחַ	פסח	תְּפַסַח
		שמר	שׁוֹמֵר	רצה	תִּרְצָה

245

Hebrew Union College Annual, Vol. 14 (1939), pp. 153-249

HEBREW BASED UPON BIBLICAL PASSAGES
IN PARALLEL TRANSMISSION

ALEXANDER SPERBER

Jewish Theological Seminary, New York

As the title indicates, this study is a continuation of my investigation relating to Hebrew grammar, inaugurated by my monograph "Hebrew based upon Greek and Latin Transliterations," *HUCA* XII-XIII. I derive the material from three sources, each of them representing *one and the same* historic narrative, legal text or prophetic vision in two recensions: 1) the Hebrew Pentateuch as represented by the Masoretic Text and the Samaritan Bible; 2) Parallel passages in the Hebrew Bible, mainly Sam.-Kings as compared with Chronicles; and 3) textual variants recorded by the Masora as Ketib-Qere, Ma'arbae-Madinḥae, Sebirin. Thus, the very nature of my source material marks this research as a comparative study: each example consists of two readings of *the same* passage, demonstrating the two possibilities of morphology (§§44–87), syntax (§§88–124) or vocabulary (§§125–131). It is, therefore, essential to emphasize right at the outset that in all instances the two quotations forming one example are taken from the *very same text*, which has been handed down to us in two recensions, the variants of which are grouped and classified herein.

The introductory chapters I–XII (§§1–43) have been included in order to exhaust the material emanating from our sources. They will undoubtedly be of use to the student of Hebrew Palaeography and Phonetics.

The following abbreviations are used: MT = Masoretic Text.— S = Samaritan Pentateuch, according to Gall and Kennicott; both texts and critical notes are utilized.— Q = Qere; K = Ketib; Ma = Ma'arbae; Md = Madinḥae; Seb = Sebirin. This Masoretic material is derived from Ch. D. Ginsburg's *The Massorah compiled from Manuscripts*, I, London 1880, pp. 591–9; II, London

1883, pp. 55–93 and 324–9. In indicating the vowel signs I follow MT, irrespective of whether Ginsburg assigns the word thus vocalized to the Q or K, Ma or Md.—Var K = Variant reading according to Kennicott, *Vetus Testamentum cum variis lectionibus*, 2 vols., Oxford 1776 and 1780.—BHK = *Biblia Hebraica* ed. Kittel, Leipzig 1913.—B-L = Hans Bauer und Pontus Leander, *Historische Grammatik der hebräischen Sprache des Alten Testaments*, Halle (Saale) 1918 seq.—Bergstr. = G. Bergsträsser, *Hebräische Grammatik*, Leipzig 1918 seq. Part II is indicated by a 2 before the paragraph quoted. Both B-L and Bergstr. are quoted merely in order to bring into sharp relief the difference between the current explanation of these grammatical phenomena as offered by them and the new approach as elaborated here.—TRL = A. Sperber, "Hebrew based upon Greek and Latin Transliterations," *HUCA* XII-XIII.—MdW = Paul Kahle, *Masoreten des Westens*, I (Stuttgart 1927), II (1930).—Frequent reference is made in footnotes to readings of the first Biblia Rabbinica, Venice 1515–17 and its marginal notes; they are quoted as Venice 1515 and marg. respectively.

These studies in biblical philology will be continued. The next instalment to follow is an examination of the interrelation between the "New Testament and Septuagint," thus extending the scope of these researches so as to include the ancient Bible versions. Their close connection with the Hebrew Bible will help us towards a better understanding of the problems we are dealing with. Only then will we be able to discuss the three sources, upon which our present study is based, in a way similar to that offered in our Introduction to the preceding monograph on the transliterations.

I thankfully acknowledge the kind assistance rendered to me by the libraries of our Jewish Theological Seminary and of the Union Theological Seminary, both of which proved most helpful in the execution of these somewhat complicated researches.

TABLE OF CONTENTS

A. THE PHONETIC VALUE OF THE LETTERS

§36: Metathesis; α) with confusion of one letter; β) with confusion of two letters.

§37: Division of words; α) involving the final letters ם and ן; β) resulting in haplography.

C. THE VOWELS AND THEIR PHONOGRAPHY

XII. Vocalization by the Letters א ה ו י:

§38: The vowel a is indicated: a) in medial position by א; α) omission of the root letter א; b) in final position by א or ה.

§39: The vowel i is indicated by י: a) corresponding to i (‎ִ‎); b) corresponding to e (‎ֵ‎ or ‎ֶ‎).

§40: The vowel o is indicated by ו: a) corresponding to ‎ָ‎; b) corresponding to ‎ֳ‎; c) corresponding to ‎ֹ‎.

§41: The diphthong au is indicated: a) by יו; b) by וי or יו.

§42: The diphthong ai is indicated: a) by אי; b) by י.

§43: The dagesh lene: a) in the ב; b) in the כ; c) in the פ; d) in the ת.

D. THE VERB

§44: 2. pers. masc. sing. perf. ending in תה or ת: 1) the personal pronoun; 2) the verb: a) ḳal; b) pi'el; c) niph'al; d) hiph'il.

§45: 2. pers. fem. sing. perf. ending in ת or תי: 1) the personal pronoun; 2) the verb: A. ḳal: a) regular verbs; b) weak verbs: α) tertiae ה; β) mediae ו or י; γ) נתן; B. pi'el; C. niph'al; D. hiph'il; E. hithpa'el; 3) participle fem.

§46: 3. pers. fem. plur. perf. ending in ו or ה: a) ḳal; b) niph'al; c) reduplicated stem.

§47: 3. pers. fem. plur. imperf.: a) ending in ן or נה: α) ḳal; β) derived stems; b) ending in ן or הן; c) ending in נה or הן.

§48: Jussive or shortened forms: 1) with preservation of the י of the hiph'il: a) imperfect; b) perfect; c) infinitive: α) regular verbs; β) weak verbs; d) imperative; 2) with preservation of the ה of verbs tertiae ה: a) 3. pers. masc.

sing. imperf.; α) derived stems; b) 3. pers. fem. sing. imperf. c) 1. pers. plur. imperf.; d) imperative; 3) jussive forms with אל: a) with preservation of the י of the hiph'il; b) with preservation of the ה of verbs tertiae ה.

§49: Imperfect with consecutive waw and preservation of the final vowel: 1) hiph'il with preservation of the י: a) 3. pers. masc. sing.; α) weak verbs; b) 3. pers. fem. sing.; c) 1. pers. plur.; 2) mediae ו ḳal with preservation of the ו; 3) tertiae ה with preservation of the ה: A. ḳal: a) 3. pers. masc. sing.; b) 3. pers. fem. sing.=2. pers. masc. sing.; c) 1. pers. sing.; d) 1. pers. plur.; B. hiph'il: e) 3. pers. masc. sing.; f) 3. pers. fem. sing.; g) 1. pers. sing.; h) 1. pers. plur.; C. niph'al: i) 3. pers. masc. sing.; j) 1. pers. sing.; D. pi'el: k) 3. pers. masc. sing.; l) 1. pers. sing.; E. hithpa'el: m) 3. pers. masc. sing.

§50: The i-imperfect ḳal: a) imperf. with second vowel i; b) inf. with second vowel i: α) inf. absol.; β) inf. constr.

§51: Verbs primae ו or י: a) ḳal; b) derived stems.

§52: Verbs mediae ו or י: a) imperf. ḳal; b) inf. absol.; c) inf. constr.

§53: Verbs tertiae ה with interchange between ה and י: α) full forms; β) shortened forms.

§54: Verbs tertiae ו or ה: a) inf. absol. ḳal; b) perfect ḳal.

§55: Verbs tertiae א or ה.

§56: Inf. constr. of verbs tertiae ה.

§57: Verbs of weak roots; α) mediae geminatae.

§58: Assimilation of the ת in the hithpa'el.

§59: Preservation of the second vowel in inflected verbal forms: a) inflected forms of the participle: α) part. fem. sing.; β) part. masc. plur.; b) imperf. forms; c) perfect forms; d) imperative; e) inf. constr.; f) the verb in Sandhi: α) imperf.; β) imperative; γ) inf. constr.

§60: The use of the tenses: a) perf. or imperf.; b) participle or imperf.; c) participle or perfect; d) imperative or imperf.

§61: Active or passive construction: a) niph'al or ḳal: α) imperf.; β) perfect; b) niph'al or hiph'il; c) pu'al or pi'el; d) hoph'al or ḳal; e) hoph'al or hiph'il: α) imperf. β) perfect.

§62: The use of the derived stems: a) ḳal or hiph'il; b) pi'el or hiph'il; c) pu'al or niph'al; d) pi'el or ḳal· α) active; β) passive.

E. THE NOUN

§63: Substantives derived from verbs with imperf. in o or i; α) substantives with preformative (ת, ש).

§64: Substantives derived from verbs primae ו or י.

§65: Substantives derived from verbs mediae ו or י; α) substantives with preformative (ת, מ, י).

§66: Substantives derived from verbs tertiae ו or י; α) substantives with preformative (ת, מ).

§67: Substantives derived from verbs tertiae א or ה.

§68: Substantives derived from verbs tertiae ה with interchange between ה and י.

§69: Substantives derived from verbs of weak roots.

§70: Substantives of which the second radical is vocalized i; α) feminine forms; β) substantives with preformative מ.

§71: Substantives of which the first radical is vocalized i.

§72: miḳtal or miḳtol forms.

§73: Substantives of which the second radical is vocalized o or i.

§74: The absolute state ending in ה or ת.

§75: Formation of the plural masc.: α) ending in ים or ין; β) ending in מ or ים; γ) substantives with masc. or fem. ending.

§76: Inflected nominal forms with preservation of the second vowel; α) the substantive in Sandhi; β) construct state fem. plur.

§77: The substantive unchanged in the construct state: a) dual forms; b) plural forms: c) fem. sing.; d) cardinals; e) the substantive taking the article.

F. NOMINAL AND VERBAL SUFFIXES

I. The Helping Vowel י in Connection with the Suffixes:

§78: The pronominal suffix of the 2.
pers. masc. sing.: A. The masculine
noun: a) MT vocalizes pausal form
sing.; b) MT vocalizes context
form sing. B. The feminine noun:
c) MT vocalizes pausal form sing.;
d) MT vocalizes context form sing.

§79: The pronominal suffix of the 2.
pers. fem. sing.: A. The masculine
noun: a) MT vocalizes the noun
as sing.; α) particles; b) MT vocalizes the noun as plur. B. The
feminine noun: c) MT vocalizes the
noun as sing.; d) MT vocalizes the
noun as plur.

§80: The pronominal suffix of the 3.
pers. masc. sing.: a) the masculine
noun; α) particles; b) the feminine noun.

§81: The pronominal suffix of the 1.
pers. plur.

§82: The pronominal suffix of the 2.
pers. masc. plur.: a) the masculine
noun; b) the feminine noun.

§83: The pronominal suffix of the 3.
pers. fem. plur.

II. The Suffixes:

§84: 2. pers. masc. sing.: ךְ or אךְ;
α) כה or ךְ; β) (ךְ)כה or יךְ.

§85: 2. pers. fem. sing.: ךְ or כי.

§86: 3. pers. masc. sing.: a) ו or ה:
α) nouns; β) verbal forms; b) of
forms ending in a consonant: ו or
הו; c) of forms ending in a vowel:
הו or ו.

§87: 3. pers. masc. plur.: ם or הם;
α) particles.

G. SYNTAX

I. Subject and Predicate:

§88: The gender of the noun; α) adjustment in gender; β) the nomen
regens a construct state; γ) names
of nations.

§89: Agreement in number between
subject and predicate: a) the verb
precedes the noun; b) the verb
follows the noun.

§90: Agreement in number between
several verbs: a) adjustment to
the preceding verb; b) adjustment
to the following verb.

§91: Collective nouns used in the
sing. or plural.

§92: The subject: a collective noun —
the predicate: in the plur. or sing.;
α) names of nations.

II. The Article:

§93: The article is used: a) in a construct state formation; b) in connection with a preposition; c) when
the noun is rendered emphatic in
other ways; d) when the noun is
otherwise undetermined.

§94: The emphatic state is indicated
by the article or suffix; α) the
article is assimilated to an inseparable preposition.

§95: The article includes the meaning
of a demonstrative pronoun:
α) masc. sing.; β) fem. sing.;
γ) plural.

§96: Preservation of the article with
an inseparable preposition: a) with
the preposition בְּ; b) with the

preposition כ; c) with the preposition ל; d) the prefixed ה in verbal formations.

III. The Verb:

§97: The use of the consecutive waw: a) with the perfect; b) with the imperfect.

§98: The use of the inf. absol. or imperative.

§99: Particle and verb: the verb in the inf. constr. or finite tense: a) עד; b) למען ;לבלתי; c) אחרי; d) ביום.

§100: Inf. constr. with בכלם and pronominal suffixes: a) with the preposition ב; b) with the preposition כ; c) with the preposition ל; d) with the preposition מ.

§101: Finite verb continued by inf. absol. or finite tense.

§102: Verbal forms with pronominal suffixes.

IV. The ה Euphonicum:

A. with verbal forms

§103: Ḳal: a) 1. pers. sing. imperf.: 1) the regular verb: α) imperf. in o; β) imperf. in a; 2) weak verbs: γ) imperf. in i; δ) imperf. in a; ε) primae א; ζ) primae נ; η) mediae ו and י; b) 1. pers. plural imperf.: 1) the regular verb: α) imperf. in o; β) imperf. in a; 2) weak verbs: γ) imperf. in i; δ) imperf. in a; ε) primae א; ζ) mediae ו; c) imperative: α) imperfect in o; β) imperfect in a; γ) imperfect in i; δ) mediae ו; d) infinitive.

§104: Pi'el: a) 1. pers. sing. imperf.; b) 3. pers. fem. sing. imperf.; c) imperative.

§105: Niph'al: a) 1. pers. sing. imperf. b) imperative; c) infinitive.

§106: Hiph'il: a) 1. pers. sing. imperf.; α) primae י; β) mediae ו; b) 1. pers. plur. imperf.; c) imperative.

§107: Hithpa'el: a) 1. pers. sing. imperf.; b) 1. pers. plur. imperf.

B. with nouns and particles

§108: The so-called ה locativum: a) the noun in the construct state; b) the noun in the emphatic state; c) proper names; d) the ה clearly a euphonic ending only.

§109: Particles and pronouns.

V. Prepositions and Particles:

§110: The prepositions כ–ב.

§111: The locative preposition ב.

§112: The ל finalis: a) in connection with היה; b) in connection with other verbs; c) in connection with a particle.

§113: The use of מן or מ.

§114: Imperfect with אל or לא.

§115: The use of אשר; α) the use of the article or אשר.

§116: The direction is indicated by the accusative or ל, אל.

§117: The use of אל or ל: a) with verbs of speech; b) with other verbs; c) addition of אל or ל.

§118: The government of prepositions: a) preposition אל; b) preposition את; c) preposition על; d) preposition ב; e) preposition כ; f) preposition ל; g) preposition מ; h) nouns and phrases.

§119: The use of the particle את.

§120: The prepositions אל and על.

§121: The word-order in the sentence: 1) inseparable prepositions; 2) particle אל; 3) particle את; 4) preposition כל; 5) particle עוד; 6) particle על; 7) personal pronouns; 8) verb and object; 9) noun and apposition; 10) the accusative-object; 11) coupled words.

§122: Insertion of the subject or apposition thereof: a) subject; b) apposition.

§123: Appositions to ישראל; a) בני ישראל; b) בית ישראל; c) variae.

§124: Insertion of various nouns and particles: a) nouns; b) particles.

H. THE VOCABULARY

§125: The personal pronoun.

§126: masc. or fem. formation of the noun; α) substantival adjectives; β) particles and pronouns.

§127: Formation by metathesis.

§128: Formation by prefix: a) prefix מ; b) prefix ת.

§129: Substantives derived from verbs tertiae ה.

§130: Particles ending in י.

§131: Formation of theophorous names: a) ending in יהו or יה; b) by prefix יו or יהו.

A. THE PHONETIC VALUE OF THE LETTERS

Due to the similarity of their phonetic value, certain letters could be misunderstood for one another, thus leading to scribal errors. They can be grouped as follows:[1]

I. THE GUTTURALS א ה ח ע.[1a]

§1: א – ה:[2]

Gen. 21.24 MT אִשָּׁבֵעַ
S השבע

Gen. 14.23 MT הֶעֱשַׁרְתִּי
S אעשרתי

Gen. 19.29 MT הַהֲפֵכָה
S האפכה

Gen. 41.25 MT הִגִּיד
S אגיד

Ex. 2.9 MT וְהֵינִקֵהוּ
S ואינקהו

α) proper names (B–L §62x):[3]

Gen. 8.4 MT אֲרָרָט
S הררט

Gen. 10.27 MT הֲדוֹרָם
S אדורם

2 Chron. 10.18 הֲדֹרָם
1 Ki. 12.18 אֲדֹרָם

2 Chron. 22.5 הָרַמִּים
2 Ki. 8.28 אֲרַמִּים

1 Chron. 11.35 הַהָרָרִי
2 Sam. 23.33 הָאָרָרִי

β) various forms:

Jer. 52.15 הָאָמוֹן
2 Ki. 25.11 הֶהָמוֹן

2 Sam. 6.9 אֵיךְ
1 Chron. 13.12 הֵיךְ

§2: א – ח:

2 Ki. 17.21 Q וַיַּדַּח
K וידא

Lev. 11.16 MT הַשַּׁחַף
S השאף

1 Chron. 9.41 וְתַחְרֵעַ
1 Chron. 8.35 וְתָאְרֵעַ

---

[1] Only the consonants matter; the vocalization is here immaterial; cf. also TRL ¶ I.

[1a] Cf. TRL paragraphs XI, XII, and XXIII sub א, ה, ח, ע.

[2] Cf. Gen. 34.1: MT ותצא — Var K ותצה; ib. 29.19: MT שבה — Var K שבא; ib. 33.15: MT אצינה — Var K אצינא. [3] Cf. also § 38 b.

161

§3: א - ע [4]

Gen. 23.18	MT	בָּאֵי
	S	בעי
Ex. 22.29	MT	אִמּוֹ
	S	עמו
Ex. 4.12	MT	עָם
	S	אם
1 Ki. 1.18	MT	וְעַתָּה (2°)
	seb	ואתה

§5: ע - ה [6]

Gen. 27.19	MT	שָׁבָה
	S	שבע
Ex. 4.7	MT	שָׁבָה
	S	שבע
Lev. 13.6	MT	פָּשָׂה
	S	פשע
Num. 24.6	MT	נָטַע
	S	נטה

§4: ה - ח [5]

Prov. 20.21	Q	מְבֹהֶלֶת
	K	מבחלת
Cant. 1.17	Q	רַהִיטֵנוּ
	K	רחיטנו
Gen. 2.14	MT	חִדָּקֶל
	S	הדקל
Gen. 25.9	MT	צֹחַר
	S	צהר

§6: ח - ע [7]

Gen. 10.22	MT	עוּץ
	S	חוץ
Ex. 28.26	MT	עֵבֶר
	S	חבר
2 Ki. 20.13		וַיִּשְׁמַע
Isa. 39.2		וַיִּשְׂמַח [7a]
1 Sam. 17.7	Q	וְעֵץ
	K	וחץ

[4] Cf. Gen. 29.7: MT רעו — Var K ראו; ib. 41.2: MT ותרעינה — Var K ותראינה; ib. 9.12: MT אות — Var K עות.

[5] Cf. TRL paragraph VIII: Gen. 14.5: MT בהם — Jerome: בחם; also Gen. 4.20: MT אהל — Var K אחל; ib. 29.3: MT והשיבו — Var K וחשיבו; ib. 11.31: MT ויקח — Var K ויקה. The interchange between ה and ח could be explained as a graphic error, too. But then we would have to assume that these confusions were committed at a time when the Bible was already written in the Square Alphabet; and I am most anxious to avoid here, as far as possible, a discussion of the interrelation between the change in the Hebrew Alphabet and the textual errors of the Bible, which may and may not have been the result thereof.

[6] Cf. Jer. 48.28: MT ערים — Var K הרים.

[7] Cf. Gen. 12.15: MT ותקח — Var K ותקע; Jer. 16.6: MT יקרח — Var K יקרע; cf. also Paul Kahle in ZAW 1921, p. 235: "Dass ח und ע in der Aussprache zusammengefallen sein müssen, geht daraus hervor, dass mehrfach Wörter, die auf diese Konsonanten ausgehen, miteinander reimen." See also MdWI, p. 47.

[7a] On the interchange שׂ-שׁ, cf. § 10.

II. The Sibilants שׁ צ ס ז.[8]

§7: ז – צ:[9]

Ex. 15.5 MT בִּמְצוֹלֹת
S במזלות

Num. 22.39 MT חָצוֹת
S חיזות

Ezek. 45.8 K וְהָאָרֶץ
Q והארז

§8: ס – שׁ:[10]

α) Gen. 1.21 MT הָרֹמֶשֶׂת
S הרמסת

Gen. 27.31 MT וַיַּעַשׂ
S ויעס

Gen. 40.9 MT שַׂר
S סר

Gen. 42.25 MT שִׂקוֹ
S סקו

Num. 15.29 MT יִשְׂרָאֵל
S ישראל

β) Isa. 17.14 Q שׁוֹסֵנוּ
K שושנו

Isa. 10.13 Q שׁוֹסֵתִי
K שושתי

§9: צ – שׁ:[11]

Num. 16.30 MT וּפָצְתָה
S ופשתה

1 Chron. 18.3 לְהַצִּיב
2 Sam. 8.3 לְהָשִׁיב

§10: שׂ – שׁ:[12]

2 Ki. 20.13 וַיִּשְׁמַע
Isa. 39.2 וַיִּשְׂמַח[12a]

Ezek. 30.18 Ma חָשַׂךְ
Md חָשַׁךְ

---

[8] Cf. TRL paragraph XIII.

[9] The possibility of regional difference in the pronunciation must be taken into consideration; cf. Ps. 96.12: יַעֲלֹז — 1 Chron. 16.32: יַעֲלֹץ; Ex. 2.23: MT וַיִּזְעָקוּ — s ויצעקו; Gen. 18.20: MT זָעֲקַת — s צעקת (B-L. §2v).

[10] Cf. Job 17.7: Venice 1515 מִבַּעַס, marg.: מכעש; ibid. 20.22: שְׂפְקוֹ, Venice 1515 marg. ספקו; further: Gen. 6.11: MT חָמָס — Var K חמש; ib. 9.2: MT תרמש — Var K תרמס; ib. 40.3: MT בַּמִּשְׁמָר — Var K במסמר.

[11] Cf. also 1 Chron. 16.16: לְיִצְחָק — Ps. 105.9: לְיִשְׂחָק (B-L §2v; Bergstr. §14f); for explanation cf. our note 9 on §7. Cf. further Gen. 21.33: MT אֶשֶׁל — Var K אצל; ib. 24.63: MT וַיֵּשֵׁא — Var K ויצא; ib 43.4: MT מִשְׁלַח — Var K מצלח.

[12] Cf. Jer. 36.9: Venice 1515 תַּשִּׂיאוּ; marg.: תַּשִּׂיאוּ; Ps. 89.23: יַשִּׂיא, Venice 1515 marg.: יַשִּׂיא; Ps. 50.23: Ven. 1515: שָׂם ן, marg.: שָׂם ן. See also TRL paragraphs XIV, and XXXIII 2.

[12a] On the change between ח–ע, cf. §6.

III. THE LABIALS ‫ב מ פ‬.

§11: ‫ב – ו‬:[13]

Ex. 12.29 MT ‫הַשְּׁבִי‬
S ‫השוי‬

Gen. 25.8 MT ‫וַיִּגְוַע‬
S ‫וינבע‬

Gen. 8.12 MT ‫הַיּוֹנָה‬
S ‫היבנה‬

a) ‫ב – יו‬:

Jer. 29.22 Q ‫וּכְאָחָיו‬
K ‫וכאחב‬

§12: ‫ב – מ‬:[14]

Num. 12.8 MT ‫וּתְמֻנַת‬
S ‫ותבונת‬

1 Chron. 20.4 ‫מִילִידֵי‬
2 Sam. 21.18 ‫בִּילִידֵי‬

2 Chron. 10.2 ‫מִמִּצְרַיִם‬
1 Ki. 12.2 ‫בְּמִצְרָיִם‬

2 Sam. 5.13 ‫מִירוּשָׁלִַם‬
1 Chron. 14.3 ‫בִּירוּשָׁלִַם‬

Ezra 1.1 ‫מִפִּי‬
2 Chron. 36.22 ‫בְּפִי‬

2 Chron. 25.23 ‫מְשַׁעַר‬
2 Ki. 14.13 ‫בְּשַׁעַר‬[15]

2 Ki. 23.33 Q ‫מִמְּלֹךְ‬
K ‫במלך‬

Josh. 3.16 Q ‫מֵאָדָם‬
K ‫באדם‬

Josh. 22.7 K ‫מעבר‬
Q ‫בְּעֵבֶר‬

Josh. 24.15 Q ‫מֵעֵבֶר‬
K ‫בעבר‬

2 Ki. 12.10 Q ‫מִיָּמִין‬
K ‫בימין‬

Job 34.14 Ma ‫יָשִׂים‬
Md ‫ישיב‬[16]

a) proper names:

Isa. 39.1 ‫מְרֹאדַךְ‬
2 Ki. 20.12 ‫בְּרֹאדַךְ‬.

2 Ki. 5.12 Q ‫אֲמָנָה‬
K ‫אבנה‬

§13: ‫ב—פ‬:[17]

Gen. 31.35 MT ‫וַיְחַפֵּשׂ‬
S ‫ויחבש‬

---

[13] Cf. Gen. 7.16: MT ‫צוה‬ — Var K ‫צבא‬; Jer. 42.14: MT ‫וללחם‬ — Var K ‫בללחם‬; Gen. 22.13: MT ‫בסבך‬ — Var K ‫בסוך‬; cf. also TRL s. v. ‫אָֽן‬.

[14] Cf. Gen. 33.10: MT ‫מִידִי‬ — Var K ‫בידי‬; Jer. 4.8: MT ‫שב‬ — Var K ‫שם‬; ib. 23.18: MT ‫הקשיב‬ — Var K ‫הקשים‬; further: Ezek. 14.9: ‫מתוך‬, Venice 1515 marg.: ‫בתוך‬.

[15] Cf. Md–Ma on 2 Ki. 14.13.

[16] On the interchange between ‫ש‬ and ‫שׂ‬ involved hereby, cf. §10.

[17] Cf. Gen. 31.35: MT ‫ויחפש‬ — Var K ‫ויחבש‬; ib. 48.4: MT ‫מפרך‬ — Var K ‫מברך‬; Jer. 15.9: MT ‫השפעה‬ — Var K ‫השבעה‬.

Gen. 31.49	MT	וְהַמִּצְפָּה	1 Chron. 19.16		וְשׁוֹפַךְ
	S	והמצבה	2 Sam. 10.16		וְשׁוֹבַךְ
Ex. 15.10	MT	נָשַׁפְתָּ	1 Chron. 17.6		שֹׁפְטֵי
	S	נשבת	2 Sam. 7.7		שִׁבְטֵי
Num. 3.6	MT	לִפְנֵי	Ps. 80.3	MT	לִפְנֵי
	S	לבני		seb	¹⁹לבני

§14: פ – מ :

Isa. 37.27		וּשְׂדֵמָה
2 Ki. 19.26		וּשְׂדֵפָה
Isa. 65.4	Q	וּמְרַק
	K	ומרק

IV. THE PALATALS — VELARS ג כ ק.

§15: כ – ג :²⁰

Gen. 14.23	MT	שְׂרוֹךְ
	S	שרוג
Gen. 21.23	MT	וּלְנֶכְדִּי
	S	ולנגדי

Lev. 11.19	MT	הַדּוּכִיפַת
	S	הדניפת

§16: ק – כ :²¹

Deut. 15.7	MT	תִקְפֹּץ
	S	תכפץ

V. THE DENTALS ט ד ת.

§17: ת – ד :²²

Ex. 31.10	MT	הַשְּׂרָד
	S	השרת

Ezek. 22.4	Q	עַד
	K	עת
Gen. 10.3	MT	וְרִיפַת
	S	ריפד

¹⁸ On the spelling with or without the mater lectionis ו, cf. §40.
¹⁹ Cf. K-Q on Prov. 4.3 and seb-MT on Job 19.17.
²⁰ Cf. Jer. 3.2: MT שֻׁגַּלְתְּ — Var K שכלת.
²¹ Cf. Gen. 23.15: MT שֶׁקֶל — Var K שכל; ib. 42.33: MT קְחוּ — Var K כחו; ib. 33.4: MT וַיִּבְכּוּ — Var K ויבקו; cf. also TRL paragraph XXIII sub כ; and here §43 b.
²² Cf. Gen. 22.2: MT אַחַד — Var K אחת; Jer. 49.1: MT נֶגֶד — Var K נת; ib. 8.7:MT עֵת — Var K עד. Cf. also TRL paragraph XXIII sub ד, and paragraph XXXI subdivision 1.

Isa. 66.17 Q   אַחַת
        K   אחד

Gen. 19.26 MT   וַתְּבֵּט
          S   וטביט

§18: ת – ט :[23]

Deut. 12.3 MT   וְנִתַּצְתָּם
          S   ונטצתם

Gen. 15.10 MT   בָּתְרוֹ
        S   בטרו

VI. The Liquids ל מ נ ר.

§19: ר–נ ; ר–מ ; נ–מ ; ר–ל :[24]

2 Sam. 12.31   וַיָּשֶׂם
1 Chron. 20.3   וַיָּשַׂר

Isa. 37.24   מְרוֹם
2 Ki. 19.23   מְלוֹן

Ps. 18.33   וַיִּתֵּן
2 Sam. 22.33   וַיַּתֵּר

B. THE GRAPHIC FORM OF THE LETTERS

Certain letters could, on account of their resemblance in script, be confused with one another; the result was an obvious mistake in the spelling of a given word. Scribal errors of this kind can be classified as follows:[24a]

VII. The Group ב ד ר.

§20: ר – ב :

Lev. 6.5 MT   בַּבֹּקֶר (2°)
      S   בבקב

Gen. 11.29 MT   אַבְרָם
        S   ארדם

Lev. 16.18 MT   הַמִּזְבֵּחַ
      S   המזרח

Gen. 13.8 MT   אַבְרָם
        S   אבבם

Num. 3.5 MT   וַיְדַבֵּר
      S   וידרר

Gen. 25.27 MT   וְיַעֲקֹב
        S   ויעקר

Num. 9.19 MT   מִשְׁמֶרֶת
      S   משמבת

---

[23] Cf. Gen. 4.7: MT לפתח — Var K לפטח; Ex. 7.4: MT בשפטים — Var K בשפתים; Gen. 33.14: MT לאטי — Var K לאתי.

[24] Cf. Gen. 8.1: MT רוח — Var K לוח; ib. 3.24: MT וישכן — Var K וישכם; Jer. 6.27: MT ובחנת — Var K ובחרת.   [24a] Cf. note 1.

Num. 15.16 MT	וְלַגֵּר	
S	ולגב	
Num. 16.30 MT	יִבְרָא	
S	יבבא	
1 Ki. 22.32	וַיָּסֻרוּ	
2 Chron. 18.31	וַיָּסֹבּוּ	
Ezek. 3.15 Q	וָאֵשֵׁב	
K	ואשר	

§21: ר – ד ²⁵

Gen. 13.6 MT	יַחְדָּו
S	יחרו
Gen. 14.14 MT	וַיָּרֶק
S	וידק
Gen. 22.13 MT	אַחַר
S	אחד
Deut. 1.22 MT	וְיַחְפְּרוּ
S	ויחפדו
Deut. 28.49, 51 MT	יִדְאֶה
S	יראה
Ps. 18.43	אֲרִיקֵם
2 Sam. 22.43	אֲדִקֵּם
Ps. 18.11	וַיֵּרֶא
2 Sam. 22.11	וַיֵּרָא
Jer. 2.20 Q	אֶעֱבוֹר
K	אעבוד
Jer. 31.40 Q	הַשְּׁדֵמוֹת
K	השרמות

Prov. 19.19 Q	גְּרָל
K	גרל
Ezek. 6.14 Md	דִּבְלָתָה
Ma	רבלתה

α) proper names:

Gen. 10.4 MT	וְדֹדָנִים
S	ורודנים
Gen. 14.2 MT	וְשַׁמְאָבָר
S	ושמאבד
Num. 2.14 MT	רְעוּאֵל
S	דעואל
Gen. 10.4	וְדֹדָנִים
1 Chron. 1.7	וְרוֹדָנִים
Gen. 36.26	חֶמְדָּן
1 Chron. 1.41	חַמְרָן
2 Sam. 8.3	הֲדַדְעֶזֶר
1 Chron. 18.3	הֲדַרְעֶזֶר ²⁵ᵃ
2 Ki. 16.6 Q	וַאֲדוֹמִים
K	וארומים

§22: ד – ב ²⁶

2 Sam. 23.29	חֵלֶב
1 Chron. 11.30	חֵלֶד
Josh. 15.47 K	הגבול
Q	הגדול

²⁵ Cf. Gen. 4.2: MT ללדת — Var K ללרת; ib. 31.53: MT בפחד — Var K בפחר; ib. 49.26: MT נזיר — Var K נזיד; further Ps. 54.5: זרים‎, Venice 1515 marg.: זדים.

²⁵ᵃ Cf. vv. 5, 7, 8 in these parallel chapters.

²⁶ Cf. Judg. 20.34: מנגד; Venice 1515 marg.: מנגב.

VIII. THE GROUP ‏ב כ ר‎.

§23: ‏כ – ב‎:[27]

2 Sam. 7.22	‏כְּכֹל‎
1 Chron. 17.20	‏בְּכֹל‎
2 Sam. 24.19	‏כִּדְבַר‎
1 Chron. 21.19	‏בִּדְבַר‎
1 Ki. 22.20	‏בְּכֹה‎
2 Chron. 18.19	‏כָּכָה‎
2 Sam. 12.31 Q	‏בְּמַלְבֵּן‎
K	‏במלכן‎
2 Ki. 3.24 Q	‏וַיַּכּוּ...וְהַכּוֹת‎
K	‏ויבו...והבות‎
Isa. 63.6 K	‏וַאֲשַׁכְּרֵם‎
Q	‏ואשברם‎

Hos. 13.9 Q	‏בְּעֶזְרֶךָ‎
K	‏כעזרך‎
Prov. 21.29 Q	‏יָבִין‎
K	‏יכין‎
Job 21.13 Q	‏יְכַלּוּ‎
K	‏יבלו‎

§24: ‏כ – ר‎:

Gen. 31.15 MT	‏מְכָרָנוּ‎
S	‏מככנו‎
Ps. 18.12	‏חָשְׁכַת‎
2 Sam. 22.12	‏חַשְׁרַת‎

IX. THE GROUP ‏ב כ נ פ‎.

§25: ‏ב – נ‎:[28]

Jer. 33.3 K	‏וּבְצֻרוֹת‎
Q	‏ונצורות‎

§26: ‏כ – נ‎:[29]

Gen. 3.2 MT	‏הַנָּחָשׁ‎
S	‏הכחש‎
2 Ki. 14.10	‏הַכֵּה‎
2 Chron. 25.19	‏הִנֵּה‎

§27: ‏כ – פ‎:

2 Sam. 24.13	‏אֱנֻסְךָ‎[30]
1 Chron. 21.12	‏נִסְפָּה‎

§28: ‏פ – נ‎:

2 Sam. 23.35	‏פַּעֲרַי‎
1 Chron. 11.37	‏נַעֲרַי‎

[27] Cf. Gen. 31.25: MT ‏לָבָן‎ — Var K ‏לכן‎; Jer. 2.15: MT ‏מִבְּלִי‎ — Var K ‏מכלי‎; Gen. 43.22: MT ‏אָכַל‎ — Var K ‏אבל‎. Only obvious graphic errors are dealt with in this paragraph. On the stylistic difference in the use of the prepositions ‏ב‎ and ‏כ‎, cf. §110.

[28] Cf. Jer. 27.18: MT ‏נא‎ — Var K ‏בא‎.

[29] Cf. Jer. 43.11: MT ‏והכה‎ — Var K ‏והנה‎.

[30] Lege ‏נסכה‎; cf. §84 a.

X. THE GROUP הוי.

§29: ‏:ו – ה

Ex. 34.31	MT	וַיָּשֻׁבוּ
	s	וישבה
Gen. 1.16	MT	וַיַּעַשׂ . . . וְאֶת
	s	היעש . . . האת
Gen. 7.12, 17	MT	וַיְהִי
	s	היהי
Gen. 7.23	MT	וַיִּשָּׁאֶר
	s	הישאר
Gen. 14.13	MT	וַיַּגֵּד
	s	הינד
Gen. 19.2	MT	וַיֹּאמֶר
	s	היאמר
Gen. 22.24	MT	וְאֶת
	s	האת
Gen. 17.21	MT	הָאַחֶרֶת
	s	ואחרת
Gen. 22.9	MT	הָעֵצִים
	s	ועצים
Gen. 25.12	MT	הַמִּצְרִית
	s	ומצרית
Ex. 1.10	MT	תִּקְרֶאנָה
	s	תקראנו
Ex. 15.1	MT	אָשִׁירָה
	s	אשירו
1 Ki. 10.8		הַשֹּׁמְעִים
2 Chron. 9.7		וְשֹׁמְעִים

2 Sam. 7.23		הָלְכוּ אֱלֹהִים
1 Chron. 17.21		³¹הָלַךְ הָאֱלֹהִים

§30: ‏³²ו – י:

1 Sam. 22.17	Q	אָבוּ
	K	אבי
2 Sam. 22.51	Q	מִגְדּוֹל
	K	מגדיל
Jer. 48.18	Q	וּשְׁבִי
	K	ישבי
Zech. 14.6	Q	וְקִפָּאוֹן
	K	יקפאון
Job 10.17	Q	וְצָבָא
	K	יצבא
2 Ki. 17.13	Q	נְבִיאַי
	K	נביאו
Isa. 47.13	Q	הֹבְרֵי
	K	הברו
Isa. 52.2	Q	מוֹסְרֵי
	K	מוסרו
Isa. 60.21	Q	מַטָּעַי
	K	מטעו
Jer. 48.31	Q	יֶהְגֶּה
	K	והגה
Jer. 49.12	Q	יִשְׁתּוּ
	K	ושתו
Ps. 10.10	Q	יִדְכֶּה
	K	ודכה

³¹ Cf. also §37.

³² Cf. Codex Petropolitanus, Isa. 14.18: בביתו; further TRL s. v. הגית:
Ps. 49.4: MT והגות — o; s. v. חדל: Ps. 49.9: MT וחדל — o; s. v. יחדל — o; Ps. 46.6: MT עזרה — o; s. v. עזר: Ps. 46.6: MT יעזרה — o; s. v. הכין — J; Amos 4.12: MT הכון — o: כון.

Ps. 102.24 Q	כחי	Jer. 40.8 Q	עֵיפִי
K	כחו	K	עופי
Ps. 108.7 Q	וַעֲנֵנִי	Gen. 36.39	פָּעוּ
K	וענונו	1 Chron. 1.50	פָּעִי
Ps. 119.79 Q	וְיֹדְעֵי	Gen. 36.11	צְפוֹ
K	וידעו	1 Chron. 1.36	צְפִי
Prov. 11.3 Q	יְשָׁדֵּם	1 Ki. 16.34 Q	וּבִשְׂגוּב
K	ושדם	K	ובשניב
Prov. 17.27 Q	יְקַר	1 Ki. 14.25 Q	שִׁישַׁק
K	וקר	K	שושק
Prov. 31.4 Q	אֵי	Gen. 36.23	שְׁפוֹ
K	או	1 Chron. 1.40	שְׁפִי
		2 Sam. 8.9	תֹּעִי
		1 Chron. 18.9	תֹּעוּ

α) proper names:

§31: ה – י:[35]

1 Sam. 25.18 Q	אֲבִינָיִל	α) Ex. 3.13 MT	אָנֹכִי
K	אבוניל	S	אנכה
Gen. 10.27 MT	אוזָל	Ex. 28.26 MT	שְׁתֵּי
S	איזל	S	שתה
Gen. 36.22	וְהֵימָם	Lev. 10.19 MT	אֹתִי
1 Chron. 1.39	וְהוֹמָם	S	אתה
Gen. 36.27	וַעֲקָן	Lev. 13.52 MT	הַשְׁתִּי
1 Chron. 1.42	יַעֲקָן	S	השתה
1 Ki. 10.11	חִירָם	Lev. 26.12 MT	וְהִתְהַלַּכְתִּי
2 Chron. 9.10	חוּרָם	S	והתהלכתה
2 Ki. 23.31 Q	חֲמוּטַל	β) Lev. 23.19 MT	שְׂנָה
K	חמיטל[33]	S	שני
2 Sam. 21.16 Q	וְיִשְׁבִּי	Josh. 18.24 Q	הָעַמוֹנָה
K	וישבו	K	העמוני
Gen. 10.28	עוֹבָל		
1 Chron. 1.22	עֵיבָל[34]		

[33] Cf. similarly 2 Ki. 24.18; Jer. 52.1.
[34] Cf. MT-s on Gen. 10.28.
[35] Cf. also §53.

2 Sam. 16.10	Q	כֹּה
	K	כִּי
Gen. 31.31	MT	כִּי
	s	כֹה

2 Sam. 23.18	Q	הַשְּׁלֹשָׁה
	K	השלשי
Micah 6.5	Q	מַה
	K	מִי

XI. Various Other Confusions.

§32: 1) א – ת :[36]

Gen. 4.12	MT	תַּח
	s	אָת
Gen. 19.32	MT	אָבִינוּ
	s	תבינו

2) ו – ג :

2 Sam. 23.36	יִגְאָל
1 Chron. 11.38	יוֹאֵל

3) ו – ג :

Ezek. 25.7	Q	לְבַז
	K	לבג

4) ו – ד :

1 Ki. 12.33	Q	מִלְּבוֹ
	K	מלבד

5) ד – ך :[37]

1 Sam. 4.13	Q	יַד
	K	יך

6) ם – ה :[38]

1 Chron. 8.32	שִׁמְאָה
1 Chron. 9.38	שִׁמְאָם
1 Ki. 14.31	אֲבִיָּם
2 Chron. 12.16	אֲבִיָּה
2 Ki. 11.3	אֹתָהּ
2 Chron. 22.12	אֹתָם

Isa. 30.32	Q	בָּם
	K	בה
Prov. 20.16; 27.13	Q	נָכְרִיָּה
	K	נכרים
Isa. 6.13	MT	בָּם
	seb	בה

7) ז – ן :[39]

Isa. 44.14	Q	אֹרֶן
	K	ארז
Jer. 39.13	Q	וּנְבוּשַׁזְבָּן
	K	ונבושזבו
Prov. 16.28	Q	וְנִרְגָּן
	K	ונרגו

[36] Cf. Gen. 15.5: MT אם — Var K חם; ib. 31.27: MT נחבאת — Var K נחבתת.
[37] Cf. Gen. 4.1: MT ותלד — Var K ותלך.
[38] Cf. Gen. 9.11: MT יהיה — Var K יהים; ib. 12.10: MT מצרימה — Var K מצרימם; Jer. 38.5: MT הנה — Var K הנם.
[39] Cf. Codex Petropolitanus: Isa. 9.14: זקן; ib. 23.11: הרגיז and כנען.

8) ח – ת: [40]

Eccl. 12.6 Q יֵרָתֵק
        K ירחק

9) ט – שׁ:

1 Sam. 14.32 Q וַיַּעַט
          K ויעש

10) צ – י:

Gen. 25.29 MT וַיָּזֶד
         S וצוד

Lev. 13.23 MT הַשְּׁחִין
         S השחצן

11) ך – ן: [41]

Gen. 47.15 MT כְּנַעַן
         S כנעך

12) כ – ס:

1 Ki. 7.40 הַכִּירוֹת
2 Chron. 4.11 הַסִּירוֹת

13) ך – ף:

Gen. 27.13 MT אַךְ
         S אַף

14) מ – ת: [42]

Gen. 4.5 MT מִנְחָתוֹ
      S מנחמו

15) ק – ר: [43]

Num. 11.12 MT תֹאמַר
       S תאמק

16) ר – ה:

1 Ki. 7.43 עָשָׂר . . . עֲשָׂרָה
2 Chron. 4.14 עָשָׂה . . . עָשָׂה

1 Ki. 22.49 Q עָשָׂה
        K עשר

17) ט – ון:

2 Sam. 23.26 הַפַּלְטִי
1 Chron. 11.27 הַפְּלוֹנִי

18) ם – נו:

2 Ki. 22.4 וְיַתֵּם
2 Chron. 34.9 וַיִּתְּנוּ

Josh. 5.1 Q עָבְרָם
        K עברנו

---

[40] Cf. Gen. 7.23: MT וַיִּמַח — Var K וימחו.

[41] Cf. Josh. 8.9: וַיֵּלֶן יהושע בלילה ההוא בתוך העם.
Josh. 8.13: וַיֵּלֶךְ יהושע בלילה ההוא בתוך העמק; cf. also Jer. 9.6, 18: MT אֵיךְ — Var K אין.

[42] Cf. Gen. 42.9, 26: MT אֵת — Var K אם.

[43] Cf. Judg. 5.15: בפלגות ראובן גדלים חִקְקֵי לב.
Judg. 5.16: בפלגות ראובן גדלים חִקְרֵי לב; cf. also Gen. 7.17: MT ותרם — Var K ותקם.

§33: Confusion of groups of letters:			
2 Sam. 23.30	הֲדָי		
1 Chron. 11.32	חוּרַי		
2 Sam. 23.27	מְבֻנַּי		
1 Chron. 11.29	סִבְּכַי[44]		
2 Sam. 23.33	שָׁרָר		
1 Chron. 11.35	שָׂכָר[46]		
2 Sam. 23.36	הַגָּדִי		
1 Chron. 11.38	חַגְרִי[45]		
2 Ki. 23.2	וְהַנְּבִיאִים		
2 Chron. 34.30	וְהַלְוִיִּם[47]		
2 Sam. 23.25	הַחָרֹדִי		
1 Chron. 11.27	הַהֲרוֹרִי		

The following classes of textual confusion can also be assigned to the oversight of the copyists:

§34: Haplography (Bergstr. §20e):

Jer. 51.3	K	אֶל יִדְרֹךְ ידרך
	Q	>

Ezek. 7.21 Q וְחִלְּלוּהוּ (:והסבתי)
K וחללוה

2 Ki. 20.18 Q יֻקְּחוּ (והיה)
K יקח

2 Sam. 7.12 כִּי יִמְלְאוּ
1 Chron. 17.11 כִּי מָלְאוּ[48]

2 Sam. 22.15 K ויהמם
Q וַיָּהֹם

β) letters:[49]

2 Ki. 9.33	K	שמטוהו (וַיִּשְׁמְטוּהָ)
	Q	שְׁמְטוּהָ
2 Ki. 11.1	K	(אֲחַזְיָהוּ) וראתה
	Q	רָאֲתָה
Ezek. 44.3	K	יצאו (וַיְבִיאֶנִי)
	Q	יֵצֵא
Ezek. 46.6	K	תְּמִימִם (1°)
	Q	תמים

§35: Dittography:
a) words:

Ezek. 48.16 K חֲמֵשׁ חמש
Q >

γ) with confusion of letters:

2 Ki. 19.23	K	ברכב (רִכְבִּי)
	Q	בְּרֹב[50]

---

[44] Cf. Jer. 20.8: MT ולקלם — Var K ולקלם.
[45] Cf. §§4 and 21.
[46] Cf. §§10 and 24.
[47] Cf. §§11 and 19.
[48] For another possible explanation, cf. §60 a.
[49] Cf. Gen. 42.26: MT שברם על — Var K שברם מעל.
[50] =Isa. 37.24; on כ-ב cf. §23.

§36: Metathesis
(Bergstr. §20d):[51]

Gen. 23.9	MT	קֶבֶר
	S	קרב
Gen. 28.20	MT	יַעֲקֹב
	S	יעבק
Gen. 47.19	MT	וְהָאֲדָמָה
	S	והאמדה
Lev. 13.21	MT	שִׁבְעָת
	S	בשעת
Num. 1.38	MT	מִבֶּן
	S	מנב
Num. 4.6	MT	בֶּגֶד
	S	בדג
Num. 7.29	MT	בֶּן
	S	נב
Num. 21.11	MT	בְּמִדְבָּר
	S	במדרב
Deut. 12.17	MT	לָאֱכֹל
	S	לאלך
2 Sam. 23.31		הַבַּרְחֻמִי
1 Chron. 11.33		הַבַּחֲרוּמִי
1 Ki. 8.7		וַיָּסֹכּוּ
2 Chron. 5.8		וַיְכַסּוּ
1 Ki. 10.11		אַלְמֻגִּים
2 Chron. 9.10		אַלְגּוּמִים

2 Sam. 22.12		סֻכּוֹת
Ps. 18.12		סָבָתוֹ
2 Sam. 22.13		בָּעֲרוּ
Ps. 18.13		עָבְרוּ
2 Sam. 22.46		וְיַחְגְּרוּ
Ps. 18.46		וְיַחְרְגוּ
2 Ki. 19.29		סָחִישׁ
Isa. 37.30		שָׁחִיס
2 Ki. 20.12		חִזְקִיָּהוּ
Isa. 39.1		וַיֶּחֱזָק
1 Sam. 27.8	Q	וְהַגִּזְרִי
	K	והגרזי
2 Sam. 15.28; 17.16	Q	בְּעַרְבוֹת
	K	בעברות
2 Sam. 20.14	Q	וַיִּקָּהֲלוּ
	K	ויקלהו
1 Ki. 7.45	Q	הָאֵלָּה
	K	האהל
Isa. 38.11	Q	חָדֶל
	K	חלד[52]
Ezek. 17.7	Q	כנפה
	K	כָּפְנָה
Ezek. 42.16	Q	מָאוֹת
	K	אמות
Eccl. 9.4	Q	יְחֻבַּר
	K	יבחר

---

[51] Cf. Gen. 27.11: MT שָׂעִיר — Var K עָשִׂיר; ib. 35.17: MT בהקשתה — Var K בהשקתה; ib. 47.14: MT וילקט — Var K ויקטל.

[52] For another possible explanation of this variant, cf. §127.

α) with confusion of one letter:

Josh. 21.20	גֹּרְלָם
1 Chron. 6.51	גְּבוּלָם[53]
2 Sam. 21.18	וַתְּהִי עוֹד
1 Chron. 20.4	וַתַּעֲמֹד[54]
2 Sam. 23.12	וַיַּעַשׂ
1 Chron. 11.14	וַיּוֹשַׁע[55]

β) with confusion of
two letters:

2 Sam. 6.5	עֲצֵי בְרוֹשִׁים
1 Chron. 13.8	עֹז וּבְשִׁירִים[56]
2 Sam. 23.11	עֲדָשִׁים
1 Chron. 11.13	שְׂעוֹרִים[57]
2 Ki. 8.21	צָעִירָה
2 Chron. 21.9	עִם שָׂרָיו[58]

§37: Division of words.

2 Sam. 5.2	Q	הָיִיתָ הַמּוֹצִיא
	K	הייתה מוציא
1 Ki. 20.33	Q	וַיַּחְלְטוּ הֲמִמֶּנּוּ
	K	ויחלטו ממנו

Jer. 8.4	Q	(אִם) יָשׁוּבוּ לֹא (יָשׁוּב)
	K	יָשׁוּב וְלֹא
Ezek. 42.9	Q	וּמִתַּחַת הַלְּשָׁכוֹת
	K	ומתחתה לשכות
Job 38.12	Q	יִדַּעְתָּ הַשַּׁחַר
	K	ידעתה שחר

α) involving the final letters
ם and ן:

2 Sam. 21.12	Q	שָׁמָה פְלִשְׁתִּים
	K	שם הפלשתים
Isa. 9.6	Q	לְמַרְבֵּה
	K	לם רבה
Job 38.1	Q	מִן הַסְּעָרָה
	K	מנהסערה[59]
Job 40.6	Q	מִן סָעָרָה
	K	מנסערה

β) resulting in haplography:

Jer. 18.3	Q	וְהִנֵּה הוּא
	K	והנהו
Ezek. 8.6	Q	מָה הֵם
	K	מהם
Ps. 123.4	Q	לִגְאֵי יוֹנִים
	K	לגאיונים

---

[53] ר-ב, cf. §20.

[54] מ-ה, cf. §32 6; on the spelling with or without the matres lectionis, cf. §§39 and 40.

[55] שׂ-שׁ, cf. §10; on the possibility of the defective spelling of ויושע cf. the instance from 2 Sam. 8.6 in §40 a.

[56] ז-צ, cf. §7; ו-י, cf. §30.

[57] ר-ד, cf. §21; שׂ-שׁ, cf. §10.

[58] ה-ם, cf. §32 6; שׂ-ע, cf. §9.

[59] Cf. 1 Chron. 27.12: Venice 1515: לִבְנָ־יָמִינִי, marg.: לָבֶן יְמִינִי.

C. THE VOWELS AND THEIR PHONOGRAPHY

As evidenced by the textual variations listed here, Hebrew then had three vowels: a, i, o. No conclusions can be drawn from our sources as to their quantity or quality.

XII. Vocalization by the Letters א ה ו י.[60]

§38: *The vowel a is indicated:*
a) in medial position by א:

Gen. 18.11	MT	(אֹרַח) כָּנָשִׁים
	S	כאנשים
Num. 31.35	MT	הַנָּשִׁים
	S	האנשים
Gen. 37.7	MT	קָמָה
	S	קאמה
Ex. 23.31	MT	וְשַׁתָּי
	S	ושאתי
Deut. 23.25	MT	בְקָמַת ... קָמַת
	S	בקאמת ... קאמת
Deut. 28.7	MT	הַקָּמִים
	S	הקאמים
Josh. 21.36		רָמֹת
1 Chron. 6.65		רָאמֹות
Josh. 21.30		מִשָׁאָל
1 Chron. 6.59		מָשָׁל
Isa. 37.12		בִּתְלַשָּׂר
2 Ki. 19.12		בִּתְלָאשָׂר
2 Sam. 11.1		הַמַּלְאָכִים
1 Chron. 20.1		הַמְּלָכִים

Judg. 4.21	Q	בְּלָט
	K	בלאט
Judg. 9.41	Q	בְרוּמָה
	K	בארומה
2 Sam. 10.17	Q	חֶלָמָה
	K	חלאמה
2 Sam. 12.1	Q	רָשׁ
	K	ראשׁ[61]
2 Sam. 12.4	Q	הָרָשׁ
	K	הראש
2 Sam. 23.33	Q	הָרָרִי
	K	האררי
Isa. 10.13	Q	כָּבִיר
	K	כאביר
Isa. 27.8	Q	בְּסַסְאָה
	K	בסאסאה
Isa. 33.20	Q	נָוֶה
	K	נאוה
Jer. 40.1	Q	בַּזִּקִּים
	K	באזקים
Jer. 40.4	Q	הַזִּקִּים
	K	האזקים

[60] On the three basic vowels of Hebrew, a, i, o, cf. also TRL paragraph XXVI b. Correspondingly, Hebrew has *three* vowel letters; for ה is a substitute either for י (cf. §§53 and 68), or for א (cf. §§38 b, 55 and 67).

[61] Cf. similarly Prov. 10.4.

Ezek. 27.26	Q	הַשָּׁטִים		
	K	השאטים⁶²		
Hos. 10.14	Q	וְקָם		
	K	וקאם		
Joel 2.6	Q	פְרור		
	K	פָּארור⁶³		
Hag. 2.2	Q	שְׁלְתִּיאֵל		
	K	שאלתיאל		

a) omission of the root letter א:⁶⁴

Ps. 18.40		וַתְּאַזְרֵנִי
2 Sam. 22.40		וַתַּזְרֵנִי
2 Ki. 7.1, 16	Q	וְסָאתַיִם
	K	וסתים
Jer. 29.22	Q	וּכְאַחְאָב
	K	וכאחב

b) in final position by א or ה:⁶⁵

Gen. 10.7	וְסַבְתָּה וְרַעְמָה
1 Chron. 1.9	וְסַבְתָּא וְרַעְמָא
2 Sam. 21.18	הָרָפָה
1 Chron. 20.4	הָרָפָא
2 Ki. 15.33	יְרוּשָׁא
2 Chron. 27.1	יְרוּשָׁה
2 Ki. 18.18	וְשֶׁבְנָה
Isa. 36.3	וְשֶׁבְנָא

Ezek. 36.5	Q	כלה
	K	כָּלָא
2 Ki. 17.24	Md	וּמֵעַוָּא
	Ma	ומעוה
Ezek. 27.31	Md	קָרְחָא
	Ma	קרחה

§39: The vowel *i* is indicated by י.

a) corresponding to i (ִ):

2 Sam. 5.22	וַיִּסְפּוּ
1 Chron. 14.13	וַיִּסִיפוּ
2 Sam. 6.3	וַיַּרְכִּבוּ
1 Chron. 13.7	וַיַּרְכִּיבוּ
2 Sam. 6.9	וַיִּרָא⁶⁶
1 Chron. 13.12	וַיִּירָא
2 Sam. 6.17	וַיָּבֹאוּ ... וַיַּצִּגוּ
1 Chron. 16.1	וַיָּבִיאוּ ... וַיַּצִּינוּ
2 Sam. 7.9	וָעֶשְׂתִּי
1 Chron. 17.8	וָעֶשִׂיתִי
2 Sam. 23.23	וַיְשִׂמֵהוּ
1 Chron. 11.25	וַיְשִׂימֵהוּ
1 Ki. 8.40	יִרָאוּךָ
2 Chron. 6.31	יִירָאוּךָ
Ezek. 6.6 Q	תשמנה
K	תִּישַׁמְנָה

⁶² Cf. also ib. 28.24, 26.
⁶³ Cf. similarly Nah. 2.11.
⁶⁴ Cf. 1 Sam. 25.8: בְּנוּ, Venice 1515 marg.: באנו; 1 Ki. 12.12: וַיָּבֹו, Venice 1515 marg.: ויבא.
⁶⁵ Cf. also §1 α.
⁶⁶ Cf. Gen. 8.10: וַיָּחֶל עוֹד שִׁבְעַת יָמִים.
Gen. 8.12: וַיִּיָּחֶל עוֹד שִׁבְעַת יָמִים.

Ezek. 7.7 Md	הצפרה		2 Sam. 8.6	וַיֹּשַׁע
Ma	הַצְּפִירָה		1 Chron. 18.6	וַיּוֹשַׁע
Ezek. 7.22 Md	פרצים		2 Sam. 23.17	הַגִּבֹרִים
Ma	פָּרִיצִים		1 Chron. 11.19	הַגִּבּוֹרִים

2 Sam. 23.18   בַּשְּׁלֹשָׁה
1 Chron. 11.20   בַּשְּׁלוֹשָׁה

b) corresponding to e (= ֵ or ֶ):67

1 Sam. 31.4   יָבוֹאוּ
1 Chron. 10.4   יָבֹאוּ

Ex. 1.16 MT   בְּיַלֶּדְכָן...וּרְאִיתָן
S   בילדכין...וראיתין

Ezek. 17.6 Q   פֹּארוֹת
K   פארת

Ex. 1.18 MT   עֲשִׂיתָן
S   עשיתין

Ex. 2.18 MT   מְהַרְתָּן
S   מהרתין

b) corresponding to ָ:

Ex. 2.20 MT   עֲזַבְתָּן
S   עזבתין

Jer. 27.20 Q   יְכָנְיָה
K   יכוניה

1 Ki. 8.1   יַקְהֵל
2 Chron. 5.2   יַקְהִיל

Jer. 33.8 Q   לְכָל
K   לכול

Jer. 42.20 Q   הִתְעֵיתָם
K   התעתים

Josh. 15.63 Q   יָכְלוּ
K   יוכלו

Ezek. 11.6 Q   וּמִלֵּאתָם
K   ומלאתים

Ezek. 23.42 Q   סָבָאִים
K   סובאים

Ezek. 32.7 Q   וכסתי
K   וְכִסֵּיתִי

Ezek. 27.15 Q   וְהָבְנִים
K   והובנים

§40: The vowel o is indicated by ו.

Ezek. 34.25 Q   בְּיָעָרִים
K   ביעורים

a) corresponding to ֹ:

c) corresponding to ָ:68

1 Sam. 31.13   עַצְמֹתֵיהֶם
1 Chron. 10.12   עַצְמוֹתֵיהֶם

1 Sam. 31.13   וַיָּצְמוּ
1 Chron. 10.12   וַיָּצוֹמוּ

---

67 Cf. §83; further: אֹתִים 1 Sam. 13.21 and אֹתִים Isa. 2.4; stat. constr. בְּאֵרֹת Gen. 26.18 and בְּאֵרֹת ib. 14.10; הַגֹּלָם Jer. 20.4 and הַגֹּלָם 1 Chron. 8.7; also Jer. 29.4, 7: הַגְלֵיתִי, Venice 1515 marg.: הַגְלֹתִי.

68 Cf. TRL paragraph XXIII sub ו and s. v. זרע: Ps. 18.35: MT זְרוֹעֹתַי — o זְרֹעֹתַי; cf. also Jer. 13.14: Ma אָחוֹס — Md אָחֹס; further: 2 Sam. 5.14:

2 Sam. 5.6	הַיְבֻסִי	
1 Chron. 11.4	הַיְבוּסִי	
2 Sam. 6.2	הַכְּרֻבִים	
1 Chron. 13.6	הַכְּרוּבִים	

§41: The diphthong au is indicated

a) by יו (B-L §17z):[69]

Zech. 7.1	Q	בכסליו
	K	בְּכִסְלָו
Cant. 2.11	Q	הַסְּתָיו
	K	הסתו
Num. 12.3	Q	עָנָיו
	K	ענו
Ps. 105.40	Q	שָׂלָיו
	K	שלו
Ex. 16.13	Q	הַשְּׂלָיו
	K	השלו[70]
Ezek. 9.4	Q	תָיו
	K	תו
1 Sam. 21.14	Q	וַיְתָיו
	K	ויתו

b) by וי or יו:[71]

Jer. 48.30	Q	בַּדָּיו
	K	בדוי[72]
Ex. 16.13	MT	הַשְּׂלָיו
	S	השלוי[73]

§42: The diphthong ai is indicated

a) by אי (B-L §21g; Bergstr. §15g):

Isa. 53.4	Q	חלאינו
	K	חֳלָיֵנוּ
Ps. 104.12	Q	עֳפָיִם
	K	עפאים
Judg. 13.18	Q	פֶּלִי
	K	פלאי
Ps. 139.6	Q	פְּלִיאָה
	K	פלאיה
Hos. 11.8	Q	כִּצְבֹיִם
	K	כצבאים[74]
Ex. 12.37	MT	רַגְלִי
	S	רגלאי[75]

הַיְלָדִים — 1 Chron. 14.4: הַיְלוּדִים; Gesenius-Buhl's Dictionary s. v. אָקְנָם and אָקְנָם, אַשְׁמוּרָה and אַשְׁמֹרֶת; גְּדֻלוֹ Deut. 5.21 and גָּדְלוֹ Ps. 150.2; Isa. 54.15: גּוּר יָגוּר.

[69] Cf. TRL s. v. צֹא sau; קוֹ cau; שׁוֹא σαυ; and §133, subdivision 1; see also here §80.

[70] Cf. also Num. 11.32.

[71] Cf. TRL §133, subdivision 2.

[72] Cf. Ma–Md on Job 18.13.

[73] Cf. similarly Num. 11.32.

[74] Cf. TRL s. v. צְבִי sabai; see also B-L §21h.

[75] Cf. also Num. 11.21.

Isa. 41.18 Q שפאים

K שְׁפָיִים[76]

b) by י (B-L §2v and §63b' on צהרים)[77]

Isa. 36.2 Q ירושלימה

K יְרוּשָׁלְמָה

Ezek. 46.19 Q בְּיַרְבָּתַיִם

K בירכתם

Ezek. 25.9 Q וְקִרְיָתָיְמָה

K וקריתמה

2 Sam. 21.9 K שבעתים

Q שְׁבַעְתָּם

§43: The dagesh lene (B-L §19; Bergstr. §18).

It is put inconsistently, and no rules can be established.[78]

a) in the ב:[79]

1 Ki. 12.16 ‹וְלֹא נַחֲלָה› בְּבֶן ‹ישי›

2 Chron. 10.16 בְּבֶן

2 Ki. 8.26 ‹אֲחַזְיָהוּ› בְּמָלְכוֹ

2 Chron. 22.2 בְּמָלְכוֹ

---

2 Ki. 21.1 ‹מְנַשֶּׁה› בְּמָלְכוֹ

2 Chron. 33.1 בְמָלְכוֹ

2 Ki. 22.1 ‹יֹאשִׁיָּהוּ› בְּמָלְכוֹ

2 Chron. 34.1 בְמָלְכוֹ

2 Ki. 22.4 ‹הַמּוּבָא› בֵּית

2 Chron. 34.9 בֵית

2 Ki. 24.18 ‹צִדְקִיָּהוּ› בְּמָלְכוֹ

2 Chron. 36.11 בְמָלְכוֹ

2 Ki. 24.20 ‹הָיְתָה› בִּירוּשָׁלַם

Jer. 52.3 בִירוּשָׁלַם

Josh. 21.17 ‹וּמִמַּטֵּה› בְּנְיָמִין

1 Chron. 6.45 בְנְיָמִן

Ps. 105.15 ‹אַל תִּגְּעוּ› בִמְשִׁיחָי

1 Chron. 16.22 בְּמְשִׁיחָי

2 Ki. 8.29 ‹לְהִתְרַפֵּא› בְּיִזְרְעָאל

2 Chron. 22.6 בְּיִזְרְעָאל

1 Chron. 8.28 ‹יָשְׁבוּ› בִּירוּשָׁלַם

1 Chron. 9.34 בִירוּשָׁלַם

b) in the כ:[80]

2 Sam. 7.23 ‹וּמִי› כְעַמְּךָ

1 Chron. 17.21 כְּעַמְּךָ

---

[76] Cf. similarly ib. 49.9; Jer. 3.21.

[77] Cf. 1 Sam. 9.4: שָׁעֲלִים, Venice 1515 marg.: שעלים; cf. also TRL s. v. אִיתֹן a and b, and the cross-references there.

[78] Cf. TRL paragraph XXVIII subdivision 5 and paragraph XXIII sub ב, כ, פ and ת; see also Paul Kahle in Marti-Festschrift (Giessen 1925), p. 171, and MdWI, p. 48.

[79] Cf. Ps. 72.2: Venice 1515: בְמִשְׁפָּט, marg.: בְּמשפט; Prov. 20.1: בּוֹ, Venice 1515 marg.: בֹ; Prov. 20.7: בְּנָיו, Venice 1515 marg.: בניו; Prov. 31.31: Venice 1515: בִּשְׁעָרִים, marg.: בשערים.

[80] Cf. Ps. 109.16: Venice 1515: וְנִכְאָה; marg.: וְנִכְאָה; Job 9.2: Venice 1515: כִּי; marg.: כִּי; cf. further: Job 33.32: Venice 1515: צַדְּקֶךָ, marg.: צדקך; Ps. 81.8: וָאֲחַלְּצֶךָּ, Venice 1515 marg.: ואחלצך; and Ps. 86.7: אֶקְרָאֶךָּ, Venice 1515 marg.: אקראך.

273

Ps. 18.25   (לִי) כְּצִדְקִי   d) in the ח:[82]

2 Sam. 22.25   כְּצִדְקָתִי[80a]   1 Sam. 31.10   (גְוִיָתוֹ) תָּקְעוּ

                                 1 Chron. 10.10   עֲלָנֻלְתוֹ) תָּקְעוּ

                     2 Sam. 22.28   (עָנִי) תּוֹשִׁיעַ

         c) in the פ:[81]   Ps. 18.28   תּוֹשִׁיעַ

1 Sam. 31.2   (וַיַּדְבְּקוּ) פְלִשְׁתִּים   2 Sam. 22.36   (וַעֲנֹתְךָ) תַּרְבֵּנִי

1 Chron. 10.2   פְלִשְׁתִּים   Ps. 18.36   תַּרְבֵּנִי

2 Sam. 23.11   (מִפְּנֵי) פְלִשְׁתִּים   2 Sam. 22.37   (צַעֲדִי) תַּחְתֵּנִי

1 Chron. 11.13   פְלִשְׁתִּים   Ps. 18.37   תַחְתָּי

D. THE VERB

§44: 2. pers. masc. sing. perf.   2) the verb

       ending in תה or ת.[83]   (Bergstr. 2, §4a).

    1) the personal pronoun   a) ḳal:

       (B-L §28 l):   Gen. 21.23 MT   גָּרַתָּה

                                   S   גרת

Num. 11.15 MT (עָשָׂה) אַתְּ

           S   אתה   2 Sam. 7.27   גָּלִיתָה

                                    1 Chron. 17.25   גָּלִיתָ

Deut. 5.24 MT (וְתִדְבֵּר) וְאַתְּ

           S   ואתה   2 Sam. 10.11   וְהָיָתָה

                                    1 Chron. 19.12   וְהָיִיתָ

Job 1.10 K   את

        Q   אַתָּה[84]   Josh. 13.1 Ma   זָקַנְתָּה

                                       Md   זקנת

1 Sam. 24.19 K   ואת

            Q   וְאַתָּה[85]   Jer. 38.17 K   וְחָיְיתָה

                                        Q   וחיית

[80a] On the difference between צדק and צדקה cf. §126.

[81] Cf. Prov. 30.20: Venice 1515: פִּיךָ, marg.: פִֽיהָ.

[82] Cf. 2 Chron. 36.16: Venice 1515: וּמִתַּעְתְּעִים; marg.: וּמִתְעַתְעִים; Josh. 8.28: Venice 1515: תֵּל; marg.: תֵּֽל.

[83] Cf. TRL paragraph XXIX B, subdivision 2; also Paul Kahle in ZAW 1921, p. 234: "Nur wo in diesen Formen (scil. 2. pers. sing. masc. perf.) ausdrücklich ein ה am Ende steht, wird das a geschrieben und also auch gelesen." Cf. also here §84a.

[84] Cf. similarly Eccl. 7.22.

[85] Cf. also Jer. 18.23; Ps. 6.4.

Deut. 23.14 MT וְחָפַרְתָּה
         S   וחפרת

Deut. 17.14 MT וְיָשַׁבְתָּה
         S   וישבת

Ex. 12.44 MT וּמַלְתָּה
       S   ומלת

2 Ki. 14.10   וְנָפַלְתָּה
2 Chron. 25.19 וְנָפַלְתָּ

Num. 14.19 MT נָשָׂאתָה
         S   נשאת

2 Chron. 6.30 וְנָתַתָּה
1 Ki. 8.39   וְנָתַתָּ

Deut. 25.12 MT וְקַצֹּתָה
         S   וקצת

Num. 27.13 MT וְרָאִיתָה
         S   וראית

Ps. 90.8 Q   שַׁתָּה
      K   שת

b) pi'el:

Num. 27.19 MT וְצִוִּיתָה
         S   וצוית

c) niph'al:

Gen. 31.30 MT נִכְסַפְתָּה
         S   נכספת

d) hiph'il:[86]

Ex. 18.20 MT וְהִזְהַרְתָּה
         S   והזהרת

Num. 14.15 MT וְהֵמַתָּה
         S   והמת

Ex. 19.23 MT הַעֵדֹתָה
         S   העדת

Isa. 37.23   הֲרִימֹתָה
2 Ki. 19.22   הֲרִימֹתָ

Ex. 5.22 MT הֲרֵעֹתָה
       S   הרעת

§45: 2. pers. fem. sing. perf. ending in ת *or* תי (B-L §42k, 1).[87]

1) the personal pronoun (B-L §28m; Bergstr. 2, §4a):

Gen. 12.11 MT אַתְּ
         S   אתי[88]

1 Ki. 14.2 Q אַתְּ
       K   אתי[89]

2) the verb.
  A. ḳal.

a) regular verbs:

Isa. 47.10 Ma אָמַרְתְּ
         Md אמרתי[90]

---

[86] Cf. Micah 4.13: וַהֲדִקּוֹת; Venice 1515 marg.: וְהֲדִיקוֹת.

[87] Cf. Judg. 5.7: שַׁקַּמְתִּי, mistaken for 1. pers. (B-L §56u" s. v. קום). Cf. also שָׁבְרְתִּי and נְתַקְתִּי in Jer. 2.20, followed by 2. pers. וַתֹּאמְרִי. See also TRL paragraph XXXIII subdivision 3, sub 2.

[88] Cf. also ib. v. 13; 24.23; 47.60 etc.

[89] Cf. similarly 2 Ki. 4.16, 23 etc.

[90] Cf. similarly Isa. 57.10

Ezek. 16.13 Q אָכָלְתְּ
K אכלתי

Jer. 31.21 Q הָלָכְתְּ
K ⁹¹הלכתי

Ezek. 16.22, 43 Q זָכַרְתְּ
K זכרתי

Ezek. 16.20 Q יָלָדְתְּ
K ילדתי

Ruth 3.3 Q וְיָרַדְתְּ
K ירדתי

Gen. 18.15 MT צָחַקְתְּ
S צחקתי

Gen. 16.11 MT וְקָרָאת
S ⁹²וקראתי

Ruth 3.4 Q וְשָׁכַבְתְּ
K ושכבתי

Jer. 4.19 Q שָׁמַעַתְּ
K שמעתי

Gen. 30.15 MT ⁹³וְלָקַחַתְּ
S ולקחתי

b) weak verbs.

α) tertiae ה:

Ezek. 16.31 Q הָיִית
K הייתי

Gen. 3.13 MT עָשִׂית
S ⁹⁴עשיתי

Num. 5.19, 20 MT שָׂטִית
S שטיתי

β) mediae ו or י:

Gen. 16.8 MT בָּאת
S באתי

Ruth 3.3 Q וְשָׁמְתְּ
K ושמתי

γ) נתן:

Ezek. 16.18, 36 Q נָתַתְּ
K נתתי

B. pi'el:

Jer. 3.5 Q דִּבַּרְתְּ
K דברתי

Jer. 2.33 Q לִמַּדְתְּ
K ⁹⁵למדתי

c. niph'al:

Jer. 22.23 Q נֵחַנְתְּ
K נחנתי

Num. 5.20 MT נִטְמֵאת
S נטמאתי

D. hiph'il

Jer. 46.11 Q הִרְבֵּית
K הרביתי

---

⁹¹ Cf. similarly Ezek. 16.47.
⁹² Cf. similarly Q–K on Jer. 3.4.
⁹³ This form is a perf. =ולקחת, and not an inf.; cf. Ezek. 16.4: הָמְלַחַתְּ,
Venice 1515 marg.: הָמְלָחַתְּ; see also our note 278 on §86 a.
⁹⁴ Cf. Q–K on Ezek. 16.31.
⁹⁵ Cf. also 13.21.

276

E. hithpa'el:

Num. 22.29	MT	הִתְעַלַּלְתָּ
	S	התעללתי
1 Ki. 14.2	Q	וְהִשְׁתַּנִּית
	K	והשתניתי

3) participle fem.:

Hos. 10.11	Q	אהבת
	K	אֹהַבְתִּי
2 Ki. 4.23	Q	הֹלָכְת
	K	הלכתי
Gen. 16.11	MT	וְיֹלַדְתְּ
	S	וילדתי
Jer. 10.17	Q	יֹשַׁבָת
	K	יושבתי[96]
Jer. 22.23	Q	יֹשַׁבְתְּ
	K	ישבתי
Jer. 51.13	Q	שֹׁכַנְתְּ
	K	שכנתי
Jer. 22.23	Q	מְקֻנַּנְתְּ
	K	מקננתי

Gen. 48.10 MT כָּבְדוּ
S כבדה

1 Sam. 4.15	Q	קָמוּ
	K	קמה
Deut. 21.7	Q	שָׁפְכוּ
	K	שפכה

b) niph'al:

Jer. 22.6	Q	נוֹשָׁבוּ
	K	נושבה
Jer. 2.15	Q	נִצְּתוּ
	K	נצתה
Gen. 7.11	MT	נִפְתָחוּ
	S	נפתחה
1 Ki. 22.49	Q	נִשְׁבְּרוּ
	K	נשברה
Jer. 48.41	Q	נתפשו
	K	נִתְפָּשָׂה

c) reduplicated stem:

Job 16.16	Q	חֳמַרְמְרוּ
	K	חמרמרה

§46: 3. pers. fem. plur.
perf. ending in ו or ה[96a]
(Bergstr. 2, §4b).

a) ķal:

Num. 34.5	MT	וְהָיוּ
	S	והיה[97]

§47: 3. pers. fem. plur. imperf.

a) ending in ן or נה
(Bergstr. 2, §5a).

α) ķal:[98]

Ex. 2.19	MT	וַתֹּאמַרְן,
	S	ותאמרנה

---

[96] Cf. similarly Lam. 4.21; Ezek. 27.3.
[96a] Indicating u (cf. §40c) and a (cf. §38b), respectively;
[97] Cf. Q–K on Josh. 8.12.   [98] Cf. Gen. 41.7: ותבלענה השבלים הדקות
Gen. 41.24: ותבלען השבלים הדקות.

Gen. 41.24 MT וַתִּבְלַעְןָ
        s ותבלענה

Ex. 27.2 MT תִּהְיֶיןָ
      s תהיינה

Gen. 19.36 MT וַתַּהֲרֶיןָ
      s ותהרנה

Gen. 30.39 MT וַתֵּלַדְןָ
      s ותלדנה

Ex. 15.20 MT וַתֵּצֶאןָ
      s ותצאנה

Ex. 1.17 MT וַתִּירֶאןָ
      s ותיראנה

Gen. 27.1 MT וַתִּכְהֶיןָ
      s ותכהינה

Deut. 31.21 MT תִּמְצֶאןָ
       s תמצאנה

Gen. 33.6 MT וַתֻּגַּשְׁןָ
      s ותגשנה

Num. 25.2 MT וַתִּקְרֶאןָ
       s ותקראנה

similarly:

Ruth 1.12 K לכן
       Q לְכֶנָה

β) derived stems:

Ex. 1.17 MT וַתְּחַיֶּיןָ
      s ותחינה

Gen. 33.6 MT וַתִּשְׁתַּחֲוֶיןָ
       s ותשתחוינה

b) ending in ן or הן:[99]

Gen. 30.38 MT תָּבֹאןָ
      s תבאהן

Gen. 19.33 MT וַתַּשְׁקֶיןָ
      s ותשקיהן

c) ending in הן or נה:[100]

Gen. 41.21 MT וַתָּבֹאנָה
      s ותבאהן

Deut. 1.44 MT תַּעֲשֶׂינָה
      s תעשיהן

§48: *Jussive or shortened forms*
(B-L §26b; Bergstr. §21).

1) with preservation of the י
of the hiph'il.

a) imperfect:

Num. 6.25 MT יָאֵר
      s יאיר

Eccl. 10.20 Q יגד
       K יַגִּיד

Ps. 21.2 Q יָגֵל
      K יגיל

Num. 30.13, 16 MT יָפֵר
            s יפיר

Gen. 24.8 MT חָשֵׁב
      s תשיב

Gen. 19.9 MT נָרַע
      s נריע

---

[99] Cf. similar nominal forms: Ex. 35.26: MT לבן — s לבהן; Gen. 30.38: MT בבאן — s בבאהן.

[100] Cf. similar nominal forms: Ex. 35.26: MT אָתָנֶה — s אתהן; 21.29: MT קרבנה — s קרבהן (B-L §29p, p'); 41.21: MT לבדהן — s לבדנה.

278

b) perfect:

Ezek. 17.16 Q הֵפֵר
K הפיר

c) infinitive.

α) regular verbs:

Deut. 7.2 MT הַחֲרֵם
S החרים[101]

Deut. 32.8 MT בְּהַנְחֵל
S בהנחיל

Deut. 15.8 MT וְהַעֲבֵט
S והעביט

Lev. 9.2 MT וְהַקְרֵב
S והקריב

Amos 9.8 Q הַשְׁמֵד
K הַשְׁמִיד

β) weak verbs:

Jer. 36.16 Q הַגֵּד
K הַגֵּיד

Jer. 44.17 Q וְהַסֵּךְ
K והסיך

Deut. 22.4 MT הָקֵם
S הקים[102]

d) imperative:

Ex. 16.33 MT וְהַנַּח
S והניח

2 Ki. 8.6 Q הָשֵׁב
K הָשִׁיב

Gen. 19.12 MT הוֹצֵא
S הוציא[103]

Ex. 33.5 MT הוֹרֵד
S הוריד

2) with preservation of the ה
of verbs tertiae ה.[104]

a) 3. pers. masc. sing. imperf.:

Gen. 30.34 MT יְהִי
S יהיה[105]

Ex. 32.11 S יִחַר[106]
MT יֶחֱרֶה

Gen. 44.33 MT יַעַל
S יעלה

Ruth 1.8 Q יַעַשׂ
K יעשה

Gen. 41.33 MT יֵרֶא
S יראה[107]

Gen. 1.22 MT יִרֶב
S ירבה

---

[101] Cf. similarly ib. 13.16; 20.17.
[102] Cf. also Q–K on Jer. 44.25.
[103] Cf. similarly Lev. 24.14.
[104] Cf. §53β.
[105] Cf. Ezek. 45.10: יְהִי, Venice 1515 marg.: יְהְיֶה.
[106] Cf. also Deut. 6.15.
[107] Cf. similarly K–Q on Jer. 17.8.

a) derived stems:

Deut. 28.8 MT   יְצַו

         S   יצוה

Lev. 9.6 MT   וְיֵרָא

         S   ויראה

b) 3. pers. fem. sing. imperf.:

Gen. 26.28 MT   תְּהִי

          S   תהיה

c) 1. pers. plur. imperf.:

Gen. 38.23 S   נהי

         MT   נִהְיֶה[108]

Isa. 41.23 K   ונרא

         Q   וְנִרְאָה

d) imperative:

Ps. 51.4 Q   הֶרֶב

       K   הרבה

Deut. 9.14 MT   הֶרֶף

         S   הרפה

3) jussive forms with אַל.

a) with preservation of the י
of the hiph'il:

Ex. 23.1 MT   תָּשֵׁת

         S   תשית

Deut. 9.26 MT   תַּשְׁחֵת

          S   תשחית

Gen. 49.4 MT   חוֹתַר

         S   חותיר

Ex. 16.19 MT   יוֹתַר

         S   יותיר

b) with preservation of the ה
of verbs tertiae ה:

Gen. 37.27 MT   תְּהִי

          S   תהיה

Jer. 40.16 K   תעש

         Q   תַּעֲשֶׂה[109]

Lev. 10.9 MT .   תַּשְׁתְּ

         S   תשתה

Ex. 34.3 MT   יֵרָא

         S   יראה

*§49: Imperfect with consecutive
waw and preservation of the
final vowel.*

1) hiph'il with preservation of
the י (Bergstr. 2, §5d).

a) 3. pers. masc. sing.:[110]

Gen. 2.9 MT   וַיַּצְמַח

         S   ויצמיח

Lev. 9.20 MT   וַיַּקְטֵר

         S   ויקטיר

Num. 16.10 MT   וַיַּקְרֵב

          S   ויקריב

Gen. 50.25 MT   וַיַּשְׁבַּע

         S   וישביע

---

[108] Cf. also Gen. 47.19.

[109] Cf. similarly MT–S on Gen. 22.12.

[110] Cf. TRL paragraph XXVII subdivision 3.

a) weak verbs:

Gen. 31.42 MT וַיּוֹכַח
        S   ויוכיח

Gen. 6.10 MT וַיּוֹלֶד
        S   ויוליד

Ex. 14.21 MT וַיּוֹלֶךְ
        S   ויוליך

Ex. 14.30 MT וַיּוֹשַׁע
        S   ויושיע

Gen. 8.21 MT וַיָּרַח
        S   ויריח

b) 3. pers. fem. sing.:

Gen. 21.15 MT וַתַּשְׁלֵךְ
        S   ותשליך

Gen. 24.28 MT וַתַּגֵּד
        S   ותגיד

Lev. 18.25 MT וַתָּקָא
        S   ותקיא

c) 1. pers. plur.:

Num. 31.50 MT וַנַּקְרֵב
        S   ונקריב

Gen. 43.7 MT וַנַּגֶּד
        S   ונגיד

Gen. 43.21 MT וַנָּשֶׁב
        S   ונשיב

2) mediae ו ḳal with preservation of the ו:

Judg. 19.21 Q וַיָּבֶל
        K   ויבול

Gen. 25.17 MT וַיָּמָת
        S   וימות

Num. 17.15 MT וַיָּשָׁב
        S   [112]וישוב

2 Sam. 13.8 Q וַתָּלָשׁ
        K   [112]ותלוש

3) tertiae ה with preservation of the ה.[113]

A. ḳal.

a) 3. pers. masc. sing.:

Num. 3.43 MT וַיְהִי
        S   ויהיה

Job 42.16 K וירא
        Q   וַיִּרְאֶה

b) 3. pers fem. sing. = 2. pers. masc. sing.:

Lev. 15.24 MT וַתְּהִי
        S   ותהיה

2 Chron. 34.27 וַתִּבַּךְ
2 Ki. 22.19 וַתִּבְכֶּה

2 Chron. 18.34 וַתַּעַל
1 Ki. 22.35 וַתַּעֲלֶה

Jer. 3.7 Q וַתֵּרֶא
        K   ותראה

[111] Cf. Q–K on Ezek. 18.28.
[112] Cf. Ruth 1.6: Venice 1515: ותקום, marg.: ותקם.
[113] Cf. §53 β.

c) 1. pers. sing.:

Ps. 18.24   וָאֱהִי

2 Sam. 22.24   וָאֶהְיֶה

Deut. 10.3 MT   וָאַעַשׂ... וָאַעַל

        s   ואעשה... ואעלה

Gen. 41.22 MT   וָאֵרֶא

        s   ואראה[114]

Gen. 24.46 MT   וָאֵשְׁתְּ

        s   ואשתה

d) 1. pers. plur.:

Deut. 3.1 MT   וַנֵּפֶן וַנַּעַל

        s   ונפנה ונעלה

B. hiph'il.

e) 3. pers. masc. sing.:

2 Chron. 18.23   וַיַּךְ

1 Ki. 22.24   וַיַּכֶּה[115]

f) 3. pers. fem. sing.:

Gen. 35.16 MT   וַתֵּקֶשׁ

        s   ותקשה

Ezek. 23.19 K   ותרב

        Q   וַתַּרְבֶּה

g) 1. pers. sing.:

Ex. 9.15 MT   וָאַךְ

        s   ואכה

Num. 23.4 MT   וָאַעַל

        s   ואעלה

Josh. 24.3 K   וארב

        Q   וָאַרְבֶּה

h) 1. pers. plur.:

Deut. 2.33 MT   וַנַּךְ

        s   ונכה

c. niph'al.

i) 3. pers. masc. sing.:

Lev. 9.23 MT   וַיֵּרָא

        s   ויראה

j) 1. pers. sing.:

Ex. 6.3 MT   וָאֵרָא

        s   ואראה

D. pi'el.

k) 3. pers. masc. sing.:

Ex. 1.22 MT   וַיְצַו

        s   ויצוה

l) 1. pers. sing.:

Deut. 3.18 MT   וָאֲצַו

        s   ואצוה

E. hithpa'el.

m) 3. pers. masc. sing.:

1 Chron. 11.17   וַיִּתְאָו

2 Sam. 23.15   וַיִּתְאַוֶּה

---

[114] Cf. Q–K on Josh. 7.21.

[115] Cf. similarly 2 Chron. 18.33 — 1 Ki. 22.34; 2 Chron. 21.9 — 2 Ki. 8.21.

§50: *The i-imperfect ḳal*
(Bergstr. 2, §14h).[116]

a) imperf. with second vowel i:

Ex. 35.3	MT	תְּבַעֲרוּ	S	תבעירו
Num. 35.20	MT	יֶהְדָּפֶנּוּ	S	יהדיפנו
Ps. 77.12	Q	אֶזְכּוֹר	K	אזכיר
Ex. 34.19	MT	תִּזָּכָר	S	תזכיר
Deut. 29.22	MT	תִזָּרַע	S	תזריע
Ex. 21.35	MT	יֶחֱצוּן	S	יחיצון
Deut. 22.10	MT	תַּחֲרשׁ	S	תחריש
Jer. 34.11	Q	וַיִּכְבְּשׁוּם	K	ויכבישום
Deut. 2.6	MT	תִּכְרוּ	S	תכירו
Deut. 20.19	MT	תִכְרֹת	S	תכרית
Gen. 4.14	MT	אֶסָּתֵר	S	אאסתיר[117]
Lev. 25.46	MT	תַּעֲבֹדוּ	S	תעבידו

Num. 14.41	MT	[118]תִצְלָח	S	תצליח
Ps. 56.7	Q	יִצְפּוֹנוּ	K	[119]יצפינו
Deut. 22.9	MT	תִקְדַּשׁ	S	תקדיש
Job 24.6	Q	יִקְצוֹרוּ	K	יקצירו
Gen. 41.56	MT	וַיִּשְׁבֹּר	S	וישביר
Deut. 2.6	MT	תִּשְׁבְּרוּ	S	תשבירו
Lev. 23.32	MT	תִּשְׁבָּתוּ	S	תשביתו

b) infinitive with second vowel i.

α) inf. absol.:

Isa. 22.18	Q	צָנוֹף	K	צניף

β) inf. constr.:

Deut. 9.4	MT	בַּהֲדֹף	S	בהדיף
Deut. 6.19	MT	לַהֲדֹף	S	להדיף
2 Sam. 18.3	Q	לַעְזוֹר	K	לעזיר

---

[116] Cf. Ch. Yalon in לשוננו, II (Tel-Aviv תר"ץ), p. 113 seq.; cf. also here §63.

[117] Cf. Ps. 89.47: MT תַסְתֵּר, Origen: θεσθερ; cf. TRL s. v. סתר.

[118] The a-imperf. has no consistent laws; cf. Jer. 5.7: Q אֶסְלָח, K אסלוח; 1 Ki. 22.30: לְבַשׁ, Venice 1515 marg.: לְבֹשׁ; see also TRL s. v. לחם: Ps. 35.1: MT לְחַם — o: לָחֵם; further: Ps. 10.2: MT יִדְלָק — Var K ידלוק.

[119] Cf. in §59b the instance MT–s on Ex. 2.2.

§51: Verbs primae ו or י.[120]

a) ḳal:[121]

1 Sam. 13.8	Q	וַיּוֹחֶל[122]
	K	וייחל[123]
2 Sam. 20.5	Q	וַיֹּחַר
	K	וייחר
Ezek. 16.13	K	ותופי
	Q	וַתִּיפִי
Jer. 17.4	Q	תּוּקַד[124]
	K	תיקד[125]
Num. 21.32	Q	וַיּוֹרֶשׁ[126]
	K	וייִרשׁ[127]
Gen. 24.33	Q	וַיּוּשַׂם
	K	וַיִּישֶׂם[128]

b) derived stems:

Isa. 45.2	K	אושר
	Q	אֲיַשֵּׁר
Gen. 8.17	K	הוצא[129]
	Q	הַיְצֵא[130]

Ps. 5.9 K הוֹשַׁר
Q הַיְשַׁר

§52: Verbs mediae ו or י.[131]

a) imperf. ḳal:

Deut. 31.7	MT	תָּבוֹא[132]
	S	תביא[133]
Prov. 23.24	K	יגול
	Q	יָגִיל
Ezek. 30.16	Q	תָּחוּל
	K	תחיל
Ex. 16.2	Q	וַיִּלּוֹנוּ
	K	וילינו
Num. 16.11	K	תלונו
	Q	תלּינו
Num. 14.36	K	וילונו
	Q	וַיַּלִּינוּ
Ezek. 45.3	Q	תָּמוֹד
	K	תמיד
Ps. 140.11	Q	יָמֹטוּ
	K	ימיטו

---

[120] Cf. §64.
[121] The context excludes the explanation of these forms as hoph'al.
[122] Cf. the derivative תּוֹחֶלֶת.
[123] Cf. יָחִיל.
[124] Cf. the derivative מוֹקֵד.
[125] Cf. יְקֹד and יקוד.
[126] Cf. מוֹרָשָׁת.
[127] Cf. יְרָשָׁה.
[128] On the interchange of the weak roots שים-ישם, cf. §57.
[129] Cf. מוֹצָא.
[130] Cf. יְצִיא.
[131] Cf. §65.
[132] Cf. the derivative מָבוֹא.
[133] Cf. בָּאָה.

Ezek. 48.14	Q	יְמֹר	Ps. 89.18	Q	תָּרוּם[136]
	K	יָמֵר		K	תרים[137]
Ex. 13.22; 33.11	S	ימוש	Ps. 66.7	Q	יָרוּמוּ
	MT	יָמִיש		K	ירימו
Prov. 17.13	Q	תָמֹש	Jer. 50.44	K	ארוצם
	K	תמיש		Q	אָרִיצֵם
Num. 32.7	K	תנואון	Joel 4.1	K	אשוב[138]
	Q	תְנִיאוּן		Q	אָשִׁיב[139]
Ps. 72.17	Q	יִנּוֹן	Ps. 54.7	K	ישוב
	K	ינין		Q	יָשִׁיב[140]
Judg. 7.21	Q	וַיָּנֻסוּ	2 Sam. 15.8	Q	יָשׁוּב
	K	וינסו		K	ישיב[141]
2 Sam. 15.20	K	אנועך	Ezek. 16.55	Q	תְּשׁוּבֶנָה
	Q	אֲנִיעֲךָ		K	תשיבנה
Ps. 59.16	K	ינועון	Lam. 3.20	Q'	וְתָשׁוּחַ[142]
	Q	יְנִיעוּן		K	ותשיח[143]
Lam. 2.13	K	אֲעוּדֵךְ[134]	Ex. 4.11	MT	יָשׂוּם
	Q	אֲעִידֵךְ[135]		S	ישים
Prov. 23.5	K	התעוף			
	Q	הֲתָעִיף			

b) inf. absol.:

Job 41.2	Q	יְעוּרֶנּוּ	Prov. 23.24	K	נול
	K	יעירנו		Q	נִיל
Prov. 3.30	K	תרוב	Deut. 17.15	MT	שׂוֹם
	Q	תָרִיב		S	שִׂים[144]

[134] Cf. the derivative תְּעוּדָה.
[135] Cf. עֵדָה.
[136] Cf. תְרוּמָה.
[137] Cf. יְרִמוֹת.
[138] Cf. שׁוּבָה.
[139] Cf. שִׁיבָה; cf. similarly Jer. 33.26.
[140] Cf. similarly Prov. 12.14; Job 39.12.
[141] Cf. also Ps. 73.10.
[142] Cf. שׁוּחָה.
[143] Cf. שִׁיחָה.
[144] Cf. K–Q on 2 Sam. 14.7.

Ps. 71.12 Q   חוּשָׁה
        K   חישה

c) inf. constr.:

Hos. 10.11 Q   לָדוּשׁ[145]
         K   לָדִישׁ[146]

Gen. 24.25 MT   לָלוּן
          S   ללין

Judg. 21.22 K   לרוב
          Q   לָרִיב

Ps. 119.148 K   לשוח
          Q   לָשִׂיחַ

Gen. 45.7 MT   לָשׂוּם
         S   לשים[147]

Isa. 10.6 Q   וּלְשׂוּמוֹ
        K   ולשימו

1 Sam. 18.6 K   לשור
          Q   לָשִׁיר

§53: Verbs tertiae ה with interchange between ה and י.[148]

a) full forms:

Num. 24.4 MT   יֶחֱזֶה
         S   יחזי

Gen. 29.35 MT   אוֹדֶה
         S   אודי

Gen. 29.34 MT   יִלָּוֶה
         S   ילוי

Gen. 30.31 MT   אֶרְעֶה
         S   ארעי

Gen. 24.48 MT   וָאֶשְׁתַּחֲוֶה
         S   ואשתחוי

Deut. 5.9 MT   תִשְׁתַּחֲוֶה
        S   תשתחוי

Gen. 22.5 MT   וְנִשְׁתַּחֲוֶה
        S   ונשתחוי

Gen. 6.14 MT   עֲשֵׂה
        S   עשי

Num. 8.7 MT   הַזֵּה
       S   הזי

β) shortened forms:[149]

Lev. 24.2 MT   צַו
       S   צוי

Gen. 7.23 MT   וַיִּמַח
       S   וימחי

Num. 20.11 MT   וַתֵּשְׁתְּ
        S   ותשתי

Ex. 18.7 MT   וַיִּשְׁתַּחוּ
       S   וישתחוי

---

[145] Cf. מְדוּשָׁה.
[146] Cf. דִּישׁ.
[147] Cf. also Num. 11.11; Deut. 12.5.
[148] Cf. §31; see further §68 and our note 222 there.
[149] Cf. §48 2 and §49 3.

§54: *Verbs tertiae* ו *or* ה
(Bergstr. §17c, r).[150]

a) inf. absol. ḳal:

Hos. 4.2	Q	אלו
	K	אָלה
Ex. 15.1	Q	וָנאו[151]
	K	ונאה[152]
Amos 5.5	Q	נלו[153]
	K	נָלה[154]
Ex. 2.19	Q	דָלו
	K	דלה
Hos. 1.2	Q	זנו
	K	זָנה
Ezek. 18.9	Q	חיו
	K	חָיה[155]
Ex. 19.13	Q	יָרו
	K	ירה
Ex. 17.14	Q	מָחו
	K	מחה
Jer. 49.12	Q	נקו
	K	נָקה

2 Sam. 24.24		קנו
1 Chron. 21.24		קנה
Ex. 3.7	MT	ראה[156]
	S	ראו[157]
Jer. 49.12	Q	שתו (2°)
	K	שתה

b) perfect ḳal:

Ezek. 26.4	K	וסחותי
	Q	וסחיתי[158]

§55: *Verbs tertiae* א *or* ה:[159]

Job 19.2	K	תְדַכְּאוּנַנִי[160]
	Q	תדכונני[161]
2 Chron. 18.24		לְהֵחָבֵא[162]
1 Ki. 22.25		לְהֵחָבֵה[163]
Job 1.21	Q	יָצָאתִי
	K	יצתי
Ex. 15.25	S	ויראהו
	MT	ויורהו
2 Sam. 11.24	K	ויראו המוראים
	Q	וַיֹּרוּ הַמֹּרִים[164]

---

[150] ה stands for ', cf. §53; cf. also §66.
[151] Cf. the derivative נַאֲוָה.
[152] Cf. נָאה.
[153] Cf. נְלוֹת.
[154] Cf. גּוֹלָה.
[155] Cf. also ib. 33.16.
[156] Cf. מַרְאָה.
[157] Cf. רָאֶה.
[158] סחה-סחו, with the final ה changed into ', cf. §53.
[159] Cf. §§1, 38 b and 67; also TRL s. v. מצא: Zech. 12.5: MT אמצה — J אמצא.
[160] Cf. דְּכָא.
[161] Cf. דְּכִי.
[162] Cf. מְחַבָּא.
[163] Cf. חָבְיוֹן.
[164] Verb and noun from the root ירה-ירא.

Jer. 26.9	Q	נְבָאָת
	K	נבית
Zech. 5.9	Q	ותשאנה
	K	וַתִּשֶּׁנָה
Ex. 9.4	s	והפלא
	MT	וְהִפְלָה
Gen. 27.20	s	הקרא
	MT	הִקְרָה
Ex. 3.18	s	נקרא
	MT	נִקְרָה[165]
Gen. 24.12	s	הקרא
	MT	הִקְרֵה
Jer. 51.9	K	רפאנו
	Q	רְפִינוּ
Hos. 11.3	K	רְפָאתִים
	Q	רפתים
Ezek. 47.8	K	ונרפאו
	Q	וְנִרְפּוּ
2 Ki. 25.29		וְשִׁנָּא
Jer. 52.33		וְשִׁנָּה
2 Sam. 21.12	Q	תְּלָאוּם
	K	תלום
Isa. 37.26		לְהַשְׁאוֹת[166]
2 Ki. 19.25		לְהְשׁוֹת

§56: *Inf. constr. of verbs tertiae* ה
(B-L §2v; Bergstr. §2g):[167]

Ex. 2.4	MT	לִרְעֶה
	s	לדעת
Gen. 50.20	MT	עֲשֹׂה
	s	עשות
Ex. 18.18	MT	עֲשֹׂהוּ
	s	עשותו
Gen. 46.3	MT	מֵרְדָה
	s	מרדת

§57: *Verbs of weak roots:*

Judg. 12.3	K	וָאִשְׂמָה[168]
	Q	וָאָשִׂימָה[169]
Ezek. 35.9	K	תישבנה
	Q	תָשֹׁבְנָה[170]
1 Ki. 12.2		וַיֵּשֶׁב
2 Chron. 10.2		וַיָּשָׁב
Prov. 23.26	K	תרצנה
	Q	תָּצֹרְנָה[171]
2 Sam. 14.30	K	והוציתיה
	Q	וְהַצִּיתוּהָ[173]
1 Sam. 14.27	K	ותראנה
	Q	וַתָּאֹרְנָה[174]

[165] Cf. 2 Sam. 1.6: נקרא נקריתי.

[166] This form is a combination of tertiae ה and א.

[167] Cf. the following paragraph; I, therefore, assume here an interchange between primae ' and tertiae ה: דעה-ידע; רדה-ירד.

[168] Root שׂם; cf. on §51a.

[169] Root שׂים. [170] שׁיב-ישׁב.

[171] נצר-רצה (or metathesis? cf. §36).

[173] נצת-יצת; cf. Ex. 2.4: MT ותתצב and ותתיצב — s (יצב-נצב); and similarly Gen. 42.1: MT תתראו — s תתיראו (ירא-ראה).

[174] אור-ראה.

1 Ki. 10.26   וַיַּנְחֵם   Ps. 18.45   יְכַחֲשׁוּ

2 Chron. 1.14   וַיַּנִּיחֵם[175]   2 Sam. 22.45   יִתְכַּחֲשׁוּ

Jer. 30.16 K   שׁאסיך[176]   Gen. 38.14 MT   וַתְּכַס

       Q   שׁסָיִךְ[177]   s   ותכס

1 Sam. 18.29 K   ויאסף   Num. 26.55 MT   יְנָחֲלוּ

           Q   וַיּוֹסֶף[178]   s   יתנחלו

Isa. 30.5 K   הבאיש   Num. 24.7 MT   וְתִנָּשֵׂא

       Q   הבִישׁ[179]   s   ותנשא

                             Isa. 66.17 K   המקדשים

a) mediae geminatae   Q   הַמִּתְקַדְּשִׁים

(B-L §21r, s):[180]   similarly:

                          2 Sam. 10.6   נִבְאֲשׁוּ

Deut. 3.7 MT   בְּזוֹנוּ   1 Chron. 19.6   הִתְבָּאֲשׁוּ

         s   בזנו

Gen. 31.19 s   לנו   **§59: Preservation of the second**

         MT   לְוֹ   **vowel in inflected verbal forms.[182]**

2 Sam. 22.6   סַבְּנִי   a) inflected forms of the

Ps. 18.6   סְבָבוּנִי   participle (B-L §26t).[183]

                             a) part. fem. sing.:

§58: Assimilation of the ת in

the hithpa'el (B-L §15e–g;   Deut. 22.6 MT   רֹבֶצֶת

Bergstr. §19b):[181]   s   רביצת

Num. 21.27 MT   וְתִכּוֹנֵן   Num. 5.15 MT   מַזְכֶּרֶת

              s   ותתכונן   s   מזכירת

---

[175] נוח–נחה.

[176] On the א, cf. §38 a; consequently, this form is a participle with suffix of the root שׁוס.

[177] שסה–שוס.

[178] יסף–אסף.

[179] יבש–באש.

[180] Cf. MT לֵב — s לבב: Gen. 18.5; Ex. 4.14; Deut. 4.11; also 2 Chron. 6.38 — 1 Ki. 8.48; Isa. 38.3 — 2 Ki. 20.3; note further מַמְתִּי Zech. 8.14 and זַמֹּתִי Jer. 4.28; חָנַן Amos 5.15 and חֹן Deut. 28.50.

[181] Cf. Ch. Yalon in *Tarbiz*, III (Jerusalem תרצא), p. 99 seq.

[182] Cf. §76; also TRL paragraphs XXVI a and XXIX B 8.

[183] Cf. TRL §15 a.

Lev. 11.3	MT	מַפְרֶסֶת
	S	מפריסת

β) part. masc. plur.:

Gen. 40.6	MT	זֹעֲפִים ·
	S	זעיפים
Ex. 5.6	MT	הַנֹּגְשִׂים
	S	הנגישים
Num. 3.46	MT	הָעֹדְפִים
	S	העדיפים
Gen. 29.2	MT	רֹבְצִים
	S	רביצים
Gen. 47.14	MT	שֹׁבְרִים
	S	שברים

b) imperfect forms:[184]

Isa. 18.4	Q	אֶשְׁקֳטָה
	K	אשקוטה
Jer. 32.9	Q	וָאֶשְׁקֳלָה
	K	ואשקולה
Deut. 32.7	MT	וְיַגֵּדְךָ
	S	ויגדך
Jer. 1.5	Q	אֶצָּרְךָ
	K	אצורך

Ex. 2.2	MT	וַתִּצְפְּנֵהוּ
	S	ותצפינהו [185]
Jer. 5.6	Q	יְשָׁדְדֵם
	K	ישודדם

c) perfect forms:[186]

Lev. 20.24	MT	הִבְדַּלְתִּי
	S	הבדילתי
Num. 10.29	MT	וְהֵטַבְנוּ
	S	והטיבנו
Deut. 2.34	MT	הִשְׁאַרְנוּ
	S	השאירנו
Num. 36.4	MT	וְנוֹסְפָה
	S	ונוספה

d) imperative
(Bergstr. 2, §14k):

Judg. 9.8	Q	מָלְכָה
	K	מלוכה
Ps. 26.2	Q	צָרְפָה
	K	צרופה
Judg. 9.12	Q	מָלְכִי
	K	מלוכי
1 Sam. 28.8	Q	קָסֳמִי
	K	קסומי

[184] Some of these formations might be explained as "pausal forms"; but since no rules exist, when context forms should be used, and when the corresponding pausal forms, I introduced in TRL the new terminology: Preservation of the 2nd vowel (paragraph XXIX A 1). Cf. f. i. Job 19.24: Ma יַחְצְבוּן — Md יַחְצֹבוּן; Ps. 50.3: וְשָׂעֲרָה, Venice 1515 marg.: נשערה; Josh. 24.15: תַּעַבְדוּן, Venice 1515 marg.: תַּעֲבֹדוּן; TRL s. v. ידה: Ps. 35.18: MT אוֹדְךָ — o אוֹדֶךָ. Cf. also here §78 A a (note 247).

[185] Cf. in §50a the instance Q–K on Ps. 56.7.

[186] Cf. 1 Chron. 4.10: וְהִרְבִּיתָ; Venice 1515 marg.: וְהַרְבִּיתָ: preservation of the vowel a in the first syllable.

290

Num. 31.3 MT   הַחָלְצוּ
         S   החליצו

Gen. 18.4 MT   וְהִשָּׁעֲנוּ
         S   והשענו

Deut. 3.28 MT   וְאַמְּצֵהוּ
         S   ואמיצהו

Deut. 3.28 MT   וְחַזְּקֵהוּ
         S   וחזיקהו

e) inf. constr. (Bergstr. 2, §14n[f]):

Ex. 32.34 MT   פָּקְדִי
         S   פקודי

Ps. 38.21 Q   רָדְפִי
       K   רדופי

f) the verb in Sandhi.

a) imperfect:

Josh. 9.7 Q   אָכְרָת
      K   אכרות[187]

Hos. 8.12 Q   אָכְתָב
      K   אכתוב

Ps. 89.29 Q   אָשְׁמָר
      K   אשמור

Ps. 10.15 Q   תדרש
      K   תִּדְרוֹשׁ

Isa. 44.17 Q   יָסְגָד
      K   יסגוד

Isa. 26.20 Q   יַעֲבָר
      K   יעבור

Prov. 22.14 Q   יִפָּל
      K   יפול

Prov. 22.8 Q   יִקְצָר
      K   יקצור

β) imperative:[188]

Ezek. 24.2 Q   כְתָב
      K   כתוב

γ) inf. constr.:

Amos 7.8 Q   עבר
      K   עֲבוֹר

Ezek. 21.28 Q   בִקְסָם
      K   בקסום

Ezek. 44.3 Q   לָאֱכָל
      K   לאכול

Ruth 4.6 Q   לִגְאָל
      K   לגאול

Isa. 44.14 Q   לִכְרָת
      K   לכרות

Nah. 2.1 Q   לַעֲבָר
      K   לעבור

2 Sam. 8.10   לִשְׁאָל
1 Chron. 18.10   לִשְׁאוֹל

1 Sam. 25.31 Q   וְלִשְׁפָּךְ
      K   ולשפוך[189]

---

187 Cf. Venice 1515 marg.: אכרת.
188 Cf. Ps. 119.49: זְכָר; Venice 1515 marg.: זכר.
189 Cf. Ezek. 22.27: לִשְׁפָּךְ, Venice 1515 marg.: לשפך.

§*60: The use of the tenses.*[190]

a) perfect or imperfect:

Deut. 30.1	MT	הֲדִיחֲךָ
	S	ידיחך
2 Chron. 22.6		הִכָּהוּ
2 Ki. 8.29		יַכֻּהוּ
Isa. 37.34		בָא
2 Ki. 19.33		יָבֹא
Isa. 1.11	seb	אמר
	MT	יֹאמַר

b) participle or imperfect
(Bergstr. §2i):[191]

Gen. 15.3	MT	יוֹרֵשׁ
	S	יירש
2 Chron. 18.7		מִתְנַבֵּא
1 Ki. 22.8		יִתְנַבֵּא

c) participle or perfect:[192]

1 Sam. 31.1		נִלְחָמִים
1 Chron. 10.1		נִלְחֲמוּ
1 Ki. 10.1		שֹׁמַעַת
2 Chron. 9.1		שָׁמְעָה

d) imperative or imperfect:

Ex. 17.5	MT	קַח
	S	תקח
2 Ki. 11.15		הֹמֵת
2 Chron. 23.14		יוּמַת

§*61: Active or passive construction.*

a) niph'al or ḳal.[193]

α) imperfect:

Num. 28.17	MT	יֵאָכֵל
	S	תאכלו
Lev. 11.13	MT	יֵאָכְלוּ
	S	תאכלו
Lev. 25.34	MT	יִמָּכֵר
	S	ימכרו
Num. 28.15	MT	יֵעָשֶׂה
	S	יעשו
2 Ki. 16.20		וַיִּקָּבֵר
2 Chron. 28.27		וַיִּקְבְּרֻהוּ[194]
Deut. 16.16	MT	יֵרָאֶה
	S	יראו

---

[190] Cf. Hos. 7.14: יַעְקֹ; Venice 1515 marg.: יִ[ע]קֹ; cf. also
Lev. 17.4: וְאֶל פֶּתַח אֹהֶל מוֹעֵד לֹא הֱבִיאוֹ
Lev. 17.9: וְאֶל פֶּתַח אֹהֶל מוֹעֵד לֹא יְבִיאֶנּוּ.
[191] Cf. also §115 α (Lev. 17.10).
[192] Cf. also §115 α (Deut. 6.12).
[193] Cf. 1 Sam. 25.12: וַיַּהַפְכוּ; Venice 1515 marg.: וַיַּהָפְכוּ; Nah. 3.3: Venice
1515: יִכְשְׁלוּ; marg.: יָכְשְׁלוּ; 1 Chron. 11.1: Venice 1515: וַיִּקְבְּצוּ; marg.: וַיִּקָּבְצוּ.
[194] Cf. similarly: 2 Ki. 21.18 — 2 Chron. 33.20; 1 Ki. 11.43 — 2 Chron.
9.31; cf. further in conjunction with §102: 2 Ki. 14.20 — 2 Chron. 25.28 and
2 Ki. 15.38 — 2 Chron. 27.9.

β) perfect:

Lev. 13.25	MT	נֶהְפַּךְ
	S	הפך
1 Chron. 14.8		נִמְשַׁח
2 Sam. 5.17		מָשְׁחוּ
Ex. 25.28	MT	וְנִשָּׂא
	S	ונשאו
Gen. 9.2	MT	נִתָּנוּ
	S	נתתיו

b) niph'al or hiph'il: [195]

Gen. 10.1	MT	וַיִּוָּלְדוּ
	S	ויולידו
2 Sam. 5.13		וַיִּוָּלְדוּ
1 Chron. 14.3		וַיּוֹלֶד

c) pu'al or pi'el: [196]

Ex. 34.34	MT	יְצֻוֶּה
	S	יצוהו
Num. 3.16	MT	צֻוָּה
	S	צווהו

d) hoph'al or ḳal:

Lev. 6.23	MT	יוּבָא
	S	יבוא

Num. 35.17 MT יוּמָת

               S   יָמוּת [197]

2 Ki. 14.6   יוּמְתוּ

2 Chron. 25.4   יָמוּתוּ

Lev. 11.35 MT   יֻתָּץ [198]

            S   יתצו

e) hoph'al or hiph'il.

α) imperfect:

2 Ki. 11.15	תּוּמָת
2 Chron. 23.14	תָּמִיתוּהָ
2 Ki. 11.16	וַתּוּמַת
2 Chron. 23.15	וַיְמִיתוּהָ
Lev. 4.35 MT	יוּסָר
S	יסיר

β) perfect:

Ex. 27.7	MT	וְהוּבָא
	S	והבאת
Deut. 17.4	MT	וְהֻגַּד
	S	והגידו
Lev. 4.31	MT	הוּסָר
	S	יסיר

---

[195] Cf. TRL s. v. סתר: Ps. 89.47: MT תָּסָתֵר — o תַּסְתִּיר.

[196] Cf. 2 Chron. 15.6: וְכִתְּתוּ, Venice 1515 marg.: וְכִתְּתוּ; TRL s. v. שבר: Ps. 46.10: MT יְשַׁבֵּר — o יְשֻׁבַּר.

[197] Cf. K–Q on Prov. 19.16; Q–K on 2 Ki. 14.6 and S–MT on Num. 35.12.

[198] Cf. §62c; the term "Passive Ḳal" (B-L §38 l'–r') will have to be discarded as a mere invention of the grammarians. This term is based upon the assumption that the verbs in question either do not occur in the pi'el at all, or if they do, at least in a different connotation. Thus, the MT is the sole basis for this grammatical phenomenon; cf. TRL paragraph XXV on פנה, where I showed that the change in the stem does not involve a change in the meaning, as intended by the Masoretes. Cf. also here note 211.

§62: The use of the derived
stems.

a) ḳal or hiph'il:[199]

2 Ki. 22.9   וַיָּבֵא
2 Chron. 34.16   וַיְבָא

1 Sam. 31.12   וַיָּבֹאוּ
1 Chron. 10.12   וַיְבִיאוּם

Lev. 20.5   MT   לִזְנוֹת
       S   להזנות[200]

Gen. 21.18   S   וחזקי
       MT   וְהַחֲזִיקִי[201]

Num. 1.51   MT   וּבַחֲנֹת
       S   ובהחנת

Ex. 21.35   MT   וְחָצוּ
       S   והחצו

Num. 21.2   S   וחרמתי
       MT   וְהַחֲרַמְתִּי

Num. 30.5   S   וחריש
       MT   וְהֶחֱרִישׁ[202]

Gen. 22.23   MT   יָלַד
       S   הוליד[203]

1 Sam. 27.4   Q   יָסַף
       K   יוסף

Deut. 20.8   MT   וְיָסְפוּ
       S   ו' יוסיפו

2 Sam. 7.15   יָסוּר
1 Chron. 17.13   אָסִיר

2 Sam. 22.23   אָסוּר
Ps. 18.23   אָסִיר

Ex. 12.12   MT   וְעָבַרְתִּי
       S   והעברתי

Deut. 29.11   MT   לְעָבְרְךָ
       S   להעברך

1 Ki. 10.29   וַתַּעֲלֶה וַתֵּצֵא
2 Chron. 1.17   וַיַּעֲלוּ וַיּוֹצִיאוּ

Gen. 34.1   MT   לִרְאוֹת
       S   להראות

Lev. 26.22   S   ושלחתי
       MT   וְהִשְׁלַחְתִּי

b) pi'el or hiph'il:

Num. 33.52   MT   תְּאַבְּדוּ
       S   תאבידו

Deut. 7.24   S   ואבדת
       MT   וְהַאֲבַדְתָּ[204]

Gen. 12.2   MT   וַאֲגַדְּלָה
       S   ואגדילה

[199] Cf. 2 Chron. 16.2: וַיֵּצֵא, Venice 1515 marg.: וַיֹּצֵא; 2 Chron. 21.13:
Venice 1515: וַתִּזְנֶה; marg.: וַתַּזְנֶה.
[200] Cf. Lev. 20.6; 21.9; Num. 25.1; Deut. 22.21.
[201] Cf. Lev. 25.35: MT וְהֶחֱזַקְתָּ — s וחזקת.
[202] Cf. Num. 30.15.
[203] Cf. Gen. 6.4; 10.8; 25.3.
[204] Cf. Lev. 23.30; Deut. 9.3.

Ex. 14.4 MT	וְחִזַּקְתִּי		Lev. 11.38 MT	יֻתַּן
S	והחזקתי		S	²⁰⁹ינתן
Gen. 7.3 MT	לַחְיוֹת		2 Sam. 21.20	יֻלַּד
S	להחיוֹת²⁰⁵		1 Chron. 20.6	נוֹלַד
1 Chron. 11.18	וַיְנַסֵּךְ		2 Sam. 21.22	יֻלְּדוּ
2 Sam. 23.16	וַיַּסֵּךְ		1 Chron. 20.8	נוֹלְדוּ²¹⁰
2 Chron. 34.25 Q	וַיְקַטְּרוּ²⁰⁶			
K	ויקטירו			

d) pi'el or ḳal.²¹¹

α) active:

2 Sam. 24.16	לְשַׁחֲתָה		Gen. 22.17 MT	בָּרֵךְ
1 Chron. 21.15	לְהַשְׁחִיתָה²⁰⁷		S	ברוך
2 Ki. 19.12	שִׁחֲתוּ		Isa. 14.23 Q	וְטֵאטֵאתִיהָ
Isa. 37.12	הִשְׁחִתוּ		K	וטאטאתיה²¹²

c) pu'al or niph'al
(B-L §38m'–r'):²⁰⁸

β) passive;

Gen. 40.15 MT	גֻּנַּבְתִּי		Gen. 25.10 MT	קֻבַּר
S	גננבתי		S	קבור
Ex. 22.6 MT	וְגֻנַּב		Lev. 10.16 MT	שֹׂרָף
S	וגננב		S	שרוף

²⁰⁵ Cf. Deut. 6.24.
²⁰⁶ Cf. 2 Ki. 22.17.
²⁰⁷ Cf. Gen. 19.13; further Gen. 6.17; 9.11, 15; 19.29 in conjunction with §96d.
²⁰⁸ Cf. our note 198 on §61d.
²⁰⁹ Cf. Q–K on 2 Sam. 21.6.
²¹⁰ Cf. Venice 1515 marg.: נולדו; similarly in 1 Chron. 3.5.
²¹¹ Cf. TRL paragraph XXV on פנה; further: s. v. חבל: Ps. 7.15: MT תְּחַבֵּל — o חָבַל; s. v. נגר: Ps. 89.45: MT מִגַּרְתָּה — o מָגַרְתָּה; s. v. נחת: Ps. 18.35: וְנִחֲתָה — o וְנָחֲתָה; s. v. שלם: Ps. 31.24: MT וּמְשַׁלֵּם — o וְשָׁלֵם; s. v. שמח: Ps. 46.5: MT יְשַׂמְּחוּ — o יִשְׂמְחוּ. Cf. also Jer. 51.36: Venice 1515: וְנִקַּמְתִּי; marg.: וְנָקַמְתִּי; Prov. 28.8: Venice 1515: יְקַבְּצֶנּוּ; marg.: יִקְבְּצֶנּוּ; 2 Chron. 33.3: Venice 1515: נָתַץ; marg.: נִתַּץ; 1 Ki. 20.27: Venice 1515: מָלְאוּ; marg.: מִלְּאוּ; Ezek. 34.4: חִזַּקְתֶּם; Venice 1515 marg.: חֲזַקְתֶּם
²¹² Cf. §38 a.

E. THE NOUN

§63: *Substantives derived from verbs with imperf. in o or i:*[213]

Isa. 23.13	Q	בְּחוּנָיו
	K	בחיניו
Zech. 11.2	K	הבצור
	Q	הַבָּצִיר
Nah. 2.6	K	בהלוכתם
	Q	בַּהֲלִיכָתָם
Jer. 37.4	Q	הַכְּלוּא
	K	הכליא
Judg. 7.13	K	צלול
	Q	צָלִיל
Isa. 62.3	K	וצנוף
	Q	וּצְנִיף
Ps. 17.14	Q	וּצְפוּנְךָ
	K	וצפינך
Ezek. 4.15	K	צפועי
	Q	צְפִיעֵי
1 Ki. 6.21	Q	בְּרַתוּקוֹת
	K	ברתיקות
Jer. 18.15	K	שבולי
	Q	שְׁבִילֵי

α) substantives with preformative (ת, שׁ):

Jer. 5.30	Q	וְשַׁעֲרוּרָה
	K	ושערירה
Jer. 43.10	K	שפרורו
	Q	שַׁפְרִירוֹ
Prov. 20.30	Q	תַּמְרוּק
	K	תמריק

§64: *Substantives derived from verbs primae ו or י:*[214]

Gen. 11.30	MT	וְלָד[215]
	S	ילד[216]
Ruth 2.1	Q	מוֹדַע
	K	מידע
2 Ki. 16.18	Q	מוּסַךְ
	K	מיסך
Ezek. 41.8	Q	מוּסְדוֹת
	K	מיסדות

§65: *Substantives derived from verbs mediae ו or י:*[217]

Jer. 6.7	K	בור
	Q	בַּיִר[218]

[213] Cf. §50.
[214] Cf. §51.
[215] Cf. מוֹלֶדֶת.
[216] Cf. לִיד; cf. also Q–K on 1 Sam. 6.23.
[217] Cf. §52.
[218] Cf. TRL s. v. בּאר

Deut. 6.11 MT וּבֹרֹת
S בירות

Ezek. 47.10 K דוגים
Q דַיָּגִים

Job 6.2 Q וְהַוָּתִי
K והיתי

Ps. 74.11 K חוקך
Q חֵיקְךָ

Prov. 23.31 Q בַּכּוֹס
K בכיס

2 Sam. 3.15 K לוש
Q לַיִשׁ

Isa. 57.19 K נוב
Q נִיב

Ezek. 22.18 K לסוג
Q לְסִיג

Isa. 30.6 K עורים
Q עֲיָרִים

Ps. 49.15 Q וְצוּרָם
K וצירם

Jer. 18.22 Q שׁוּחָה
K שיחה

Isa. 28.15 Q שׁוֹט
K שיט

a) substantives with preformative (ת, מ, י):

1 Ki. 6.5 K יצוע
Q יָצִיעַ

Isa. 11.8 Q מְאוּרַת
K מאירת

Prov. 18.19 K ומדונים
Q וּמִדְיָנִים

Prov. 18.20 Q תְּבוּאַת
K תביאת

§66: Substantives derived from verbs tertiae ו *or* י*:*[219]

2 Ki. 23.12 K עלות
Q עֲלִיַּת

Ps. 9.13 Q עֲנָוִים
K עֲנִיִּים[220]

Eccl. 5.10 Q רְאוּת
K ראית

Jer. 30.3 Q שְׁבוּת
K שבית

a) substantives with preformative (ת, מ):

Ps. 129.3 K למענותם
Q לְמַעֲנִיתָם

Jer. 14.14 K ותרמות
Q וְתַרְמִית

§67: Substantives derived from verbs tertiae א *or* ה*:*[221]

2 Chron. 9.18 לַכִּסֵּא
1 Ki. 10.19 לַכִּסֵּה

[219] Cf. §54; the ה there is equivalent to a '; cf. §53.
[220] Cf. TRL s. v. עני: Ps. 76.10: MT עַנְוֵי — O עֲנִיֵּי.
[221] Cf. §55; also §§1 and 38 b.

2 Chron. 1.16	מִקְוֵא	Gen. 47.4 MT	מִרְעֶה
1 Ki. 10.28	מִקְוֵה	s	מרעי

§68: Substantives derived from verbs tertiae ה, with interchange between ה and י:²²²

		Lev. 26.36 MT	עָלֶה
		s	עלי
Deut. 18.1 s	אשה	2 Chron. 34.10	עֹשֵׂה
MT	אִשֵּׁי	2 Ki. 22.5	עֹשֵׂי
Deut. 28.60 MT	מַדְוֶה	Ex. 25.32 s	קנה
s	מדוי	MT	קָנֵי
Num. 19.21 MT	וּמַזֶּה	Deut. 9.13 MT	קְשֵׁה
s	ומזי	s	קשי²²⁴
Num. 24.16 MT	מַחֲזֶה	Gen. 21.20 MT	רֹבֶה
s	מחזי	s	רבי
Mal. 3.5 Q	ומטה	Gen. 47.3 MT	רֹעֵה
K	וּמַטֵּי	s	רעי
2 Ki. 22.17	מַעֲשֵׂה	Deut. 22.1 s	שהו
2 Chron. 34.25	מַעֲשֵׂי	MT	שֶׁיוֹ

§69: Substantives derived from verbs of weak roots:

1 Ki. 7.46	בְּמַעֲבֵה	2 Sam. 3.25 Q	מוֹבָאֶךָ
2 Chron. 4.17	בַּעֲבִי²²³	K	מבואך²²⁵
Deut. 23.11 MT	מִקְרֵה	Deut. 26.8 MT	וּבְמֹרָא
s	מקרי	s	ובמראה²²⁶
Eccl. 11.9 Q	וּבְמַרְאֵה	1 Ki. 12.15	סִבָּה
K	ובמראי	2 Chron. 10.15	נְסִבָּה²²⁷

²²² Cf. §53; the context of these forms makes it evident that neither does the ending in ה indicate a sing., nor the י a plural; cf. §78 seq., and especially §81 seq.

²²³ On the difference in the nominal formation: with or without prefix מ, cf. §128 a.

²²⁴ Cf. K–Q on Ezek. 2.4.

²²⁵ בוא–יבא.

²²⁶ ראה–ירא; cf. similarly Gen. 9.2; Deut. 4.34; 11.25; 34.12.

²²⁷ נסב–סבב; cf. Gen. 19.4: סָבּוּ: Ḳal with preservation of the second vowel; cf. TRL paragraph XXIX B 3.

§70: *Substantives of which the second radical is vocalized i:*[228]

Ex. 2.6	MT	הַיֶּלֶד
	S	היליד
Ex. 1.17	MT	הַיְלָדִים
	S	הילידים
Ex. 2.6	MT	מְיַלְּדִי
	S	מילידי
Gen. 30.26	MT	יְלָדַי
	S	ילידי
Gen. 33.7	MT	וִילָדֶיהָ
	S	ולידיה
Gen. 32.23	MT	יְלָדָיו
	S	ילידיו
Gen. 33.2	MT	יַלְדֵיהֶן
	S	ילידיהן
Ezek. 4.6	Q	הַיְמָנִי
	K	הימיני
Num. 23.10	MT	יְשָׁרִים
	S	ישירים
Num. 16.27	MT	נִצָּבִים
	S	נציבים[229]
Deut. 12.5	MT	לְשִׁכְנוֹ
	S	לשכינו

a) feminine forms:[230]

Deut. 32.11	MT	אֶבְרָתוֹ
	S	אבירתו

Gen. 4.23	MT	אָמַרְתִּי
	S	אמירתי
Deut. 33.9	MT	אִמְרָתֶךָ
	S	אמירתך
Num. 32.16	MT	גְּדֵרֹת
	S	נדירות[231]
Prov. 31.27	K	הילכות
	Q	הֲלִיכוֹת
Gen. 34.4	MT	הַיַּלְדָּה
	S	הילידה
Lev. 5.2	MT	בְּנִבְלַת
	S	בנבילת
Ex. 33.22	MT	בְּנִקְרַת
	S	בנקירות
Lev. 23.21	MT	עֲבֹדָה
	S	עבידה
Ex. 5.9	MT	הָעֲבֹדָה
	S	העבידה
Num. 7.5	MT	עֲבֹדָתוֹ
	S	עבידתו
Num. 7.7	MT	עֲבֹדָתָם
	S	עבידתם
Num. 32.3	MT	עֲטָרֹת
	S	עטירות
Gen. 15.6	MT	צְדָקָה
	S	צדיקה
Deut. 33.21	MT	צִדְקַת
	S	צדיקת

[228] Cf. Jer. 11.20: צָדָק, Venice 1515 marg.: צַדִּיק; Ezek. 17.24: Venice 1515: שָׁפֵל; marg.: שָׁפָל.
[229] Cf. 1 Ki. 4.7: נִצָּבִים; Venice 1515 marg.: נְצָבִים; cf. further: Q–K on 2 Chron. 8.10.
[230] Cf. TRL s. v. זמרה.   [231] Cf. TRL s. v. גדרה.

Gen. 30.33 MT צִדְקָתִי

S צדיקתי

Lev. 27.10 MT וּתְמוּרָתוֹ

S ותמירתו

β) substantives with preformative מ:

Num. 32.36 MT מִבְצָר

S מבציר

Num. 13.19 MT בְּמִבְצָרִים

S מבצירים

Lev. 6.2 MT מוֹקְדָה

S הַמוּקִידָה[232]

§71: Substantives of which the first radical is vocalized i:

Deut. 28.65 MT וְדַאֲבוֹן

S ודיבון

Gen. 27.37 MT וְדָגָן

S ודיגן

Deut. 17.12 MT בְּזָדוֹן

S בזידון

§72: miktal or miktol forms:

Isa. 37.24 מִבְחַר

2 Ki. 19.23 מִבְחוֹר

Lam. 1.11 Q מַחֲמַדֵּיהֶם

K מחמודיהם

Lev. 26.26 MT בְּמִשְׁקָל

S במשקול

§73: Substantives of which the second radical is vocalized o or i:

Gen. 43.33 MT הַבְּכוֹר

S הבכיר

Jer. 50.45 K צעורי

Q צְעִירֵי

Jer. 48.4 K צעוריה

Q צְעִירֶיהָ

Jer. 14.3 K צעוריהם

Q צְעִירֵיהֶם

Num. 15.40 MT קָדְשִׁים

S קדישים[233]

Ex. 32.27 MT קָרְבוֹ

S קריבו

Lev. 10.3 MT בִּקְרֹבַי

S בקריבי

§74: The absolute state ending in ה or ת (B-L §25i'–l'):

Jer. 52.4 בְּשָׁנָה

2 Ki. 25.1 בִּשְׁנַת[234]

Jer. 49.25 K תהלה

Q תְּהִלָּת

§75: Formation of the plur. masc.

a) ending in ים or ין (B-L §63t):

Job 32.11 Md מִלִּים

Ma מלין

---

[232] On the Article in s, cf. §93 b.

[233] Cf. Lev. 11.44, 45; 19.2; 20.7, 26; 21.6; 24.9; Num. 5.17; 16.3.

[234] Cf. Q–K on Jer. 28.1; 32.1; 51.59.

2 Chron. 23.12   הָרָצִים

2 Ki. 11.13   הָרָצִין

Lam. 4.3   Q   תַּנִים

         K   תנין

β) ending in ם or ים :[235]

Ezek. 29.4   Q   חַחִים

        K   חחיים

Ezek. 23.14   Q   כַּשְׂדִים

         K   כשדיים

Isa. 23.12   Q   כִּתִּים

        K   כתיים[236]

Gen. 10.13   לוּדִים

1 Chron. 1.12   לוּדְיִים

γ) substantives with masc. or fem. ending (B-L §63p) :[237]

Num. 13.20   MT   בְּכוּרֵי

           S   בכרות

Gen. 25.16   MT   בְּחַצְרֵיהֶם

           S   בחצרותם

Ex. 28.12   MT   כְּתַפָיו

           S   כתפתיו

Ps. 18.8   וּמוֹסְדֵי

2 Sam. 22.8   מוֹסְדוֹת

§76: Inflected nominal forms with preservation of the second vowel:[238]

Ex. 17.6   MT   זְקְנֵי

         S   זקיני

Lev. 8.21   MT   וְהַכְּרָעַיִם

          S   והכורעים

Lev. 4.11   MT   כְּרָעָיו

          S   כורעיו

Ex. 36.32   MT   לְיַרְכָתַיִם

          S   לירכותים

Num. 6.3   MT   מִשְׁרַת

         S   משארת

Deut. 7.13   MT   וְעַשְׁתְּרֹת

          S   ועשתארות

Lev. 14.4   MT   צִפֳּרִים

         S   צפורים

α) the substantive in Sandhi:

Nah. 1.3   Q   וּגְדָל

        K   וגדול[239]

Prov. 22.11   Q   טְהָר

          K   טהור

β) construct state fem. plur. (B-L §63q):

Deut. 33.13   Q   בָּמֱתֵי

          K   במותי

---

[235] Cf. Josh. 2.17, 20: נְקִיִם; Venice 1515 marg.: נקיים; on the letter י as an indicator of the vowel i, cf. §39 a.

[236] Cf. K–Q on Ezek. 27.6.

[237] Cf. §126.

[238] Cf. §59; also TRL paragraphs XXVI a and XXIX B 6.

[239] Cf. Ps. 145.8.

Ex. 26.22 MT וּלְיַרְכְּתֵי
S ולירכותי

1 Ki. 6.16 Q מִיַּרְכְּתֵי
K מירכותי

§77: *The substantive unchanged in the construct state.*²⁴⁰
a) dual forms:

Deut. 33.11 MT מָתְנַיִם קָמָיו
S ... מתני

2 Chron. 4.3 שְׁנַיִם טוּרִים
1 Ki. 7.24 ....²⁴¹ שְׁנֵי

Lev. 24.6 MT שְׁתַּיִם מַעֲרָכוֹת
S ..... שתי

b) plural forms:

Num. 13.32 S אנשים מדות
MT ... אַנְשֵׁי

Ex. 32.28 S אלפים איש
MT ... אַלְפֵי

Num. 3.38 MT²⁴² שֹׁמְרִים מִשְׁמֶרֶת
S ..... שמרי

c) fem. sing.:

Deut. 21.11 S אשה יפת תאר
MT ...... אֵשֶׁת

Gen. 17.17 MT מֵאָה שָׁנָה
S ... מאת²⁴³

Num. 28.3 MT עֹלָה תָמִיד
S ... עלת

Jer. 52.21 K קומה העמד
Q .... קוֹמַת

d) cardinals:

Lev. 27.7 MT עֲשָׂרָה שְׁקָלִים
S .... עשרת

1 Ki. 12.5 שְׁלֹשָׁה יָמִים
2 Chron. 10.5 ... שְׁלֹשֶׁת

Ezek. 46.6 Q וששה כבשים
K .... וְשֵׁשֶׁת

Lev. 23.18 S שבעה כבשים
MT .... שִׁבְעַת

e) the substantive taking the article:

1 Sam. 26.22 K החנית המלך
Q .... חֲנִית

2 Ki. 7.13 K ההמון ישראל
Q .... הֲמוֹן

Jer. 32.12 K²⁴⁴ הַסֵּפֶר הַמִּקְנָה
Q .... סֵפֶר

---

²⁴⁰ Cf. TRL paragraphs XXVI c, XXIX B 4 and §138 seq.

²⁴¹ Cf. MT–S on Ex. 25.18 and Deut. 17.6; also: 2 Chron. 4.13 — 1 Ki. 7.42: further K–Q on Judg. 11.38; 2 Ki. 17.16.

²⁴² Cf. Ex. 26.26: בְּרִיחִם עֲצֵי שִׁטִּים חֲמִשָּׁה
Ex. 36.31: בְּרִיחֵי עֲצֵי שִׁטִּים חֲמִשָּׁה.

²⁴³ Cf. Gen. 23.1.

²⁴⁴ Cf. Ex. 28.24: שְׁתֵּי עֲבֹתֹת הַזָּהָב
Ex. 39.17: שְׁתֵּי הָעֲבֹתֹת הַזָּהָב

2 Sam. 10.7	הַצָּבָא הַגִּבּוֹרִים	Isa. 39.2	הַשֶּׁמֶן הַטּוֹב
1 Chron. 19.8	..... צָבָא²⁴⁵	2 Ki. 20.13	שֶׁמֶן ...
Isa. 36.16	²⁴⁶הַמֶּלֶךְ אַשּׁוּר	Num. 34.2 MT	הָאָרֶץ כְּנַעַן
2 Ki. 18.31	מֶלֶךְ	seb	... אֶרֶץ

F. NOMINAL AND VERBAL SUFFIXES

I. THE HELPING VOWEL י IN CONNECTION WITH THE SUFFIXES

The pronominal suffixes to the noun in the sing. and in the plur. are the same; י is merely a helping vowel and does not indicate the number of the noun; cf. the number of the respective predicates in the instances listed in this chapter.

§78: *The pronominal suffix of the 2. pers. masc. sing.*

(B-L §29r).

A. The masculine noun.

  a) MT vocalizes pausal form sing.:²⁴⁷

Deut. 20.1	MT		אֹיִבְךָ
	s		איביך
Gen. 30.34	MT		כִּדְבָרְךָ
	s		כדבריך²⁴⁸

Ex. 33.13	MT	דַּרְכְּךָ
	s	דרכיך
Deut. 2.7	MT	יָדְךָ
	s	ידיך²⁴⁹
Ruth 3.9	Ma	כְּנָפֶךָ
	Md	כנפיך
Lev. 25.5	MT	נְזִירֶךָ
	s	נזיריך
Isa. 37.17		עֵינֶךָ
2 Ki. 19.16		עֵינֶיךָ

---

²⁴⁵ Cf. Venice 1515 marg.: צְבָא.

²⁴⁶ Cf. 2 Ki. 25.11: וְאֵת הַנֹּפְלִים אֲשֶׁר נָפְלוּ עַל הַמֶּלֶךְ בָּבֶל Jer. 52.15: וְאֵת הַנֹּפְלִים אֲשֶׁר נָפְלוּ עַל מֶלֶךְ בָּבֶל.

²⁴⁷ The pausal-form is an arbitrary vocalization; cf. Ps. 143.10: Venice 1515: רְצוֹנֶךָ; marg.: רְצוֹנֶךָ; Ps. 68.30: מֵהֵיכָלֶךָ; Venice 1515 marg.: מהיכלך; Ezek. 4.8: צִדֶּךָ; Venice 1515 marg.: צדך; Ps. 79.6: חֲמָתְךָ; Venice 1515 marg.: חֲמָתָךְ; cf. also §59 b note 184.

²⁴⁸ Cf. Gen. 47.30; Num. 14.20.

²⁴⁹ Cf. Deut. 6.8.

b) MT vocalizes context
form sing.:

Prov. 24.17: Q   אֹיִבְךָ
        K   אֹיביך[250]

Deut. 24.14 MT: מֵגֵרְךָ
         s: מגריך

Ex. 8.6: MT: כִּדְבָרְךָ
      s: כדבריך[251]

2 Sam. 1.16: Q   דָּמְךָ
         K: דמיך

Ps. 16.10: Q: חֲסִידְךָ
        K: חסידיך

Gen. 49.8 MT   יָדְךָ
         s   ידיך[252]

Ex. 9.19 MT   מִקְנְךָ
        s   מקניך[253]

1 Ki. 1.27 Q   עַבְדְּךָ
       K   · עבדיך

Lev. 2.13 MT   קָרְבָּנְךָ
       s   קרבניך

Deut. 4.4 MT   וְרַגְלְךָ
       s   ורגליך[254]

Prov. 3.28 Q   לְרֵעֶךָ
       K   לרעיך

Ps. 77.20 Q   וּשְׁבִילְךָ
       K   ושביליך

B. The feminine noun.

c) MT vocalizes pausal
form sing.:[255]

Lev. 2.13 MT   מִנְחָתֶךָ   (2°)
       s   מנחתיך

Num. 23.3 MT   עֹלָתֶךָ
       s   עלתיך

d) MT vocalizes context
form sing.:

Isa. 26.20 Q   דְּלָתֶךָ
       K   דלתיך

Lev. 2.13 MT   מִנְחָתֶךָ   (1°)
       s   מנחתיך

§79: *The pronominal suffix of
the 2. pers. fem. sing.*

A. The masculine noun.

a) MT vocalizes the noun as
sing. (B-L §29b'):

Gen. 20.13 MT   חַסְדֵּךְ
       s   חסדיך

Ezek. 23.29 Q   יְגִיעֵךְ
       K   יגיעיך

---

[250] Cf. 1 Sam. 24.5; 26.8.

[251] Cf. Q–K: Judg. 13.12, 17; 1 Ki. 8.26; 18.36; 22.13; Jer. 15.16; Ps. 119.147, 161.

[252] Cf. Q–K: Josh. 10.8; 1 Ki. 22.34; Prov. 3.7.

[253] Cf. Gen. 30.29; Ex. 9.3; 34.19.

[254] Cf. Q–K: Eccl. 4.17.

[255] The inconsistency of the pausal vocalization is shown in our note 247 on subdivision a.

Gen. 21.18	MT	יָדֵךְ
	S	ידיך
Gen. 24.14	MT	כַּדֵּךְ
	S	כדיך[256]
Cant. 2.14	Q	וּמַרְאֵךְ
	K	ומראיך
Ex. 2.9	MT	שְׂכָרֵךְ
	S	שכריך

a) particles:

Gen. 20.16	MT	אֹתָךְ
	S	אתיך
Gen. 12.12	MT	אֹתָךְ
	S	אתיך
Gen. 20.16	MT	לָךְ
	S	ליך
Gen. 12.13	MT	בִּגְלָלֵךְ
	S	בגליך
Gen. 12.13	MT	בַּעֲבוּרֵךְ
	S	בעבוריך

b) MT vocalizes the noun as plur.:

Ezek. 36.13	K	נויך
	Q	גּוֹיָיִךְ
Ezek. 27.12	K	עזבונך
	Q	עִזְבוֹנָיִךְ

B. The feminine noun.

c) MT vocalizes the noun as sing.:

Ezek. 16.26	Q	תַזְנוּתֵךְ
	K	תזנותיך

d) MT vocalizes the noun as plur.:

Ezek. 16.57	K	אחותך
	Q	אֲחוֹתַיִךְ
Ezek. 16.25	K	תזנותך
	Q	תַזְנוּתָיִךְ
Ruth 3.3	K	שמלתך
	Q	שִׂמְלֹתַיִךְ

§80: The pronominal suffix of the 3. pers. masc. sing.[257]

a) the masculine noun (B-L §29s):

Prov. 30.10	K	אדנו
	Q	אֲדֹנָיו
2 Sam. 18.17	K	לאהלו
	Q	לְאֹהָלָיו[258] .
1 Ki. 8.37		אִיבוֹ
2 Chron. 6.28		אֹיְבָיו
Lev. 17.14	S	אכלו
	MT	אֹכְלָיו[259]

---

[256] Cf. Gen. 24.43.
[257] Cf. §41a.
[258] Cf. 2 Sam. 20.22; 2 Ki. 14.12.
[259] Cf. Lev. 19.8.

1 Sam. 23.5 K ואנשו
         Q וַאֲנָשָׁיו

2 Ki. 21.6 בְנוֹ
2 Chron. 33.6 בָּנָיו[260]

Ps. 10.5 K דרכו
       Q דְּרָכָיו[261]

1 Ki. 8.15 וּבְיָדוֹ
2 Chron. 6.4 וּבְיָדָיו[262]

Job 38.41 K ילדו
       Q יְלָדָיו

Eccl. 4.8 Q עֵינוֹ
      K עֵינָיו[263]

α) particles:

2 Sam. 23.9 K ואחרו
       Q וְאַחֲרָיו

1 Sam. 22.13 K אלו
       Q אֵלָיו[264]

Josh. 8.11 K בינו
       Q בֵּינָיו[265]

1 Sam. 2.10 K עלו
       Q עָלָיו[266]

2 Sam. 3.12 K תחתו
       Q תַּחְתָּיו[267]

b) the feminine noun:

Jer. 15.8 K אלמנותו
       Q אַלְמְנוֹתָיו

Prov. 6.13 K באצבעתו
       Q בְּאֶצְבְּעֹתָיו

Prov. 22.25 K ארחתו
       Q אֹרְחֹתָיו

2 Ki. 11.18 K מזבחתו
       Q מִזְבְּחֹתָיו

Ezek. 40.26 K עלותו·
       Q עֲלוֹתָיו[268]

Ezek. 3.20 K צדקתו
       Q צִדְקֹתָיו[269]

§81: The pronominal suffix of the 1. pers. plur.:[270]

Isa. 53.4 Ma ומכאבנו
       Md וּמַכְאֹבֵינוּ

Gen. 5.29 MT מִמַּעֲשֵׂנוּ
       s ממעשינו

---

[260] Cf. K–Q on Deut. 2.33; 33.9; 1 Sam. 30.6.

[261] Cf. 1 Sam. 8.3; 18.14; Jer. 17.10; Ezek. 18.23; Job 26.14.

[262] Cf. MT–s on Ex. 17.11; also K–Q on Ex. 32.19; Lev. 9.23; 16.21; Isa. 25.11; Ezek. 43.26; Job 5.18.

[263] Cf. MT–s on Lev. 13.55; 21.20; also K–Q on 1 Sam. 3.2, 18; 2 Sam. 10.12; 12.9; 13.34; 19.19; 24.22; Jer. 32.4; Job 21.20.

[264] Cf. Ezek. 9.4; Zech. 2.8.

[265] Cf. Josh. 3.4.

[266] Cf. 2 Sam. 20.8.

[267] Cf. 2 Sam. 2.23; 16.8; Job 9.13.

[268] Cf. MT–s on Num. 23.6, 17.

[269] Cf. Ezek. 18.24; 33.13.

[270] Cf. Josh. 2.20: דְּבָרֵנוּ זֶה; Venice 1515 marg.: דברינו.

Num. 32.16 MT   לְמִקְנֵנוּ
        s   למקנינו

Ex. 34.9 MT   לַעֲוֹנֵנוּ
       s   לעונינו

§82: The pronominal suffix of the 2. pers. masc. plur.

a) the masculine noun:[271]

Ex. 12.11 MT   וּמַקֶּלְכֶם
       s   ומקליכם

Gen. 45.20 MT   וְעֵינְכֶם
        s   [272]ועיניכם

Lev. 26.19 MT   עֻזְּכֶם
       s   עזיכם

Lev. 1.2 MT   קָרְבַּנְכֶם
      s   קרבניכם

b) the feminine noun:

Gen. 47.23 MT   אַדְמַתְכֶם
        s   אדמתיכם

Ex. 32.30 MT   חַטָּאתְכֶם
       s   [273]חטאתיכם

Num. 18.26 MT   בְּנַחֲלַתְכֶם
        s   בנחלתיכם

Num. 10.10 MT   שִׂמְחַתְכֶם
      s   שמחתיכם

§83: The pronominal suffix of the 3. pers. fem. plur.:[274]

Num. 27.5 MT   מִשְׁפָּטָן
       s   משפטין

Num. 36.12 MT   נַחֲלָתָן
        s   נחלתין

Lev. 18.10 MT   עֶרְוָתָן
      s   ערותין

a) Lev. 8.16 MT   חֶלְבְּהֶן
       s   חלביהן

β) Num. 31.9 MT   מִקְנֶהֶם
        s   מקניהם

II. THE SUFFIXES.

§84: 2. pers. masc. sing.: ךָ or אָךְ (B-L §29i, j, f'):[275]

Gen. 22.2 MT   יְחִידְךָ
       s   יחידאך

Hos. 4.6 Q   וְאֶמְאָסְךָ
      K   ואמאסאך

Deut. 32.6 MT   קָנֶךָ
       s   קנאך

[271] Cf. TRL paragraphs XXVI f 2 and XXIX B 16; also s. v. יד: Mal. 2.13: MT מִיֶּדְכֶם — o מִידִיכֶם; cf. further: Jer. 44.25: Venice 1515: וּבִיֶדְכֶם, marg.: וּבִידָכֶם.

[272] Cf. Q–K on Ezek. 9.5; also K–Q on Ezek. 33.25.

[273] Cf. Num. 32.23; Deut. 9.18, 21.

[274] Cf. also §39b.

[275] Cf. TRL paragraph XXIX B 1; cf. also 1 Sam. 13.13: צִוְּךָ; Venice 1515 marg.: צִוָּךְ.

Deut. 25.18 MT   קָרְךָ
          s   קראך

Num. 11.23 MT   הֲיִקְרְךָ
          s   היקראך

a) כה or ך:[276]

Num. 22.33 MT   אֹתְכָה
          s   אתך

2 Sam. 22.30   בְּכָה
Ps. 18.30   בְּךָ

Ex. 15.11 MT   כָּמֹכָה
         s   כמוך

Gen. 3.9 MT   אַיֶּכָּה
        s   איך

Deut. 28.22 MT   יַכְּכָה
          s   יכך

β) יך or (ך)כה (B-L §29i):[277]

Ex. 13.16 MT   יָדְכָה
         s   ידיך

Gen. 48.4 MT   מַפְרְךָ
        s   מפריך

§85: 2. pers. fem. sing.: ך or כי:

2 Ki. 4.7 Q   וּבָנַיִךְ
       K   בניכי

---

2 Ki. 4.7 Q   נִשְׁיֵךְ
       K   נשיכי

2 Ki. 4.3 Q   שְׁכֵנַיִךְ
       K   שכניכי

1 Ki. 17.13 Q   וְלָךְ
       K   ולכי

§86: 3. pers. masc. sing.

a) ו or ה (B-L §29k).[278]

α) nouns:

Ex. 22.4 Q   בְּעִירוֹ
       K   בעירה

Ex. 22.26 Q   כְּסוּתוֹ
       K   כסותה

Lev. 23.13 Q   וְנִסְכּוֹ
        K   ונסכה

Gen. 49.11 Q   עִירוֹ
        K   עירה

Isa. 37.24   קִצּוֹ
2 Ki. 19.23   קִצֹּה

β) verbal forms:

2 Ki. 6.10 Q   וְהִזְהִירוֹ
       K   והזהירה

Num. 10.36 Q   וּבְנֻחוֹ
       K   ובנחה

---

[276] Cf. our note 83 on §44.

[277] Cf. TRL §124 subdivision 2, and §74a.

[278] Hence, passages like: Gen. 24.36: MT זָקְנָה — s זקנתו; Num. 30.16: MT צָוָּה — s עונו; Gen. 50.11: MT שָׁמָּה — s שמו, according to the interpretation of s, will have to be vocalized as זקנתה, עונה and שמה respectively. Cf. our notes 93 on §45 2a and 279 on §86 b.

Ex. 32.25 Q   פְּרָעֹו
       K   פרעה

Num. 23.8 Q   קַבֹּו
       K   קבה

Ex. 32.17 Q   בְּרֵעֹו
       K   ברעה

b) of forms ending in a consonant: וֹ or הוּ:[279]

Gen. 27.27 MT   בָּרֲכֹו
       s   ברכהו

Deut. 34.10 MT   יְדָעֹו
       s   ידעהו

Deut. 33.8 MT   נִסִּיתֹו
       s   נסיתהו

Ex. 2.3 MT   הַצְפִינֹו
       s   הצפינהו

Ex. 20.8 MT   לְקַדְּשֹׁו
       s   לקדשהו

Ex. 4.28 MT   שְׁלָחֹו
       s   שלחהו

1 Sam. 18.1 K   ויאהבו
        Q   וַיֶּאֱהָבֵהוּ

c) of forms ending in a
vowel: הוּ or וֹ:

Num. 11.12 MT   יְלִדְתִּיהוּ
       s   ילדתיו

Ex. 2.10 MT   מְשִׁיתִהוּ
      s   משיתיו

1 Chron. 17.9   וּנְטַעְתִּיהוּ
2 Sam. 7.10   וּנְטַעְתִּיו

1 Chron. 16.12   פִּיהוּ
Ps. 105.5   פִּיו[280]

§87: 3. pers. masc. plur.:
ם or הם (B-L §29e, q, s):

1 Ki. 8.34   לַאֲבֹותָם
2 Chron. 6.25   וְלַאֲבֹתֵיהֶם

Ex. 36.34 MT   טַבְעֹתָם
      s   טבעתיהם

Ex. 34.13 MT   מִזְבְּחֹתָם
      s   מזבחתיהם[281]

2 Sam. 22.46   מִמִּסְגְּרֹותָם
Ps. 18.46   מִמִּסְגְּרֹותֵיהֶם

Ex. 34.13 MT   מַצֵּבֹתָם
      s   מצבתיהם[282]

2 Chron. 6.37   שֶׁבְיָם
1 Ki. 8.47   שֹׁבֵיהֶם[283]

1 Ki. 8.49   תְּחִנָּתָם[284]
2 Chron. 6.39   תְּחִנֹּתֵיהֶם

1 Ki. 14.27   תַּחְתָּם
2 Chron. 12.10   תַּחְתֵּיהֶם[285]

[279] Consequently, in instances like: Ex. 18.7: MT וַיָּבֹאוּ — s ויבאהו; Num. 20.27: MT וַיַּעֲלוּ — s ויעלהו; Ex. 15.22: MT וַיֵּצְאוּ — s ויצאהו, the MT will have to be understood as: וַיֵּצְאֹו and וַיָּבֹאֹו respectively; cf. our note 278.

[280] Cf. MT–s on Ex. 4.15.

[281] Cf. Deut. 12.3.   [282] Cf. Deut. 12.3.

[283] Lege שֹׁבֵיהֶם?   [284] Lege תְּחִנָּתָם?

[285] Cf. MT–s on Deut. 2.12, 21, 22, 23.

Ex. 32.12 MT   הוֹצִיאָם
       S   הוציאהם

a) particles:

Gen. 32.1 MT   אָתְהֶם
        S   אאתם[286]

1 Chron. 16.6   בָּהֶם
1 Ki. 15.22   בָּם[287]

Num. 22.12 MT   עִמָּהֶם
          S   עמם[288]

G. SYNTAX

I. SUBJECT AND PREDICATE.

§88: *The gender of the noun*
(B-L §62c'):

Gen. 13.6 MT   נָשָׂא ... הָאָרֶץ
        S   נשאה ....

Jer. 48.45 MT   אֵשׁ יָצָא
        seb   .. יצאה

1 Ki. 22.43   דָּרַךְ ... מִמֶּנּוּ
2 Chron. 20.32   מִמֶּנָּה ..... [289]

Ex. 38.24 MT   תֵּשַׁע ... כִּכָּר
        S   תשעה ...

Gen. 49.20 MT   שְׁמֵנָה לַחְמוֹ
        S   שמן ....

2 Sam. 5.12   נִשֵּׂא מַמְלַכְתּוֹ
1 Chron. 14.2   נשאת .....

Gen. 49.15 MT   מְנוּחָה ... טוֹב
          S   טובה .... [290]

Judg. 19.13 K   בְּאַחַד הַמְּקֹמוֹת
         Q   באחת ..... [291]

Ex. 37.22 MT   מִקְשָׁה אַחַת
        S   אחד .... [292]

Num. 31.28 MT   אֶחָד נֶפֶשׁ
          S   אחת ... [293]

Cant. 4.9 K   בְּאַחַד מֵעֵינַיִךְ
        Q   בְּאַחַת ....

1 Sam. 31.7   הֶעָרִים .. בָּהֶן
1 Chron. 10.7   בָּהֶם ......

2 Sam. 23.8 K   בְּפַעַם אֶחָד
        Q   אֶחָת ....

---

[286] Cf. Ex. 18.20; Num. 21.3.
[287] Cf. MT–S on Ex. 19.22; 29.29, 33; 32.10; also S–MT on Ex. 25.28; Lev. 15.27; Num. 4.12.
[288] Cf. S–MT on Deut. 29.24.
[289] Cf. MT–S on Deut. 28.7, 25; also MT–seb on Judg. 2.22; Isa. 30.21.
[290] Cf. MT–seb on Lev. 6.8.
[291] Cf. Q–K: 2 Sam. 17.9, 12.
[292] Cf. Ex. 25.36.
[293] Cf. Gen. 46.22, 25; Lev. 20.6; also Md–Ma on Jer. 38.16.

Gen. 30.39 MT וַיֵּחַמוּ הַצֹּאן

S וְיֵחמנה . . .[294]

Ex. 37.3 MT צַלְעֹו הַשֵּׁנִית

S השני . . . .

Ex. 11.6 MT כָּמֹהוּ . . וְכָמֹהוּ . . כָּצְעָקָה

S כמוה . . . וכמוה . . . . .

Dan. 8.9 MT יָצָא קֶרֶן אַחַת

seb יצאה . . . .

Ex. 10.13 MT וְרוּחַ . . . נָשָׂא

S נשאה . . . . . .

1 Ki. 19.4 K רֹתֶם אַחַת

Q אֶחָד . . .

Gen. 48.22 MT שְׁכֶם אֶחָד

S אחת . . .

Gen. 19.23 MT הַשֶּׁמֶשׁ יָצָא

S יצאה . . . . .[295]

Deut. 23.17 MT בְּאַחַד שְׁעָרֶיךָ

S באחת . . . .[296]

1 Ki. 8.38 תְּחִנָּה . . . תִּהְיֶה

2 Chron. 6.29 יִהְיֶה . . . .

a) adjustment in gender:

Ex. 1.16 MT בֵּן . . . וְחָיָה

S וחיתה . . . . .

2 Sam. 24.12 אַחַת מֵהֶם

1 Chron. 21.10 מֵהֵנָּה . . .

β) the nomen regens a construct state:[297]

Jer. 17.24 Q בֹו . . . יֹום הַשַּׁבָּת

K בה . . . .

Num. 7.61 MT קַעֲרַת כֶּסֶף אַחַת

S אחד . . . .

Gen. 47.26 MT אַדְמַת הַכֹּהֲנִים לְבַדָּם

S לבדה . . . .

Num. 28.31 MT עֹלַת הַתָּמִיד וּמִנְחָתֹו

S ומנחתה . . . .

γ) names of nations:

2 Sam. 8.5 וַתָּבֹא אֲרָם

1 Chron. 18.5 וַיָּבֹא . . .[298]

2 Sam. 24.9 וַתְּהִי יִשְׂרָאֵל

1 Chron. 21.5 וַיְהִי . . . . .

§89: *Agreement in number between subject and predicate.*

a) the verb precedes the noun:

Gen. 9.29 MT וַיְהִי כָל יְמֵי

S ויהיו . . . .[299]

Num. 9.6 MT וַיְהִי אֲנָשִׁים

S ויהיו . . . .

Gen. 30.42 MT וְהָיָה הָעֲטֻפִים

S והיו . . . . .

[294] Cf. s–MT on Ex. 21.37; Num. 31.37; also: 1 Ki. 22.17 — 2 Chron. 18.16.
[295] Cf. Ex. 16.21; also Q–K: Jer. 15.9.
[296] Cf. Deut. 15.7; 16.5; 17.2; 18.6.
[297] Cf. Deut. 28.61: בְּסֵפֶר הַתֹּורָה הַזֹּאת
Deut. 29.20: בְּסֵפֶר הַתֹּורָה הַזֶּה.
[298] Cf. 2 Sam. 8.6 — 1 Chron. 18.6.
[299] Cf. Gen. 5.23, 31.

311

Num. 32.25 MT   וַיֹּאמֶר בְּנֵי גָד
S   .... ויאמרו

Ex. 4.29 MT   ³⁰⁰וַיֵּלֶךְ מֹשֶׁה וְאַהֲרֹן
S   .... וילכו

Gen. 10.25 MT   יֻלַּד שְׁנֵי בָנִים
S   ..... ³⁰¹ילדו

Deut. 21.19 S   ותפש בו אביו ואמו
MT   .... ³⁰²וְתָפְשׂוּ

b) the verb follows the noun:

Gen. 46.27 MT   וּבְנֵי יוֹסֵף אֲשֶׁר יֻלַּד
S   .... ³⁰³ילדו

Lev. 25.31 MT   וּבָתֵּי הַחֲצֵרִים .. יֵחָשֵׁב
S   .... יחשבו

Gen. 13.7 MT   וְהַכְּנַעֲנִי וְהַפְּרִזִּי אָז יֹשֵׁב
S   .... ישבים

2 Ki.9.11 MT   עַבְדֵי אֲדֹנָיו וַיֹּאמֶר לוֹ
seb   .... ³⁰⁴ויאמרו

Num. 27.3 S   וּבָנִים לֹא הָיָה לוֹ
MT   ...... הָיוּ ...

§90: Agreement in number between several verbs.

a) adjustment to the preceding verb:

Ex. 39.3 MT   וַיְרַקְּעוּ ... וְקִצֵּץ
S   .... וקצצו

Lev. 14.42 MT   .. וְהֵבִיא ... וְלָקְחוּ
יַקַּח וְשָׂח
S   .... יקחו וטחו

Lev. 19.27 MT   לֹא תַקִּפוּ ... וְלֹא תַשְׁחִית
S   .... תשחיתו

Num. 13.2 MT   שְׁלַח ... תִּשְׁלָחוּ
S   .... תשלח

Num. 21.32 MT   וַיִּלְכְּדוּ ... וַיּוֹרֶשׁ
S   .... ויורישו

Deut. 12.5 MT   תִדְרְשׁוּ וּבָאתָ
S   ..... ובאתם

b) adjustment to the following verb:

Ex. 10.17 MT   שָׂא ... וְהַעְתִּירוּ
S   .... ³⁰⁵שאו

Ex. 12.46 MT   לֹא תוֹצִיא .. לֹא תִשְׁבְּרוּ
S   .... תוציאו

Num. 31.29 MT   תִּקְחוּ וְנָתַתָּה
S   ..... תקח

Num. 33.54 MT   תָּמְעִיט ... תַּרְבּוּ
S   .... תרבה

Deut. 4.25 MT   כִּי תוֹלִיד ...
וְנוֹשַׁנְתֶּם ... וְהִשְׁחַתֶּם
S   .... תולידו .

³⁰⁰ Cf. Ex. 29.10, 19: וסמך אהרן ובניו
Ex. 29.15: וסמכו אהרן ובניו.
³⁰¹ Cf. Gen. 41.50; Num. 26.33.
³⁰² Cf. Lev. 8.14.
³⁰³ Cf. Gen. 35.26.
³⁰⁴ Cf. Josh. 6.19; Judg. 11.15; 1 Ki. 20.3; Ezek. 44.9.
³⁰⁵ Cf. Judg. 18.9: קומה ונעלה, Venice 1515 marg.: קומו ונעלה.

312

Deut. 12.16 MT לֹא תֹאכְלוּ .. תִּשְׁפְּכֶנּוּ
s .... תֹאכַל ..

Isa. 36.7 תֹאמַר ... בָּטָחְנוּ
2 Ki. 18.22 ...... תֹאמְרוּן

§91: Collective nouns used in the sing. or plur. (B-L §63x):

Lev. 20.27 MT בְּאֹבֶן
s באבנים

Lev. 8.13 MT אַבְנֵט
s אבניטים

1 Chron. 10.7 אִישׁ
1 Sam. 31.7 אֲנָשֵׁי³⁰⁶

2 Ki. 25.17 K אמה
Q אַמּוֹת

1 Ki. 10.22 אֳנִי (1°)
2 Chron. 9.21 אֳנִיּוֹת

Gen. 41.57 MT הָאָרֶץ
s הארצות

2 Ki. 21.3 אֲשֵׁרָה
2 Chron. 33.3 אֲשֵׁרוֹת

1 Chron. 19.10 בָחוּר
2 Sam. 10.9 בָחוּרֵי

Num. 3.50 MT בְּכוֹר
s בכורי³⁰⁷

2 Ki. 21.3 לַבַּעַל
2 Chron. 33.3 לַבְּעָלִים

Ex. 35.28 MT הַבֹּשֶׂם
s הבשמים

1 Ki. 12.24 דְּבַר
2 Chron. 11.4 דִּבְרֵי³⁰⁸

Ex. 22.1 s דם
MT דָּמִים

2 Ki. 16.3 בְּדֶרֶךְ
2 Chron. 28.2 בְּדַרְכֵי³⁰⁹

Ps. 18.49 חָמָס
2 Sam. 22.49 חֲמָסִים

2 Ki. 11.10 הַחֲנִית
2 Chron. 23.9 הַחֲנִיתִים

1 Sam. 20.38 K החצי
Q הַחִצִּים

2 Ki. 12.12 K יד
Q יָדֵי

Gen. 17.13 MT יְלִיד
s יְלִידֵי³¹⁰

1 Ki. 10.14 כִּכַּר
2 Chron. 9.13 כִּכְּרֵי

2 Chron. 9.19 (וְכָל) מַמְלָכָה
1 Ki. 10.20 מַמְלָכוֹת

³⁰⁶ Cf. 1 Chron. 10.1 — 1 Sam. 31.1.
³⁰⁷ Cf. Num. 3.46.
³⁰⁸ Cf. MT–s on Deut. 5.5.
³⁰⁹ Cf. 2 Ki. 8.27 — 2 Chron. 22.3; 2 Ki. 22.2 — 2 Chron. 34.2; also
2 Chron. 21.13: בְּדֶרֶךְ, Venice 1515 marg.: בְּדַרְכֵי.
³¹⁰ Cf. Lev. 22.11.

Num. 4.15 MT   מַשָּׂא
s   משאי

Lev. 25.5 MT   סְפִיחַ
s   ספיחי

Deut. 32.14 MT   עֵנָב
s   ענבים

Lev. 23.40 MT   וַעֲנַף
s   וענפי

2 Sam. 5.11   עֵץ[311]
1 Chron. 14.1   עֵצִים

1 Chron. 6.45   עִיר
Josh. 21.19   עָרִים

Num. 15.38 MT   צִיצִת
s   ציציות

Gen. 15.10 MT   הַצִּפֹּר
s   הצפרים

Ex. 26.20 MT   קֶרֶשׁ
s   קרשים

Num. 11.31 s   שְׂלָו
MT   שְׂלָיו

2 Ki. 22.1   שָׁנָה
2 Chron. 34.1   שָׁנִים[312]

---

§92: The subject: a collective noun — the predicate: in the plur. or sing.:

Josh. 9.7 Q   [313]וַיֹּאמֶר אִישׁ יִשְׂרָאֵל
K   ויאמרו ......

Ex. 15.24 MT   וַיִּלֹּנוּ הָעָם
s   [314]וַיִּלֶן ...

1 Chron. 11.13   וְהָעָם נָסוּ
2 Sam. 23.11   [315]... נָס

2 Chron. 36.1   וַיִּקְחוּ עַם הָאָרֶץ
2 Ki. 23.30   [316]וַיִּקַּח ......

Gen. 15.16 MT   וְדוֹר רְבִיעִי יָשׁוּבוּ
s   ישוב ......

2 Chron. 18.18   עֹמְדִים ... צָבָא
1 Ki. 22.19   עֹמֵד ......

Num. 22.4 MT   יְלַחֲכוּ הַקָּהָל
s   ילחך .....

a) names of nations:

1 Chron. 18.13   וַיִּהְיוּ כָל אֱדוֹם
2 Sam. 8.14   וַיְהִי......

Hos. 12.9 seb   וַיֹּאמְרוּ אֶפְרַיִם
MT   וַיֹּאמֶר .....

1 Chron. 19.16   אֲרָם ... נִגְּפוּ
2 Sam. 10.15   נִגַּף ......

---

[311] Cf. Ezek. 15.6: בְּעֵץ, Venice 1515 marg.: בָּעֵץ.

[312] Cf. MT–s on Gen. 17.24; K–Q on 2 Ki. 8.17; and 2 Ki. 24.8 — 2 Chron. 36.9; cf. also 2 Sam. 2.10: שנים (ושתים), Venice 1515 marg.: שָׁנָה.

[313] Cf. Judg. 18.11: שש מאות איש חָגוּר כְּלֵי מלחמה   Judg. 18.16: שש מאות איש חֲגוּרִים כלי מלחמה.

[314] Cf. Num. 14.1; Ex. 16.30; also 1 Ki. 12.5 — 2 Chron. 10.5.

[315] Cf. MT–s on Ex. 24.2; also s–MT on Num. 12.15.

[316] Cf. 2 Chron. 23.21 — 2 Ki. 11.20; 2 Chron. 33.25 — 2 Ki. 21.24.

1 Chron. 11.4	הַיְבוּסִי יֹשְׁבֵי הָאָרֶץ	1 Chron. 18.2	וַיְהִי מוֹאָב
2 Sam. 5.6	יוֹשֵׁב .... [317]	2 Sam. 8.2	וַתְּהִי[318]....
2 Chron. 10.1	בָּאוּ כָל יִשְׂרָאֵל	Ex. 14.10 MT	מִצְרַיִם נֹסֵעַ
1 Ki. 12.1	בָּא	S	נֹסְעִים ... [319]

II. THE ARTICLE.

§93: *The article is used* (Bergstr. §21)		Ezek. 18.2 K	וְשָׁנִי בנים
		Q	הַבָּנִים ...
a) in a construct state formation:[320]		2 Ki. 15.25 K	בֵּית מלך
		Q	הַמֶּלֶךְ ...[321]
1 Chron. 8.28	רָאשֵׁי אָבוֹת	2 Ki. 25.28 K	כִּסֵּא מלכים
1 Chron. 9.34	הָאָבוֹת	Q	הַמְּלָכִים ...[322]
Ps. 96.12	עֲצֵי יָעַר	Eccl. 7.2 Ma	בֵּית מִשְׁתֶּה
1 Chron. 16.33	הַיָּעַר ...	Md	המשתה ...
2 Sam. 8.13	בְּנִיא מֶלַח	2 Ki. 11.20 K	עַם ארץ
1 Chron. 18.12	הַמֶּלַח ...	Q	הָאָרֶץ ..[323]
2 Sam. 7.2	בְּבֵית אֲרָזִים	2 Chron. 4.1 Ma	מִזְבַּח נְחֹשֶׁת
1 Chron. 17.1	הָאֲרָזִים	Md	הנחשת ....
2 Sam. 5.24	קוֹל צְעָדָה	2 Chron. 8.9	אַנְשֵׁי מִלְחָמָה
1 Chron. 14.15	הַצְּעָדָה ...	1 Ki. 9.22	הַמִּלְחָמָה ...
Jer. 17.19 K	בְּנֵי עם	2 Chron. 9.14	מַלְכֵי עֶרֶב
Q	הָעָם ...	1 Ki. 10.15	הָעֶרֶב ....
Jer. 32.19 K	בְּנֵי אדם	Jer. 38.11 Q	בְּלוֹיֵ סְחָבוֹת
Q	הָאָדָם ...	K	הסחבות ...

[317] Cf. Md–Ma on Judg. 1.21.
[318] On the difference in the gender of the verb, cf. §88 γ.
[319] Cf. Ex. 14.25.
[320] Cf. TRL s. v. רשע: Ps. 1.1: MT רשעים (בעצת) — o הרשעים; s. v. עצבים:
Ps. 127.2: MT העצבים (לחם) — o עצבים.
[321] Cf. 2 Ki. 11.20; 15.18.
[322] Cf. Jer. 52.32.
[323] Cf. Jer. 10.13.

b) in connection with a
preposition:

1 Sam. 14.32	K	אֶל שְׁלָל
	Q	...הַשָּׁלָל

1 Ki. 22.31	אֶת קָטֹן וְאֶת גָּדוֹל
2 Chron. 18.30	הַגָּדוֹל ...הַקָּטֹן...

2 Sam. 23.21	אֶת אִישׁ מִצְרִי
1 Chron. 11.23	...הָאִישׁ הַמִּצְרִי

2 Ki. 15.25	K	וְאֶת אַרְיֵה
	Q	...הָאַרְיֵה

Lam. 1.18	K	כָּל עַמִּים [324]
	Q	...הָעַמִּים

1 Ki. 7.21	K	לְעֹבֵר שבכה
	Q	...הַשְּׂבָכָה

2 Sam. 5.23	מִמּוּל בְּכָאִים
1 Chron. 14.14	...הַבְּכָאִים

2 Sam. 7.16	עַד עוֹלָם (1°)
1 Chron. 17.14	...הָעוֹלָם

1 Ki. 4.7	K	עַל אֶחָד
	Q	...הָאֶחָד

c) when the noun is rendered
emphatic in other ways:[325]

Jer. 40.3	K	דבר הֶזֶּה
	Q	...הַדָּבָר

Jer. 27.3	K	מַלְאָכִים הַבָּאִים
	Q	...הַמלאכים

2 Sam. 23.30	בְּנָיְהוּ פִרְעָתֹנִי
1 Chron. 11.31	....הַפִּרְעָתֹנִי

1 Ki. 9.17:	בֵּית חֹרֹן תַּחְתּוֹן
2 Chr. 8. 5:	.....הַתַּחְתּוֹן

d) when the noun is otherwise
undetermined:[326]

2 Sam. 7.5	תִּבְנֶה לִי בָיִת
1 Chron. 17.4	......הַבָּיִת

2 Chron. 9.6	לֹא הֻגַּד לִי חֲצִי
1 Ki. 10.7	.......הַחֵצִי

1 Chron. 20.5	וַתְּהִי עוֹד מִלְחָמָה
2 Sam. 21.19	......הַמִּלְחָמָה

*§94: The emphatic state is indi-
cated by the article or suffix:*

Gen. 38.21	MT	מְקֹמָהּ
	S	המקום

Lev. 3.8	MT	דָּמוֹ [327]
	S	הדם

1 Chron. 10.7	עָרֵיהֶם
2 Sam. 31.7	הֶעָרִים

---

[324] Cf. Deut. 11.24: כל הַמָּקוֹם אשר תדרך כף רגלכם בו
Josh. 1.3: כל מָקוֹם אשר תדרך כף רגלכם בו.
[325] Cf. Ex. 29.39: את הכבש הָאֶחָד תעשה בבקר
Num. 28.4: את הכבש אֶחָד תעשה בבקר; cf. also Ezek. 40.31: חָצֵר
הַחֲצוֹנָה; Venice 1515 marg.: הֶחָצֵר.
[326] Cf. Josh. 15.18: ויהי בבואה ותסיתהו לשאול מאת אביה שָׂדֶה
Judg. 1.14: ויהי בבואה ותסיתהו לשאול מאת אביה הַשָּׂדֶה; cf. also TRL
s. v.: אֶרֶץ: Ps. 46.3: MT אֶרֶץ (בהמיר) o — הָאָרֶץ.
[327] Cf. Lev. 1.11: חרקו בני אהרן הכהנים את דָּמוֹ
Lev. 3.2: חרקו בני אהרן הכהנים את הַדָּם.

2 Chron. 23.13 עֲמוּדוֹ
2 Ki. 11.14 הָעַמּוּד328

2 Sam. 10.18 צְבָאוֹ
1 Chron. 19.18 הַצָּבָא

1 Sam. 31.5 חַרְבּוֹ
1 Chron. 10.5 הֶחָרֶב

a) the article is assimilated to an inseparable preposition:

2 Sam. 24.13 בְּאַרְצֶךָ
1 Chron. 21.12 בָּאָרֶץ
2 Chron. 9.6 לְדִבְרֵיהֶם
1 Ki. 10.7 לַדְּבָרִים
1 Ki. 22.34 לְרִכְבּוֹ
2 Chron. 18.33 לָרֶכֶב
Ezek. 29.7 K בכפך
      Q בְּכַף

§95: The article includes the meaning of a demonstrative pronoun (B-L §30i):329

a) masc. sing.:

Gen. 3.3 MT הָעֵץ
    S העץ הזה

Gen. 19.12 MT הַמָּקוֹם
    S המקום הזה

Num. 22.4 MT הַקָּהָל
    S הקהל הזה

Num. 29.12 MT לַחֹדֶשׁ הַשְּׁבִיעִי
    S לחדש השביעי הזה

2 Ki. 20.9 אֶת הַדָּבָר
Isa. 38.7 אֶת הַדָּבָר הַזֶּה

2 Chron. 10.10 לָעָם
1 Ki. 12.10 לָעָם הַזֶּה330

β) fem. sing.:

Gen. 21.13 MT הָאָמָה
    S האמה הזאת

1 Ki. 8.44 הָעִיר
2 Chron. 6.34 הָעִיר הַזֹּאת

γ) plural:

Gen. 48.16 MT אֶת הַנְּעָרִים
    S את הנערים האלה

2 Ki. 18.35 הָאֲרָצוֹת
Isa. 36.20 הָאֲרָצוֹת הָאֵלֶּה

§96: Preservation of the article with an inseparable preposition (B-L §25 w, x; Bergstr. §16b):331

a) with the preposition ב:

Deut. 21.1 MT בָּאֲדָמָה
    S בהאדמה

---

328 Cf. 2 Chron. 34.31 — 2 Ki. 23.3.
329 Cf. *MGWJ* 1937, p. 64, on Ruth 3.13.
330 Cf. MT–s on Deut. 10.11.
331 The vocalization of the בכל with a pataḥ does not necessarily imply the assimilation of the Article; cf. TRL paragraph XXVI e. Similarly, no consistent rules can be established for their vocalization with pataḥ or ḳamez (Bergstr. §28p.); cf. 1 Ki. 8.12: בָּעֲרָפֶל — 2 Chron. 6.1: בְּעַרפל; 2 Chron. 1. 15: כָּאֲבָנִים — 1 Ki. 10.27: כַּאבנים; Ezek. 7.19: בְּחוצוֹת, Venice 1515 marg.: בַּחֻצוֹת.

Gen. 8.5 MT   בָּעֲשִׂירִי

       s   בהעשירי

2 Ki. 7.12 Q   בַּשָּׂדֶה

       K   בהשדה

b) with the preposition כ:

Gen. 3.5 MT   כֵּאלֹהִים

       s   כהאלהים

Deut. 6.24 s   כיום הזה

       MT   כְּהַיּוֹם הַזֶּה

c) with the preposition ל:

Gen. 1.5 MT   לָאוֹר

       s   להאור

Ex. 1.20 MT   לַמְיַלְּדֹת

       s   להטילדות

1 Ki. 12.7   לָעָם הַזֶּה

2 Chron. 10.7   לְהָעָם הַזֶּה

d) the prefixed ה in verbal formations:

Deut. 1.33 MT   לַחֲנֹתְכֶם

        s   להחנותכם

Ex. 13.21 MT   לַנְחֹתָם

        s   להנחתם

Deut. 1.33 MT   לַרְאֹתְכֶם

        s   להראותכם

2 Ki. 9.15 K   לנגיד[332]

        Q   לְהַגִּיד

2 Ki. 7.15 Q   בְּחָפְזָם

        K   בהחפזם

III. THE VERB.

§97: *The use of the consecutive waw* (Bergstr. §2i).

a) with the perfect:

Ex. 8.12 MT   וְהָיָה

       s   ויהי

Josh. 19.29 Q   וְהָיוּ

        K   ויהיו[333]

Gen. 27.4 s   והבאת

        MT   וְהֵבֵיאָה

Ex. 3.10 s   והוצאת

      MT   וְהוֹצֵא[334]

2 Chron. 18.33   וְהוֹצִיאֵנִי

1 Ki. 22.34   וְהוֹצִיאֵנִי

Ex. 8.23 MT   וְזָבַחְנוּ

       s   ונזבחה

1 Chron. 14.10   הַאֶעֱלֶה ... וּנְתַתָּם

2 Sam. 5.19   הַאֶעֱלֶה ... הַתִּתְּנֵם

---

[332] Cf. Jer. 39.7: MT לְבִיא for לְהָבִיא.

[333] Cf. K–Q on Jer. 18.23.

[334] On the difference between this example and the preceding one, cf. §106 c.

Lev. 26.43 s   והרצתה[335]
      MT   וְתִרֶץ

b) with the imperfect:

Gen. 27.22 MT   וַיְמֻשֵּׁהוּ
          s   והמשהו

Isa. 36.21   וַיַּחֲרִישׁוּ
2 Ki. 18.36   וְהַחֲרִישׁוּ

2 Sam. 19.41 K   ויעברו
            Q   הֶעָבִירוּ

Prov. 22.3 K   רָאָה . . . וַיִּסָּתֵר
          Q   . . . . . . וְנִסְתָּר

1 Ki. 12.16   וַיַּרְא כָּל יִשְׂרָאֵל
2 Chron. 10.16   וְכָל יִשְׂרָאֵל רָאוּ

2 Ki. 19.26   וַיֵּבֹשׁוּ
Isa. 37.27   וּבֹשׁוּ

1 Chron. 15.29   וַיְהִי
2 Sam. 6.16   וְהָיָה

Gen. 37.3 s   ויעש
        MT   וְעָשָׂה

§98: The use of the inf. absol.or imperative (Bergstr. 2, §12k):

Deut. 31.26 MT   לָקֹחַ
          s   ללקחו[336]

Num. 25.17 MT   צָרוֹר
          s   צררו

Num. 15.35 MT   רָגוֹם
          s   רגמו

Deut. 1.16 MT   שָׁמֹעַ
          s   שמעו

Deut. 27.1 MT   שָׁמֹר
          s   שמרו

2 Sam. 24.12   הָלוֹךְ
1 Chron. 21.10   לָךְ

Ps. 105.8   זָכַר[337]
1 Chron. 16.15   זִכְרוּ[338]

§99: Particle and verb: the verb in the inf. constr. or finite tense (Bergstr. 2, §11):

a) אחרי:

Gen. 46.30 MT   אַחֲרֵי רְאוֹתִי
          s   רָאִיתִי . . . .

Deut. 12.30 MT אַחֲרֵי הִשָּׁמְדָם
          s   הַשְׁמִידָם . . . .

b) למען; לבלתי:

Deut. 17.20 MT לְבִלְתִּי רוּם
          s   רָאם . . . . .[339]

Jer. 17.23 Q   לְבִלְתִּי שְׁמוֹעַ
          K   שׁוֹמֵעַ . . . . .

Jer. 25.7 Q   לְמַעַן הַכְעִיסֵנִי
          K   הַכְעַסוּנִי . . . .

---

[335] On this form, cf. Lev. 26.34: MT וְהִרְצָת — s והרצתה; 25.21: MT וְעָשָׂת —
s וְעָשְׂתָה; 2 Ki. 9.37: K והית — Q וְהָיְתָה.
[336] Cf. Ex. 29.1: לָקַח; 1 Ki. 17.11: לָקְחִי.
[337] Lege זְכֹר.
[338] Cf. MT–s on Ex. 13.3.
[339] Cf. §38 a.

c) עַד:

Gen. 39.16	MT	עַד בּוֹא
	s	...בָּא.[340]
Gen. 27.45	MT	עַד שׁוּב
	s	...שׁב.
Num. 32.18	MT	עַד הִתְנַחֵל
	s	...התנחלו.
Deut. 28.20	MT	עַד הִשָּׁמֶדְךָ
		וְעַד אֲבָדְךָ
	s	...הׁשמידוך.[341]
		האבידוך

d) בְּיוֹם:

Num. 3.13	MT	בְּיוֹם הַכֹּתִי
	s	....הכיתי.
Num. 9.15	MT	וּבְיוֹם הָקִים
	s	....הוקם.[342]

§100: Inf. constr. with בכלם
and pronominal suffixes.

a) with the preposition בְּ:

| Gen. 19.29 | MT | בַּהֲפֹךְ |
| | s | בהפכו |

b) with the preposition כְּ:

Gen. 33.10	MT	כִּרְאֹת
	s	כראותי
Gen. 24.30	MT	כִּרְאֹת
	s	כראותו

c) with the preposition לְ:

Gen. 28.4	s	לרשת
	MT	לְרִשְׁתְּךָ
Ex. 28.1	s	לכהן
	MT	לְכַהֲנוֹ
Deut. 21.5	s	לשרת
	MT	לְשָׁרְתוֹ
1 Chron. 17.4		לָשֶׁבֶת
2 Sam. 7.5		לְשִׁבְתִּי
2 Ki. 21.6		לְהַכְעִיס
2 Chron. 33.6		לְהַכְעִיסוֹ

d) with the preposition מְ:

Deut. 16.9	MT	מֵהָחֵל
	s	מהחלך
1 Chron. 11.19		מַעֲשׂוֹת
2 Sam. 23.17		מַעֲשֹׂתִי

§101: Finite verb continued by
inf. absol. or finite tense (B-L
§36e', h'; Bergstr. 2, §12h):[343]

Gen. 8.3	MT	וַיָּשֻׁבוּ ... הָלוֹךְ וָשׁוֹב
	s	......הלכו ושבו
Gen. 8.5	MT	הָיוּ הָלוֹךְ וְחָסוֹר
	s	...הלכו וחסרו
Gen. 8.7	MT	וַיֵּצֵא יָצוֹא וָשׁוֹב
	s	.. יצא ושב
Gen. 12.9	MT	וַיִּסַּע ... הָלוֹךְ וְנָסוֹעַ
	s	.......הלך ונסע

[340] Cf. Gen. 43.24.
[341] Cf. Deut. 7.23; further: Jer. 52.3: (עַד)הִשְׁלִיכוֹ, Venice 1515 marg.:
הַשְׁלִיכוּ.
[342] On the change from hiph'il to hoph'al cf. §61e.
[343] Cf. TRL paragraph XXXIII subdivision 3 sub 1.

ALEXANDER SPERBER

Ex. 8.11 MT	וַיַּרְא ... וְהַכְבֵּד	2 Chron. 25.28	וַיִּשָּׂאֻהוּ
s	...... ויכבד	2 Ki. 14.20	וַיִּשְׂאוּ אֹתוֹ
Isa. 37.18, 19	הֶחֱרִיבוּ ... וְנָתֹן	2 Chron. 36.1	וַיַּמְלִיכֻהוּ
2 Ki. 19.17, 18	וְנָתְנוּ	2 Ki. 23.30	וַיַּמְלִיכוּ אֹתוֹ
Isa. 37.30 K	זְרְעוּ וְקִצְרוּ וְנִטְעוּ ...	2 Chron. 23.14	הוֹצִיאוּהָ
	וְאָכוֹל	2 Ki. 11.15	הוֹצִיאוּ אֹתָהּ
Q	וְאִכְלוּ 344	Num. 24.10 MT	קְרָאתִיךָ
		s	קראתי לך

§102: Verbal forms with pronominal suffixes (Bergstr. §2i)[345]

The pronominal suffix is added to the verb or to the particle את (cf. §119):

		1 Chron. 19.12	וְהוֹשַׁעְתִּיךָ
		2 Sam. 10.11	לְהוֹשִׁיעַ לָךְ
Lev. 10.5 MT	וַיִּשָּׂאֻם	Ps. 18.20	וַיּוֹצִיאֵנִי
s	וישאו אתם	2 Sam. 22.20	וַיֹּצֵא ... אֹתִי
Deut. 9.28 MT	לַהֲבִיאָם	2 Chron. 10.13	וַיַּעֲנֵם
s	להביא אתם	1 Ki. 12.13	וַיַּעַן .. אֶת הָעָם
		1 Ki. 10.1	לְנַסֹּתוֹ
		2 Chron. 9.1	לְנַסּוֹת אֶת שְׁלֹמֹה

IV. THE ה EUPHONICUM.

A. With verbal forms.
§103: Ḳal.
a) 1. pers. sing. imperf.
1) the regular verb.
a) imperfect in o:

		Ps. 18.38	אֶרְדּוֹף
		2 Sam. 22.38	אֶרְדְּפָה
Gen. 30.32 MT	אֶעֱבֹר	Ex. 6.5 MT	וָאֶזְכֹּר
s	אעברה	s	ואזכרה
		Deut. 10.2 MT	וְאֶכְתֹּב
		s	ואכתבה

344 = 2 Ki. 19.29. Cf. likewise 2 Ki. 21.13: ...... כַּאֲשֶׁר יָמָחָה...מָחָה וְהָפַךְ; the proposed correction in מחה והפך (BHK) is, therefore, basically erroneous.

345 Cf. Lev. 6.22: כל זכר בכהנים יאכל אתה; Lev. 7.6: כל זכר בכהנים יאכלנו; Num. 18.11: כל טהור בביתך יאכל אתו; Num. 18.13: כל טהור בביתך יאכלנו. Consequently, readings like: Ex. 2.6: MT ותראהו את הילד (cf. s ותרא); ib. 35.5: יָבִיאָהָ את תרומת יהוה (cf s יביא) represent doublets; cf. our note 419 on §124 b 8.

321

Deut. 10.3 MT וָאֶפְסֹל
S ואפסלה

Lev. 26.13 MT וָאֶשְׁבֹּר
S ואשברה

Deut. 9.21 MT וָאֶשְׂרֹף
S ואשרפה

Deut. 9.17 MT וָאֲתַפֵּשׂ
S ואתפשה

β) imperfect in a:[346]

Deut. 22.14 MT וָאֶקְרַב
S ואקרבה

Deut. 2.26 MT וָאֶשְׁלַח
S ואשלחה

Jer. 8.6 K וָאַשְׁמַע
Q ואשמעה

2) weak verbs.

γ) imperfect in i:

Ex. 3.8 MT וָאֵרֵד
S וארדה

Gen. 34.12 s ואתן
MT וְאֶתְּנָה

δ) imperfect in a:

Gen. 18.5 s ואקח
MT וְאֶקְחָה

Num. 22.19 s ואדע
MT וְאֵדְעָה[347]

ε) primae א:

Ex. 3.17 MT וָאֹמַר
S ואמרה

Gen. 27.25 s ואכל
MT וָאֹכְלָה

ʃ) primae נ:

Deut. 9.21 MT וָאַכֹּת
S ואכתה

1 Chron. 21.13 אֶפֹּל
2 Sam. 24.14 אֶפְּלָה

η) mediae ו and י:

Isa. 37.24 וָאָבוֹא
2 Ki. 19.23 וְאָבוֹאָה
Ex. 3.3 s אסור
MT אָסֻרָה
Deut. 10.5 MT וָאָשִׂם
S ואשימה

b) 1. pers. plur. imperf.

1) the regular verb.

a) imperfect in o:

Gen. 41.11 s ונחלם
MT וַנַּחַלְמָה

Deut. 3.4 MT וַנִּלְכֹּד
S ונלכדה

Deut. 2.13 MT וַנַּעֲבֹר
S ונעברה

---

[346] Cf. TRL s. v. שמח: Ps. 31.8: MT וְאֶשְׂמְחָה — o וָאֶשְׂמַח.
[347] Cf. K–Q on Ruth 4.4.

ALEXANDER SPERBER

β) imperfect in a:[348]

Ex. 8.22 MT נִזְבַּח
S נזבחה

Gen. 43.21 S ונפתח
MT וַנִּפְתְּחָה

Gen. 24.57 S ונשאל
MT וְנִשְׁאֲלָה

2) weak verbs.

γ) imperfect in i:

Ex. 8.23 MT נֵלֵךְ
S נלכה

Num. 14.4 S נתן
MT נִתְּנָה

δ) imperfect in a:

Gen. 19.5 S ונדע
MT וְנֵדְעָה

Deut. 1.19 MT וַנִּסַּע
S ונסעה

ε) primae א:

Num. 11.13 S ונאכל
MT וְנֹאכְלָה

Gen. 34.23 S נאות
MT נֵאוֹתָה

ζ) mediae ו:

Gen. 35.3 s תקום
MT וְנָקוּמָה

Num. 14.4 s ונשוב
MT וְנָשׁוּבָה[349]

c) imperative (Bergstr. 2, §5f).

α) imperfect in o:

Num. 21.16 MT אֱסֹף
S אספה

β) imperfect in a:

Isa. 37.17 Q פְּקַח
K פקחה

Gen. 15.9 s קח
MT קְחָה

Gen. 43.8 s שלח
MT שִׁלְחָה

Num. 23.18 MT וּשְׁמַע
S ושמעה

γ) imperfect in i:

Gen. 19.9 MT נַּשׁ
S נשה

2 Chron. 25.17 לֵךְ
2 Ki. 14.8 לְכָה

2 Ki. 14.10 וְשֵׁב
2 Chron. 25.19 שְׁבָה

[348] Cf. in §50a the instance from Num. 14.41, and our note 118 thereon.
[349] Cf. K-Q on Lam. 5.21.

323

Gen. 14.21 MT קַן
      S תנה

δ) mediae ו:[350]

Num. 23.18 MT קום
      S קומה

Gen. 27.3 S וצוד
      MT וְצוּדָה

d) infinitive:

Ex. 36.2 S לקרב
      MT לְקָרְבָה

Gen. 1.30 S לאכל
      MT לְאָכְלָה

§104: Pi'el.

a) 1. pers. sing. imperf.:

Gen. 12.3 S ואברך
      MT וַאֲבָרְכָה

Num. 24.13 MT אֲדַבֵּר
      S אדברה

2 Sam. 22.50 אֲזַמֵּר
Ps. 18.50 אֲזַמְּרָה

Ex. 32.30 S אכפר
      MT אֲכַפְּרָה

Ex. 9.28 S ואשלח
      MT וַאֲשַׁלְּחָה

b) 3. pers. fem. sing. imperf.:

Ezek. 23.16 K ותעגב
      Q וַתַּעְגְּבָה

c) imperative:

2 Chron. 18.8 מַהַר
1 Ki. 22.9 מַהֲרָה

§105: Niph'al.

a) 1. pers. sing. imperf.:

Gen. 19.20 S אמלט
      MT אִמָּלְטָה

Hag. 1.8 K ואכבד
      Q וְאֶכָּבְדָה

b) imperative:

Gen. 25.33 S השבע
      MT הִשָּׁבְעָה

c) infinitive:

Num. 12.15 MT הֵאָסֵף
      S האספה

§106: Hiph'il.

a) 1. pers. sing. imperf.:

1 Chron. 17.8 וָאַכְרִית
2 Sam. 7.9 וָאַכְרִתָה

Deut. 32.20 S אסתיר
      MT אַסְתִּירָה

Deut. 32.26 S אשבית
      MT אַשְׁבִּיתָה

Deut. 9.21 MT וָאַשְׁלַךְ
      S ואשליכה

[350] Cf. TRL s. v. קום: Ps. 35,2: MT וְקוּמָה — o קום.

324

a) primae י:

Gen. 32.10 s ואיטב
        MT וְאֵיטִיבָה

Gen. 19.8 s אוצא
        MT אוֹצִיאָה

β) mediae ו:

Josh. 24.8 Q וָאָבִיא
        K ואביאה

b) 1. pers. plur. imperf.:

Deut. 3.6 MT וַנַּחֲרֵם
       s ונחרימה

c) imperative:

Gen. 27.7 s הבא
      MT הָבִיאָה

Lam. 5.1 K הביט
      Q הַבִּיטָה

2 Chron. 16.3   הָפֵר
1 Ki. 15.19   הָפֵרָה

Deut. 26.15 s השקף
       MT הַשְׁקִיפָה

§107: Hithpa'el.

a) 1. pers. sing. imperf.:

Deut. 9.18 MT וָאֶתְנַפַּל
       s ואתנפלה

Deut. 9.20 MT וָאֶתְפַּלֵּל
       s ואתפללה

Ps. 18.24   וָאֶשְׁתַּמֵּר
2 Sam. 22.24   וָאֶשְׁתַּמְּרָה

b) 1. pers. plur. imperf.:

2 Sam. 10.12   וְנִתְחַזַּק
1 Chron. 19.13   וְנִתְחַזְּקָה

Ex. 1.10 s נתחכם
      MT נִתְחַכְּמָה

B. With nouns and particles.

§108: The so-called ה locativum.

a) the noun in the construct state (B-L §65n):[351]

Gen. 12.5 MT אַרְצָה כְּנָעַן
      s ....ארץ.[352]

Ex. 34.26 s ביתה יהוה
      MT בֵית ....

Ex. 10.19 MT יָמָה סוּף
      s ים ....

Num. 34.5 MT נַחְלָה מִצְרַיִם
      s נחל ......

b) the noun in the emphatic state:

Ex. 33.9 MT הָאֹהֱלָה
      s האהל

---

[351] Cf. Deut. 4.41: בעבר הירדן מִזְרָחָה שמש;
    Deut. 4.47: בעבר הירדן מִזְרָח שמש. See also TRL paragraph XXXIII, subdivision 3, sub 3.
[352] Cf. similarly Gen. 20.1; 29.1; 32.4; 46.28; Ex. 4.20.

Gen. 37.24	MT	הַבֹּרָה	Num. 13.21 s	חמתה
	s	הבור	MT	חֲמָת
1 Sam. 9.26	Q	הַגָּגָה	Isa. 36.2	יְרוּשָׁלְמָה
	K	הגג	2 Ki. 18.17	יְרוּשָׁלִַם
Ex. 1.22	MT	הַיְאֹרָה	2 Chron. 36.4	מִצְרָיְמָה
	s	היאר	2 Ki. 23.34	מִצְרַיִם
Num. 14.25 s		המדברה	Gen. 13.10 s	צערה
	MT	הַמִּדְבָּר	MT	צֹעַר
Lev. 5.12	MT	הַמִּזְבֵּחָה	2 Chron. 10.1	שְׁכֶמָה
	s	המזבח	1 Ki. 12.1	שְׁכֶם
Ex. 7.15	MT	הַמַּיְמָה	2 Ki. 14.14	שֹׁמְרוֹנָה
	s	המים	2 Chron. 25.24	שֹׁמְרֹן
Gen. 24.16	MT	הָעַיְנָה		
	s	העין		

d) the ה clearly a euphonic
ending only:

1 Chron. 19.15		הָעִירָה
2 Sam. 10.14		הָעִיר
Gen. 19.16	MT	הַפֶּתְחָה
	s	הפתח
2 Chron. 6.13		הַשָּׁמַיְמָה
1 Ki. 8.22		הַשָּׁמַיִם³⁵³

Deut. 3.17 MT וְהָעֲרָבָה וְהַיַּרְדֵּן
s ......והירדנה

Deut. 23.14 MT בְּשִׁבְתְּךָ חוּץ
s ..... החוצה

c) proper names:

Gen. 10.4 וְתַרְשִׁישׁ
1 Chron. 1.7 וְתַרְשִׁישָׁה

Ex. 15.27	MT	אֵילִמָה
	s	אילים
2 Ki. 20.17		בָּבֶלָה
Isa. 39.6		בָּבֶל

1 Chron. 10.12 בְּיָבֵשׁ
1 Sam. 31.13 בְּיָבֵשָׁה

Ex. 38.12 MT וְלִפְאַת יָם
s .....ימה³⁵⁴

Gen. 46.1 MT בְּאֵרָה שֶׁבַע
s באר .....

Num. 34.3 MT גְּבוּל נֶגֶב
s נגבה...³⁵⁵

353 Cf. similarly MT–s on Gen. 15.5; 28.12; Ex. 9.8, 10; Deut. 4.19; 30.12.
354 Cf. Ex. 27.12.
355 Cf. Ex. 27.9; 36.23; 38.9.

Ex. 36.25   MT   לִפְאַת צָפוֹן
     S   צפונה .... [356]

Gen. 50.3   MT   וַיִּבְכּוּ אֹתוֹ מִצְרַיִם
     S   מצרימה ....

§109: Particles and pronouns (B-L §28p, q; §65x):

Deut. 7.17   MT   אֵיכָה
     S   איך [357]

Gen. 27.39   MT   הִנֵּה
     S   הן [358]

Gen. 43.30   MT   שָׁמָּה
     S   שׁם [359]

Num. 17.11   MT   מְהֵרָה
     S   מהר [360]

Gen. 31.6   MT   וְאַתֵּנָה
     S   ואתין

2 Chron. 8.9   הֵמָּה [361]
1 Ki. 9.22   הֵם

Num. 9.7   MT   הָהֵמָּה
     S   הָהֵם [362]

Ex. 36.1   MT   בָּהֵמָּה [363]
     S   בהם

Lev. 5.22   MT   בָּהֵנָּה
     S   בהן [364]

Gen. 41.19   MT   כָּהֵנָּה
     S   כהן

Lev. 4.2   MT   מֵהֵנָּה
     S   מהן

V. PREPOSITIONS AND PARTICLES.

§110: The prepositions ב and כ:

Est. 3.4   K   באמרם
    Q   כְּאָמְרָם

1 Sam. 11.9   K   בחם
     Q   כְּחֹם

Jer. 44.23   K   ביום
     Q   כְּיוֹם

Judg. 19.25   K   בעלות
     Q   כַּעֲלוֹת [365]

---

[356] Cf. Ex. 26.20, 35; 27.10; 38.11; cf. also Jer. 23.8: צפונה (מארץ), Venice 1515 marg.: צפון.

[357] Cf. Deut. 12.30; 18.20; 32.30; also Q-K on Jer. 48.17.

[358] Cf. Ex. 1.9; Num. 22.5, 10; 23.20; also Q-K: Isa. 54.16.

[359] Cf. also K-Q: Joel 4.7; and Md-Ma on 1 Ki. 17.4.

[360] Cf. Deut. 11.17.

[361] Cf. TRL s. v. הם: Ps. 9.7: MT הֵמָּה — o הם; further
Deut. 3.20: עד אשר יניח יהוה לאחיכם ככם וירשו גם הם את הארץ
Josh. 1.15: עד אשר יניח יהוה לאחיכם ככם וירשו גם הֵמָּה את הארץ.

[362] Cf. Md-Ma on Jer. 50.20.

[363] Cf. Ex. 30.4: לשאת אתו בָּהֵמָּה
Ex. 37.27: לשאת אתו בָּהֶם.

[364] Cf. Num. 13.19.   [365] Cf. Josh. 4.18; 6.15; 1 Sam. 9.26.

Jer. 36.23 K בקרוא
     Q כְּקָרוֹא
Josh. 6.5 K בשמעכם
     Q כְּשָׁמְעֲכֶם³⁶⁶

§111: The locative preposition ב
(B-L §22a; Bergstr. §20e[e]):

Gen. 24.23 MT בֵּית³⁶⁷
     S בבית³⁶⁸
2 Chron. 23.9 בֵּית
2 Ki. 11.10 בְּבֵית³⁶⁹
1 Ki. 7.40 בֵּית
2 Chron. 4.11 בְּבֵית³⁷⁰

§112: The ל finalis
(Bergstr. 2, §11i–p).

a) in connection with היה:

2 Sam. 5.2 תִּהְיֶה לְנָגִיד
1 Chron. 11.2 נָגִיד . .
2 Sam. 8.2 וַתְּהִי . . . לַעֲבָדִים
1 Chron. 18.2 עֲבָדִים . . . . . .³⁷¹
Ps 18.19 וַיְהִי . . . לְמִשְׁעָן
2 Sam. 22.19 מִשְׁעָן . . . . . .

2 Chron. 18.21 וְהָיִיתִי לְרוּחַ
1 Ki. 22.22 רוּחַ . . . . .

b) in connection with other verbs:

Gen. 22.2 MT וְהַעֲלֵהוּ . . . לְעֹלָה
     S עלה . . . .
2 Chron. 18.7 מִתְנַבֵּא לְטוֹבָה . . . לְרָעָה
1 Ki. 22.8 טוֹב . . רָע . . . .³⁷²
2 Chron. 5.1 עָשָׂה . . . לַבַּיִת
1 Ki. 7.51 בַּיִת . . . . . .
2 Chron. 18.12 לִקְרֹא לְמִיכָיְהוּ
1 Ki. 22.13 מִיכָיְהוּ . . . .
2 Sam. 7.23 לִפְדּוֹת לוֹ לְעָם
1 Chron. 7.21 עָם . . . .

c) in connection with a particle:

Num. 32.19 MT מֵעֵבֶר הַיַּרְדֵּן
     S לירדן . . . .³⁷³
2 Sam. 10.3 בַּעֲבוּר חָקֹר
1 Chron. 19.3 לַחְקֹר . . . . .

³⁶⁶ Cf. 1 Sam. 11.6; 2 Sam. 5.24.
³⁶⁷ Cf. Num. 20.17: דֶּרֶךְ הַמֶּלֶךְ נֵלֵךְ.
Num. 21.22: בְּדֶרֶךְ הַמֶּלֶךְ נֵלֵךְ.
³⁶⁸ Cf. Num. 30.7; also Q–K: 2 Ki. 22.5; Jer. 52.11; further: MT–seb on Ex. 8.20; 2 Ki. 2.3; 10.29.
³⁶⁹ Cf. 2 Chron. 26.21 — 2 Ki. 15.5; 2 Chron. 34.30 — 2 Ki. 23.2.
³⁷⁰ Cf. 2 Sam. 23.14 — 1 Chron. 11.16; 1 Ki. 10.17 — 2 Chron. 9.16; 2 Ki. 11.3 — 2 Chron. 22.12; 2 Ki. 14.14 — 2 Chron. 25.24; also S–MT on Gen. 39.2.
³⁷¹ Cf. 2 Sam. 8.6 — 1 Chron. 18.6.
³⁷² On the difference between רעה, טובה (fem.) and רע, טוב (masc.). cf. §126.
³⁷³ Cf. 1 Ki. 14.15: (מעבר) לנהר, Venice 1515 marg.: הנהר.

§113: The use of מן or מ

(B-L §81p' seq; §15k;

Bergstr. §19a):374

2 Sam. 23.13	מֵהַשְּׁלֹשִׁים
1 Chron. 11.15	מִן הַשְּׁלוֹשִׁים
2 Sam. 23.20	מִקַּבְצְאֵל
1 Chron. 11.22	מִן קַבְצְאֵל
1 Ki. 9.22	וּמִבְּנֵי
2 Chron. 8.9	וּמִן בְּנֵי375
2 Ki. 15.2	מִירוּשָׁלַם
2 Chron. 26.3	מִן יְרוּשָׁלַם376
1 Sam. 24.8 Q	מֵהַמְּעָרָה
K	מן המערה377
Num. 23.7 MT	מִן אֲרָם
S	מארם

§114: Imperfect with אַל
or לֹא:378

Gen. 3.17	MT	לֹא תֹאכַל
	S	אל.....

Ex. 12.22	MT	לֹא תֵצְאוּ
	S	אל.....
Ex. 23.7	MT	לֹא תִקָּח
	S	אל.....
Lev. 19.17	MT	וְלֹא תִשָּׂא
	S	אל....
2 Ki. 11.15		אַל (תּוּמַת)379
2 Chron. 23.14		לֹא ...
Ex. 5.9	MT	וְאַל יִשְׁעוּ
	S	ולא ...

§115: The use of אשר

(Bergstr. §21):380

Gen. 39.4	MT	וְכָל יֶשׁ לוֹ
	S	אשר..
Ex. 13.20	MT	בִּקְצֵה הַמִּדְבָּר
	S	אשר.........
Ex. 18.20	MT	הַדֶּרֶךְ יֵלְכוּ בָהּ
	S	אשר.....
Lev. 17.6	MT	פֶּתַח אֹהֶל מוֹעֵד
	S	אשר.........

374 Cf. TRL s.v. שאול: Ps. 30.4: MT מן שאול — o משאול; s. v. בטן: Isa. 46.3: MT מני בטן — J מבטן; s. v. רחם: Isa. 46.3: MT מני רחם — J מרחם; cf. also 1 Ki. 18.5: Venice 1515: מן בהמה, marg.: מהבהמה.

375 Cf. s–MT on Lev. 1.14; 14.30; Ex. 9.18.

376 Cf. 2 Chron. 25.1 — 2 Ki. 14.2; Isa. 36.2 — 2 Ki. 18.17.

377 Cf. 1 Ki. 18.5; Joel 1.12; Lam. 1.6; also 2 Chron. 7.1: מהשמים, Venice 1515 marg.: מן השמים.

378 Cf. Num. 13.2: תִּשְׁלָחוּ; here the Masora parva in the edition Venice 1524-5 reads: ב ויאמר אל תשלחו. But the passage 2 Ki. 2.16 referred to, has: ויאמר לא תשלחו.

379 Cf. 1 Ki. 3.26: תנו לה את הילוד החי והמת אַל תמיתהו
1 Ki. 3.27: תנו לה את הילוד החי והמת לֹא תמיתהו.

380 Cf. Judg. 6.26: במערכה, Venice 1515 marg.: אשר במערכה; 1 Sam. 26.3: Venice 1515: על פני הישימן; MT praemittit: אשר.

Isa. 36.2	בְּמְסִלַּת
2 Ki. 18.17	אֲשֶׁר.....
2 Sam. 10.5	עַד יִצְמַח
1 Chron. 19.5	....אֲשֶׁר....

2 Sam. 24.16	וַיִּשְׁלַח...יְרוּשָׁלַם
1 Chron. 21.15	........לִירוּשָׁלַם.
Ex. 17.10 MT	עֲלוּ רֹאשׁ
S	...אֶל רֹאשׁ[384]

a) the use of the article
or אֲשֶׁר:[381]

2 Ki. 22.13	הַנִּמְצָא
2 Chron. 34.21	אֲשֶׁר נִמְצָא
Deut. 6.12 S	הַמּוֹצִיאֲךָ
MT	אֲשֶׁר הוֹצִיאֲךָ[382]
Lev. 17.10 MT	הַגֵּר
S	אֲשֶׁר יָגוּר[383]

**§116: The direction is indicated
by the accusative or אֶל, לְ:**

2 Sam. 10.2	וַיָּבֹאוּ...אֶרֶץ
1 Chron. 19.2	.......אֶל אֶרֶץ
2 Sam. 6.10	וַיַּטֵּהוּ בֵּית
1 Chron. 13.13	....אֶל בֵּית
1 Ki. 22.29	וַיַּעַל...רָמֹת
2 Chron. 18.28	......אֶל רָמֹת

§117: The use of אֶל or לְ.

a) with verbs of speech:[385]

Gen. 19.5 MT	וַיֹּאמְרוּ לוֹ
S	.....אֵלָיו[386]
Ex. 10.17 MT	וְהַעְתִּירוּ לַיהוה
S	......אֶל יהוה[387]
Ex. 19.20 MT	וַיִּקְרָא...לְמֹשֶׁה
S	........אֶל משה[388]
2 Chron. 34.23	וַתֹּאמֶר לָהֶם
2 Ki. 22.5	.....אֲלֵיהֶם[389]
1 Chron. 19.3	וַיֹּאמְרוּ...לְחָנוּן
2 Sam. 10.3	........אֶל חָנוּן
1 Sam. 31.4	וַיֹּאמֶר...לְנֹשֵׂא
1 Chron. 10.4	....אֶל נֹשֵׂא[390]

[381] Cf. 2 Chron. 10.8: הָעֹמְדִים — 1 Ki. 12.8: אֲשֶׁר הָעֹמְדִים; the passage in Kings thus represents a doublet; cf. B-L §32a and e. See also our note 419 on §124 b 8. 1 Ki. 21.11: אֲשֶׁר הַיֹּשְׁבִים is a doublet, too.

[382] On the difference in the tense cf. §60 c.

[383] On the difference in the tense cf. §60 b.

[384] Cf. Deut. 3.27.

[385] Cf. Judg. 21.22: אֲלֵיהֶם (ואמרנו), Venice 1515 marg.: להם; 1 Ki. 18.44: אֶל אחאב (אמר), Venice 1515 marg.: לאחאב.

[386] Cf. Gen. 27.32; 42.1; Ex. 3.14; 8.5; Num. 21.16; 22.28; 23.3, 17.

[387] Cf. Gen. 25.21.

[388] Cf. Ex. 8.21.

[389] Cf. 1 Chron. 21.24 — 2 Sam. 24.24.

[390] Cf. s–MT on Gen. 21.29; 24.58; 37.9; Ex. 18.6; 35.30; also 2 Ki. 19.6 — Isa. 37.6.

b) with other verbs:

Gen. 24.56 MT   וְאֵלְכָה לַאדֹנִי
S   אל אדני .....

Num. 31.47 MT   וַיִּתֵּן ... לַלְוִיִּם
S   אל הלוים ......

Num. 36.9 MT   וְלֹא תִסֹּב ... לְמַטֶּה
S   אל מטה ....

Gen. 32.10 MT   שׁוּב לְאַרְצְךָ
S   אל ארצך ...

2 Ki. 19.7   וְשָׁב לְאַרְצוֹ
Isa. 37.7   אֶל אַרְצוֹ ...

2 Chron. 10.16   לֹא שָׁמַע ... לָהֶם
1 Ki. 12.16   אֲלֵהֶם ....

Ps. 96.2   בַּשְּׂרוּ מִיּוֹם לְיוֹם
1 Chron. 16.23   אֶל יוֹם ....

c) addition of אל or ל:

Gen. 18.29 MT   וַיֹּאמֶר
S   אֵלָיו 391

2 Chron. 18.13   יֹאמַר
1 Ki. 22.14   אֵלַי 392

Isa. 36.12   וַיֹּאמֶר
2 Ki. 18.27   אֲלֵיהֶם.....

Gen. 29.7 MT   וַיֹּאמֶר
S   לָהֶם....393

2 Ki. 20.14   בָּאוּ
Isa. 39.3   אֵלַי ...

Ex. 34.32 MT   נִגְּשׁוּ
S   אֵלָיו ...

1 Chron. 10.11   וַיִּשְׁמְעוּ
1 Sam. 31.11   אֵלָיו....

§118: The government of prepositions (Bergstr. §21).

a) preposition אל:

Gen. 30.25 MT   אֶל מְקוֹמִי וּלְאַרְצִי
S   וּאל ארצי......

Gen. 31.3 MT   אֶל אֶרֶץ אֲבוֹתֶיךָ וּלְמוֹלַדְתֶּךָ
S   וּאל מולדתך ....

Lev. 10.6 MT   אֶל אַהֲרֹן וּלְאֶלְעָזָר וּלְאִיתָמָר
S   ..... וּאל אלעזר
וּאל איתמר

Ex. 12.43 MT   אֶל מֹשֶׁה וְאַהֲרֹן
S   וּאל אהרן ......

1 Chron. 17.4   אֶל דָּוִד עַבְדִּי
2 Sam. 7.5   אֶל עַבְדִּי אֶל דָּוִד

b) preposition את:

Ex. 12.28 MT   אֶת מֹשֶׁה וְאַהֲרֹן
S   וּאת אהרן ......

Num. 22.6 MT   אֵת אֲשֶׁר תְּבָרֵךְ ... וַאֲשֶׁר תָּאֹר
S   וּאת אשר... ....

Deut. 22.4 MT   אֶת חֲמוֹר אָחִיךָ אוֹ שׁוֹרוֹ
S   או את.. ....

Num. 15.31 MT   כִּי דְבַר.. וְאֶת מִצְוָתוֹ
S   כי את ....

---

391 Cf. Gen. 47.1; also 2 Chron. 18.14 — 1 Ki. 22.15.
392 Cf. MT–S on Num. 24.13; also K–Q: Ruth 3.5.
393 Cf. Gen. 12.7; Num. 13.30.

2 Chron. 11.1   אֶת ‹בֵּית יְהוּדָה› וּבִנְיָמִן

1 Ki. 12.21   וְאֶת ‹שֵׁבֶט בִּנְיָמִן› ... [394]

c) preposition עַל:

1 Chron. 17.7   עַל עַמִּי יִשְׂרָאֵל

2 Sam. 7.8   עַל עַמִּי עַל יִשְׂרָאֵל

d) preposition בְּ:

Josh. 8.17 MT   בָּעַי וּבֵית אֵל

seb   ...וּבְבֵית

Jer. 52.3   בִּירוּשָׁלַם וִיהוּדָה

2 Ki. 24.20   ...וּבִיהוּדָה

Prov. 28.8 Q   בְּנֶשֶׁךְ וְתַרְבִּית

K   ...וּבְתַרְבִּית

e) preposition כְּ:

Gen. 48.5 MT   כִּרְאוּבֵן וְשִׁמְעוֹן

s   ...וְכַשִׁמְעוֹן

1 Chron. 17.21   כְּעַמְּךָ יִשְׂרָאֵל

2 Sam. 7.23   ...כְּיִשְׂרָאֵל

f) preposition לְ:

Ex. 2.14 MT   לְאִישׁ שַׂר וְשֹׁפֵט

s   ...וּלְשֹׁפֵט

1 Chron. 17.9   לְעַמִּי יִשְׂרָאֵל

2 Sam. 7.10   ...לְיִשְׂרָאֵל

2 Chron. 9.22   לְעֹשֶׁר וְחָכְמָה

1 Ki. 10.23   ...וּלְחָכְמָה

g) preposition מִ:

Num. 29.39 MT   מִנִּדְרֵיכֶם וְנִדְבֹתֵיכֶם [395]

s   ...וּמִנִּדְבֹתֵיכֶם

2 Ki. 17.24 K   וּמֵעַוָּא וּמֵחֲמָת וּסְפַרְוַיִם

Q   ...וּמִסְפַרְוַיִם

Gen. 7.8 MT   וּמִן הָעוֹף וְכֹל אֲשֶׁר

s   ...וּמִכֹּל

h) nouns and phrases:

2 Chron. 35.18   מִימֵי ...וְכָל מַלְכֵי

2 Ki. 23.22   וְכֹל יְמֵי.

2 Chron. 10.11, 14   אָבִי יִסַּר אֶתְכֶם...וַאֲנִי

1 Ki. 12.11, 14   ...וַאֲנִי אֲיַסֵּר אֶתְכֶם

Deut. 17.6 MT   עַל פִּי...אוֹ

s   ...אוֹ עַל פִּי

Ps. 18.1   מִכַּף...וּמִיַּד [396]

2 Sam. 22.1   וּמִכַּף

Ps. 18.32   מִבַּלְעֲדֵי...זוּלָתִי

2 Sam. 22.32   מִבַּלְעֲדֵי...

§119: The use of the particle אֵת (Bergstr. §21): [397]

Gen. 44.26 MT   לִרְאוֹת פְּנֵי הָאִישׁ

s   ...אֵת......

Ex. 2.9 MT   וַתִּקַּח הָאִשָּׁה הַיֶּלֶד

s   ...אֵת....... .

---

[394] On the insertion of שבט here, cf. §123 c.

[395] Cf. Zech. 1.4: מִדַּרְכֵיכֶם...וּמַעַלְלֵיכֶם; Venice 1515 marg.: וּמִמַּעַלְלֵיכֶם.

[396] Cf. Ezek. 19.2: בֵּין אֲרָיוֹת בְּתוֹךְ כְּפִרִים; Venice 1515 marg.: בֵּין...בֵּין.

[397] On אֵת with the pronomen suffixum, cf. §102.

Lev. 4.17 MT   וְטָבַל הַכֹּהֵן אֶצְבָּעוֹ
s ..... את ....

Num. 22.41 MT   וַיַּרְא מִשָּׁם קְצֵה הָעָם
s ..... את ......

Deut. 26.2 MT   לְשַׁכֵּן שְׁמוֹ שָׁם
s ..... את ....·

1 Chron. 17.26   וַתְּדַבֵּר ‹עַל עַבְדְּךָ›
הַטּוֹבָה הַזֹּאת
2 Sam. 7.28 .... אֶת ....

1 Chron. 19.17   וַיַּעֲבֹר הַיַּרְדֵּן
2 Sam. 10.17   .... אֶת ....

2 Chron. 18.26   שִׂימוּ זֶה
1 Ki. 22.27   ... אֶת ...

2 Sam. 24.13   מָה אָשִׁיב שֹׁלְחִי
1 Chron. 21.12 ... אֶת ......

§120: The prepositions אֶל and עַל:

1) Gen. 50.21 MT   וַיְדַבֵּר עַל לִבָּם
s   .... אֶל ....

Ex. 40.23 MT   וַיַּעֲרֹךְ עָלָיו עֵרֶךְ לֶחֶם
s   אֵלָיו ....

Lev. 16.14 MT   וְהָיָה... עַל פְּנֵי הַכַּפֹּרֶת
s   ..... אֶל ....

1 Chron. 10.3   וַתִּכְבַּד הַמִּלְחָמָה עַל
1 Sam. 31.3   אֶל ....

1 Chron. 19.2   לְנַחֲמוֹ עַל אָבִיו
2 Sam. 10.2   .... אֶל ...

1 Chron. 18.7   אֲשֶׁר הָיוּ עַל עַבְדֵי
2 Sam. 8.7   ...... אֶל ....

2 Chron. 18.16   נְפוֹצִים עַל הֶהָרִים
1 Ki. 22.17   ..... אֶל .....

2 Chron. 34.24   מֵבִיא רָעָה עַל הַמָּקוֹם
2 Ki. 22.16   .... אֶל .....

2) Num. 13.30 MT   וַיַּהַס כָּלֵב אֶת הָעָם
אֶל מֹשֶׁה
s   .... עַל ...

Ex. 32.34 MT   נְחֵה אֶת הָעָם אֶל אֲשֶׁר
דִּבַּרְתִּי
s   .... עַל .....

Deut. 30.1 MT   וַהֲשֵׁבֹתָ אֶל לְבָבֶךָ
s   .... עַל .....

2 Chron. 16.4   וַיִּשְׁלַח... אֶל עָרֵי
1 Ki. 15.20   ... עַל ....

2 Chron. 34.28   אֹסִפְךָ אֶל אֲבֹתֶיךָ
2 Ki. 22.20   .... עַל ....

2 Chron. 34.15   וַיֹּאמֶר אֶל שָׁפָן
2 Ki. 22.8   ... עַל ....

§121: The word-order in the sentence.

1) inseparable prepositions:

Ex. 40.38 MT   וְאֵשׁ תִּהְיֶה לַיְלָה בּוֹ
s   ...... בו לילה

Lev. 18.23 MT   לֹא תִתֵּן שְׁכָבְתְּךָ
לְטָמְאָה בָהּ
s   .... בה לטמאה

Gen. 50.12 MT   וַיַּעֲשׂוּ בָנָיו לוֹ
s   ... לו בניו

Ex. 30.19 MT וְרָחֲצוּ אַהֲרֹן וּבָנָיו מִמֶּנּוּ
s .....ממנו אהרן ובניו

2) particle אֶל:

Gen. 31.16 MT ³⁹⁸וַאמֶר אֱלֹהִים אֵלַיִךְ
s ...אליך אלהים

Ex. 3.2 MT וַיֵּרָא מַלְאַךְ יהוה אֵלָיו
s ... אליו מלאך יהוה

1 Chron. 19.10 כִּי הָיְתָה פְּנֵי הַמִּלְחָמָה אֵלָיו
2 Sam. 10.9 ....אֵלָיו פְּנֵי הַמִּלְחָמָה

3) particle אֵת:

Ex. 35.29 MT אֲשֶׁר נָדַב לִבָּם אֹתָם
s ³⁹⁹......אתם לבם

Lev. 13.27 MT וְטִמֵּא הַכֹּהֵן אֹתוֹ
s ... אתו הכהן

4) preposition כֹּל:

Gen. 19.28 MT וְעַל כָּל פְּנֵי אֶרֶץ
s ...פני כל....

Gen. 41.56 MT עַל כָּל פְּנֵי הָאָרֶץ
s ...פני כל....

Num. 8.16 MT תַּחַת פִּטְרַת כָּל רֶחֶם בְּכוֹר
s .. כל בכור פטר רחם

Num. 1.20 MT בְּמִסְפַּר שֵׁמוֹת לְגֻלְגְּלֹתָם כָּל זָכָר
s ...כל זכר לגלגלתם

5) particle עוֹד:

Gen. 8.21 MT לֹא אֹסֵף לְקַלֵּל עוֹד
s ......עוד לקלל

Gen. 35.10 MT לֹא יִקָּרֵא שִׁמְךָ עוֹד
s ......עוד שמך

Deut. 34.10 MT וְלֹא קָם נָבִיא עוֹד
s ⁴⁰⁰.....עוד נביא

1 Chron. 14.3 וַיּוֹלֶד דָּוִיד עוֹד
2 Sam. 5.13 ....עוד לדוד

1 Chron. 19.19 לְהוֹשִׁיעַ אֶת בְּנֵי עַמּוֹן עוֹד
2 Sam. 10.19 ... עוֹד אֶת בְּנֵי עַמּוֹן

6) particle עַל:

Ex. 19.18 MT אֲשֶׁר יָרַד עָלָיו יהוה
s ......יהוה עליו

7) personal pronouns:

Gen. 20.12 MT אֲחֹתִי בַת אָבִי הִוא
s ....היא בת אבי

Ex. 29.18 MT אִשֶּׁה לַיהוה הוּא
s ... הוא ליהוה

Gen. 42.32 s שְׁנֵים עָשָׂר אַחִים אֲנַחְנוּ
MT ....אֲנַחְנוּ אַחִים

8) verb and object:

Lev. 21.21 MT אֵת לֶחֶם אֱלֹהָיו לֹא יִגַּשׁ לְהַקְרִיב
s לא יגש להקריב לחם אלהיו

³⁹⁸ Cf. Lev. 9.12: וימצאו בני אהרן אליו את הדם
Lev. 9.18: וימצאו בני אהרן את הדם אליו.
³⁹⁹ Cf. Lev. 18.28: ולא תקיא הארץ אתכם
Lev. 20.22: ולא תקיא אתכם הארץ.
⁴⁰⁰ Cf. similarly Gen. 9.11; Deut. 19.20.

1 Chron. 17.18 וְאַתָּה אֶת עַבְדְּךָ יָדַעְתָּ

2 Sam. 7.20 .... יָדַעְתָּ אֶת עַבְדְּךָ

1 Chron. 19.13 הַטּוֹב בְּעֵינָיו
יַעֲשֶׂה

2 Sam. 10.12 יַעֲשֶׂה הַטּוֹב בְּעֵינָיו

Deut. 12.22 MT יַחְדָּו יֹאכְלֶנּוּ
S יאכלנו יחדו

9) noun and apposition:

2 Chron. 16.6 וְאָסָא הַמֶּלֶךְ

1 Ki. 15.22 וְהַמֶּלֶךְ אָסָא

1 Chron. 17.24 דָּוִיד עַבְדְּךָ

2 Sam. 7.26 עַבְדְּךָ דָוִד[401]

10) the accusative-object:

2 Chron. 15.16 עָשְׂתָה לַאֲשֵׁרָה
מִפְלָצֶת

1 Ki. 15.13 .... מִפְלֶצֶת לַאֲשֵׁרָה

2 Chron. 1.17 וַיּוֹצִיאוּ מִמִּצְרַיִם מֶרְכָּבָה

1 Ki. 10.29 ... מֶרְכָּבָה מִמִּצְרַיִם

11) coupled words:

2 Chron. 23.7 בְּבֹאוֹ וּבְצֵאתוֹ

2 Ki. 11.8 בְּצֵאתוֹ וּבְבֹאוֹ

2 Chron. 6.20 יוֹמָם וָלַיְלָה

1 Ki. 8.29 לַיְלָה וָיוֹם

2 Chron. 34.30 מִגָּדוֹל וְעַד קָטָן

2 Ki. 23.2 לְמִקָּטֹן וְעַד גָּדוֹל

1 Chron. 21.2 מִבְּאֵר שֶׁבַע וְעַד דָּן

2 Sam. 24.2 מִדָּן וְעַד בְּאֵר שֶׁבַע

§122: Insertion of the subject or apposition thereof.[402]

a) subject:

Gen. 21.33 MT וַיִּטַּע
S אברהם ...

Gen. 29.23 MT וַיָּבֵא אֵלֶיהָ
S יעקב ......

Ex. 15.25 MT וַיִּצְעַק אֶל יהוה
S .... משה .....

Ex. 2.6 MT וַתַּחְמֹל עָלָיו
S .... בת פרעה

Lev. 14.37 MT וְרָאָה
S .... הכהן

1 Chron. 18.1 וַיִּקַּח
2 Sam. 8.1 דָּוִד ...[403]

1 Chron. 18.10 וַיִּשְׁלַח
2 Sam. 8.10 ..... תֹּעִי

1 Chron. 19.1 וַיִּמְלֹךְ
2 Sam. 10.1 .... חָנוּן

2 Chron. 6.12 וַיַּעֲמֹד
1 Ki. 8.22 .... שְׁלֹמֹה

2 Ki. 20.2 וַיַּסֵּב
Isa. 38.2 .... חִזְקִיָּהוּ

2 Sam. 16.23 K כַּאֲשֶׁר יִשְׁאַל
Q אִישׁ ....

---

[401] Cf. also 1 Ki. 22.43 — 2 Chron. 20.32; Isa. 37.2 — 2 Ki. 19.2.
[402] Cf. my *Septuagintaprobleme* (Stuttgart 1929), p. 60.
[403] Cf. 1 Chron. 18.14 — 2 Sam. 8.15; 1 Chron. 11.18 — 2 Sam. 23.16.

b) apposition:

Gen. 26.5 MT אֲשֶׁר שָׁמַע אַבְרָהָם
S אָבִיךָ ....

Gen. 48.7 MT מֵתָה עָלַי רָחֵל
S אִמְּךָ ....

Gen. 38.13 MT וַיֻּגַּד לְתָמָר
S כַּלָּתוֹ ......

Gen. 48.7 MT בְּבֹאִי מִפַּדָּן
S אֲרָם ....

1 Chron. 19.3 לַחֲנוּן
2 Sam. 10.3 אֲדֹנֶיהָם ....

2 Chron. 27.9 בְּעִיר דָּוִד
2 Ki. 15.38 אָבִיו ....

2 Sam. 10.14 מִפְּנֵי אֲבִישַׁי
1 Chron. 19.15 אָחִיו ......

2 Ki. 19.37 K וְאַדְרַמֶּלֶךְ וְשַׂרְאֶצֶר
Q בָּנָיו .... [404]

§123: Appositions to יִשְׂרָאֵל.

a) בני ישראל: [405]

Ex. 3.16 MT זִקְנֵי יִשְׂרָאֵל
S ....בְּנֵי ...

Ex. 12.3 MT עֲדַת יִשְׂרָאֵל
S .... בְּנֵי ...

Ex. 9.7 MT מִמִּקְנֵה יִשְׂרָאֵל
S ..... בְּנֵי ....

Num. 10.18 MT מַחֲנֵה רְאוּבֵן
S ....בְּנֵי....

Num. 26.58 MT מִשְׁפְּחֹת לֵוִי
S ... בְּנֵי .....

2 Chron. 8.7 מִיִּשְׂרָאֵל
1 Ki. 9.20 מִבְּנֵי יִשְׂרָאֵל

1 Chron. 17.5 אֶת יִשְׂרָאֵל [406]
2 Sam. 7.6 בְּנֵי ....

b) בית ישראל:

1 Chron. 13.8 וְכָל יִשְׂרָאֵל
2 Sam. 6.5 בֵּית ....

2 Chron. 11.1 עִם יִשְׂרָאֵל
1 Ki. 12.21 בֵּית .. ....

c) variae:

2 Chron. 10.3 וְכָל יִשְׂרָאֵל [407]
1 Ki. 12.23 קְהַל ...

2 Chron. 11.1 וּבִנְיָמִן
1 Ki. 12.21 שֵׁבֶט בִּנְיָמִן

1 Chron. 11.1 כָּל יִשְׂרָאֵל
2 Sam. 5.1 שִׁבְטֵי .. ....

§124: Insertion of various nouns and particles:

a) nouns:

1)Lev. 5.24 MT מִכֹּל אֲשֶׁר יִשָּׁבַע עָלָיו
S דְּבַר ....

---

[404] Cf. Isa. 37.38.
[405] Cf. Josh. 7.1: בְּבְנֵי יִשְׂרָאֵל; Venice 1515 marg.: בִּישְׂרָאֵל; Josh. 8.27: בְּנֵי יִשְׂרָאֵל; Venice 1515 marg.: (לָהֶם) יִשְׂרָאֵל.
[406] Cf. Venice 1515: אֶת בְּנֵי יִשְׂרָאֵל, marg.: בס"א לית (scil. בְּנֵי).
[407] Cf. Ex. 12.15: וְנִכְרְתָה הַנֶּפֶשׁ הַהִוא מִיִּשְׂרָאֵל
Ex. 12.19: וְנִכְרְתָה הַנֶּפֶשׁ הַהִוא מֵעֲדַת יִשְׂרָאֵל; cf. also our note 438 on §128 a.

Num. 23.26 MT   כל   אֲשֶׁר יְדַבֵּר
s   .... הדבר ..

2) Ex. 15.22 MT   וַיֵּלְכוּ   שְׁלֹשֶׁת יָמִים
s   ..... דרך....

3) Gen. 48.14 MT   וַיִּשְׁלַח.. אֶת יְמִינוֹ
s   .. יד ....

4) Gen. 47.16 MT   וְאֶתְּנָה לָכֶם
s   לחם ......

5) Ex. 5.20 MT   מֵאֵת פַּרְעֹה
s   .... פני ...

6) Gen. 45.23 MT   מְטוּב   מִצְרָיִם
s   .. ארץ .. [408]

2 Chron. 5.10   מִמִּצְרָיִם
1 Ki. 8.9   [409] מֵאֶרֶץ מִצְרָיִם

2 Sam. 11.1   בְּנֵי עַמּוֹן
1 Chron. 20.1   אֶרֶץ .....

7) 1 Chron. 13.6   יהוה יוֹשֵׁב הַכְּרוּבִים
2 Sam. 6.2   צְבָאוֹת ....

1 Chron. 16.2   בְּשֵׁם יהוה
2 Sam. 6.18   צְבָאוֹת ......

2 Ki. 20.16   דְּבַר יהוה
Isa. 39.5   [410] צְבָאוֹת ....

2 Ki. 19.31 K   קִנְאַת יהוה
Q   צְבָאוֹת ....

b) particles:

1) Deut. 12.22 MT   הַטָּמֵא וְהַטָּהוֹר
s   .... בְּךָ .....

Ex. 13.3 MT   הַיּוֹם אֲשֶׁר יְצָאתֶם
s   בו ....

Ex. 20.10 MT   לֹא תַעֲשֶׂה כָל מְלָאכָה
s   [411] ..... בו ......

Ex. 29.33 MT   לְמַלֵּא אֶת יָדָם
s   .... בָּם ....

Ex. 37.5 MT   לָשֵׂאת אֶת הָאָרֹן
s   [412] .... בהם

2) Gen. 21.7 MT   כִּי יָלַדְתִּי
s   ...... לוֹ

Ex. 18.21 MT   תֶחֱזֶה
s   .... לָךְ

Isa. 36.6   הִנֵּה בָטַחְתָּ
2 Ki. 18.21   .... לְּךָ

Jer. 50.29 K   אַל יְהִי
Q   ..... לָהּ

Num. 31.19 MT   וְאַתֶּם חֲנוּ
s   ...... לכם

3) Gen. 24.4 MT   כִּי
s   [413] .. אם

2 Chron. 6.9   כִּי
1 Ki. 8.19   [414] כִּי אם

---

[408] Cf. similarly: Ex. 6.27; 11.4; 13.3; Deut. 16.12.
[409] Cf. similarly 1 Ki. 8.16 — 2 Chron. 6.5.
[410] Cf. similarly 2 Ki. 19.15 — Isa. 37.16.
[411] Cf. also Deut. 5.14; 16.16.
[412] Cf. similarly: Ex. 36.1.
[413] Cf. Q–K on 2 Ki. 14.6; 2 Sam. 13.33; 15.21; Jer. 39.12; Ruth 3.12; cf. also Jer. 22.12: כי, Venice 1515 marg.: כי אם.
[414] Cf. similarly: 2 Chron. 25.4 — 2 Ki. 14.6.

4) Gen. 2.12 MT   טוֹב
         S   מְאֹד ...

Ex. 8.20 MT   עָרֹב כָּבֵד
        S   מְאֹד ......

1 Chron. 10.3   וַיָּחֶל
2 Sam. 31.3   מְאֹד ...[415]

1 Ki. 8.65   קָהָל גָּדוֹל
2 Chron. 7.8   מְאֹד ....

5) Gen. 47.29 MT   וְעָשִׂיתָ עִמָּדִי
         S   נָא ....

Ex. 12.3 MT   דַּבְּרוּ
        S   נָא ....[416]

2'Chron. 6.17   יֵאָמֵן
1 Ki. 8.26   נָא ...

2 Chron. 18.12   הִנֵּה
1 Ki. 22.13   נָא ...[417]

2 Ki. 5.18 Q   יִסְלַח
       K   נָא ....

6) Gen. 2.19 MT   וַיִּצֶר יהוה אֱלֹהִים
         S   עוֹד ....

Deut. 13.12 MT   וְלֹא יֹסִפוּ
        S   עוֹד ......

2 Chron. 10.2   וְהוּא בְמִצְרַיִם
1 Ki. 12.2   עוֹדֶנּוּ ....

7) Gen. 26.7 MT   כִּי יָרֵא לֵאמֹר אִשְׁתִּי
        S   היא ....

Gen. 37.33 MT   כְּתֹנֶת בְּנִי
        S   היא ......

Ex. 21.8 MT   אִם רָעָה בְּעֵינֵי אֲדֹנֶיהָ
        S   ....היא......

Ex. 8.16 MT   הִנֵּה יֹצֵא
        S   הוא ...

Gen. 42.28 MT   וְגַם הִנֵּה בְּאַמְתַּחְתִּי
        S   הוא ....

Ex. 28.12 MT   זִכָּרֹן לִבְנֵי יִשְׂרָאֵל
        S   הנה ...

2 Chron. 9.5   אֶמֶת הַדָּבָר
1 Ki. 10.6   הָיָה ....

1 Chron. 17.24   וּבֵית דָּוִד עַבְדְּךָ
נָכוֹן לְפָנֶיךָ
2 Sam. 7.26 ... יִהְיֶה ....[418]

8) Ex. 32.7 MT   וַיְדַבֵּר יהוה אֶל מֹשֶׁה
        S   לֵאמֹר ....[419]

---

[415] Cf. similarly: 2 Chron. 9.1 — 1 Ki. 10.2.

[416] Cf. also Ex. 14.12.

[417] Cf. also Isa. 37.20 — 2 Ki. 19.19.

[418] Cf. Ex. 28.21: והאבנים תהיין על שמת בני ישראל
Ex. 39.14: והאבנים < על שמת בני ישראל;
Lev. 27.25: עשרים גרה יהיה השקל
Num. 3.47: עשרים גרה > השקל.

[419] Cf. Ex. 33.1; Num. 27.12. On לאמר as an introductory phrase to the direct speech, see my *Septuagintaprobleme*, p. 60. Instead of לאמר, the form ויאמר may be used, too; cf. 2 Sam. 6.9 — 1 Chron. 13.12; Isa. 38.2, 3 — 2 Ki. 20.2; 2 Ki. 19.15 — Isa. 37.15. Consequently, I am inclined to regard the passage 2 Sam. 5.1: ויאמרו לאמר as a doublet; note that the parallel report 1 Chron. 11.1 reads only: לאמר. See also our notes 345 on §102 and 381 on §115a.

Num. 5.6 MT	דַּבֵּר אֶל בְּנֵי יִשְׂרָאֵל	1 Chron. 11.5	וַיֹּאמְרוּ . . . לְדָוִיד
s	. . . . לֵאמֹר	2 Sam. 5.6	לֵאמֹר 420
		2 Sam. 24.12	וְדִבַּרְתָּ אֶל דָּוִד
		1 Chron. 21.10	לֵאמֹר . . . .

H. THE VOCABULARY

§125: *The personal pronoun*
(B-L §28d, o; Bergstr. §2i):

Gen. 14.23 MT	אֲנִי
s	אָנֹכִי421
Gen. 42.11 MT	נַחְנוּ
s	אֲנַחְנוּ422
Jer. 42.6 K	אנו
Q	אֲנַחְנוּ

§126: *masc. or fem. formation of the noun* (B-L §62z):423

Num. 24.9 MT	כַּאֲרִי
s	כאריה424
2 Sam. 23.20 Q	הָאֲרִי
K	האריה425

1 Ki. 10.20	אֲרָיִים
2 Chron. 9.19	אֲרָיוֹת
Lev. 5.23 s	הגזל
MT	הַגְּזֵלָה
Gen. 48.10 MT	מִזֹּקֶן
s	מזקנה
Ex. 30.21 MT	חָק
s	חקת
2 Chron. 34.31	וְחֻקָּיו
2 Ki. 23.3	וְאֶת חֻקֹּתָיו426
Gen. 9.2 MT	וְחִתְּכֶם
s	וחתתכם
Ex. 12.42 MT	לֵיל
s	לילה
Prov. 31.18 K	בליל
Q	בַּלַּיְלָה427

420 Cf. 1 Ki. 20.28: אָמְרוּ אָדָם, Venice 1515 marg. adds: לֵאמֹר.

421 Cf. Ex. 22.26; Deut. 32.39; further: 1 Chron. 17.16 — 2 Sam. 7.18; 1 Chron. 21.10 — 2 Sam. 24.12; 1 Chron. 21.17 — 2 Sam. 24.17; 2 Chron. 34.27 — 2 Ki. 22.19; also Hos. 7.13: וְאָנֹכִי, Venice 1515 marg.: וַאֲנִי.

422 Cf. Ex. 16.7, 8; Num. 32.32.

423 Cf. TRL s. v. ישועה: Hab. 3.13: MT לישע — J לישועה; s. v. נשפה: Jer. 13.16: MT נשף — J נשפה; s. v. עור: Ps. 46.2: MT עזרה — o עזר; cf. further Ps. 70.6: עָזְרִי, Venice 1515 marg.: עזרתי.

424 Cf. Num. 23.24.

425 Cf. Lam. 3.10.

426 Cf. Deut. 27.10: MT and s.

427 Cf. Lam. 2.19.

Job 31.7	Q	מְאוּם	
	K	מאומה	
1 Chron. 11.7		בְּמָצָד	
2 Sam. 5.9		בִּמְצֻדָה	
Gen. 34.12	MT	וּמַתָּן	
	S	ומתנה	
2 Ki. 5.4	K	הנער	
	Q	הַנַּעֲרָה	
Gen. 27.3	Q	צֵיד	
	K	צידה	
Ps. 18.21		כְּצִדְקִי	
2 Sam. 22.21		כְּצִדְקָתִי	
Jer. 31.39	Q	קַו	
	K	קוה[428]	
2 Chron. 8.1		מָקֵץ	
1 Ki. 9.10		מְקְצֵה[429]	
Prov. 27.10	Q	וְרֵעַ	
	K	ורעה	
Ps. 96.12		שָׂדַי	
1 Chron.16.32		הַשָּׂדֶה[430]	
1 Ki. 7.26		שׁוֹשָׁן	
2 Chron. 4.5		שׁוֹשַׁנָּה	

α) substantival adjectives:

Amos 5.15	Q	רָע
	K	רעה[431]
Deut. 28.11	S	לטוב
	MT	לְטוֹבָה

β) particles and pronouns:

Gen. 4.9	MT	אֵי
	S	איה[432]
2 Ki. 19.13		אַיּוֹ
Isa. 37.13		אַיֵּה[433]
1 Chron. 20.8		אֵל
2 Sam. 21.22		אֵלָּה
Gen. 26.3	MT	הָאֵל
	S	האלה[434]
Gen. 24.65	S	הַלָּז
	MT	הַלָּזֶה[435]

§127: Formation by metathesis:

1) Lev. 4.32	MT	כֶּבֶשׂ
	S	כשבה
Ex. 12.5	MT	הַכְּבָשִׂים
	S	הכשבים[436]

[428] Cf. 1 Ki. 7.23; Zech. 1.16.
[429] Cf. Gen. 8.3; Deut. 14.28: MT and s.
[430] See B-L §2v; cf. also K–Q on Hos. 2.22.
[431] Cf. also Jer. 18.10 and Micah 3.2: K and Q; further: Gen. 44.34; Num. 22.34 and 32.13: MT and s.
[432] Cf. Deut. 32.37.
[433] Cf. K–Q on Jer. 37.19.
[434] Cf. Gen. 19.8, 25; 26.4; Lev. 18.27; Deut. 4.42; 7.22; 19.11.
[435] Cf. Gen. 37.19.
[436] Cf. Num. 15.11.

ALEXANDER SPERBER

2) Ex. 22.8 MT שַׂלְמָה
       S שמלה

Ex. 22.25 MT שַׂלְמָת
       S שמלת

Deut. 24.13 MT בְּשַׂלְמָתוֹ
       S בשמלתו

2 Chron. 9.24 Q וּשְׂלָמוֹת
       K ושמלות

Deut. 29.4 MT שַׂלְמֹתֵיכֶם
       S שמלתיכם

3) Deut. 28.25 MT לְזַעֲוָה
       S לזועה[437]

4) Prov. 1.27 K כשאוה
       Q כְּשׁוֹאָה

1 Chron. 11.16 וּנְצִיב
2 Sam. 23.14 וּמַצָּב

Num. 3.38 S הקדש
       MT הַמִּקְדָּשׁ

Ezek. 44.24 K לשפט
       Q לְמִשְׁפָּט

Ex. 7.4 MT בִּשְׁפָטִים
       S במשפטים[440]

b) prefix ת:

Lev. 25.37 MT וּבְמַרְבִּית
       S ובתרבית

2 Sam. 10.11 לִישׁוּעָה
1 Chron. 19.12 לִתְשׁוּעָה

§128: Formation by prefix.
a) prefix מ:[438]

Ex. 26.4 MT בַּחֹבָרֶת
       S במחברת

Ex. 21.25 MT כְּוִיָּה
       S מכוה

2 Chron. 7.18 מַלְכוּתֶךָ
1 Ki. 9.5 מַמְלַכְתְּךָ

1 Chron. 14.2 מַלְכוּתוֹ
2 Sam. 5.12 מַמְלַכְתּוֹ[439]

§129: Substantives derived from
verbs tertiae ה:[441]

Gen. 3.16 MT וְהֵרֹנֵךְ
       S והריונך

1 Chron. 17.15 הֶחָזוֹן
2 Sam. 7.17 הַחִזָּיוֹן

§130: Particles ending in י:

Gen. 9.28 MT אַחַר
       S אחרי[442]

---

[437] Cf. Jer. 15.4; 24.9; 29.18; 34.17; Ezek. 23.46: Q and K.
[438] Cf. Ex. 12.15: כי כל אכל חָמֵץ ונכרתה הנפש ההוא
    Ex. 12.19: כִּי כל אכל מַחֲמֶצֶת ונכרתה הנפש ההוא; cf. our note 407
on §123 c.
[439] Cf. 1 Chron. 17.11 — 2 Sam. 7.12.
[440] Cf. Ex. 6.6.
[441] Cf. in this connection also: 1 Ki. 10.5: וְעֹלָתוֹ — 2 Chron. 9.4: וַעֲלִיָתוֹ.
[442] Cf. Gen. 10.1, 32; 11.10; 37.17; Lev. 14.36, 43; Num. 6.19; 25.8·
further: 2 Ki. 23.3 — 2 Chron. 34.31.

Hos. 9.16 Q	בָּל		2 Chron. 26.1	עֻזִּיָּהוּ
K	בְּלִי		2 Ki. 14.21	עֲזַרְיָה
Job 7.1 K	עַל		2 Chron. 22.10	וַעֲתַלְיָהוּ
Q	עֲלִי		2 Ki. 11.1	וַעֲתַלְיָה
1 Ki. 20.41 K	מֵעַל		2 Chron. 18.10	צִדְקִיָּהוּ
Q	מֵעֲלִי		1 Ki. 22.11	צִדְקִיָּה

§*131: Formation of theophorous names* (B-L §25c', d'; Bergstr. §16c).

a) ending in יָהוּ or יָה:

2 Chron. 10.15	אֲחִיָּהוּ		2 Chron. 11.2	שְׁמַעְיָהוּ
1 Ki. 12.15	אֲחִיָּה		1 Ki. 12.22	שְׁמַעְיָה
2 Chron. 25.17	אֲמַצְיָהוּ		2 Sam. 23.30	בְּנָיָהוּ
2 Ki. 14.8	אֲמַצְיָה		1 Chron. 11.31	בְּנָיָה
2 Chron. 29.1	זְכַרְיָהוּ			
2 Ki. 18.2	זְכַרְיָה		b) by prefix יוֹ or יְהוֹ:	
2 Chron. 34.18	חִלְקִיָּהוּ		2 Chron. 36.2	יוֹאָחָז
2 Ki. 22.10	חִלְקִיָּה		2 Ki. 23.31	יְהוֹאָחָז
2 Chron. 36.22	יִרְמְיָהוּ		2 Chron. 24.1	יֹאָשׁ
Ezra 1.1	יִרְמְיָה		2 Ki. 12.1	יְהוֹאָשׁ
			1 Chron. 10.2	יוֹנָתָן
			1 Sam. 31.2	יְהוֹנָתָן
			2 Ki. 8.21	יוֹרָם
			2 Chron. 21.9	יְהוֹרָם

-- THE END OF VOLUME ONE --

www.ingramcontent.com/pod-product-compliance
Lightning Source LLC
Chambersburg PA
CBHW020452100426
42813CB00031B/3343/J